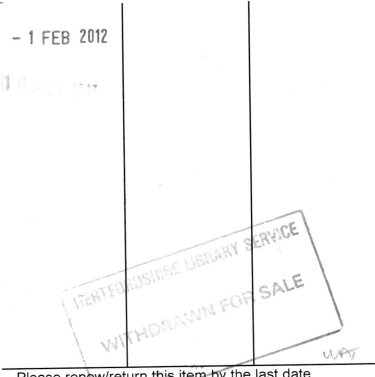
Please renew/return this item by the last date
shown. Please call the number below:

Renewals and enquiries: 0300 123 4049

Textphone for hearing or   0300 123 4041
speech impaired users:

www.hertsdirect.org/librarycatalogue

Hertfordshire

D1357008

What's Wrong with the British Constitution?

IAIN McLEAN

OXFORD
UNIVERSITY PRESS

OXFORD

UNIVERSITY PRESS

Great Clarendon Street, Oxford OX2 6DP

Oxford University Press is a department of the University of Oxford.
It furthers the University's objective of excellence in research, scholarship,
and education by publishing worldwide in

Oxford New York

Auckland Cape Town Dar es Salaam Hong Kong Karachi
Kuala Lumpur Madrid Melbourne Mexico City Nairobi
New Delhi Shanghai Taipei Toronto

With offices in

Argentina Austria Brazil Chile Czech Republic France Greece
Guatemala Hungary Italy Japan Poland Portugal Singapore
South Korea Switzerland Thailand Turkey Ukraine Vietnam

Oxford is a registered trade mark of Oxford University Press
in the UK and in certain other countries

Published in the United States
by Oxford University Press Inc., New York

British Library Cataloguing in Publication Data
Data available

Library of Congress Cataloging in Publication Data
Data available

Typeset by SPI Publisher Services, Pondicherry, India
Printed in Great Britain
on acid-free paper by the
MPG Books Group, Bodmin and King's Lynn

ISBN 978–0–19–954695–4

5 7 9 10 8 6 4

Contents

Preface

Well, what is wrong with the British Constitution?

For a start, nobody knows what it is. That is not to say (as people often and lazily do) that it is unwritten. Parts of it are very written indeed. Nobody ever denies that the Parliament Acts 1911 and 1949, which limit the right of the unelected House of Lords to amend bills sent up by the elected House of Commons, are part of the constitution. Those Acts also set the maximum possible time between general elections, which is as fundamental a constitutional rule as one can imagine. Without it, there would be nothing to prevent the House of Commons from prolonging its existence indefinitely.

Equally, the Representation of the People and Parliamentary Constituencies Acts are undoubtedly part of the Constitution. These Acts determine who is allowed to vote, and how the boundaries of the single-member districts in which they vote are to be drawn. Another class of constitutional legislation ratifies international treaties which define the very extent or powers of the UK government and parliament. The Act of Union 1706, still in force, is the third of a triplet of documents that created Great Britain as we know it by uniting the legislatures of England and Scotland. These three documents are normally confused and conflated, especially by English commentators. The European Communities Act 1972 and the European Communities (Amendment) Acts 1986 and subsequently define the terms of the UK's membership of the European Union.

Slightly further from the core of the constitution lie, for instance, the Human Rights Act 1998 and the Freedom of Information Act 2000. These Acts give individual rights against government and public bodies. To some people, this is an essentially constitutional matter. Similar protections of individual rights were added very early in the life of the US Constitution. The Constitution was ratified in 1788, but several of the ratifying states complained that it needed to be strengthened by a set of amendments protecting individual rights. Some of them tried to make their ratification conditional on a bill of rights. Ten such amendments were ratified in 1791, and they are indeed known as the US 'Bill of Rights'. Some of them echo rights asserted by Parliament in the English Bill of Rights Act 1689.

Other constitutionalists, however, would deny that Acts such as the Human Rights Acts either are or should be regarded as part of the constitution. Unlike the US Bill of Rights, they are in fact subject to repeal and amendment just like any other Act of Parliament. But then, so is the Act of Union 1706, so this in itself does not establish a difference. The difference is rather *normative*: some people argue that while the Act of Union needs to have a special status, the Human Rights and Freedom of Information Acts are in a different normative category.

The magic circle of those entitled to say what the constitution is includes judges, law professors, and a few journalists. One important move is by those judges who discover constitutional principles in the common law. This book will examine the most prominent recent effort of this sort, by Sir John Laws, who has been a Lord Justice of Appeal since 1999.

However, the custodians of the magic circle have always been reluctant to allow political scientists into it. 'We live,' said the constitutional commentator and journalist Sidney Low in 1904, 'under a system of tacit understandings. But the understandings themselves are not always understood' (Low 1904: 12). An example discussed in this book is that in May 1950 an anonymous letter writer calling himself 'Senex' wrote to *The Times* about the terms on which a UK monarch may or may not refuse a dissolution of parliament to the Prime Minister. Normally, anonymous letters to the papers have little authority. Nowadays the serious papers refuse to publish them at all, except from whistle-blowers, victims of sexual abuse, and so on. However, to those in the know, it appears that 'Senex' was the king's private secretary; and that the doctrines he announced 'in so far as this matter can be publicly discussed' (Senex 1950) form part of the British Constitution. Those content with the idea that a constitution may be defined by anonymous letter writers to the papers will probably find this book very annoying and should perhaps stop reading now.

It is a pleasure to acknowledge the invisible college of friends and colleagues who have helped me with this book. As I trespass into fields not my own, I am more indebted than usual to the following, who have all made constructive comments, or helped with requests for information, or both:

Bruce Ackerman, Andrew Adonis, James Alt, Nick Bamforth, Hugh Bayley MP, Richard Bellamy, Thom Brooks, Roger Congleton, Nick Crafts, Frank Cranmer, Dennis Galligan, Brigid Hadfield, David Hayton, Cameron Hazlehurst, Gwilym Hughes, Doug Irwin, Peter Jay, Tony King, Cécile Laborde, Laurence Lustgarten, Neil MacCormick, Diarmaid Macculloch, Marjory MacLean, David Marquand, Bob Morris, Ruairi O'Donnell, Scot Peterson, Jack Rakove, Julian Rivers, David Robertson, John Robertson, Meg Russell, Maria Sciara, Hew Strachan, Alan Trench, Albert Weale, Stuart White, Stewart Wood, and Alison Young.

Like everyone else in this field, I was deeply saddened by the death of Sir Neil MacCormick in April 2009. He had been a role model for me from the moment I arrived in Oxford as a naive 18-year-old, who had scarcely ever left Scotland. Neil was then a Snell Exhibitioner at Balliol College and a glittering prizewinner in the Oxford Union and elsewhere. He was one of the inspirations of this project and offered it his warm and practical support throughout.

I tried out themes from the book at numerous academic seminars. I am very grateful to organizers, respondents, and those who commented, at:

University College, London Constitution Unit seminar
University of Essex Government seminar
University of Edinburgh Scottish History seminar
Australian National University Politics Program,
Research School of Social Sciences seminar.

Finally, the Oxford University Public Policy Unit kindly hosted a one-day workshop to discuss the complete draft manuscript in February 2009. I am very grateful to the historians and lawyers (especially) who dissected the historical and legal claims in the book and put them under (sometimes withering) scrutiny. They bear no responsibility for the results.

I used several archives, listed in the References at the end. All were helpful, but without making invidious distinctions I wish especially to thank the archivists at the National Archives of Australia; Churchill College, Cambridge; Nuffield College, Oxford, and the Royal Archives, Windsor, for dealing with my questions. The Royal Archives are quoted by the permission of Her Majesty Queen Elizabeth II.

Whilst writing this book, I was also working on two main concurrent projects. The first is *Options for a New Britain*, published in March 2009, for which I acknowledge financial support from the Economic & Social Research Council under research grant RES-177-25-0003; Gatsby Charitable Trust; John Fell Fund, Oxford University; and Gwilym Gibbon Fund, Nuffield College. The second is the Independent Expert Group reporting to the Calman Commission of the Scottish Parliament on options to reform or replace the Barnett Formula. The three projects are mutually supportive. I therefore acknowledge the support of my *Options* research officers, Varun Uberoi and Adam Coutts (Adam also helped with copy preparation for this book); my *Options* and Barnett co-authors, Guy Lodge and Katie Schmuecker; my fellow members of the Independent Expert Group; and the Commissioners and secretariat of the Calman Commission. I thank Lluis Orriols for compiling Figure 11.1 with his signature cheerfulness and enthusiasm.

Three chapters emanate from joint work with colleagues or former students. I thank Jennifer Nou, Alistair McMillan, and Tom Lubbock for their work on those chapters. With those exceptions, I take full responsibility for all errors and omissions.

Finally, a note on references. This book draws on three main academic disciplines: political science, law, and history. Each has a different standard method of referencing. I have standardized on the Harvard author–date system, which most political scientists use. Historical references can be assimilated to the Harvard system fairly easily, but in deference to historians I retain a few more footnotes than a political science book would normally have. Law references are more difficult. Lawyers have a unique referencing system. I have taken the liberty of changing the form of citation of law review articles to the Harvard style. There are no separate Tables of Statutes or of Cases, but all statutes and cases referred to are given their full legal citation forms, where available on standard databases, in the general index.

Additional note, July 2009. Vernon Bogdanor's eagerly-awaited *The New British Constitution* (Oxford: Hart Publishing 2009) is just out. It modifies some positions he has previously taken, which are criticized in this book; but it is too late for me to change the main text of this book.

List of Tables

List of Figures

List of Abbreviations

AV	Alternative Vote
BES	British Election Survey
BNP	British National Party
BSA	British Social Attitudes
CBE	Commander of the Order of the British Empire
DCA	Department of Constitutional Affairs
ECHR	European Convention on Human Rights
ECtHR	European Court of Human Rights
ECJ	European Court of Justice
EEC	European Economic Community
EU	European Union
IRA	Irish Republican Army
JCHR	Joint Committee on Human Rights
JCPC	Judicial Committee of the Privy Council
JP	Justice of the Peace
MSP	Member of the Scottish Parliament
NIRA	National Industrial Recovery Act
ODNB	Oxford Dictionary of National Biography
QMV	Qualified Majority Voting
SEA	Single European Act
SNP	Scottish National Party
STV	Single Transferable Vote
SVR	Scottish Variable Rate
UVF	Ulster Volunteer Force
WLQ	West Lothian Question

Part I

The Old Constitution:
Two Approaches

Introduction

Yet if he [Robert the Bruce, King of Scotland] should give up what he has begun, and agree to make us or our kingdom subject to the King of England or the English, we should exert ourselves at once to drive him out as our enemy and a subverter of his own rights and ours, and make some other man who was well able to defend us our King; for, as long as but a hundred of us remain alive, never will we on any conditions be brought under English rule.

It is in truth not for glory, nor riches, nor honours that we are fighting, but for freedom—for that alone, which no honest man gives up but with life itself.

(Declaration of Arbroath, 1320, translation at
http://heritage.scotsman.com/declarationofarbroath/
The-text-of-the-Declaration.2600645.jp. Original Latin text available
at http://www.geo.ed.ac.uk/home/scotland/arbroath_latin.html)

For really I think that the poorest he that is in England hath a life to live, as the greatest he; and therefore truly, sir, I think it's clear, that every man that is to live under a government ought first by his own consent to put himself under that government; and I do think that the poorest man in England is not at all bound in a strict sense to that government that he hath not had a voice to put himself under.

(Speech of Col. Thomas Rainborough at Putney Debates,
October 1647; text (modernized spelling)
at http://courses.essex.ac.uk/cs/cs101/PUTNEY.HTM)

There is nocht tua nations vndir the firmament that ar mair contrar and different fra vthirs, nor is inglis men and scottis men quhoubeit that thai be vitht in ane ile and nythtbours, and of ane langage: for inglis men ar subtil and scottis men ar facile, inglis men ar ambitius in prosperite, and scottis men ar humain in prosperite. inglis men ar humil quhen thai ar subieckit be forse and violence, and scottis men ar furious quhen thai ar violently subiekit[.] inglis men ar cruel quhene thai get victorie, and

scottis men ar merciful quhen thai get victorie. and to conclude it is
onpossibil that scottis men and inglis men can remane in concord vndir
ane monarche or one prince be cause there naturis and conditions ar as
indefferent as is the nature of scheip and voluis [wolves].

(Complaynt of Scotland, c. 1549, at
http://www.scotsindependent.org/features/scots/complaynt/chap13.htm).

This book is about how four neighbours of two (main) isles and one (main)
language have remained, more or less, in concord for three centuries. It may
or may not be true that Englishmen are humble when they are subjected by
force and violence, and cruel when they get victory, but in constitutional
matters this book shows that Englishmen (they are mostly men) tend to be far
from humble; therefore they systematically misunderstand and misrepresent
the British Constitution.

The traditional story of the British (English, United Kingdom) Constitution does not make sense. It purports to be both positive and normative: that
is, to describe both how people actually behave and how they ought to behave.
It fails to do either. It is not a correct description and it has no persuasive
force. This book offers a reasoned alternative. The UK government's 2007
Green Paper, *The Governance of Britain* (HM Government 2007), starts down
the road proposed in this book, but it does not go nearly far enough. The
succeeding White Paper (HM Government 2008*a*) was widely regarded as
backsliding—for instance, in rejecting change to the role of Attorney-General.
One aim of this book is to encourage policy-makers to be bold—and consistent.

The view that still dominates the thoughts of constitutional lawyers is
parliamentary sovereignty (or *supremacy*). According to this view, the supreme
lawgiver in the United Kingdom is Parliament. Some writers in this tradition
go on to insist that Parliament in turn derives its authority from the people,
for the people elect Parliament. An obvious problem with this view is
that Parliament, to a lawyer, comprises three houses: monarch, Lords, and
Commons. The people elect only one of those three houses.

However, the rival idea that the people themselves are sovereign is ancient,
as my first two epigraphs show. The Declaration of Arbroath was written in
1320. It was addressed by fifty Scots barons to the pope at Avignon, asking
him to recognize Scottish independence from England. The signatories
claimed to speak on behalf of the 'entire community of the realm of Scotland'
(*tota Communitas Regni Scocie*). In the first epigraph I quoted, the signatories
claim that their war hero Robert the Bruce, who had defeated the English at
Bannockburn in 1314, was king only by their consent, and that if he 'sub-
verted' their rights (*sui nostrique Juris subuersorem*), they would depose him.

In 1647, after the parliamentary armies had defeated King Charles I in the first English civil war, they argued among themselves about what that defeat implied. A faction of soldiers and civilians, known as the Levellers, put forward a programme ('An Agreement of the People') for limited government, universal male franchise, and frequent general elections. This horrified the leaders of the Parliamentary Army, but they nevertheless debated the proposals for two weeks with the Levellers, beginning in Putney church. The (now) best-known speech at Putney was made by Col. Thomas Rainborough. He was rescued from utter obscurity by the discovery of the transcript in 1890, followed after a further century by a prize-winning exhibition in Putney church and the accolade of TV serialization (*The Devil's Whore*, 2008). Rainborough's ideas were reinvented independently by John Locke, whose *Second Treatise of Government* was published in 1690 after the abdication of King James II (of England) and VII (of Scotland). After the writing, but before the publication, of Locke's *Second Treatise*, Convention Parliaments[1] in both countries had separately chosen William of Orange and his wife Mary to be king and queen. An elected monarchy, as perhaps foreseen by the Scots in 1320, was thus a reality. The parliaments rearranged the rules of royal succession again in 1701 (in England) and 1705–7 (in Scotland).

That this history should have led for three centuries to the legal convention, and rule of common law, that *Parliament*, rather than the people, is sovereign is slightly mysterious. The Framers of the US Constitution, students of Locke and his successors in the Scottish Enlightenment, declared in 1787 '*We the People of the United States . . . do ordain and establish this Constitution.*' They did not know about Rainborough, but some of them, including Thomas Jefferson,[2] were close students of the English Civil War. Similar declarations have been made in numerous other democracies including France and Australia. This book explores how the British Constitution would look if its writers were to do what the American Framers did in 1787.

The British Constitution is changing fast. The biggest generators of change were UK membership of the European Union (EU) in 1973; the first, and so far only, nationwide referendum, on whether Britain should remain in the EU,[3] in 1975; and the devolution of power to elected governments in Scotland, Wales, and intermittently Northern Ireland, enacted in 1997–8 and beginning in 1999. Through all these changes, and others described in this book, some writers of textbooks on law and constitutional theory have clung to an outdated framework defined for them by a deeply prejudiced law professor with a long beard, whose most famous book was published in 1885. Even as they argue with him (as most of them do), they continue to take his theories as their starting point. One problem is that he seemed to know very little about Scotland, although he coauthored a book about the Union of England and Scotland in 1707. That Union created Great Britain, a new state with a single Parliament and executive.

The incoherence of the British Constitution is not a new problem. It dates back to that union of 1707, when two constitutional traditions were awkwardly merged. A symbol of this awkwardness has endured for three centuries with almost no comment. The Treaty and Acts of Union 1706/7 unite the executives and legislatures of England and Scotland into Great Britain. They comprise three documents in temporal sequence. In the first (the Treaty), English and Scots negotiators agreed a set of terms for union. In the second (the last Act of the Scottish Parliament), the Scots enacted the articles of the treaty, but announced in advance that their assent would be withdrawn if the English failed to accept the incorporated Act for the Security of the Church of Scotland. The English were welcome to add an Act of their own for the security of the Church of England. In the final document, namely the last Act of the English Parliament, the English did just that, while reciting and incorporating the Scottish Act.

Whether this third document is viewed as the last act of the English Parliament or (as the various collections of Statutes do) the first Act of the Parliament of Great Britain, it imposes two conflicting duties on the monarch of Great Britain. The incorporated Scottish Act is an Act for securing the true Protestant religion and Presbyterian Church Government. Each incoming monarch must, by the Acts of Union, 'inviolably maintain and preserve the foresaid Settlement of the true Protestant Religion'. The English Act requires that

> for ever hereafter every King or Queen succeeding and coming to the Royal Government of the Kingdom of Great Britain at His or Her Coronation shall in the presence of all persons who shall be attending assisting or otherwise then and there present take and subscribe an Oath to maintain and preserve inviolably the said Settlement of the Church of England and the Doctrine Worship Discipline and Government thereof as by Law established within the Kingdoms of England and Ireland the Dominion of Wales and Town of Berwick upon Tweed and the Territories thereunto belonging.

Because the English Parliament incorporated the Scottish Act as the Scots had forced it to do, these two incompatible requirements are found in a single Act of Parliament, the (English) Union with Scotland Act 1706 c.11.[4] There can be at most one true Protestant religion. The monarch of the United Kingdom is legally required to protect inconsistent truths.

Despite that anomaly, the Union of England and Scotland was successful after a rocky start. It was bitterly unpopular in Scotland when it was negotiated, and its unpopularity enabled the Jacobites (supporters of the deposed King James VII and II—*Jacobus* in Latin—and his descendants the 'Old Pretender' and 'Young Pretender') to mount their unsuccessful risings in 1715 and 1745. Bonnie Prince Charlie, the 'Young Pretender' to loyalists, arrived in Edinburgh in 1745 and set up his court at Holyrood Palace (just across the road from the present-day Scottish Parliament). The Edinburgh militia of university intellectuals failed to resist him, and he soon defeated a government army at Prestonpans, east of Edinburgh. However, his invasion of England petered out at Derby, and his forces were routed on the retreat at Culloden, near Inverness, in 1746.

Soon after Culloden, the Scottish Enlightenment of Adam Smith and David Hume burst forth in astonishing profusion. Scotland suddenly changed from the dirt-poor theocracy it had been only fifty years earlier, when an Edinburgh student was hanged for blasphemy, to a prosperous and cultured society, whose elites believed that the Union had been very good for Scotland. Nobody seriously challenged that view until the 1880s, and then only because nationalism started to seep back from Ireland.

The Union of Great Britain with Ireland in 1800–1 looked superficially like the Union with Scotland of a century earlier. But there was one fatal difference. In both cases, the MPs and negotiators of the smaller country demanded conditions in return for their agreement to dissolve its parliament. In Scotland, those conditions were subsequently honoured (with an exception, described below, which lasted from 1712 to 1843 and caused a great deal of trouble but did not threaten the Union itself after 1746). In Ireland, they were not. Ireland was overwhelmingly Catholic; its second religion was the Presbyterianism of the Ulster Scots; the established Anglican religion was only the third in size. A faction of its all-Protestant Parliament had demanded greater civil rights for Catholics and Presbyterians as part of the Union bargain. Prime Minister William Pitt the Younger had promised them. But after the Act of Union had passed and the Irish Parliament had dissolved itself, King George III decided that Catholic emancipation, as it was called, would violate his Coronation oath to protect the Protestant religion, and he vetoed it. Pitt resigned, and the Union was illegitimate from the start in the eyes of most Irish people. When they got the vote, they used it to elect politicians who demanded a weakening (but not a dissolution) of the Union. They were called 'nationalists'. Their opponents were called 'Unionists'. By the 1880s, Protestants from the north-east of Ireland tended to be fervent Unionists, but so did many English and Scottish people.

In spite of the Scottish and Irish difficulties, a traditional narrative of the British Constitution continued to develop, due principally to the nineteenth-century jurist and Unionist ideologue A.V. Dicey (1835–1922), who was an Oxford law professor. After the Hanoverian succession, 'the King' became to a large extent 'the government, acting in the king's name'. The government inherited the Royal Prerogative from the king. Under the Royal Prerogative, which is part of the customary common law and is not codified, the government may do lots of things without seeking the consent of legislature or people. Here as elsewhere, English commentators have assumed without hesitation that legal doctrines derived from English history apply throughout Great Britain, although Scots law remained distinct under the terms of the Treaty and Acts of Union.

Throughout his writings Dicey refers to 'England' and the 'English Constitution' to mean the United Kingdom and the British Constitution, respectively. His last book, however, written jointly with R. S. Rait, the Historiographer-Royal for Scotland, was a study of the 1707 Act of Union. Here Dicey and Rait (1920) acknowledge that Scotland might be different, although even in this book they refer only to a singular Act of Union. However, Dicey is most famous for his *Introduction to the Law of the Constitution* (Dicey 1885/1915), a text which went through eight editions in his lifetime and is still a reference point for constitutional law despite frequent attacks on it by public lawyers. He announced two fundamental doctrines: parliamentary sovereignty and the rule of law. These were intended to be both descriptions of the British Constitution and normative statements. In other words, they claimed to describe both how constitutional actors, such as judges and soldiers, actually behaved and how they ought to behave.

But Dicey was also a fervent Unionist who hated the idea of devolution to Ireland. This hatred led him to undermine his own constitutional doctrine and to encourage others to do so. He was one of the main godfathers of the Unionist revolt of 1912–14, described later. A coalition including the king, the leaders of the Opposition, the House of Lords, and a group of contingently mutinous[5] army officers vetoed the policies of the elected government. What happened in spring 1914 was no less than a successful coup d'état. It would have made a civil war in Ireland almost inevitable had it not been providentially overtaken by the First World War.

Dicey's own actions helped to make his doctrine descriptively wrong. Parliament was not sovereign, nor did the rule of law apply, in 1914. Dicey and other Unionists groped for a rival doctrine of popular sovereignty, but did not produce a credible one. He also destroyed his own normative theory.

By 1913 he had reduced it to the proposition: 'Parliament is sovereign except when I think it should not be: in which case those who think it should remain sovereign are fools.' In his last and most strident blast against Irish Home Rule, *A Fool's Paradise* (Dicey 1913), he writes that 'oppression, and especially resistance to the will of the nation, might justify what was technically conspiracy or rebellion'. In Ireland, soldiers at the Curragh and gunrunners at Larne took him at his word in 1914. In the name of what they took (without evidence) to be the will of the nation, they destroyed parliamentary supremacy, as this book relates.

Nevertheless, modern texts on constitutional law still operate in the shadow of Dicey (but see Weill 2003). Despite a formidable onslaught from (Sir) Ivor Jennings in the 1930s, standard texts would say until recently, 'Dicey's word has in some respects become the only written constitution we have' (Jowell and Oliver 1985, second edition 1989: p. v). Vernon Bogdanor, quoting this, sets about 'exorcising Dicey's ghost' in his copious writings about the UK Constitution (Bogdanor 1995, 1996, 2003). He fails to. Although Jowell and Oliver now refer to 'hammer blows against our . . . Diceyan traditions' delivered since 1997 (Jowell and Oliver 1985, fourth edition 2000: p. v), the undead Dicey still hovers over discussions of sovereignty and the rule of law. For instance, in the most important constitutional case to reach the Law Lords so far in the twenty-first century, one of the Law Lords giving judgment describes Dicey as 'our greatest constitutional lawyer'.[6] As a consequence, professional discussions of such matters as Crown prerogative, church establishment, the role of the UK monarchy in its constitution, devolution, Europe, and the status of fundamental constitutional law have a century-old conservative slant.

This book aims to exorcize Dicey's ghost. It is both political history and political science. The history aims to explain why Dicey's legacy is bankrupt. By examining the creation of the United Kingdom in 1705–7 and 1800–1, I try to show how Dicey's anglocentrism blinded him, and almost everybody who has followed him, to the real nature of the two unions. I then focus on the Unionist campaign of (initially civil) disobedience against the elected governments between 1909 and 1914, which began with the House of Lords' rejection of government bills including the 1909 Budget and culminated in the illegal arming of Ulster Protestant paramilitaries with 30,000 rifles and three million ammunition rounds from a dealer in Hamburg. (The price was high because German arms dealers were also arming both sides in the Mexican civil war.) This operation was bankrolled by, among others, Rudyard Kipling, Lord Milner, and possibly the Unionist frontbencher

Walter Long. The most revered commander in the British Army, Field-Marshal Lord Roberts, approved a letter to be issued in his name encouraging soldiers to disobey orders.[7] The coup was masterminded by Sir Edward Carson and encouraged by the Leader of his Majesty's Loyal Opposition, Andrew Bonar Law. Law probably had advance knowledge of, and may even have financed, the Hamburg-to-Larne gunrunning. His Majesty King George V was loyal to his opposition, not to his government. All of these believed that the Parliament Act 1911 had removed Parliament's legitimacy.

The reader may say that this was a long time ago, and that the possibilities for later coups have been modified by such developments as the abdication of Edward VIII and the Parliament Act 1949. But these events need only have happened once to destroy Dicey's credibility, because they show that at times of heightened partisanship—exactly the times when a constitution must be most robust—the British Constitution was at its most fragile. To replace Diceyanism as positive description I introduce (in Chapter 2) veto-player theory and an American-derived theory of modified popular sovereignty.

Briefly, the more veto players there are in a political system, the more stable its outcomes. Under the normal operations of parliamentary politics, there were only two veto players in British politics up to 1911, and something like 1.5 since then. The two veto players can be represented as the median MP and the median peer. Normally, with single-party governments, the median MP is a member of the governing party. The median peer was always a Conservative up to 1999 and is now a Liberal Democrat, a Lord Spiritual (i.e. bishop), or a cross-bencher. The median peer held a veto over all legislation (except, it was believed, money bills) up to 1909. In 1909, he vetoed the Budget. This led, after two general elections forced by successive kings' veto on creating peers without an election, to the curbing of his powers in the Parliament Act 1911, limiting, but not eliminating, his veto. It is still effective in the last years of a Parliament, when time has run out to enforce legislation by repeated passage through the Commons under the terms of the Parliament Acts 1911 and 1949.

I then introduce the concept of the 'win set' of the status quo. The win set is the set of points that can be reached by majority decision without being vetoed. If the United Kingdom truly was the 'elective dictatorship' that politicians in opposition sometimes claim it to be, the win set would be of infinite size, because anything the median MP could be persuaded by her government to support would be carried. This would be majoritarian, but not stable, because after the next election the median MP might be of a different party. But the United Kingdom is not an elective dictatorship, except perhaps under Conservative governments before the United Kingdom's entry to the

EU. At all other times, the (Conservative till 1999) median peer is a veto player subject only to the Parliament Acts and the 'Salisbury convention' discussed later. Since EU entry, the primacy of EU over member-state law limits parliamentary sovereignty. This is brought out most starkly in the *Factortame* cases of 1990–1,[8] which I analyse below. With more veto players, policy is more stable, but some outcomes that a majority of elected legislators would prefer cannot be reached. Since EU entry, two further challenges to parliamentary sovereignty have materialized. One is devolution within the United Kingdom, which brings back to the agenda a number of issues that Scots lawyers and historians (and almost nobody else) have worried about since 1707.[9] The other is human rights law. These are discussed in detail in Chapters 9 and 10, respectively.

If parliamentary sovereignty is incoherent, what might replace it? My answer is popular sovereignty modified by entrenchment. American constitutionalism reached this point over 200 years ago (and Australian constitutionalism over 100 years ago). The US Constitution, ratified in 1787–8, declares that 'we, the people of the United States . . . do ordain this Constitution'. It is easy to be cynical. No women or slaves ordained it. Nevertheless, it was subject to ratification, and was ratified. The original Constitution therefore embodies the compromises necessary to get majorities of those entitled to vote in at least nine states to ratify it. It contains provision for its own ratification and amendment. It creates two directly elected chambers—the President and the House of Representatives. Since the Seventeenth Amendment in 1913, the Senate has also been directly elected. As they are all elected by different procedures, the median voter in each is a different person, and the win set of the status quo is the set of policies that is not vetoed by the median (unique) President, the median Senator, or the median Representative.

There is therefore a considerable amount of discussion of the US and Australian constitutions in this book. Why these two countries in particular, rather than (say) Canada, Germany, or France, which get only passing mentions? Because the United States and Australia are the only two countries with a common-law tradition whose original constitutions claim to derive from the people. (Canada was a latecomer to this party, but its 1982 constitution is discussed in Chapter 10). The US Constitution had to be ratified by constitutional conventions in at least nine states before coming into effect. It was, although some of the ratifying states demanded that a further Bill of Rights be added: it was, too. The Australian Constitution was the product of constitutional conventions in 1891 and 1897–8—the first elected by the colonial legislatures, and the second directly elected by the people. Neither Constitution may be amended unless the draft amendment is ratified by a supermajority of the people in a majority of the states.

The United States is a federal republic. So, according to Galligan (1995), is Australia. The former description is uncontroversial; the latter is controversial. Australians had a constitutional crisis in 1975, logically followed by a referendum on a republic in 1999, which the republicans lost. Nevertheless, I agree with Galligan that in all essentials Australia is both a federal and a republic. The starting point of this book is: 'How would the British Constitution look if we all agreed (1) that the Acts of Union 1706/7 enacted a treaty, not a takeover; and (2) that sovereignty ultimately comes from the people, not Parliament?' I argue that it would look like the constitution of a federal republic.

The US Constitution also guarantees rights, both procedural (e.g. against self-incrimination) and substantive (e.g. of free speech), which are intended to be proof against majorities. To that extent it restricts popular sovereignty in favour of protecting rights. As explored in Chapter 2, it does not operate as it says on its face. Analysis of the US Constitution and inferences for the United Kingdom must deal with the uncomfortable fact that all the most important amendments to the Constitution have been enacted unconstitutionally.

This book discusses what would change and what would not were the United Kingdom to become a regime of popular sovereignty modified by entrenchment. Laws to be entrenched would include those that create or amend a *rule of recognition*. A rule of recognition is a secondary rule or meta-rule that stipulates which claimants to the title of 'rules' may actually be called rules. As classically defined:

> [A] 'rule of recognition' . . . will specify some feature or features possession of which by a suggested rule is taken as a conclusive affirmative indication that it is a rule of the group to be supported by the social pressure it exerts . . . . In a developed legal system the rules of recognition . . . instead of identifying rules exclusively by reference to a text . . . do so by reference to some general characteristic possessed by the primary rules (Hart 1961).

Another class of rules about rules are 'rules of change' which give a defined set of people the right to introduce new primary rules and abolish old ones. The rule of recognition needs to recognize the rule of change (Hart 1961: pp. 92–3).

Thus the Parliament Acts, Representation of the People Acts, and Parliamentary Constituencies Acts are rules of change. They each redefine the class of people entitled to make authoritative primary rules, and the class of people entitled to elect those who make those primary rules. So do those Acts that incorporate treaties between sovereign bodies, such as the Act of Union 1706 and the European Communities Act 1972. The 1706 Act creates a Parliament of Great Britain; the 1972 Act gives EU law priority over domestic law.

Rules of change must contain a rule for their own amendment. If a branch cannot bend, it may break. The US Constitution, wonderful achievement though it was, contained no rule saying whether, and if so in what circumstances, states could secede. This omission helped to cause the bloodiest war in US history. For the same reason, it would be wrong to insist that Scotland cannot secede from the United Kingdom, or that the United Kingdom may never leave the EU. It would not only be wrong, but also pointless. If a majority of both Members of the Scottish Parliament and the Scottish people want Scotland to secede, there would be little or no resistance in the UK Parliament to repeal of the 1706 Act. Since the Scottish election of 2007, both the minority Scottish Nationalist government and the leader of the Opposition in Scotland have called for a referendum on Scottish independence (although they wanted different sorts of referendum, at different times). Parliament has already offered the same guarantee to Northern Ireland. If a majority of the people there wish to secede from the United Kingdom, nobody will stand in their way. It would be totally pointless for a UK government to say to the Scots that, since the constitution is a reserved power, a Scottish referendum vote in favour of independence was of no force.[10]

Nevertheless, Parliament and the courts already treat constitutional Acts like these two as special, in ways to be described in later chapters. It would be much clearer and simpler if the procedures for their repeal or amendment were explicitly *supermajoritarian*. All written constitutions include rules for their amendment. For instance, amendments to the US Constitution require a two-thirds vote in both houses of Congress and the assent of three-quarters of the states. Amendments to the Australian Constitution require an absolute majority of both houses of parliament and approval in a referendum. These are high thresholds; there have been few constitutional amendments in either country. If an Act or constitution cannot be repealed by a simple majority of those voting in each Parliamentary chamber, it is said to be *entrenched*. How entrenchment might work in the United Kingdom is discussed in later chapters.

Many constitutions also entrench fundamental rights. It would be possible to entrench some rights protection in the United Kingdom, including, for instance, the Human Rights Act 1998. It would also be possible to go further. One entrenchable Act protecting fundamental rights could be drawn directly from the US Constitution by simply adapting its First

Amendment: 'Parliament shall make no law respecting an establishment of religion, or prohibiting the free exercise thereof; or abridging the freedom of speech, or of the press; or the right of the people peaceably to assemble, and to petition the government for a redress of grievances.'

Under such a regime, a number of bodies that remain only because of intellectual conservatism would disappear. These would include an unelected upper house, established churches, and the remaining constitutional duties of the monarch. The 2007 Green Paper on Governance in practice disestablishes the Church of England, although it denies doing so.

The upper house of Parliament would be wholly or largely elected. After the Commons voted (perhaps cynically) for a wholly elected upper house in 2007, a cross-party Parliamentary committee with representatives from both houses (including a bishop) produced a White Paper in 2008 (Ministry of Justice 2008), analysing options and transitional arrangements for such a house. The immediate press response was cynical. But I think the White Paper is worth taking more seriously than the UK press did when it appeared. Dicey and others were scrambling around for a theory of popular sovereignty a century ago. But that theory must remain radically incoherent unless the people elect the veto players in the executive (who may be drawn from either house) and the legislature. All churches and faith communities would become voluntary bodies subject to the same regulation as all other charities. They would have no role in the legislature (whereas the 2008 White Paper proposes to retain bishops). The head of state would be either directly elected or chosen by both elected houses of Parliament. The titles 'king', queen', prince', 'lord', etc. could remain but neither duties nor privileges would be attached to them.

Constitutional law is a secret garden. Some lawyers object to people who are not lawyers setting foot in it. One lawyer told my publishers that the prospectus for this book was the worst proposal he or she had ever seen. I think this is unfortunate. It has meant that lawyers' discussion of the British Constitution has been locked away in the secret garden. But it matters to everybody. That is why I have barged in. Equally, as one trained originally in history and later in political science, I have not hesitated to barge into the secret gardens of other academic disciplines. Historians may find this book annoying for a different reason. I have not recounted the long sweep of British and Irish constitutional history, but have rather zoomed in on a few key moments. I concede that I may have wrenched my moments out of context. But with a tight word limit it was that or nothing. I want my political science to be historically informed.

My reference list is therefore a list of the works referred to in the book. It is not a list of everything I have read on British history or the British Constitution. Some may raise an eyebrow at my scanty citation of (especially) law texts. The reason is that I find that they go on an infinite regress. *What is the British Constitution? What a previous constitutional lawyer has said it is.* Some people who are not constitutional lawyers are allowed into the canon, including a mid-Victorian journalist, and a king's secretary writing to *The Times* under the pseudonym 'Senex' (old man). As related below, in late 1975, when the Australian Attorney-General's office urgently had to compile a file on whether the Governor-General of Australia could properly dismiss the Prime Minister of Australia (which he just had), they were reduced to photocopying a mutually referring cycle of mostly British constitutional law books. Most of them said he could. One of them (Sir Ivor Jennings) said he perhaps could but certainly should not. This is pretty intellectually unsatisfying.

One lawyer whose approach is quite similar to mine, namely Elizabeth Wicks (2006), is scantily cited for a different reason—I did not become aware of her book until I had written about two-thirds of this one. Like me, Wicks analyses certain critical junctures of UK constitutional history, although (except for her important chapter on the European Convention on Human Rights) she does not use archive sources. Her list of crucial junctures is similar but not identical to mine. The main difference is that, like other lawyers and historians, she seems to underestimate the (counter-)revolutionary events of 1911–14, which I analyse in detail.

For different reasons, I cite only scantily some other modern UK lawyers and political scientists whose approach is closer to mine, although I do not exactly agree with any of them. They include Adam Tomkins, Anthony King, David Marquand, and Richard Bellamy (Tomkins 2005, 2008; Bellamy 2007; King 2007; Marquand 2008a, 2008b). I have deliberately *not* kept their books beside me whilst writing mine: not because I do not respect them, but because I want to say what I want to say, rather than produce a more conventional literature review.

I am limited in time and words. Some topics for which I have no room are admirably covered in the recent review by the Constitution Unit, University College, London (Hazell 2008b). This book reviews Hazell's earlier constitutional *History of the Next Ten Years* (1999) which mostly proved prophetic. I say little about proportional representation and almost nothing about either watchdogs of the constitution or freedom of information (although I have used FOI to prise open some of the sources I use). Although I talk about upper house reform, I have no room for a discussion of lower house reform. For admirable and even-handed discussions of all of these, see Hazell (2008b).

If people outside the magic circle were allowed to nominate their most important constitutional document (other than an Act of Parliament), my vote would go to an exchange of letters between Prime Minister Asquith and King George V in autumn 1913 on the constitutional position of the sovereign. The issues they contest are at the heart of the book. I believe that, on all the main points, Asquith was right and the king was wrong. But that is for the reader to judge. Although four of the five have been published before, to the best of my knowledge, they have never been published as a set; and Asquith's final salvo has not been published before as far as I know.

I struggled to find the right place to put them in the book. In the end, I have put them as an appendix to Chapter 12. But I refer to them constantly in the book. And they are such a good read that perhaps the reader should go there first, and then decide whether or not to read the rest of this book.

1

The English Public Lawyers' Constitution

A SO-CALLED 'UNWRITTEN' CONSTITUTION

Here is the full text of the letter published in *The Times* on 2 May 1950, which I mentioned in the Preface and Introduction.

DISSOLUTION OF PARLIAMENT

Factors in Crown's choice

Sir,—It is surely indisputable (and common sense) that a Prime Minister may ask—not demand—that his Sovereign will grant him a dissolution of Parliament; and that the Sovereign, if he so chooses, may refuse to grant this request. The problem of such a choice is entirely personal to the Sovereign, though he is, of course, free to seek informal advice from anybody whom he thinks fit to consult.

In so far as this matter can be publicly discussed, it can be properly assumed that no wise Sovereign—that is, one who has at heart the true interest of the country, the constitution, and the Monarchy—would deny a dissolution to his Prime Minister unless he were satisfied that: (1) the existing Parliament was still vital, viable, and capable of doing its job; (2) a General Election would be detrimental to the national economy; (3) he could rely on finding another Prime Minister who could carry on his Government, for a reasonable period, with a working majority in the House of Commons. When Sir Patrick Duncan refused a dissolution to his Prime Minister in South Africa in 1939, all these conditions were satisfied: when Lord Byng did the same in Canada in 1926, they appeared to be, but in the event the third proved illusory.

I am &c.,   SENEX.
April 29.[1]

What should a discourse analyst, such as a constitutional lawyer, make of this? On the face of it, we do not know who wrote the letter, with what authority. The writer states that there are matters about the Sovereign's response to a Prime Minister's request for a dissolution that cannot be publicly discussed. Two things are said to be both indisputable and common sense, though in a brief letter the author does not have space to explain why. A wise sovereign is defined as one who jointly possesses three listed qualities, implying that any other sovereign is unwise. For a sovereign to be wise, it is therefore essential that he or his advisors is capable of judging whether a general election would be detrimental to the national economy. He or his advisors must therefore have skills in macroeconomic analysis.

Whether a Prime Minister may or may not expect a request for dissolution of Parliament to be granted is clearly a bedrock constitutional matter. A denial of such a dissolution means that the head of state, rather than the electorate, has chosen the government. So how can a constitutional lawyer—or anybody else—know that in this respect the UK Constitution is what Senex says it is?

Bogdanor (1995: 158) states that 'Senex' was Sir Alan Lascelles, King George VI's principal private secretary, who at the time was 63. He does not state how he knows this, but quotes letters from Lascelles in the Royal Archives on cognate matters which make the claim plausible. What, then, made Sir Alan an authority on the Constitution? Rather circularly, the fact that he had been a courtier since 1920. In his earlier career, according to the *Dictionary of National Biography,* he had

> had difficulty in settling into a job. Having failed to get into the Foreign Office he turned his hand to journalism and stockbroking but found them dispiriting. He joined the Bedfordshire yeomanry in 1913 and was mobilized on the outbreak of war. (Prochaska 2004)

He, thus, had no formal qualifications except his long service to three kings, one of whom (Edward VIII) he evidently despised. His dispiriting experience in stockbroking may or may not have qualified him to judge whether a general election would be detrimental to the national economy.

It is to uncertainties such as these that writers refer when they inaccurately call the United Kingdom's constitution 'unwritten'. Rather, a mutually referring group of writers say that constitutional conventions are what they say they are. The canon of these writers is generally held (see, e.g., King 2007: 15) to include:

- Walter Bagehot, political commentator, economist, and journalist (1826–1877);
- A. V. Dicey, jurist (1835–1922);

- Sidney Low, journalist, historian, and essayist (1857–1932);
- L. S. Amery, politician and journalist (1873–1955);
- Harold Laski, political theorist and university teacher (1893–1950); and
- Ivor Jennings, jurist (1903–1965).

The descriptions of each writer are taken from the *Oxford Dictionary of National Biography* (*ODNB*). They reveal that to be a canonical writer on the British constitution it is neither necessary nor sufficient to be a constitutional ('public') lawyer, or, as *ODNB* puts it, a 'jurist'.

Nevertheless, in the rest of this chapter I attempt to give a consensus view of what English public lawyers (and the journalists, politicians, and royal secretaries who are deemed canonical) say constitutes the British Constitution. They say that there are two fundamental principles: parliamentary sovereignty and the rule of law.

PARLIAMENTARY SOVEREIGNTY

As often, the starting point is Dicey (1885/1915: 30, 37–8):

> The duty, in short, of an English professor of law is to state what are the laws which form part of the constitution, to arrange them in their order, to explain their meaning, and to exhibit where possible their logical connection. . . .The sovereignty of Parliament is (from a legal point of view) the dominant characteristic of our political institutions. . . .Parliament means, in the mouth of a lawyer (though the word has often a different sense in ordinary conversation), the King, the House of Lords, and the House of Commons; these three bodies acting together may be aptly described as the 'King in Parliament', and constitute Parliament. The principle of Parliamentary sovereignty means neither more nor less than this, namely, that Parliament thus defined has, under the English constitution, the right to make or unmake any law whatever; and, further, that no person or body is recognised by the law of England as having a right to override or set aside the legislation of Parliament.

In 'stat[ing] what are the laws which form . . . the constitution', Dicey relied on earlier writers. He cites the eighteenth-century jurist Sir William Blackstone (1723–1780), first as to the composition of Parliament:

> THE constituent parts of a parliament are the next objects of our enquiry. And these are, the king's majesty, sitting there in his royal political capacity, and the three estates of the realm; the lords spiritual, the lords temporal, (who sit, together with the king, in one house) and the commons, who sit

by themselves in another. And the king and these three estates, together, form the great corporation or body politic of the kingdom, of which the king is said to be caput, principium, et finis. For upon their coming together the king meets them, either in person or by representation; without which there can be no beginning of a parliament; and he also has alone the power of dissolving them. (Blackstone 1765–9: I, 149)[2]

Blackstone (and Dicey, following him) locates parliamentary sovereignty in fifteenth-century decisions by judges that they have no power to inquire into the internal affairs of parliament. Dicey quotes a long passage from Blackstone to this effect. In turn Blackstone quotes the early seventeenth-century jurist Sir Edward Coke and others of that century, on the sovereignty of parliament. This reflects the common pattern (and problem) of constitutional lawyers' citations of one another: How many iterations of a constitutional lawyer's citation of a predecessor's claim that X does it require for X to be true? It is also interesting that Dicey's citation of Blackstone stops just before Blackstone goes on to write:

> IT must be owned that Mr Locke,[3] and other theoretical writers, have held, that 'there remains still inherent in the people a supreme power to remove or alter the legislative, when they find the legislative act contrary to the trust reposed in them: for when such trust is abused; it is thereby forfeited, and devolves to those who gave it.' But however just this conclusion may be in theory, we cannot adopt it, nor argue from it, under any dispensation of government at present actually existing. For this devolution of power, to the people at large, includes in it a dissolution of the whole form of government established by that people, reduces all the members of their original state of equality, and by annihilating the sovereign power repeals all positive laws whatsoever before enacted. No human laws will therefore suppose a case, which at once must destroy all law, and compel men to build afresh upon a new foundation; nor will they make provision for so desperate an event, as must render all legal provisions ineffectual. So long therefore as the English constitution lasts, we may venture to affirm, that the power of parliament is absolute and without control. (Blackstone 1765–9: I, 157)[4]

This is a very significant omission on both Blackstone's and Dicey's part. Locke argued that sovereignty lay with the people, who could reclaim it from a tyrannical government. He held that that was exactly what happened in 1688, when the people deposed James II and accepted William and Mary. This idea of popular sovereignty profoundly influenced the framers of the American and Australian Constitutions. However, Blackstone's rejection of Locke combines with his formalism that only a king can summon a parliament to leave him with an awkward question: What was the status of the 'convention parliaments' of 1660 and 1688, both of which met to invite somebody to accept the throne of England? Blackstone has no coherent answer to that question. We might now say that a revolution begets its own legality, and that this is what the English Bill of Rights Act and Scottish Claim of Right Act, both of 1689, do. They both announce that William and Mary have accepted their thrones on conditions laid down by the two convention parliaments. But then Blackstone's invocation of 'the king's majesty, sitting there in his royal political capacity' sits awkwardly with his claim, a mere eight pages on, that Parliament is sovereign because the courts have held back from interfering with it. What if there is a row between the king and the rest of parliament? Is that not what the English Civil War (1640–9) was about?

Dicey resolves any such tension by saying that since 1688 'the King occupies his throne under a parliamentary title; his claim to reign depends upon and is the result of a statute', namely, the Act of Settlement 1701, which itself recites the Bill of Rights Act 1689 (Dicey 1885/1915: 41). Neither Blackstone nor Dicey mentions the situation in Scotland (see later).

In other books (especially Dicey 1905 and the anti-Home Rule polemics analysed in Chapter 6) and in other times Dicey was willing to admit that Parliament was in turn influenced, and partly elected, by the people. But here he claims to be stating 'what the laws are' as if that were an entirely separate exercise. In this, most English public lawyers have followed him. Even when they disagree with him (as most now do), they argue within an intellectual framework that he largely created. If I can persuade readers that that framework is fundamentally broken, a radical reconstruction may be possible. But that is a task for later chapters.

Parliamentary sovereignty thus means that Parliament may enact anything it chooses. There is nothing it cannot do except, paradoxically, bind a later Parliament. For if an Act should contain a section such as

> That the foresaid true Protestant Religion, contained in the above-mentioned Confession of Faith, with the Form and Purity of Worship presently in use within this Church, and its Presbyterian Church Government and Discipline (that is to say) the Government of the Church by Kirk Sessions, Presbyteries, Provincial Synods, and General Assemblies, all established by the foresaid Acts of Parliament, pursuant to the Claim of Right, shall remain and continue unalterable, and that the said Presbyterian Government shall be the only Government of the Church within the Kingdom of *Scotland*. (Act of Union 1706, s.2)

what is the force of 'shall remain and continue unalterable'? If Parliament is to be sovereign, a later Parliament, or even a later session of the current Parliament, must have the right to change its mind. The Parliament of 1711, after a Tory General Election victory, changed the 'unalterable' government of the Church of Scotland in a way which some of its supporters regarded as clear breach of the Treaty and Acts of Union. To Dicey and his followers, this merely reflects parliamentary sovereignty: It did it because it could.

Furthermore, according to Dicey and his followers, repeal need not be explicit. In another of his more notorious phrases:

> Should the Dentists Act, 1878, unfortunately contradict the terms of the Act of Union, the Act of Union would be *pro tanto* repealed (Dicey 1885/1915: 141)

This is the doctrine of implied repeal. A later statute trumps an earlier one, even if the later statute does not explicitly repeal the section of the previous statute with which it is found to be inconsistent.

What is it that Parliament is sovereign over? One formula is as given in the Government of Ireland Act 1920 at s.75:

> Notwithstanding the establishment of the Parliaments, of Southern and Northern Ireland, or the Parliament of Ireland, or anything contained in this Act, the supreme authority of the Parliament of the United Kingdom shall remain unaffected and undiminished over all persons, matters, and things in Ireland and every part thereof.

Here the political scientist and the lawyer tend to part company. The political scientist may say: *But that is ridiculous. The whole point of the 1920 Act was to set up subordinate parliaments in Ireland. Of these, one (in Northern Ireland) succeeded and the other failed. The very enactment of the Act arguably made s.75 false. If its enactment did not, then certainly the treaty recognizing the independence of the Irish Free State in December 1921 did so. The Parliament of the United Kingdom no longer had supreme authority over persons, matters, and things in Ireland. The same comments apply to all divestments of power by the UK Parliament, including the statutes giving self-government to Canada and Australia.*

Warming to the theme, the political scientist may continue: *The Australian Constitution is a schedule to the UK Commonwealth of Australia Constitution Act 1900. The UK Colonial Secretary, Joseph Chamberlain, insisted on adding, to the constitution agreed by the Australian Constitutional Conventions, a section broadening the acceptable classes of appeals from the Australian High Court to the Privy Council. This forms part of s.74 of the Constitution:*

> Except as provided in this section, this Constitution shall not impair any right which the Queen may be pleased to exercise by virtue of Her Royal prerogative to grant special leave of appeal from the High Court to Her

Majesty in Council. The Parliament may make laws limiting the matters in which such leave may be asked, but proposed laws containing any such limitation shall be reserved by the Governor-General for Her Majesty's pleasure.

At this point a historian may take over. The Australian Constitution was drafted at two constitutional conventions the second of which was directly elected, approved by the requisite popular majorities in five of the six states (not western Australia) and presented to the UK government as a *fait accompli*—or so the Australians hoped. However, Chamberlain insisted on broadening appeals to the Privy Council 'because the interests of the British Empire—really of British interests in Australia—were concerned' (Galligan 1995: 28). During the constitutional crisis of 1975 occasioned by Governor General Sir John Kerr's dismissal of the government of Gough Whitlam, discussed below, Whitlam and his supporters appealed to Queen Elizabeth and her advisors to become involved. They refused, stating:

> The Australian Constitution (written by Australians, and which can only be changed by Australians) gives to the Governor-General (who is appointed by The Queen on the advice of her Australian Prime Minister) certain very specific constitutional functions and responsibilities. The written constitution, and accepted constitutional conventions, preclude The Queen from intervening personally in those functions once the Governor-General has been appointed.... (From standard letter by Queen's assistant private secretary to those who wrote to her to complain about the dismissal, November 1975, in Whitlam 1979: 176–7)

However, the Queen's assistant secretary, although an Australian himself, was not quite right. Section 74 of the Australian Constitution was not wholly written by Australians. It was changed, and then enacted, by non-Australians.

Did the extension of appeals to the Judicial Committee of the Privy Council (JCPC) matter? Yes and no. Private law cases continued to be referred to the JCPC (presumably at huge expense to litigants) until shortly before the abolition of appeals to it in 1986. Public law cases did not. The High Court of Australia has only ever referred one case to the Judicial Committee of the Privy Council, and then only because the Court was deadlocked. One other early public law case had gone on appeal to the Privy Council from a decision of the Supreme Court of Victoria.[5] The JCPC argued that it had jurisdiction to hear the case, and issued a ruling—which the Australian courts simply refused to accept. In the words of a later Chief Justice of the High Court:

> In *Webb* v. *Outtrim*, which was the first case affecting the Commonwealth
> Constitution which came before the Privy Council, it was apparent that the
> tribunal was not aware of the distinction between a unitary legislature with
> unlimited power [i.e., the UK Parliament as interpreted by Dicey] and
> a legislature operating under a federal Constitution by which it was
> bound [i.e. the Parliament of Victoria] ... [T]he High Court considered
> *Webb* v. *Outtrim* and refused to be bound by the decision. The High Court
> pointed out some obvious slips in the reasoning of *Webb* v. *Outtrim*.
> (Latham 1952: 7, 26)

By the (UK) Australia Act 1986, Parliament forwent any jurisdiction over the
Commonwealth and States of Australia, and appeals to the Privy Council were
abolished. Parallel legislation was passed by the Commonwealth and State
Parliaments in Australia (Galligan 1995: 31).

Section 74 of the Australian Constitution has not been repealed or
amended—it is simply made redundant by the Australia Acts 1986, passed
simultaneously, and in identical terms, by the United Kingdom, Australian
Commonwealth, and Australian State Parliaments. The results of appeals to
the Privy Council, imposed on the Australians by Joseph Chamberlain, were
simply ignored by the Australian courts long before 1986, whenever their
reasoning conflicted with Australian constitutional understanding. We have
the testimony of Sir John Latham, a long-serving Chief Justice of the Australian High Court, for that.

Thus, already we note some difficulties with the Diceyan concept of
parliamentary sovereignty:

*What happens if the components of the King-in-Parliament disagree with one
another?*

- Most acutely, what happens if a king purports to dismiss (the rest of) a
  Parliament, or (the rest of) a Parliament purports to dismiss a king?[6]
- How does the concept of parliamentary sovereignty sit with the anony-
  mous assertion of 'Senex' in 1950 that the king may refuse dissolution of
  Parliament?

*Can a sovereign Parliament ever bind itself not to reclaim an authority it has
devolved?*

- Specifically, can a sovereign Parliament meaningfully grant devolution to
  Scotland or (Northern) Ireland, or independence to Canada or Australia?
- Can a sovereign Parliament make meaningful promises not to intervene
  in the internal affairs of civil society organizations such as churches?

These difficulties will loom large in the chapters that follow.

THE RULE OF LAW

For Dicey, the rule of law has three components:

> We mean, in the first place, that no man is punishable or can be lawfully made to suffer in body or goods except for a distinct breach of law established in the ordinary legal manner before the ordinary Courts of the land. In this sense the rule of law is contrasted with every system of government based on the exercise by persons in authority of wide, arbitrary, or discretionary powers of constraint.

> We mean in the second place, when we speak of the 'rule of law' as a characteristic of our country, not only that with us no man is above the law, but (what is a different thing) that here every man, whatever be his rank or condition, is subject to the ordinary law of the realm and amenable to the jurisdiction of the ordinary tribunals.

> There remains yet a third and a different sense in which the 'rule of law' or the predominance of the legal spirit may be described as a special attribute of English institutions. We may say that the constitution is pervaded by the rule of law on the ground that the general principles of the constitution (as for example the right to personal liberty, or the right of public meeting) are with us the result of judicial decisions determining the rights of private persons in particular cases brought before the Courts; whereas under many foreign constitutions the security (such as it is) given to the rights of individuals results, or appears to result, from the general principles of the constitution. (Dicey 1885/1915 quoted at 183–4, 189, 191)

Dicey glosses each of these three senses. As to the first, he asserts that the rule of law in this sense is confined to 'England [*sic*], or to those countries which, like the United States of America, have inherited English traditions'—that is, to the common-law countries of the British Empire, past and contemporary. '[A] study of European politics now and again reminds English readers that wherever there is discretion there is room for arbitrariness.' Dicey was a sworn enemy of continental *droit administratif*, which, he said, gave state officials unacceptable discretion to act as they pleased.

As to the second, the law binds 'every official, from the Prime Minister down to a constable or a collector of taxes' just as it binds every non-official. Dicey does not clarify whether the law binds the monarch or not. He introduces his chapter with an untranslated statement from Norman-French law of the time of Henry VI (reigned 1422–61 and 1470–1): 'by the law he himself and all his subjects are ruled' (Dicey 1885/1915: 180; my translation). As to the third, he summarizes: 'Our constitution, in short, is a judge-made constitution, and it bears on its face all the features, good and bad, of judge-made law'.

Subsequent lawyers, working within the Diceyan tradition, have tried to separate wheat from chaff in these statements. They have accepted for a long time that Dicey's characterization of *droit administratif* owes more to prejudice than to actual knowledge of Continental legal systems (Robson 1928; Jowell 2007: 7). The issues of rules *versus* discretion, and courts *versus* administrative tribunals, are considered in the next section.

Is the King-in-Parliament subject to the rule of law? This question introduces an apparent contradiction between Dicey's two principles. To answer *yes* seems to limit parliamentary sovereignty; to answer *no* seems to limit the rule of law. The law of Henry VI could be read as stating 'by the law the King-in-Parliament and all his subjects are ruled': but the King-in-Parliament could change it. The US Constitution states: *No bill of attainder or ex post facto Law shall be passed* (US Constitution Article 1:9; article 1:10 bans the states from passing 'ex post facto' laws). An 'ex post facto' law is one that makes unlawful something that was lawful at the time it was done. Nevertheless, the doctrine of parliamentary sovereignty seems to imply that Parliament may pass an ex post facto law. The War Crimes Act 1991 is the only Act of the UK Parliament where a Conservative government had to use the Parliament Acts 1911–49 to override a veto in the Lords. The Lords' first veto was based on the claim that the bill was 'retrospective legislation' (*HL Deb 04 June 1990 vol 519 cc1080–1208* quoted at 1086).

Some commentators, such as Richard Bellamy, have disputed that there is any conflict between the rule of law and parliamentary sovereignty. 'The rule of law simply is the democratic rule of persons' (Bellamy 2007: 83). In the case of the War Crimes Act, the Lords were unelected; the Commons were elected; the Commons' use of the Parliament Acts can therefore be justified on democratic grounds. But suppose that an elected upper house had refused to pass the bill on the same grounds, claiming (as the unelected Lords did in 1990) that the bill violated the rule of law? Then there is a stark conflict between Dicey's two principles; one has to give way.

One possible way out of this dilemma is ruled out by Dicey's third gloss on the 'rule of law', where he contrasts it with the rule of entrenched bills of rights. Dicey relies instead on 'judicial decisions determining the rights of private persons' to protect human rights. This has to follow from his defence of parliamentary sovereignty. If a UK Parliament enacted the US Constitution's ban on ex post facto laws, it would be (purporting to) bind its successor, which, Dicey insists, is the one thing Parliament cannot do. Human rights, in his view, must therefore depend on judges, not on Parliament.

Critics from within English public law

The rule of law (in Dicey's stipulative definition) came under challenge before parliamentary sovereignty did. The first challenge came from the behaviour of A. V. Dicey and a number of others, when they encouraged a number of illegal acts in Protestant Ulster in 1913–14. This is discussed below. In the calmer halls of the court and lecture room, Dicey's characterization of administrative discretion as what those foreigners do was successfully challenged in 1928. The climate of public law in the United Kingdom changed with the politics of the day. In the 1930s, Jennings forcefully pointed out that there is much ideology in Dicey's definition: when Dicey wrote his text, 'the Whig section of the Liberal party, to which Dicey belonged, was still fighting what appeared to be a successful defensive action' on behalf of minimal government and against regulation. 'Dicey . . . was stating as a principle of the British Constitution what he, and many others of his generation, thought *ought to be* a principle of policy' (Jennings 1933/1959: 307–8; stress in original).

Already in 1885, Jennings points out, some classes of officials had extensive discretionary powers under the poor law or public health legislation. Such powers continued to expand in Dicey's lifetime, notably with the National Insurance scheme introduced in 1911, and during and after the First World War. Appeals against the actions of officials were (and still are) heard in various administrative tribunals, but, as Jennings (1933/1959: 313) pointed out, 'administrative courts are as "ordinary" as the civil courts'. Jennings's work remained a standard reference through the Second World War and into the 1960s. In the climate of those times, politicians and writers generally regarded the Welfare State, with its proliferation of administrative discretion, as largely or wholly benign, and the occasional writer who warned of the 'new despotism' or similar dire threats, was a throwback to the mid-Victorian era. The spirit of the times was summed up by the Labour intellectual Douglas Jay, a minister in the Attlee and Wilson governments who had written in 1937, 'in the case of nutrition and health, just as in the case of education, the gentleman in Whitehall really does know better what is good for people than the people know themselves' (Jay 1937: 317).

In recent decades, there has been a swing back towards Dicey, in the first of his three arguments for the 'rule of law'. As Jowell (2007) notes, this has been driven from the left as well as the right. For instance, benefit claimants and their advocates have succeeded in restricting the discretion of officials in deciding whether to allow claims. The courts have become more active, from a position in Jennings's day where they were most unwilling to interfere in governments' or officials' discretion. This is in part driven by a huge jump in applications for judicial review of decisions: but that is endogenous with the courts' greater willingness to side with complainants.

Are liberties better protected by judges or by a constitution? Inevitably, the answer may depend on what sort of judges there are. If courts typically side with one class of litigants against another (for instance, government officials against private citizens or, as classically claimed by Griffith [1977], the socially and morally conventional against the socially and morally unconventional), then Dicey's argument may be turned against him. One of the benefits of the rule of law, he insists, is its certainty. Well then, should not civil rights, especially for unpopular groups, be entrenched in some law such as the US Bill of Rights, which Dicey deplored?

A fast-moving situation

This book will argue that Diceyanism was fatally undermined a long time ago, by Dicey himself as much as others (Chapters 4–7). However, even readers who do not accept that argument will probably accept, as do all the constitutional law texts, that the United Kingdom's Constitution is rapidly changing. The main drivers of change have been accession to the European Union (Chapter 8); devolution to Scotland, Wales, and Northern Ireland (Chapter 9); and developments in human rights law since the United Kingdom ratified the European Convention on Human Rights (Chapter 10).

In the next chapter I introduce some concepts from political science that may help us understand what is going on in the politics of constitutions. I also make a first attempt, following through US history, to see how a constitution based (at least purportedly) on the sovereignty of the people, rather than the sovereignty of Parliament, has evolved.

2

A Fresh Start: Veto Players, Win Sets, and Constitutional Moments

VETO PLAYERS AND WIN SETS

George Tsebelis (1995, 2002) has introduced the important analytical concept of 'veto players' to political science. It is highly relevant to the themes of this book. Veto players are, as the name suggests, individuals or groups who have the power to block a proposal. According to Tsebelis, they come in two varieties: institutional and partisan. An institutional veto player is one who has the legal power to block. Such a player may be an individual (the US President) or a chamber (the House of Lords). And the veto may be unconditional (the US President's at the end of a session of Congress, when there is no time to override it; the House of Lords on all non-monetary matters before 1911). Or it may be conditional (the US President when his veto may be overridden; the House of Lords since 1911, when it remains a veto player in the last year of a parliament, and over bills to prolong the life of a parliament, but not otherwise). A partisan veto player is a party (or other) group that may block a proposal so long as the group coheres. A governing party with over half of the seats in a chamber is a unique partisan veto player over all proposals that are carried if a simple majority votes for them. More than one party may be a veto player in a chamber where no party holds half the seats, or where more than a simple majority of those present is required to pass a measure.

Now consider the *status quo*—the set of policies and constitutional arrangements currently in force. The status quo is stable if it is relatively hard to upset. The more veto players there are in a political system, or the larger the qualified majority required for a proposal to pass, the more stable is the status quo. Equivalently, as either the number of veto players or the qualified majority threshold rises, the *win set* of the status quo diminishes, and the core, or the uncovered set of the game, gets bigger. The win set means the set of alternative policies that could be carried against the status quo. The core means the area of policy which, once reached, cannot be abandoned.

Stability, thus understood, is neither good nor bad in itself. Most of us probably want the constitution to be stable and ordinary laws dividing spoils among interest groups to be unstable. An example of an unstable constitution would be that of Weimar Germany, after Hitler with a little help from his friends had drastically reduced the number of veto players to one. We would like the constitution to be protected by some sort of entrenchment, that is, a requirement for more than a simple parliamentary majority before it can be amended. The UK Constitution comprises, among other things, ordinary Acts of Parliament which, if the doctrine of parliamentary sovereignty remains intact, are no more protected from repeal, explicit or implied, than is the Dentists Act 1878. These parts are thus not entrenched, nor do they require a supermajority for their amendment. The conventions of the British Constitution were set out, for instance, in a book written by a weekly magazine journalist in 1865, and an anonymous letter from a king's secretary to *The Times* in 1950. It is hard to see what would count as a repeal of those documents. Certainly it does not seem to require a supermajority. In these respects, it may be felt that the British Constitution is insufficiently stable.

An example of an over-stable distributive law might be the Common Agricultural Policy of the European Union (EU), which is wealth-destroying, economically crazy, and vicious to the developing world (among a number of its properties), but which is protected by the multiple vetoes and high qualified-majority thresholds of the EU. Policy in multiple-veto-player regimes is more stable than in single- or small-n veto player regimes. The EU obviously has multiple veto players. So do individual member states, in the EU and elsewhere, which have proportional representation. Proportional representation goes along with multiparty government. Each coalition partner in a multiparty government is a veto player because each can threaten to leave the coalition and bring down the government.

Seen in this light, the veto-player framework is an extension of Duverger's famous Law: *The simple-majority single-ballot system favours the two-party system . . . [;] the simple-majority system with second ballot and proportional representation favour multi-partism* (1954: 217, 239). Duverger's Law comprises three propositions. The second, concerning the run-off system of election used for the French parliament, is generally held to be false. The first and the third are well-founded, when the conditions are carefully stated. The simple-majority single-ballot (i.e. 'Westminster' or 'first-past-the-post') system implies that there will be, in the long run, at most two viable parties in each constituency. As it becomes common knowledge which parties are not competitive in a given constituency, voters will withdraw support for them and vote for whichever of the two locally dominant parties they dislike less. Duverger's Law may be read as a statement of a special case of the veto-player framework. A multiparty system may be reclassified as a system with numerous partisan veto players. From this you can read off the greater stability (for both good and ill) of policy under proportional than under majoritarian electoral systems.

The UK is classically hailed as the ideal type of Duvergerian two-party system. As W.S. Gilbert wrote a long time ago:

> Then let's rejoice with loud fa-la
> (Fa la la la, fa, la la la)
> That nature always does contrive
> (Fa la la la la)
> That every boy and every gal
> That's born into the world alive
> Is either a little Liberal
> or else a little Conservative. (Gilbert 1882, opening of Act 2)

The UK was a two-party system because of Duverger's Law. But note that the Law, properly construed, states that only at most two parties are competitive *in each district*. A party may be competitive (or even dominant) in some districts while not competitive (or even present) in others. The Irish Party was dominant in most of Ireland from 1885 to 1918 inclusive. It also won one seat in Liverpool throughout that period. Otherwise, it had no presence in Britain at all. Nevertheless, it was pivotal, and hence a partisan veto player, in four parliaments, namely those elected in 1885, 1892, and twice in 1910.

We will hear a lot more about the Irish Party. But where there are no significant regional parties, the winning party's lead in seats is typically much greater than its lead in votes. This has long been known as the 'cube law', because the ratio of seats going to the top two parties has sometimes been as high as the cube of their ratio of votes. (In 1906, it was even higher; in modern conditions it is lower, but there is still an exaggerative effect.)

Two pairs of political economists have proposed extensions to this Duverger–Tsebelis framework. From their extensive and sophisticated cross-national statistical analysis, Persson and Tabellini (2005: 270) find that

> One of the central findings of this book is the strong constitutional effect of electoral rules on fiscal policy . . . [A] switch from proportional to majoritarian elections reduces overall government spending by almost 5% of GDP, welfare spending by 2–3% of GDP, and budget deficits by about 2% of GDP. Advocates in the United Kingdom of the opposite switch, from majoritarian to proportional, should take careful note of these findings.

The intuition behind this result is as follows. A majoritarian government, as normally in the UK, is dominated by a single party. There is a large win set of the status quo. The governing party can switch from current policy to anything it can persuade its followers in the House of Commons to support. This will make it relatively good at enacting important but (in the short term) unattractive proposals, such as either expenditure reductions or tax increases needed to balance the budget. In contrast, a proportional government contains numerous partisan veto players. Each of them represents a narrower segment of society than in a majoritarian regime. Each of them demands spending (including transfers) for the benefit of the group of citizens that it represents. So: more welfare spending, but less budget discipline.

Iversen and Soskice (2006) explore why some democracies redistribute more than others. In the 1990s, the United States used redistributive taxation and transfers to reduce the pre-tax-and-transfer poverty rate by 13 per cent; Sweden reduced it, on the same measure, by 82 per cent. Both are democracies. What is the relevant difference? According to Iversen and Soskice, the main relevant differences lie in the electoral system and the structure of veto players. For a country like the UK these have opposite effects. The electoral system (as shown independently by Persson and Tabellini) implies that majoritarian countries like the UK more often than not have right-wing governments hostile to redistribution, compared to countries with proportional representation. There is a tricky question of direction of causation here, which is not relevant to the main theme of this book. What is highly relevant is Iversen and Soskice's finding (page 175 and Table 5) on the effect of the number of veto points. '[M]ultiple veto points, as expected, reduce redistribution, and . . . PR has a direct (positive) effect on redistribution.' The UK has few veto points and no PR. The first effect increases redistribution, and the second reduces it, with ambiguous overall results.

But what if we transfer this framework to the study of the constitution? We might suppose that left-wing governments support constitutional reform, while right-wing governments oppose it. This is too simple—once a left-wing government has seized the levers of power in the UK, the normal absence of veto players means that it has more opportunity than elsewhere to enact its redistributive programme. This might be a fair description of the Liberal governments of 1908–14 and the Labour governments of 1945–51. Labour in its most redistributive period was indeed hostile to constitutional reform. The Liberals in theirs, on the other hand, were strongly in favour. What was the difference between the cases? Essentially, as is argued in detail in the following chapters, the number of veto players in the UK temporarily but sharply increased between 1909 and 1914 to include the House of

Lords, the kings, and sections of the army. The Liberals' substantive programme—redistribution—became impossible without their procedural programme—constitutional reform.

Thus important redistributive moments may or may not coincide with important constitutional moments. The constitutional moments for the UK examined in this book are those of 1707 and 1909–14. They are not the only constitutional moments in British history. The diffuse seventeenth-century revolutions were undoubtedly constitutional. But in one sense, 1707 was their culmination so their omission is more apparent than real. This book does not explicitly discuss the stages in the widening of the franchise, where 1832 was the most important constitutional moment. It will be mentioned in passing in this book, because in 1832 as in 1911 the unelected parts of the British parliament gave way to the elected part, under the threat of the mass creation of peers and hence of the substantial reshaping of the unelected part. But, as 1707 in a sense summarizes the seventeenth-century constitutional revolutions in England and in Scotland, so 1912–14 summarizes 1832. The unelected houses were brought face to face with the consequences of majority rule in the elected house.

The next section therefore discusses constitutional moments in another common-law Anglophone democracy: the United States.

CONSTITUTIONAL MOMENTS

The tradition of parliamentary sovereignty has traditionally not distinguished constitutional statutes from normal legislation.[1] As the UK unquestionably has constitutional statutes, which (in practice) courts now treat differently to ordinary statutes, parliamentary sovereignty has become an obstacle, not a key, to understanding the UK's Constitution. We need a new key. The place to look for such a key is in the constitutional practice of other countries. For the purposes of this book, the most appropriate comparator countries are those which, in all respects except their constitutions, are the most similar to the UK. This means looking at the other major common-law democracies: the United States, Canada, and Australia.

Is this not a blinkered selection of comparators? No: the common-law background, and the common constitutional starting point, of all four countries are vital. Before 1707, England had one of the most developed codes of common law, a phrase with multiple overlapping meanings: law common to the whole country; and/or law for (disputes among) commoners, to which the king was not party. But a feature of it, in all its meanings, was that it was judge-made law, not law made by Parliament in statutes, nor in comprehensive codes (which apply in *civil law* jurisdictions). In all four common-law democracies, judges determine what the law is unless and until it is changed by a trumping statute.

The UK, the United States, and Canada are not pure common-law jurisdictions. Scotland, Louisiana, and Quebec offer partial exceptions. The civil-law codes of Louisiana and Quebec, both former French colonies, are not relevant to the themes of this book. But the code of Scotland assuredly is. Scots could not, or chose not to, study at Oxford or Cambridge. Intellectual interchange was with the universities of the Netherlands, France, and Italy, not England. Scottish legal rules were therefore codified independently of England's, most notably in James Dalrymple, Viscount Stair's *Institutions of the law of Scotland, deduced from its originals, and collated with the civil, canon and feudal laws; and with the customs of neighbouring nations* (Dalrymple 1681). Stair's subtitle indicates that Scotland was not wholly either a common-law or a civil jurisdiction; and it had no explicit doctrine of parliamentary sovereignty before 1707. To this day, the main annotated compilation of Scots law is called the *Stair Memorial Encyclopaedia*.

Nevertheless, the United States (in 1787), the Commonwealth of Australia (1900), and Canada (as late as 1982)[2] each introduced a written constitution as a third tier of law, above judge-made, English-derived common law and statute law. As this book argues for a similar step in the United Kingdom, it is worth examining how some of those jurisdictions distinguish between constitutional law and ordinary law.

At a formal level it is easy. The US Constitution comprises the original Constitution drafted in 1787 and ratified by all the states then existing, plus its subsequent amendments, of which the first ten (the Bill of Rights) were ratified soon after the original ratification, being regarded in some states as further guarantees that must be promised before those states' conventions would sign up to the original constitution. The Constitution may be amended by the procedure (actually, by any one of the four procedures) set down in Article 5:

> The Congress, whenever two thirds of both Houses shall deem it necessary, shall propose Amendments to this Constitution, or, on the Application of the Legislatures of two thirds of the several States, shall call a Convention for proposing Amendments, which, in either Case, shall be valid to all Intents and Purposes, as part of this Constitution, when ratified by the

Legislatures of three fourths of the several States, or by Conventions in three fourths thereof, as the one or the other Mode of Ratification may be proposed by the Congress.

The Constitution of Australia, likewise, comprises the text agreed by two conventions of the Australian states at the turn of the twentieth century. It may only be amended by the procedure of Chapter VIII:

128. This Constitution shall not be altered except in the following manner:

The proposed law for the alteration thereof must be passed by an absolute majority of each House of the Parliament, and not less than two nor more than six months after its passage through both Houses the proposed law shall be submitted in each State and Territory to the electors qualified to vote for the election of members of the House of Representatives.

[paragraph dealing with differences between the Houses omitted]

When a proposed law is submitted to the electors the vote shall be taken in such manner as the Parliament prescribes. [sentence about arrangements for States without universal suffrage omitted]

And if in a majority of the States a majority of the electors voting approve the proposed law, and if a majority of all the electors voting also approve the proposed law, it shall be presented to the Governor-General for the Queen's assent.

Constitutions may include unamendable sections. In the original US Constitution, the article permitting the slave trade to continue until 1808 was made unamendable. Now, under Article 5, the only unamendable provision is that 'no State, without its Consent, shall be deprived of its equal Suffrage in the Senate'. In the Australian Constitution, nothing is absolutely unamendable, but:

No alteration diminishing the proportionate representation of any State in either House of the Parliament, or the minimum number of representatives of a State in the House of Representative, or increasing, diminishing, or otherwise altering the limits of the State, or in any manner affecting the provisions of the Constitution in relation thereto, shall become law unless the majority of the electors voting in that State approve the proposed law.

By comparison, the Basic Law of the Federal Republic of Germany makes the following matters unamendable:

79 (3) Amendments to this Basic Law affecting the division of the Federation into Länder, their participation on principle in the legislative process, or the principles laid down in Articles 1 and 20 shall be inadmissible.

Article 1 (1) states, 'Human dignity shall be inviolable. To respect and protect it shall be the duty of all state authority.' Article 20 states:

(1) The Federal Republic of Germany is a democratic and social federal state.
(2) All state authority is derived from the people. It shall be exercised by the people through elections and other votes and through specific legislative, executive, and judicial bodies.
(3) The legislature shall be bound by the constitutional order, the executive and the judiciary by law and justice.
(4) All Germans shall have the right to resist any person seeking to abolish this constitutional order, if no other remedy is available.

These constitutions set high thresholds for amendment. There have been only twenty-seven amendments to the US Constitution to date; ten of these comprise the Bill of Rights, passed in 1791. There have been only eight successful amendments to the Australian Constitution to date, out of forty-four proposals.

A formalist statement would therefore run: *The higher law of the United States (Australia, Canada, Germany . . .) is the Constitution as validly amended to date; the ordinary law is everything else, which in common law systems may be divided into statutes and common law.* But this is too simple. In a powerful two-volume (so far) critique, Bruce Ackerman (1991, 1998) develops what he calls a model of 'dualist democracy'. He takes on various enemies, including those who privilege the 'plain meaning' of the US Constitution ('hypertextualists'), and those who seek to examine the 'original intent' of its framers. But the organizing argument is that 'dualist democracy' sits between two untenable alternatives, which he calls 'monism' and 'rights foundationalism'.

Monism is the belief that

> Democracy requires the grant of plenary lawmaking authority to the winners of the last general election—so long, at least, as the election was conducted under free and fair ground rules and the winners don't try to prevent the next scheduled round of electoral challenges. (Ackerman 1991: 8)

As he goes on to explain, this formulation is 'an idealized version of British Parliamentary practice', which has been upheld by distinguished American thinkers as varied as Woodrow Wilson and Oliver Wendell Holmes. In the monist view, as characterized by Ackerman, the anti-democratic movements in American history notably include the period early in F. D. Roosevelt's New Deal when the 'Nine Old Men' of the Supreme Court overturned legislation emanating from the administration that held the largest presidential and congressional majority in US history.

At the other extreme, 'rights foundationalists' believe that 'the American constitution is concerned, first and foremost, with the protection of [rights]. Indeed, the whole point of having rights is to trump decisions rendered by democratic institutions that may otherwise legislate for the collective welfare...Rights trump democracy—provided, of course, that they're the Right rights' (Ackerman 1991: 11–12). Rights foundationalism, argues Ackerman, may correctly describe the ideology of the German Basic Law, with its list of unamendable rights provisions, but is just an incorrect description of the US Constitution. An amendment, duly passed under Article 5 procedures, that repealed the First Amendment in favour of a statement that Christianity was the official religion of the United States would be valid law—just as (though Ackerman does not here appeal to this case) Prohibition was valid higher law in the United States from the passage of the Eighteenth Amendment in 1919 until its repeal by the Twenty-first Amendment in 1933. A rights foundationalist would be horrified by the repeal of the First Amendment, as Ackerman would, but would be unable to argue that the Twenty-eighth Amendment establishing Christianity as the official religion of the United States and imposing disabilities on practitioners of other religions was invalid law.

How then should we parse the US Constitution? For this argument the three crucial parts are the Article 5 amendment procedure, the ratification rule (Article 7), and the very first sentence of the Constitution:

> We the People of the United States, in Order to form a more perfect Union, establish Justice, insure domestic Tranquility, provide for the common defence, promote the general Welfare, and secure the Blessings of Liberty to ourselves and our Posterity, do ordain and establish this Constitution for the United States of America. (US Constitution, preamble)

What does this mean? One level of the history of the preamble is its textual history. The working draft of the Constitution presented by the Committee of Detail to the plenary convention in Philadelphia, on 6 August 1787, opened 'We the people of the States of [the list of the original 13 states[3] follows] do ordain, declare, and establish the following Constitution for the Government of ourselves and our Posterity.' Towards the end of the convention, the text was referred to a Committee on Stile and Arrangement, which presented the text we know today to the Convention on 12 September 1787. The Convention accepted it (Madison 1787/1987: 385–96, 616–34).

The members of the Committee on Stile and Arrangement were Alexander Hamilton, William Johnson, Rufus King, James Madison, and Gouverneur Morris. They thus included two of the three authors of *The Federalist Papers*

(Hamilton and Madison) and the most talkative rhetorician of the Constitution, Gouverneur Morris of Pennsylvania, who is thought to have been the author of the Preamble. 'Rhetoric is concerned with the persuasion-value of sentences' (Riker 1986: x). Like every other delegate, Morris knew that the Convention and the country were divided. He was a genius at crafting persuasive sentences. The original draft of the preamble was cumbersome, and contained an obvious untruth—namely the claim that the people of Rhode Island had ordained, declared, or established anything. The final version claimed that *the people of the United States*, no less, had ordained the Constitution. This, too, was an untruth, but one that, as it turned out, was cloaked in such lofty language that it inspired eleven of the thirteen original states to ratify the Constitution by the procedure it laid down. (Rhode Island ratified, grudgingly and conditionally, in 1790; North Carolina rejected in 1788, and ratified in 1790.)

Morris was also responsible for some theatre at the end of the convention, as reported by Madison. Benjamin Franklin, the oldest delegate, wrote (and had delivered by another delegate) a witty rallying speech to the effect that they all thought the constitution had flaws but that they should nevertheless ratify. Franklin

> then moved that the Constitution be signed by the members and offered the following as a convenient form viz. "Done in Convention by the unanimous consent of *the States* present the 17th of Sept. &c—In Witness whereof we have hereunto subscribed our names".
>
> This ambiguous form had been drawn up by Mr. G[ouverneur]. M[orris]. in order to gain the dissenting members, and put into the hands of Docr Franklin that it might have the better chance of success (Madison 1787/ 1987: 654)

The trick worked. Three weighty members present (George Mason and Edmund Randolph, both of Virginia, and Elbridge Gerry of Massachusetts) refused to sign. Four other opponents of the evolving constitution—one of them the weighty but loquacious Luther Martin of Maryland—had left during the convention as its shape gradually emerged (Rakove 1999). The State of New York was left with only one delegate (Hamilton) as his two Anti-Federalist colleagues had gone home. Nevertheless, the unanimous consent of the States present was gained, attested by the signature of the lone Hamilton from New York, and three delegates from Virginia including Madison, compared to five from tiny Delaware.

Article 7 of the original constitution stipulates that 'The Ratification of the Conventions of nine States, shall be sufficient for the Establishment of this Constitution between the States so ratifying the Same.' As noted, eleven of the twelve states represented at Philadelphia did so, with varying degrees of enthusiasm. When the ninth state (New Hampshire) ratified on 21 June, 1788, the Constitution was valid.

Or was it? There are two objections to this formalist (as lawyers call it, 'black-letter') interpretation. First: on 21 June, 1788, two of the most important states, New York and Virginia, had not yet ratified. They were both in doubt until the last minute. Both had been divided at the Convention (New York throughout, and Virginia when Mason's and Randolph's objections crystallized late on), and were deeply divided in the state. The finest rhetorical efforts of Hamilton and Madison had gone into *The Federalist* designed to persuade the New York ratifying convention to say Yes. After writing thirty-odd numbers of *The Federalist*, but finishing only three-fourths of the way through the series, at number 63, Madison had to hurry back to Virginia in the hope of getting his home state to ratify, something about which he had been deeply pessimistic. The Constitution was remarkably *improbable*. The rhetoric of Morris, Madison, and Hamilton, and a few others, saved the day for it (Riker 1996). But if Virginia and New York had not both ratified, the United States would not have come into being regardless of the formal satisfaction of Article 7.

Secondly, and more startlingly, Ackerman argues that Article 7 was itself unconstitutional. The Constitution in force in 1787 was the Articles of Confederation, a document that reflected the loose alliance that the states had formed to fight the war of independence. The Philadelphia Convention was itself of dubious legitimacy, as it exceeded the instructions under which it had been called. But the rules for amending the Articles of Convention were perfectly clear: All thirteen of the treaty partners must ratify any change in the Articles. Rhode Island, governed at the time by a radically democratic assembly, was deeply suspicious of closer union and would have vetoed any alteration to the Articles. Most of the political leaders in several other states were Anti-Federalists.

Does this mean that the language of *We the People* is totally empty? Have we been hoodwinked by Gouverneur Morris for two centuries? No, says Ackerman (1991, 1998); and I largely agree with him.[4] Constitutional moments, he argues, are marked not by unanimity but by a *supermajority*. The supermajority must be reflected in the institutions of the day. It is not necessarily the supermajority specified in Article 5 of the Constitution. The two most important constitutional moments after 1787 did not go correctly through the Article 5 procedure. The Reconstruction (Thirteenth and Fourteenth) Amendments were, on a textualist view, unconstitutional. The New Deal avoided constitutional amendments altogether.

Because this is a book about UK, not US, constitutional history, I have too little space to present these startling claims except in the baldest outline.

Take Reconstruction first. One of the critical silences of the original Constitution was whether States had the right to secede from the union (Compare the British Acts of Union of 1707 and 1800, both of which declare that the union they inaugurate is perpetual. One of those unions has lasted; the other has not.) It also contained concessions and fudges designed to ensure that both free and slave states could join the Union. Slaves are referred to three times, although never under that name. The first time is in the article apportioning seats among the states in the House of Representatives. For the purpose of calculating states' qualifying population (and hence entitlement to House seats), each slave was to count as three-fifths of a person. Secondly, the slave trade was to be allowed to continue at least until 1808, and this provision was made unamendable until then. This article was the subject of an explicit log-roll in the Convention between New England and the Deep South. Gouverneur Morris (again!) arranged the log-roll ('These things may form a bargain among the Northern and Southern States'—Madison 1787/ 1987: 507; Riker 1986: 89–105). The Deep South got protection of the slave trade; New England got the threat of a federal veto on their navigation acts lifted. Finally, the 'fugitive slave' clause (Article 4 Section 2 clause 3), forbade states to which fugitive slaves had escaped from abrogating their owners' claims over them. The fugitive slave clause was agreed *nem. con.* at the Constitutional Convention (Madison 1787/1987: 552).

The main protection that the Constitution offered to the South, however, came to be none of these three provisions. It was the rule which offered each State, regardless of population, two Senators. At the outset, the slave states held roughly half the seats in the Senate. After a threat in 1819 to unbalance this, the Missouri Compromise accepted the admission of Missouri as a slave state on condition that it was balanced by the admission of Maine as a free state. This aspect of the compromise lasted until 1850, with states being admitted in pairs, one slave, one free. Its breakdown when California was admitted as a free state was one of the things that led the slide into civil war.

The American Civil War was a constitutional moment in its own right. The Union victory ensured that all the constitutional compromises just listed must be swept away, together with the institution of slavery. The Thirteenth Amendment (ratified in 1865) abolished slavery. The Fourteenth (ratified, or as Ackerman would have it 'ratified' in 1868) specified that everyone born or naturalized in the United States was a citizen of the United States and of his or her state. It also, *inter alia*, applied the 'due process' clause of the Fifth Amendment to the states.

Here is the puzzle: how many states were in the Union in 1865 and in 1868? Article 5 requires three-quarters of the states to ratify, either through their legislatures or via state conventions as Congress may specify. Immediately after the end of the Civil War, the Union Army arranged for state conventions to meet in each of the ex-Confederate states. These conventions altered the state constitutions to abolish slavery and created the first new state legislatures. Enough of these legislatures ratified the Thirteenth Amendment for the Secretary of State to announce in December 1865 that it had been ratified by three-quarters (twenty-seven out of thirty-six) states. However, when he made that announcement, the radical Republicans who controlled Congress had already refused to seat the Congressional delegations from all the Southern States except Tennessee (home of President Andrew Johnson). It was this rump Congress which proposed what became the Fourteenth Amendment to the states in 1866, thus (apparently) initiating the Article 5 process for the Fourteenth Amendment. But if there were thirty-six states in 1865, were there not still thirty-six states in 1866? If the southern delegations had been seated, historians agree that Congress would never have got the two-third majorities in each house required to initiate the Article 5 amendment process.

President Johnson had come to the White House because of the assassination of Abraham Lincoln. Lincoln had chosen him as Vice-President in 1864 in order to balance his ticket. Johnson was the only Senator from any southern state not to have joined the Confederacy. Accordingly, he was content to see the Thirteenth Amendment enacted. But he balked at the Fourteenth. The radical Republican Congress of 1866 sent the draft text to all the states, telling the southern states that their readmission to the union was contingent on their prior agreement to ratify the amendment. Article 5 assuredly gave it no power to make readmission contingent on ratification. The conflict became so acute that the House of Representatives impeached President Johnson on the ground that he had 'affirm[ed] in substance that the 39th Congress of the United States was not a Congress of the United States authorized to exercise legislative power under the same; but, on the contrary, was a Congress of only part of the States' (quoted in Ackerman 1998: 179).[5]

Johnson had a point. But he retreated from his attempt to block the Fourteenth Amendment. In the summer of 1868 he started behaving in a more conciliatory way towards Congress and the army. The impeachment failed in the Senate by a single vote.

What then makes the Fourteenth Amendment a valid part of the US Constitution, and therefore part of the entrenched higher law of the United States? Assuredly not the text of Article 5 and the proclamation of its ratification by the radical Congress of 1867–9. It is not clear what norms apply in the constitutional chaos of civil war. Ackerman (1998: 244–5) sees the final constitutional moment of Reconstruction in the Supreme Court judgement in the *Slaughterhouse Cases* of 1873. In these cases, the plaintiffs, white butchers from Louisiana, argued that their state government had violated the Fourteenth Amendment by imposing restrictive trading conditions on them. The Court dismissed their case, saying that the Amendment, one of three articles 'of vast importance [which] have been added by the voice of the people' (Mr Justice Samuel Miller quoted by Ackerman 1998: 245) is about the rights of blacks, not of whites. Interpretations of the Fourteenth Amendment have moved on; but the idea that it represents 'the voice of the people' has stayed. This despite its very dubious Article 5 history. Hardly anybody now doubts the constitutionality of the Fourteenth Amendment, but its legislative history is very dodgy indeed. Ackerman claims that it is the voice of the people, not Article 5, that is crucial. The voice of the people was heard in the elections of 1864 and (particularly) 1866. The latter election gave the radical Republicans such a supermajority in the truncated Congress that Johnson—and the Supreme Court—had to retreat.

The New Deal constitutional moment came without amending the Constitution. Soon after F. D. Roosevelt's first election in 1932, he proposed a National Industrial Recovery Act (NIRA) which was quickly enacted. It envisaged a corporatist restructuring of industry, with massive federal intervention. In 1935, in *Schechter Poultry Corporation* v. *US*, the Supreme Court unanimously ruled it unconstitutional under the Fifth and Tenth Amendments. Known to generations of students as the 'sick chicken' case, *Schechter* concerned a wholesale kosher butcher in New York that had been convicted of several violations of the Live Poultry Code, including one of supplying unfit meat. The court held that the federal government had no authority to enact, still less to delegate the enactment of, such a code, dismissing arguments that the Schechters were engaged in interstate commerce and therefore subject to federal regulation. Roosevelt immediately denounced the Court decision as the worst since *Dred Scott*.[6] Spinning to the newspapers, White House staff hinted that the President was contemplating a constitutional amendment, to be ratified by the state convention route (as the abolition of Prohibition, in the Twenty-first Amendment, had just been).

But Roosevelt did not confront the Court head-on. First, he got Congress to enact the measures of the Second New Deal, which avoided the features of the NIRA ruled unconstitutional in *Schechter*. Then, he proposed to appoint one new Justice for every serving Justice over the age of 70, up to a total of six. Roosevelt's 'court-packing' plan was widely denounced but effective. In what (again) all students have learnt to call 'the switch in time that saved nine', two swing members of the Court started to support the constitutionality of New Deal economic regulation, validating the Wagner Labor Act, the imposition of consumer standards on food products (e.g. in *Carolene Products*, discussed extensively in the following text), and the (state) regulation of labour hours for women and minors. The Court's interpretation of the regulatory powers of Congress changed, and has stayed changed, so that the Interstate Commerce clause is held to give the federal government wide powers to regulate economic activity. No extra Justices were appointed.

Roosevelt avoided seeking a formal Constitutional amendment because, in his words, 'there was no way of keeping such an affair from getting out of hand what with Coughlin[7] and other crackpots about. But there is more than one way of killing a cat' (quoted by Ackerman 1998: 317). In reaching for his court-packing plan instead, Roosevelt and his aides had in mind the parallel with the British constitutional moments of 1832 and 1909–11 (the latter discussed in Chapters 4–7), on both of which occasions a 'Lords-packing plan' removed the House of Lords' veto over constitutional reform. Roosevelt's secretary of the Interior, Harold Ickes, noted in his diary for 27 December 1935 that FDR

> had a good deal to say about what the Supreme Court is likely to do on New Deal legislation. As once before in talking to me, he went back to the period when Gladstone was Prime Minister of Great Britain and succeeded in passing the Irish Home Rule Bill through the House of Commons on two or three occasions, only to have it vetoed by the House of Lords.
>
> Later, when Lloyd George's social security act was similarly blocked, Lloyd George went to the King, who was in favour of the bill, and he asked Lloyd George whether he wanted him to create three hundred new peers. Lloyd George said that he did not but that he was going to pass through Commons a bill providing that in the future any bill vetoed by the House of Lords should, notwithstanding that, become the law of Great Britain if passed again by the Commons. He told the King that when that bill was ready to go to the Lords he would like the King to send word that if it didn't pass, he would create three hundred new Lords. This the King did, with the result that the bill was accepted by the House of Lords. (Ickes 1953: 494–5)

What is of primary interest is not Roosevelt's faulty knowledge of British history (interesting, though, that he attributes Asquith's actions to Lloyd George) but his profound understanding of veto plays. He sensed that Lloyd George and Asquith were ultimately using the People to veto the Peers.

What the US constitutional moments of 1865–8 and 1935–7 have in common, according to Ackerman, is that We the People spoke. The election sequences 1864–6–8 and 1932–4–6 each showed that a movement for radical constitutional reform had repeated popular support. President Johnson's opposition to the Fourteenth Amendment crumbled after the 1866 election. The Supreme Court's opposition to the New Deal crumbled after the 1936 election, which gave the Democrats their greatest majority in US history in the Presidency and both houses of Congress.

How much of this analysis can be applied to the UK? Quite a lot. Historians are uneasy with Ackerman's compression of complex history into brief 'switch-in-time' moments. They may be equally irritated at my parallel treatment. I claim boldly that the switch-in-time moments in British constitutional history are 1689–90, 1832, 1911, and 1914. On each of these occasions a body that can plausibly be described as the People overcame the veto of a non-elected player. In 1689, in separate revolutions in England and in Scotland, parliamentarians speaking in the name of the people deposed a line of monarchs and invited a new one. In 1707, although I cannot claim that union was made by the people, I do claim that the Union crisis was brought about by further parliamentary efforts to determine the royal succession. When these threatened to drive England and Scotland apart, the treaty partners brought them together on improved terms for Scotland. In 1832 and (as noted by FDR) 1911, the People were ultimately the force that overcame the Lords' vetoes over constitutional reform. The date 1914 may seem the strangest on my list. As I go on to record in this book, the People (in the shape of the twice re-elected House of Commons majority) were thwarted by the Lords, the King, the Ulster Unionists, and part of the Army. In the longer term, however, the episode showed that Asquith was right and George V wrong in their interpretations. The Sovereign must act, as Asquith insisted, always and only on the advice of Ministers commanding a Commons, and ultimately a popular, majority. Anything else made the Sovereign a partisan. George V and his advisers did not realize that then, but events in Australia in 1975 proved that Asquith had been right.

Perhaps to the dismay of historians, I therefore find the concept of 'constitutional moments' very useful. One could say that the British Constitution is like a series of train crashes. Since 1840, railway accidents in the UK have been investigated by HM Inspectorate of Railways. W. E. Gladstone, arguably the greatest administrative reformer in British history, was one of those who shaped the system (McLean and Foster 1992). Most inspectors' reports into accidents recommend safety improvements to prevent a repetition of the accident. In railway safety, the equivalent of the Parliament Act 1911 is the Regulation of Railways Act 1889, which demanded continuous brakes on trains after a terrible accident at Armagh, when a Sunday School train parked on a hill had run away backwards into a following locomotive and dozens of children were killed. The rule book of British railways is the consolidation of nearly two centuries of accident reports. It may be helpful to regard the rule book of British politics—the constitution—in the same way. Each constitutional moment, such as 1707 and 1911, then represents a rule change necessitated by some constitutional accident or disaster.

Part II

The Constitution from Below

3

1707 and 1800: a Treaty (Mostly) Honoured and a Treaty Broken

Iain McLean and Alistair McMillan

> The motives will be, Trade with most, Hanover with some, ease and security with others, together with a generall aversion to civill discords, intollerable poverty and . . . constant oppression. (Earl of Roxburgh,[1] a member of the *Squadrone Volante* ['Flying Squadron' of swing voters in the last Scottish Parliament] in 1706: Whatley 1989: 153).

This chapter aims to show that the Union of England and Scotland in 1707 was a genuine treaty, conducted by two bargainers of unequal power; however, the weaker partner (Scotland) had enough to force the English to the table and to extract some concessions from them. In contrast, the Union of Great Britain and Ireland in 1800–1 was not a genuine treaty, because one party unilaterally abrogated it after it had been concluded and after the Irish Parliament had ceased to exist. To make these points requires historical analysis in considerable depth. Readers who are happy to take our claims on trust may skip this chapter and fast-forward to 1909, when the detailed historical analysis resumes.

For Dicey and Rait (1920), the Union of Scotland with England and Wales of 1707 was an act of supreme statesmanship, cementing the political and geographical basis from which the British Empire could be consolidated. For Scottish nationalists it was a betrayal: 'We're bought and sold for English gold—Such a parcel of rogues in a nation!'[2] Namierite historians share the Scottish nationalist analysis without the poetry. Sir Lewis Namier powerfully influenced a generation of British political historians with his ideology that there was no ideology in eighteenth-century parliaments, only interests (Namier and Brooke 1964). The leading Namierite writing about the Union, P. W. J. Riley (1968, 1978), took it as axiomatic that the Scottish Union negotiators, and those who voted for Union in the last Scottish Parliament, were a parcel of rogues. Other views stress the advantage of a union as a free-trade area, and the Scots' need to recoup the losses from their disastrous Darien expedition, described later. None of these adequately recognizes that the Treaty of Union was a true treaty from which both sides gained, but both made concessions. Union did involve a strengthening and consolidation of the parliamentary sovereignty based at Westminster, but also entrenched the Scottish Presbyterian church, and established a unified trading, financial, and military system, which had advantages for the political establishments in both London and Edinburgh.

In our monograph, *State of the Union* (McLean and McMillan 2005), we analysed, for the first time, the flow of votes in the last Scottish Parliament to show that none of the standard explanations of Union was correct. The Earl of Roxburgh was a better guide than Dicey, Namier, Riley, or Burns. The key issues were trading relations; the succession of the monarchy (a politico-religious question); and the military situation. We repeat, more concisely, some of the analysis. Readers who wish more detail are referred to *State of the Union.*

Darien had shown that Scotland could not build an independent empire. The venture involved two expeditions to Central America (modern Panama), which sought to establish a colony by opening up trade from the Far East, as well as the Americas. The first expedition sailed in July 1698, with some 1,200 colonists, but was devastated by illness, and failed to establish 'New Edin-burgh'. The settlement was abandoned in June 1699. A second expedition was dispatched before news of the failure of the first had reached Scotland, and encountered a Spanish military force which defeated the Scots. Darien was abandoned by the Scots in April 1700 (Barbour 1907; Insh 1932; Fry 2001: ch. 2; Devine 2003: ch. 2).

King William III and Queen Mary were monarchs of both Scotland and England by parliamentary invitation—one from each parliament, therefore in principle on different terms. However, William's geopolitical interests were primarily those of a king of England. England was at war with France. Therefore, on the chessboard principle that my enemy's enemy, lying on my enemy's opposite frontier, is my friend, Spain was an ally of England. The Scots invasion of territory in Darien claimed by Spain interfered with William's statecraft.

The English agent in Scotland, Daniel Defoe, saw trading issues—striking a balance between protectionism and free trade—as one of the keys to success. So have many modern commentators. A weakened Scottish economy would be strengthened by closer political links with the booming English trading society. The humiliation of Darien, which squandered Scottish capital and exposed the Crown's promotion of English over Scottish interests, gave place to a united trading empire which the Scots were able to exploit.

However, the negotiators of Union did not know Adam Smith's or David Ricardo's arguments for free trade, because they had not yet been written.

The succession of the monarchy was a focus for the opponents of the Union in Scotland, who responded to the Act of Settlement passed in Westminster in 1701—asserting the Hanoverian succession across Britain—with their own Act of Security, which reserved the Scottish Parliament's right to choose the monarch. This challenged the 1603 union of the Crowns under James VI and I. The battles of the seventeenth century, and the English settlement through the Glorious Revolution of 1688, had a different resonance in Scotland. The Scots acceptance of William had been associated with the establishment of the Presbyterian church, but the Glencoe massacre,[3] the Darien collapse, and the obstinacy (seen from Edinburgh) of the London court had since undermined Scottish allegiance to the Crown.

In the seventeenth century, Presbyterians and Catholics had attacked the Stuarts' Anglican monarchy from opposite sides. Therefore, the Crown had to choose the lesser of two evils to be its Scottish ally. The association between the Crown and Scottish Presbyterian interests made their Jacobite[4] enemies opponents of the Union. Some Jacobites were Catholics; others (especially strong around Aberdeen) were Episcopalians. 'Such a parcel or rogues in a nation' is a Jacobite ballad (real, or invented by Burns). On the other wing, hardline ('Covenanting') Presbyterians yearned for a return to the theocratic 1640s and did not trust either William or Anne. The succession provides a cross-cutting cleavage in parliamentary politics which explains much of the failure of an alternative constitutional settlement, in both the Westminster and Edinburgh Parliaments.

Roxburgh's 'ease and security' relates to military discord. England was at war with France. In 1689–90, during the previous French war, the Jacobites had attacked the new English regime in both Scotland and Ireland, with French support. England needed to secure its north and west frontiers, with troops based in Northumberland and Ireland poised to march. Scottish troops were diffused amongst the different armies campaigning at the time, but the English knew that military conquest of Scotland was expensive and dubious. Cromwell had succeeded; but Edward I and Charles I had failed. Union offered a bulwark against a Jacobite invasion and military consolidation. The most articulate Scottish opponent of Union, Andrew Fletcher of Saltoun, sought a system of security based on local militias, rather than a united army that would be at the command of the monarch. But when Jacobite invasions did come in 1715 and 1745, unitary military command made them easier to contain than they would have been without Union (and the Edinburgh militia completely failed to stop Bonnie Prince Charlie).

An incorporating Union would tie parliamentary limitation of the Crown to a more stable form of administrative finance. Therefore, the Westminster Parliament was willing to promote Union as a policy. But why was the Scottish legislature happy to forfeit notional independence for a role in Westminster? After the accession of King William, on the terms proposed by the Scottish Parliament, it became more assertive in its right to develop its own political programmes independent of Westminster. But whereas the necessities of financing military and trading operations had led the London government to widen the tax base and improve its yield, the Scottish government, with no wars of its own to fight, had been hindered by economic stagnation and administrative weakness. Darien was financed out of a stock issue, not from taxation. This meant that Scottish control over revenue and patronage was limited. Incorporating Union was one solution to this situation, but it was not the only one. However, the status quo seemed unviable to those who thought seriously about Scotland's plight, such as the Union negotiator Clerk of Penicuik. Clerk denounced those who

> exclaim against the Union, as a thing that will ruin us; not considering that our case is such, that 'tis scarce conceivable, how any condition of life, we can fall into, can render us more Miserable and Poor, than we are (Whatley 2006: 291).

In addition, the pro-Union forces were centrists; the anti-Union forces a fissile alliance of religious extremists—extreme Presbyterians and Jacobites.

Darien and Glencoe had undermined the faith that some had placed in the joint monarchy of King William. At the instance of lobbyists for English chartered companies, William had banned English subscriptions to the Company of Scotland, and imposed restrictions on Scottish shipping in a Navigation Act, in 1696 (Whatley 2006: 169). The Union case was argued by some of the most colourful characters of the period. Daniel Defoe was sent to Scotland as a pro-Union propagandist, and William Paterson, founder of the Bank of England and driving force behind the Darien venture, also campaigned for the Union. The anti-Union campaign in Edinburgh was led by Fletcher of Saltoun, renowned for both his political radicalism and violent temper, and fitfully by the Duke of Hamilton, renowned for his dominant mother and psychosomatic toothache. Whilst Fletcher developed a plan for the radical reworking of constitutional and governmental relations between London and Edinburgh (Fletcher 1698, 1703 in Robertson 1997), his views were not influential, except that Hamilton adopted his clever threat to name someone other than the elector of Hanover to succeed Anne in Scotland.

A. V. Dicey saw the Union as the foundation of British military success, and an act of great statesmanship; its benefit shown by the failure of any move to repeal. For Dicey it was also a prime example of a conflict between a wise decision and a popular one: in England the measure received little general acclaim, and in Scotland it was greeted with widespread hostility. The Union stood, therefore, as a warning to the sensible and patriotic Englishman against a constitution which allowed the predominance of the popular over the wise (Dicey [1915] 1982: cxix). We shall see this anti-majoritarian theme in Dicey recurring in later chapters.

Economic historians (e.g. Smout 1969: Chapter 9) view the Union as a stage in the Scottish assimilation into a wider Britain. They follow Clerk of Penicuik. Smout (1969: 217) argues that the Scottish Parliament was unable to free itself from the influence of the Crown and London. For Dicey, Rait, and Smout, the Union represented a sharing of sovereignty, entrenching a British national interest in a constitutional framework which promoted political stability, military strength, and economic development.

More recent work on the passage of the Union has focused on the reasons for the Scottish acceptance of the measure. The last Scottish Parliament, which sat between 1703 and 1707, passed violently anti-English legislation at the start of its term and voted for Union at the end. At the start, relations between the parliaments in London and Edinburgh were set on collision course partly as a result of the slow arrival of the news of Marlborough's great victory at Blenheim, in 1704. The English minister Godolphin advised Queen Anne to give her assent to the Scottish Act of Security in order to gain supply required to pay the army, which was late and seen as imperative in the light of the threat of a French invasion. Queen Anne assented to the Act on 5 August 1704, without knowing that three days earlier Marlborough had beaten the French army at Blenheim (Riley 1964: 7–8). Godolphin's move created a game of beggar-my-neighbour between the two parliaments.

Our roll-call analysis (presented in McLean and McMillan [2005]) tries to explain the Scottish Parliament's swing to Union. There are no roll calls available for the English votes, but we also need to explain how the Act passed through Westminster with such serenity, when similar measures had previously attracted the objections of the trading interest and aroused 'a maelstrom of prejudice in which the Scots were eclectically damned as beggars, thieves and murderers' (Ferguson 1977: 102–3). The English placidly accepted union with a rival religion entrenched in Scotland: a religion which Charles I, Cromwell, Charles II, and James II had all tried to overthrow.

The powers of the Scottish Parliament during the seventeenth century had waxed and waned inversely with those of the monarch. At the Union of the Crowns in 1603, the parliament had little power. James VI and I commented that 'Here I sit and governe it [Scotland] with my pen, I write and it is done, and by a Clearke of the Councell I governe Scotland now, which others could not do by the sword' (quoted in Rait 1901: 101–2). From 1641 to 1650 Scotland was ruled by the Scottish Parliament, in conjunction with the General Assembly of the Presbyterian Church. Cromwell's victory over the Scots at Dunbar in 1650 saw a short-lived 'union', under which the Government of Scotland was neither ecclesiastical nor civil, but martial. The Edinburgh Parliament agreed to the Cromwellian union, 'once again because it was ordered to do so' (Rait 1901: 106). During this period, free trade with England was established, and feudality abolished. After the Restoration of the monarchy in 1660, the parliament was again reduced to subservience, and dominance of the king and the Episcopalian establishment reasserted. The feudal system of land tenure was restored, to be abolished by the Scottish Parliament in 2000.

The Scottish Parliament's acceptance of William and Mary in Scotland was formalized, through the Claim of Right Act 1689 and the Articles of Grievances, in a way which entrenched Scottish parliamentary authority (Mitchison 1983: 115–19). As in England, a pact between king and parliament extinguished the old claims of divine right. But it was a different pact. The Church of Scotland leader, William Carstares, promoted the establishment of the Scottish Convention Parliament, which met in Edinburgh in March 1689, and legitimized the accession of William to the Scottish throne (Dunlop 1967: 65–73). His influence over William eased the passage of the Act Ratifying the Confession of Faith and Settling Presbyterian Church Government on 7 June 1690. The General Assembly reaffirmed, in 1698, the independence of the Church from the state, declaring that 'Jesus Christ is the only Head and King of his Church' (Goldie 1996: 234). In return the powers of the parliament were strengthened by abolishing both the estate of the bishops and the Lords of the Articles, the parliamentary committee through which the crown's executive authority had been exercised (Devine 2003: 50). From 1695 the Crown sought to control parliament through a system of 'management' by which patronage was directed through powerful aristocratic politicians. However, the coherence of the Scottish administration was undermined by factional competition between the supporters of the prominent aristocratic leaders.

The initial confrontations with London were due to three issues which highlighted the subordination of Scottish to English politics. First, the Act of Settlement passed by the Westminster Parliament in 1701 purported to override Scottish authority over sovereignty and regal succession in Scotland. It stated that, in the absence of any natural heirs of Anne, the succession should pass to Sophia, Electress of Hanover (grand-daughter of James VI and I), and her issue. The measure was passed after Anne's last surviving child, the Duke of Gloucester, died in July 1700. Second, the delay in calling parliament in Edinburgh on the accession of Anne was seen as a challenge to Scottish parliamentary authority. Parliament was supposed to meet within twenty days of the king's death, under the Act of Security of 1696. However, it was not recalled until ninety days after William's death in March 1702, with the Duke of Queensberry (the royal manager in Scotland) and the court party reluctant to hold elections. The Duke of Hamilton therefore boycotted the 1702 session, which allowed the court party to press through key legislation, including measures designed to secure an incorporating Union (Ferguson 1977: 200–1).

Thirdly, war was declared against France in May 1702 without consulting the Scottish Parliament, contravening the 1696 Act of Security (Brown 1992: 177). The Scottish Parliament responded with a hostile and assertive programme, which emphasized Scottish interests over the succession, trade, and military affairs. The parliamentary session of 1703 rallied against English domination, and sought an alternative to the subservience of Scottish politics to the interests of the London court. How then could the same parliament vote within four years for union and extinction?

The Edinburgh Parliament was a unicameral body, with the three estates of nobles, barons, and burgh representatives voting together in Parliament House. In the 1690s, the parliament operated a system of committees, on which officers of state who were not members of the parliament could sit (but not vote). All of the key votes running up to the Act of Union were discussed by the full parliament. Votes were held with a clerk reading out the roll of members, and each member present giving his vote individually and aloud (Ditchfield et al. 1995: 140). Key votes were recorded in the *Acts of the Parliament of Scotland* (1966) alongside lists of voters drawn up by those present. This method of voting provides for a more accurate record of voting than for the Westminster Parliament, where voting was through leaving the chamber into a lobby. We, therefore, conducted a roll-call analysis of the vote in Scotland, though not in England.[5]

Three Acts passed in 1703 and 1704 seemed particularly anglophobic. *The Act for the Security of the Kingdom* (Act of Security) and *The Act anent Peace and War* asserted the right of the Scottish Parliament over the succession and declaration of war. These were part of Fletcher's campaign to impose limitations on the influence of the English court on Scottish affairs. They were carried against the wishes of Scottish ministers. The third Act, the *Act for Allowing the Importation of all Wines and Foreign Liquors* (the Wine Act) was seen in London as part of the Scottish assertion of independence and anti-Englishness—opening up Scottish trade to French imports—but was actually an administrative proposal pressed by the Edinburgh court in an attempt to gain some much needed revenue. It was bitterly opposed by the country party (including Fletcher[6]), which had pushed through the previous Acts. In fact, the records of votes against the Act of Security and the Wine Act show that only Sir Robert Dundas of Arniston voted against both, with 190 other MPs taking opposing sides. This allows us to construct a cross-section of the pro- and anti-court position in the Scottish Parliament in 1703. Those voting against the Act of Security and/or for the Wine Act are coded as 'court party'; those voting against the Wine Act (a ministerial measure) and/or for the Act of Security are coded as 'country party'. This can then be compared with the voting patterns on the Act of Union, which was passed by the same parliament in 1706, allowing an analysis of vote switching over the parliament. Although the two Acts may seem unrelated, or may even seem (to us) to be ideologically linked in the opposite way to the way contemporaries saw them, the fact that only a single MP voted against both shows a stark division along party lines.

The 1704 and 1705 sessions of the Edinburgh Parliament were chaotic. Lord Queensberry's administration fell in the aftermath of false claims of a Jacobite conspiracy (the 'Scotch plot' or 'Queensberry plot'). In Edinburgh, the new Commissioner, Lord Tweeddale, struggled to press for a resolution of the question of the succession with little parliamentary support (the 'New Party', which never commanded more than thirty votes) (Ferguson 1977: 217), amidst Queensberry's attempt to undermine his ministry and a continued agitation from the country party. The London court offered a deal, whereby in return for the Scottish Parliament's acceptance of the Hanoverian succession the parliament would gain a veto over court appointments. This addressed Fletcher's criticisms of the lack of parliamentary control over patronage. However, it did not go far enough, and instead the parliament passed a resolve, proposed by the Duke of Hamilton: 'Not to name the Successor till we have a previous Treaty with *England* for regulating our Commerce, and other Concerns with that Nation.' This resolve was cleverly worded: vague enough to unite those seeking to undermine Tweeddale, the Jacobites, and Fletcher's desire for limitations on the monarchy and a strong parliament.

In order to secure the supply necessary to support the military campaign in Europe, building up to Blenheim, Queen Anne was forced to concede the Act for Security, alongside an Act permitting the export of wool. Both these measures, although accepted by the Queen's advisors as necessary to secure supply, were seen as hostile to English interests, and led to a welling-up of popular anti-Scottish feeling (Ferguson 1977: 222). Retaliation from Westminster came in the form of the 'Act for the effectual securing of the Kingdom of England from the apparent dangers that might arise from several Acts lately passed in the Parliament of Scotland', known as the Aliens Act. This threatened to treat the Scots as aliens, and restrict trade in cattle, linen and coal: a 'naked piece of economic blackmail, designed to bring the Scottish parliament swiftly to the negotiating table' (Devine 1999: 3; see also Whatley 2006: 213–4). The Act led to riots in Edinburgh, and ended Tweeddale's spell as Commissioner. It emphasized the difficulties of running a Scottish government that was acceptable in Westminster and the London court. The Queen's two parliaments were passing Acts that contradicted one another.

Up to 1705 there was no clear majority in the Scottish Parliament for a coherent programme of government. The weakness of the constitutional institutions linking London and Edinburgh was exacerbated by a Scottish party system split between court, country, and Jacobite/Cavalier parties. The court interest was split by competition over patronage and places, most clearly seen in Queensberry's obstruction of any lasting settlement whilst out of office.

Riley (1978: 57) describes the anti-English programme pressed by the Scottish parliament in 1703–4 as a ruse to 'embarrass the court':

> On neither side were the leaders saying what they meant. The opposition talked of trade and a treaty; the court claimed that the best way to achieve such aims was by limitations and settlement of the succession. The latter were making the best of the task they had been given; the former were trying to sabotage their efforts. All the rest was just talk. (Riley 1978: 94)

Thus, it was a simple matter for the London court to influence negotiations in their own interest, using a combination of patronage and bribery, and Riley gives a detailed analysis of the financial resources used to buy votes and smooth the passage of the Act of Union through the Edinburgh Parliament.

For Robertson (1995) on the other hand, the ideology of Andrew Fletcher of Saltoun matters. Fletcher presented a blueprint for a federal constitution, whereby the dominance of London would be tempered by a limited monarchy, and parliamentary and military power diffused across a number of regional centres. This country Whig perspective challenged the centralizing vision of a United Kingdom based on Westminster Parliament controlling the regal territories. Fletcher's radical constitutional alternative, and his strong denunciation of a venal and corrupt political system, threatened the traditional basis of Scottish government as fundamentally as the Union proposals. Fletcher and the Unionists agreed that the current mode of government in Scotland was unsustainable. The English discontent with the way that the Scottish establishment operated was clearly focused on the challenge to the regal union, and a wish to suppress the religious controversy associated with the Jacobite challenge; alongside a more administrative concern to simplify the regulation of trading, military concerns, and taxation.

However, the opponents of Union failed to present a coherent alternative. In part, this was due to Hamilton's weak leadership. Hamilton 'bitterly resented' Queensberry's control of the Douglas clan of which they were both members, as well as Queensberry's role as leader of the court interest; despite marriage to a wealthy English heiress, Hamilton was in constant financial difficulty;[7] and his claim to the crown of Scotland, through descent from Mary Stuart (daughter of James II of Scotland), complicated his relations with the Jacobites and Queen Anne. These factors led to some otherwise incomprehensible decisions which undermined the anti-Union movement, notably his proposal to give Queen Anne the right to appoint the Scottish Commissioners to discuss Union (Whatley 2006: 224). He failed to support a popular rising against the Union, despite toying with the idea, and pleaded toothache when the time came to lead the parliamentary opposition to the passage of the Act of Union. (For more on Hamilton, his character, and his mother, see Whatley 2006 *passim*, esp. at 47, 172–3, 185–6.)

Fletcher's views were too radical to form a coalition across the middle ground of the Scottish establishment, and his 'temper frequently let him down' (Robertson 1997: xvii).[8] At the inception of the Scottish Parliament, in May 1703, Fletcher set out his opposition to a court demand for supply, arguing that first 'the house would take into consideration what acts are necessary to secure our religion, liberty, and trade' (quoted in Robertson 1997: 131). As a supporter and advocate of the Act of Security and the Act anent Peace and War, Fletcher led the campaign for limitations on the English court. However, his proposals also sought to entrench the role of the Scottish parliament over patronage and procedure, presenting a constructive programme as an alternative to an incorporating union. These measures included the entrenchment of the elected portion of the parliament, and the right of the parliament to select the administration and appoint government officials. The Edinburgh Parliament would also have control over the military, and appointments to all military commissions (Robertson 1997: 138–9, 151).

Fletcher was not a Scottish nationalist. There is 'no denying that he was in favour of a degree of union between Scotland and England' (Robertson 1987: 203). Despite Fletcher's skill as a spokesman against the incorporating Union, his wider constitutional prescriptions were too radical to gain widespread popular and parliamentary support. The anti-Union coalition was so disparate, containing as it did Jacobites, country Whigs, extreme Presbyterians, and disappointed office-seekers, that even without Hamilton's toothache and Fletcher's temper it would have disintegrated.

After the fall of the interim administrations led by Tweeddale and (in 1705) by Argyll, the court interest, again under the leadership of the Duke of Queensberry, was able to consolidate its support and present a united front in the votes on the Union. This may have been due to the bribery and patronage that Queensberry was able to command, but represented a greater coherence amongst the court interest that had previously been evident. It also showed that the London administration were willing to overcome their discontent with Queensberry's earlier involvement with the 'Scotch plot'. Queensberry returned as the Queen's Commissioner for the 1706 session of the Scottish Parliament. This strengthening of the Court interest in Scotland coincided with a rare conjunction of English regal, military, administrative, and parliamentary agreement. The prospect of an incorporating Union brought together Queen Anne, Marlborough, Godolphin, and Harley, each of whom was persuaded to press the Unionist cause. For Queen Anne the Union represented the solution to the issue of the succession; to Marlborough the removal of a potential military weakness; for Godolphin the extension of administrative control over a recalcitrant region; and for Harley the entrenchment of Whig parliamentary authority.

There had already been abortive negotiations over Union at the start of the new reign in 1702. Then the Scottish Commissioners had focused on trading concessions and the English were so uninterested that the proceedings had to be frequently adjourned because they could not raise a quorum (Mathieson 1905: 77–8; Ferguson 1977: 201–2). In 1706, there was a much greater sense of purpose. The Scottish Commissioners first proposed a federal union, a suggestion that was rejected out of hand by the English Commissioners. Clerk of Penicuik records that the federal scheme 'was most favoured by the people of Scotland, but all the Scots Commissioners, to a Man, considered it rediculous and impracticable' (Clerk 1892: 60). The Scottish Commissioners were also aware that the English Commissioners were unlikely to compromise on this point, being settled on an incorporating union. As it was probably common knowledge that the Scots would not, or could not, press hard for a federal scheme, once the parties settled on an incorporating union, negotiations were straightforward. The Scottish Parliament would be abolished, in return for representation within the new Great Britain Parliament (the extent of which was the only issue which forced a joint meeting of the negotiating teams; Speck 1994: 98). The monarchy was to be settled on the House of Hanover, provided that monarchs remained Protestant. There would be freedom of trade in the new state, but with certain aspects of the Scottish economy given a buffer of protection. The cost of taking on a share of the English (and Welsh) national debt would be addressed through the provision of compensation, which would also ameliorate the loss of trading rights given to the Company of Scotland. The negotiators agreed to organize the passage through the Scottish Parliament first, to be considered in London thereafter.

The Scottish Parliament opened its session on 3 October 1706, with the reading of an address from Queen Anne, which stated 'The Union has been long desired by both nations, and we shall esteem it as the greatest glory of our reign to have it now perfected' (quoted in Speck 1994: 106). The articles were read, and the First Article which stated 'That the Two Kingdoms of Scotland and England, shall . . . be United into One Kingdom by the Name of GREAT BRITAIN', was carried on 4 November 1706, by 116 votes to 83. The Scottish court were able to carry all of the twenty-five articles with only minor revision, and the Act of Union was ratified in Edinburgh on 16 January 1707 by 110 votes to 69. News of this reached London on 20 January, and the Act of Union was approved by both Houses of the Westminster Parliament by 24 February, and given the assent of Queen Anne on 6 March, with effect from 1 May 1707 (Speck 1994: 106–17).

The key group of swing voters was nicknamed the Squadrone Volante. Table 3.1 replicates Riley's allocation of party labels, set against the changing voting behaviour between 1703 and 1706 (Riley 1978: 328). Riley notes the strength of party voting across the parliament, suggesting that 'Practically all voted their normal party line to an extent that is quite beyond coincidence' (Riley 1978: 275). This is hard to square with the Namierite/nationalist parcel of rogues hypothesis. A parcel of rogues would have sought the advantages of aligning with court interest in order to gain the monetary benefits and patronage of union. Party cohesion, on the contrary, suggests that there were real ideological differences between the parliamentary groupings. Table 3.2 shows that the nobles were significantly more pro-Union than the other two orders.[9]

Riley (1969) and Ferguson (1968) place much of the weight of their explanation of the Scottish switch in attitudes towards Union on the provi-

Table 3.1 Party identification and voting in the Scottish Parliament 1703 and 1706.

	Country/Cavalier	Court	Squadrone	Total	
Unionist in 1703 and 1706	3	53	1	57	116
Anti-union in 1703, pro in 1706	2	3	20	25	
No vote 1703, pro-union 1706	1	30	3	34	
Anti-union in 1703 and 1706	43	0	0	43	83
Pro-union in 1703, anti in 1706	17	7	0	24	
No vote 1703, anti-union 1706	14	2	0	16	
Pro-union 1703, no vote 1706	3	7	0	10	29
Anti-union 1703, no vote 1706	5	0	2	7	
Other absent/abstained	6	5	1	12	
Total	94	107	27	228	228

Source for all tables in this chapter: our data.

Table 3.2 Membership of the Estates and voting in the Scottish Parliament on the First Article of the Act of Union.

	Nobles	Barons/Shire	Burgh	Total
Pro-union	46	37	33	116
Anti-union	21	33	29	83
No vote	91	31	15	137
	158	101	77	336

p of $\chi^2 < 0.001$

sion of £20,000 sterling, secretly sent from London in order to cover the arrears of past and present office holders. However, the list of recorded arrears and payments (shown in Appendix B of Riley 1969) suggests that, although a large proportion of this went to the swing voters of the Squadrone Volante, this was largely to cover expenses incurred during Tweeddale's tenure as Commissioner. Such payments are hard to distinguish from the general expenses incurred and recompensed from the treasury during the normal practice of parliamentary management. Queensberry was recorded as receiving £12,325, but this was against recorded arrears of £26,756, and he had received a larger amount in 1705, when out of favour with the London and Edinburgh courts, in recognition of arrears incurred in his earlier tenure as Commissioner. A far greater source of remuneration was through the payment of the 'Equivalent', designed to compensate for Scotland's acceptance of a national debt, discussed below.

Riley's account does expose the underlying weakness of the popular basis of the Scottish Parliament. Whilst there was widespread popular opposition to the Union amongst the Scottish population, this was apparently incidental to the voting patterns in the Edinburgh Parliament. The Scottish MPs were insulated from popular opinion by the very limited extent of electoral participation. Scottish electorates in both shire and burgh constituencies were extremely small: Midlothian, with around a hundred voters, had the largest electorate, and most burghs had an electorate of twelve or fewer (Hayton 1996: 81). This ensured that the elections were easily controlled by the aristocratic interests. And in a unicameral parliament, unelected members of the nobility voted alongside the elected members.

Fletcher saw the danger that the London court would attempt to exert influence over the parliament through the creation of new titles, which could tilt the balance within the parliament. His proposed limitations on the Crown included a provision 'That so many lesser barons shall be added to the parliament, as there have been noblemen created ... and that in all time coming, for every nobleman that shall be created, there shall be a baron added to the parliament' (quoted in Robertson 1997: 138). Table 3.2 shows voting on the First Article of the Act of Union, broken down by estates. Whilst a majority of each of the estates was pro-Union on the key vote, the majority amongst the nobles was much larger than that of the members representing the counties and burghs of Scotland.[10] Fletcher's concerns about the ability of the London court to influence the Scottish aristocracy appear to be supported, although the causal links may be more complex: 'That 1 in 7 Scottish nobles had English wives at the resumption of negotiations, testifies not only [to] their steady assimilation into the British ruling class, but also to their growing dependence on the English marriage market to build up disposable income' (McNeill and MacQueen 1996: 151). The fact that membership of the aristocracy was associated with a greater interest in trade, both with England and abroad, has also been used to explain the greater propensity of the nobility to support the Union.

Distinguishing between the responsiveness of members of the three estates of the Scottish Parliament to the debate over the Act of Union is complicated by the close kinship and patronage links between the different estates, but it appears that the nobility was more likely to swing Unionist, followed by the barons, whereas the burgh members who shifted allegiance were more likely to go to the anti-Unionist position. This may reflect a greater sensitiveness amongst the burgh members to public opinion within their constituencies.

The extent to which public opinion was directed against the Union has been gauged by the number, and complete one-sidedness, of the petitions presented to the Scottish Parliament. Petitions were received from at least fifteen out of the thirty-three counties, and twenty-one of the sixty-seven royal burghs (Macinnes 1990: 12). All were opposed to the incorporating Union. Further to this pressure, sixty-two 'exceptional and unsolicited addresses' were delivered to the parliament, three from presbyteries, nine from towns, and fifty from parishes. 'These addresses against the union came predominantly from west-central and south-western Scotland, where local communities drew consciously on covenanting traditions of supplicating in support of religious and civil liberties' (McNeill and MacQueen 1996: 151). This glut of anti-Union activity has been taken to represent the widespread popular antipathy to the measure, as well as indicating grass-roots opposition to an incorporating union from members of the Presbyterian church. However, our analysis of the effect of petitions on the voting behaviour of members of the Edinburgh Parliament suggests that petitioning had little or no effect.

Comparing positions in 1703 with the vote on the First Article of the Act of Union, controlling for whether there was a petition in the constituency, gives

Table 3.3 Petitioning and vote-switching in the Scottish Parliament 1703–6.

	Petition	No petition
Unionist in 1703 and 1706	10	29
Anti-union in 1703, pro in 1706	15	4
No vote 1703, pro-union 1706	2	10
Anti-union in 1703 and 1706	23	8
Pro-union in 1703, anti in 1706	8	10
No vote 1703, anti-union 1706	6	7
Pro-union 1703, no vote 1706	3	12
Anti-union 1703, no vote 1706	8	7
Other absent/abstained	8	8
Total	83	95

p of $\chi^2 < 0.001$

the pattern shown in Table 3.3. This shows that petitions, to a large extent, did reflect voting behaviour by constituency members. Petitions were more likely to be presented in constituencies where the member consistently opposed Union, and were less prevalent in those constituencies represented by stable pro-Union members. Similarly, of the members with no recorded position in 1703, the pro-Unionists tended not to come from constituencies where petitions were raised, whereas the anti-Unionists were more likely. The exception to this pattern is amongst the nineteen members, largely from the Squadrone Volante, who switched from an anti-Union position in 1703 to a pro-Union position in 1706. Fifteen of these faced petitions raised in their constituencies, a sign that there was popular opposition to their change in voting allegiance. The fact that the simple relationship between petitions and vote is non-significant (Macinnes 1990), whereas the more complex relationship shown in Table 3.3 is significant, shows that petitions reflected rather than induced voting behaviour. The *realpolitik* of pro-Union politicians like the duke of Argyll and the earl of Mar seems justified. Argyll suggested that the petitions were only fit to make kites of, and Mar suggested that the pro-Union campaign had left it too late, and that few pro-Union petitions would look worse than none (Ferguson 1964: 109–10).

'TRADE WITH MOST...'

Union has been presented as creating 'an Anglo-Scottish common market that was the biggest customs-free zone in Europe' (Smout 1969a: 215).

Whatley (2000: 1) suggests that famine in the 1690s caused the death of between 10 and 20 per cent of the Scottish population. This economic weakness was compounded by the expensive failure of Darien.

This free-trade interpretation of the Union can be challenged from a number of positions. First, studies of the extent to which any cross-border tariffs were effective before the Union, and the extent to which common excise duties were imposed after the Union, suggest that the Union only provided a blurred distinction between trading practices (Smout 1964: 458; Saville 1996: 65–6). Secondly, there was a shared appreciation on both sides of the border, that protectionist measures could cut both ways; which meant that free trade was not necessarily seen as a positive benefit (Whatley 1989).

Yet the demand for free trade with England had been frequently raised from Scotland, and the threat of economic sanctions was used by the English as a means of putting pressure on the Scottish Parliament to accede to a Parliamentary Union, through the Aliens Act of 1705. Promoters of the Union, such as Daniel Defoe, stressed the benefits of free trade to the Scottish economy (Smout 1964: 463–4), and Fletcher noted that the prospect of greater trading benefits was 'the bait that covers the hook' (quoted in Whatley 2001: 57). Marlborough said in 1706: 'the true state of the matter was, whether Scotland should continue subject to an English Ministry without trade, or be subject to an English Parliament with trade' (quoted in Young 1999: 25). Marlborough's position as favourite of the Queen and military destroyer of the French depended on a governmental revolution in terms of taxation and finance. In this area, rather than the expansion of free trade, lay the main benefits of Union for the English state. Scottish government had been a distraction to the Queen's English ministers. Union would remove a potential rival to the establishment of a monopolistic trading empire. It also offered scope for a more robust tax regime.

A number of historians have attempted to link voting in the Edinburgh Parliament on the Acts of Union to the specific economic interests of Scottish members of parliament. Both Riley (1978: 276) and Smout (1963: 263) note that the nobility had a particularly strong interest in the export market for Scottish goods; and that this could have explained their greater likelihood of supporting the Union (see Table 3.2). Free-market arguments cut both ways:

> although a majority of those Scots involved in the making of the Treaty clearly grasped the opportunity of access to the English and colonial markets while it was on offer, others were equally concerned to obtain as many safeguards as possible to defend vulnerable elements of what . . . was an exceedingly fragile economy. (Whatley 1989: 159)

In particular, the Scottish salt industry, and the coal production which supported it, were both extremely vulnerable to competition. Whatley (2001: 60) suggests that members of each of the estates had (or represented) significant trading interests, but that such considerations offer little additional explanatory power. The fact that the fifteen of the twenty articles of the Act of Union concerned economic aspects may seem to represent the importance of trade in the making of the treaty. However, those fifteen can be divided into three groups: those dealing with free-trade; those dealing with customs and duties and the extent of temporary measures protecting Scottish industry; and those dealing with the compensation for the adoption of English and Welsh national debt. The key free-trade Article was the fourth, which stated 'That all the Subjects of the United Kingdom of Great Britain shall from and after the Union have full Freedom and Intercourse of Trade and Navigation'. This was accompanied by four other Articles (5, 6, 17, and 18) which set out the free-trade basis of the state, establishing a British navy, a common currency, and system of weights and measures. Nine Articles (6 to 14) dealt with the unified system of customs and duties, and contained a large number of concessions designed to protect Scottish trading interests, including the beer and liquor trade, salt, fishing, paper, and coal industries. Finally, Article 15 dealt with the payment of the 'Equivalent', amounting to just under £400,000 sterling, to compensate Scotland for the higher taxation and adoption of the English and Welsh national debt. Thus, the Treaty of Union delivered free trade, tempered by a number of measures protecting supposedly vulnerable areas of the Scottish economy. It also shows that the Westminster Parliament was willing to accept significant concessions to Scottish trading interests.

Article 4 was passed with the largest majority of any Article: securing 154 supporting votes versus 19 against; 31 members who had hitherto voted against union changed sides to support Article 4. This was despite Fletcher's attempt to make Article 4 a central element of the opposition attack on Union (Riley 1978: 288). As Table 3.4 shows, the Article received support from the most consistent opponents of the Union programme.

But in 1707 (and still in 1800) free trade connoted access to markets, not removal of protection. In contrast to the smooth passage of Article 4 of the Act of Union, the Articles dealing with customs and duties (referred to as the 'explanations') were much more contentious, and led to significant amendments to the negotiated treaty, all adding elements of protection for particular aspects of Scottish trade and industry. Indeed, Article 8, dealing with the Salt Tax, involved the court's only defeat during the passage of the Act of Union (on an amendment demanding drawbacks on the export of salted beef and pork; Macinnes 1990: 17). The Scottish Parliament succeeded in adding a number of amendments to the draft treaty negotiated in London (Whatley

Table 3.4 Vote on Article 4 (free trade) and vote-switching in the Scottish Parliament 1703–6.

	For Article 4	Against Article 4
Unionist in 1703 and 1706	54	–
Anti-union in 1703, pro in 1706	25	–
No vote 1703, pro-union 1706	30	–
Anti-union in 1703 and 1706	12	13
Pro-union in 1703, anti in 1706	12	2
No vote 1703, anti-union 1706	7	3
Pro-union 1703, no vote 1706	5	1
Anti-union 1703, no vote 1706	4	–
Other absent/abstained	4	–
Total	154	19

p of χ^2 not calculated because of empty cells.

2001), much to the consternation of Godolphin who was worried that this could complicate the passage of the Act of Union through the Westminster Parliament (Riley 1978: 291). These amendments were nevertheless accepted by the court, and carried without significant numbers of defections. However, the passage of the 'explanations', and the success of the Scottish Parliament in adding protectionist measures, show the limitations of a purely free-trade explanation of the passage of the Act of Union. The Articles of Union were amended to include a number of (albeit temporary) protectionist measures.

The third economic element of the Act of Union was the payment of the 'Equivalent', ostensibly compensation for the adoption of the burden of the English and Welsh national debt. The details of this, and the way that payment would be channelled (largely to stockholders in the Company of Scotland, responsible for the Darien venture) were outlined in Article 15. The prohibition on capitalization of the Company in London (at the behest of the English East India Company) had forced the directors to focus on raising money in Scotland, and it became a great patriotic enterprise, with pledges for the revised capitalization of £400,000 reached within six months of the subscriptions opening in February 1696 (Devine 2003: 42). Andrew Fletcher wrote in 1698 that 'no Scotsman is an enemy' to the Company of Scotland (quoted in Robertson 1997: 38). Fletcher linked support for the Company of Scotland to his broader schemes of limitations on monarchy, using the obstructions imposed by King William to illustrate the weakness of the Scottish interest under the existing scheme of joint monarchy.

The Company of Scotland had highlighted the potential threat to English monopoly trading rights, most particularly associated with the East India

Companies; also the possibility that an independent Scotland could free-ride on English military expansion, undermining trade and revenue from customs and excise. But Darien also undermined Scottish economic confidence; for contemporaries 'it seemed . . . that Scotland was on the verge of economic collapse' (Smout 1964: 459). This helped swing the general debate on the trading benefits of Union towards Clerk and the Unionists, whereas the economic arguments of the anti-Unionists were 'distinctly old-fashioned and more fundamentally unrealistic' (Smout 1964: 485). However, Darien led to popular fury culminating in the judicial murder of the captain and two officers of the *Worcester*, an English ship rumoured to have sunk one of the Darien vessels, which put into Leith docks in 1705.

Thus, Darien was an economic disaster to the Scots but also a political threat to the English. The London court sought to relieve both by directing payments to stockholders in return for a union. This would remove a potential source of rivalry to the East India Company, which was subsequently free to exploit its monopolistic trading rights. The parliamentary union helped consolidate this monopolistic control of trading rights, and restricted the ability of Scottish entrepreneurs to undermine English trading interests by free-riding on the back of English military and territorial expansion.

From 1702 compensation for the losses incurred in the Darien venture, totalling £153,631—estimated to be one-quarter of Scotland's entire capital stock—were made part of the Scottish negotiations over a possible incorporating union (Riley 1978: 35, 199). This compensation was linked to the payment of the 'Equivalent', the sum of money paid to Scotland upon Union in order to assuage the burden of the English national debt, which a unitary state would have to bear.

The 'Equivalent' was calculated on the basis of English pre-Union debts, but there was no clear way of distributing this financial largesse. Whilst a great deal of consideration was given to calculating the total amount, which was agreed at £398,085 10s, much larger than the assessed losses from Darien, the issue of who should receive it was given much less consideration. Rather than defraying past or future tax payments across the Scottish nation, it was appropriated by a number of sectional interests: those who had lost out from the switch from Scottish to English coinage; the shareholders of the Company of Scotland; the Scottish woollen industry; and allowances to Commissioners who negotiated the Union. Further patronage was exercised in setting up a Committee which was designed to spend the 'Equivalent', with suitable compensation. Members were paid expenses of £920 a year (Riley 1964: 208, 214). As such, the 'Equivalent' provided a much greater source of patronage than the amount of money which was seen as being covertly shifted to Scotland to ease the passage of the Union.

The 'Equivalent' arrived belatedly in an armed convoy of wagons (Whatley 2006: 330). The English exchequer could not afford to pay it all in cash, so bills were issued; a situation that it helped establish the Bank of Scotland, which was charged with overseeing the exchange (Scott 1911: 268). The compensation was directed at those with the clearest claim, and so subscribers to the Company of Scotland and the Union Commissioners received first charge. For more ambiguous recipients, such as the woollen traders, the result was less satisfactory: They 'could not be paid because nobody had been named in the Act anent the Public Debts to receive it' (Riley 1964: 212). The rest of the Scottish population received nothing. Debates over the liabilities of creditors to the Scottish government prior to 1707 continued to 1724, and holders of 'Equivalent' debt ended up by creating a joint stock bank in the form of the Royal Bank of Scotland (Riley 1964: 229). Thus, two of the biggest banks in the present-day United Kingdom—what are now part of Lloyds Group (after its shotgun takeover of HBOS in late 2008) and the Royal Bank of Scotland owe their origins to the Scottish Equivalent.

However, support for the Darien venture does not correlate with support or opposition for an incorporating Union; two of the leading activists in the scheme took diametrically opposed views on the Union. William Paterson returned from Darien (where his wife had died) to write pro-Unionist propaganda, and he acted as an agent for the English minister Robert Harley. Andrew Fletcher, meanwhile, saw the failure of the Darien expedition (to which he had subscribed £1,000) as an illustration of the subjugation of Scottish to English trading interests, a situation which would only be worsened if the Scottish Parliament were to be abolished. Similarly, the leader of the Court interest who pushed the Union through the Edinburgh Parliament, the Duke of Queensberry, had subscribed £3,000; as had a leading opponent of the Union, Lord Belhaven. The Duchess of Hamilton opened the subscription with a promise of £1,000.

In his analysis of the socio-economic and geographical basis of the Company of Scotland subscription lists W. Douglas Jones (2001: 33–4) identifies 170 subscribers (12.0 per cent of the total number, contributing 16.4 per cent of the total capital) who served as Members of Parliament, Privy Councillors, ministers of state, or high court judges, including 57 members of Parliament who sat between 1696 and 1700. Comparing a list of all Darien subscribers (*A perfect list . . . 1696*) with our database of members of the Scottish Parliament of 1703–7, there are ninety-nine members of parliament who can be (with varying degrees of certainty) linked to a subscription to the Company of Scotland, contributing £62,850 (15.7 per cent) of the total.

Tables 3.5 and 3.6 suggest that, despite the strong incentives for Darien compensation and its association with direct recompense through

Table 3.5 Voting on the First Article in the Scottish Parliament compared to Darien stockholding.

	Stockholders' votes (%)	Average stock (£)	Non-stockholders' votes (%)	Total votes (%)
For	41 (55%)	658.54	75 (60%)	116 (58%)
Against	33 (45%)	604.55	50 (40%)	83 (42%)
Total	74	638.46	125	199

Article 1, 4th November 1706: That the two kingdoms of England and Scotland shall upon the 1st day of May next . . . , and forever after, be united into one kingdom by the name of Great Britain. p of $\chi^2 = 0.53$, not significant.

Table 3.6 Voting on the Fifteenth Article (providing an 'Equivalent') in the Scottish Parliament compared to Darien stockholding.

	Stockholders' votes (%)	Average stock (£)	Non-stockholders' votes (%)	Total votes (%)
For	44 (73%)	647.73	68 (64%)	112 (68%)
Against	16 (27%)	665.63	38 (36%)	54 (33%)
Total	60	652.50	106	166

p of $\chi^2 = 0.23$, not significant.

the 'Equivalent', it does not appear to be a significant factor in the overall passage of the Act of Union in Edinburgh. Whilst the average stockholdings in the Company of Scotland were higher amongst those who favoured the Union, possession of stock does not appear to have been an indicator of voting one way or the other. Non-stockholders were more likely to vote for the Union. The relationships in Tables 3.5 and 3.6 are not significant.

Breaking down the seventy-four members who voted on the first article of the Union according to their position in the 1703 session of parliament shows that thirteen members subscribing to Darien switched to a pro-Union stance, but ten switched the other way. It seems that the large amounts of money available in compensation for Darien subscribers included in the Union had no effect on the voting patterns in the Scottish Parliament. Riley (1978) argues that short-term gain was the incentive behind most of the voting on the Union. If this were the case, then Darien subscribers should have been much more likely to switch to a pro-Union position. They were not. Even on the vote on Article 15, which set out the conditions for repayment of the 'Equivalent', largely to stockholders of the Company of Scotland, there was very little cross-voting amongst MPs who would directly benefit.

The final recorded vote (until 1999) of the Scottish Parliament, on 10 March 1707, concerned the payment of compensation to the Company of Scotland's shareholders, and the issue of whether it should be paid to proprietors or through a committee of appointed commissioners. The vote went in favour of a commission, by thirty votes to eleven; twenty-nine MPs coded as having held Darien stock voted, with twenty-two in favour and seven against. There is no significant difference between the voting pattern of stockholders and non-stockholders (p of $\chi^2 = 0.55$).

Union brought Scotland within the ambit of what was becoming an established and efficient tax-gathering establishment (Saville 1996: 5). Furthermore, it prevented the possibility of tax competition between Scotland and England, whereby trade and investment could be easily diverted from one to the other. It also restricted, although did not totally rule out, tax evasion through imports from Scotland.

Under the guidance of Lord Godolphin, Lord Treasurer between 1703 and 1710, the tax-raising functions of the government were consolidated, and allied to a system of long-term loans which reduced uncertainty over the liquidity of government and the markets. The land tax, levied at four shillings in the pound, was the 'chief pillar of direct taxation', and underwrote approximately two-thirds of the government's long-term debt (Dickson 1967: 358). The figures for England and Wales show an expansion in the share of national income appropriated as taxation (calculated in constant price values) from 6.7 per cent in 1690 to 9.2 per cent in 1710 (O'Brien 1988: 3, table 2). Fletcher had argued in favour of a Scottish land tax, in order to place the government of Scotland on a firmer fiscal footing (1698 in Robertson 1997: 41), although this was contingent on greater autonomy over how the finances raised would be spent. He got his way through the Union he despised.

The raising of public debt was facilitated by the success of the East India Companies, which provided finance for the Exchequer, and the creation of the Bank of England in 1694. This was consolidated by the close links between these companies and parliament. Interest rates on East India bonds fell from 6 per cent between 1688 and September 1705, to 5 per cent between September 1705 and September 1708 (Dickson 1967: 411, table 67), and this was associated with a general lowering of interest rates on (English) government borrowing over the period in which the Union with Scotland was forged (Table 3.7). That the government was able to raise money at lower interest after Union than before is eloquent.

In Scotland, the Bank of Scotland and the Darien Companies had been unable to provide a comparable basis for a government debt. The Scottish economy was, somewhat surprisingly, capable of financing the capital calls of both the Company and the Bank of Scotland, but such investment was

Table 3.7 Government long-term borrowing (1704–8).

Date of royal assent to Loan Act	Sum raised (£)	Interest (%)
24 Feb 1704	1,382,976	6.6
16 Jan 1705	690,000	6.6
16 Feb 1706	2,855,762	6.4
27 Mar 1707	1,155,000	6.25
13 Feb 1708	640,000	6.25
11 March 1708	2,280,000	6.25

Source: Dickson (1967: table 3, 60–1).

unsustainable in the light of the lack of returns from both these issues, and by 1697 there was a credit crisis (Jones 2001: 38). Although the transformation of the credit culture in Scotland over this period has been described as providing 'the core of the financial revolution that occurred in Scotland during the eighteenth century' (Jones 2001: 39), it is probably safer to date the transformation from 1707, the Fifteenth Article, and the Bank of Scotland (later joined by the Royal Bank) trading in government debt. There was no adverse market reaction to Union.

'Hanover with some'

The support for an incorporating union given by King William and Queen Anne removed any possibility of the use of the Crown veto over the Acts of Union passed by the Edinburgh and Westminster Parliament. Both monarchs had lobbied hard for such a measure, and Queen Anne attended the Westminster Parliament during the final debates on the Act of Union, in an expression of her support. However, despite the influence of the Crown over the running of the executive in London and Edinburgh, and powers of patronage through the court interest, this was subject to parliamentary control. William's desire for a parliamentary union was frustrated by Westminster's indifference, and Anne was forced to endure and endorse the outcomes of a hostile parliament in Edinburgh during the 1703–5 sessions.

To understand the debate over 'Hanover', one should focus less on the possibilities of the breaking of the dual monarchy or a Jacobite alternative (although these were certainly issues at the time) than on the religious basis of government in Britain. In Scotland, the relationship between the kirk and monarchy had drawn them into the English Civil War (otherwise known as the War of Three Kingdoms). 'The Kirk became the most formidable opponent of the [union] project' (Devine 2003: 50–4). However, by the time of the vote on the Articles of the Act of Union this opposition had been neutered by concessions to the leaders of the Presbyterian church, which had entrenched itself in 1689–90 as the established church in Scotland. William Carstares, the Scottish Presbyterian leader, acted as chaplain of William of Orange, and played a crucial role in establishing the kirk in the Williamite constitutional settlement. Whilst less close to Queen Anne, Carstares was active in the promotion of the Union from his position as Principal of the University of Edinburgh, minister of Greyfriars' church, and a prominent member of the General Assembly of the Presbyterian church.

When the Articles were brought before the Scottish Parliament, Presbyterians were dismayed to find that they contained no protection for them. One minister wrote, in the psalter-metre of the metrical 124th Psalm:

> If that our church had fully been secured
> And if that we had finallie procur'd
> Establishment, we should not have gainstood
> The work, had it been for religious good.[11] (Quoted in Stephen 2007: 90).

The central issue was entrenchment of the Presbyterian established church in Scotland, against the episcopal and Jacobite movements, by *An Act for the Security of the True Protestant Religion and Government of the Church*, passed alongside the Acts of Union (and incorporated with them so that it is still in force). As Carstares wrote to Harley in October 1706, 'the desire I have to see our Church secured makes me in love with the Union as the most probable means to preserve it' (quoted in Dunlop 1967: 115). Whilst this was not the unanimous view of the Presbyterian clergy, the pro-Union leaders were able to prevent outright hostility to the Union becoming an issue associated with the church (Macree 1973: 71–3; Stephen 2007). The approach of Carstares was supported and encouraged by Daniel Defoe, whose role as propagandist for the Union involved reassurance that the change in the constitution would not threaten the Presbyterian church. In September 1706, Defoe described his own role in Edinburgh being 'To remove the jealousies and uneasiness of people about secret designs here against the Kirk' (quoted in Macree 1973: 65).

The presbyteries had proved a source of organized opposition to an incorporating Union, associated with various petitions raised against the measure. The vote on the Act was held on 12 November 1706, in between the votes on the First and Second Articles of the Act of Union. The timing of this vote was perhaps determined by Lord Belhaven's effective speech against the First Article of Union. The Act was passed by 113 to 38; a larger majority than the key vote on the First Article. There was a very strong association between support for the First Article of the Act of Union and support for the *Act for the Security of the . . . Church*. Ninety-five members of the Edinburgh Parliament supported both measures, and no pro-Union members voted against the establishment of the Presbyterian church. However, the opponents of the Union were more clearly divided on the measure, with eleven of the eighty-three members who had voted against the First Article voting for Presbyterian establishment. Whilst opponents of the Union made up nearly all of the thirty-eight votes against the *Act for the Security of the . . . Church*, more abstained on this than voted against. Comparing voting patterns between 1703, the First Article of the Act of Union, and the *Act for the Security of the . . . Church* shows that there was very little difference in the abstention rate within those members who had been solidly pro-Union and those who had switched to a pro-Union stance between 1703 and 1706 (McLean and McMillan 2005). However, those who had switched from pro- to anti-Union positions, or had newly joined the anti-Union camp were less likely to vote against the *Act for the Security of the . . . Church* when compared to those who had consistently opposed unionist measures from 1703. This gives some support to the argument that the issue of Presbyterian establishment cut across the anti-Unionist support base.

Thus, the incorporation of Presbyterian church establishment played the same role in the creation of Great Britain as the US Bill of Rights (the first ten amendments of the US Constitution) played in the creation of the United States. In each case the concession to the anti-federalists won enough of them over for union to pass, where it would otherwise have failed. Establishment brought the leadership of the kirk into sympathy with the court party, and exposed the divisions on religious issues amongst the opponents of Union in Scotland. Further to this, a similar process occurred in London, where a similar Act entrenching the Church of England was passed alongside the Act of Union at Westminster. Whilst there is limited evidence on voting patterns in the Westminster Parliament on this issue, it undoubtedly helped assuage Tory doubts as to the religious basis of the constitution. There was opposition from high-church Tories, led by Sir John Pakington, who saw a conflict between the Queen's roles as head of the Church of England and upholder of the Church of Scotland; but opposition in both the House of Lords and House of Commons was limited. In the Commons the third reading of the Act of Union was passed 274 votes to 116. In the Lords, attempts to challenge the role of the Scottish church were defeated fifty-five to nineteen (Speck 1994: 114–16). Because the Scots had brought credible threats to the table, the English were forced to swallow the establishment of a rival church in Scotland.

'Ease and security'

The Cromwellian Union, imposed through conquest in 1654 after the battles of Dunbar (1650) and Worcester (1651), had raised the question of whether Scotland could survive as an independent nation. The issue of military security was reinforced in 1706 by the mobilization of troops northwards. Godolphin told the Earl of Leven that forces were stationed 'to bee in a readiness in case this ferment should continue to give any farther disturbance to the publick peace' (Ferguson 1977: 256).

However, the focus of English military concerns in 1706 was not Scotland, but Europe. Whilst the negotiations over the basis of an incorporating Union were being thrashed out at Westminster, Marlborough was winning the battle of Ramillies on 12 May. Union with Scotland may have had a military advantage in consolidating the base of the British military territory (although this was challenged in 1708, 1715, and 1745), but it also absorbed Scotland into the English model of governmental and military relations. Again, this is associated with the 'financial revolution' in England, which was closely tied in to the expansionist military commitments of the government under William and Mary and Queen Anne. Military expenditure between 1702 and 1713 accounted for some 72 per cent of total government expenditure, and amounted to some £93,644,560, a third of which was financed by loans (O'Brien 1988: 2, table 1; Dickson 1967: 10, table 1). According to the English Commissioners for Union in 1702, Scotland gained from the success of the British military state:

> the sayd [English Government] debts have been contracted by a long War entered into more particularly for the Preservation of England & the dominions thereunto belonging, yet that Scotland has tasted of the Benefits which have accrued to Great Brittain in general from the Opposition that has been made to the Growth and Power of France. (quoted in Dickson 1967: 8)

The relationship between the military and the government provided one of the focuses for the anti-Union campaign in Scotland. Fletcher's militia campaign was overshadowed by the importance of the war against France in the run up to 1707. The presence of a standing army was less controversial during war—the main debate centred on how the military forces of the state should be maintained during peacetime. The European campaign also brought together Scots fighting in the Scottish, English, and Dutch armies; a common cause that would be enhanced by a more coherent organization.

Fletcher's ideas about a militia took root not in Great Britain but in the United States. The 'country Whigs', of whom he was one, argued as he did that militias preserved freedom whereas standing armies threatened it. The leaders of the American Revolution, above all Thomas Jefferson, took over country Whig ideology wholesale as it suited their politics and their temperaments. The protection of state militias is therefore written into the US Constitution in the Second Amendment, which guarantees 'the right to bear arms' to their members.

Representation and finance

England and Wales returned 513 members to the House of Commons, and Scotland was first offered 38 (it had had 30 under Cromwell). This was above the ratio of tax contributions, which were closer to 28:513, but below the population ratio, on which basis Scotland should have returned perhaps 100 seats—although no reliable population estimates were yet available for either country (Speck 1994: 100). The Scottish Commissioners proposed a representation of fifty seats, and a compromise was struck at forty-five, alongside sixteen members of the House of Lords. This settlement was entrenched in the Twenty-Second Article of the Act of Union.

The passage of Article 22 was meant to be the last-ditch stand of the opponents of the incorporating Union, but was the occasion of the Duke of Hamilton's toothache. The importance of the Article lay not only in the general principle of Scottish representation, but in the mechanics by which the Scottish members of the Westminster Parliament would be chosen. The fact that the Westminster Parliament had decided that the passage of the Union would not be accompanied by a general election across the newly constituted state before the (English and Welsh) general election required by 1708 meant that the Scottish Parliament had to select its own method of representation in the first British Parliament in Westminster. This led to a period of intensive (and antagonistic) bargaining amongst members of the three estates (Riley 1978: 293), over the basis of Scottish representation. In the end, the parliament decided to choose its own delegates to Westminster on the basis of the existing parliamentary majority in Edinburgh. If the motives behind Scottish members of parliament voting for Union were largely determined by patronage, then 112 burgh and shire, and 144 noble, turkeys voted for Christmas (albeit with many receiving a rich stuffing). Acceptance of the incorporating Union would deny a huge swathe of the Scottish political establishment the future possibility of patronage and preferment.

Neither statesmen nor rogues

From 1690 the Scottish Parliament had become more assertive and independent, but it had not established the fiscal or administrative basis which would
support such an independent role. Its assertiveness brought it into conflict
with the trading, military, and regal interests of the English state. An alternative constitutional structure could perhaps have embraced these competing
interests, but the opposition to an incorporating union was divided along
ideological and pragmatic lines. Scottish members of parliament were willing
to exchange direct involvement in a system of administrative patronage
which delivered limited returns, in favour of a more powerful system of
executive authority.

We have grouped interpretations of the 1707 Union into:

- Diceyan (incorporating union as a supreme act of statesmanship)
- Nationalist/Namierite (a parcel of rogues in a nation were bought and
  sold for English gold)
- Free-trading (Roxburgh's *Trade with most*)
- Uncertainty-reducing (*Hanover with some*)
- Welfare-maximizing (*a general aversion to civil discords, intolerable pov-
  erty and . . . constant oppression*).

On our historical and statistical evidence, the eighteenth-century Earl was
nearer the truth than twentieth-century scholars.

The Dicey view, seeing only an incorporating Union, overlooks the extent
to which the Union of 1707 was a *compromise* and a *bargain* between
Westminster and Edinburgh Parliaments. The Act of Union as approved by
the Parliament of Scotland included a number of concessions to the trading
interests of the Scottish members of parliament. More importantly, it entrenched the Presbyterian church in Scotland. This helped neutralize opposition to the Union within Scotland, but also ended Tory aspirations for an
Episcopalian settlement. The entrenchment of two different versions of Protestant truth, via the Scottish and English church establishment Acts that are
both incorporated in the final Act of Union, has remained a fundamental
feature of the British Constitution ever since. We return to it in later chapters.

Perhaps our most important finding is negative. The relationship between
Darien holding and vote on Union is not statistically significant (Tables 3.5
and 3.6). That non-significance is of great substantive significance. It destroys
the Namierites' central contention. Those who held Darien stock were no
more prone to be bought and sold with English gold than those who did not.
Trade was a big issue, but commentators schooled in (neo)classical economics

misconstrue it. The classical view, developed by Adam Smith and David Ricardo, is that both sides of a customs union always gain from trade. Smith had seen the huge growth of the Scottish economy in his own lifetime. But it did not immediately follow the union. The negotiators of the Union thought of trade as a weapon, not as a positive-sum game. The two nations could threaten one another's trade—Scotland could threaten the East India Company, and England could counter-threaten by harassing the Darien Company or by the anti-Scottish Acts mentioned above. A trade treaty was a promise to put down the weapons, not a chance to gain from Ricardian comparative advantage, which was not understood in 1706.

Because so many modern commentators forget that Union was a bargain, they miss Roxburgh's last two points. Bargainers do not strike a deal unless both parties think that they will gain. Union was uncertainty-reducing and welfare-maximizing for both the English and the Scottish negotiators. For the English, reducing uncertainty about the succession meant that the northern frontier was secured and the Jacobite threat contained. Most of the voters for the Duke of Hamilton's Resolve were not Jacobites. They were shrewd bargainers, whose credible threat brought the English to the table. Though they would have preferred a federal union, the Scottish negotiators did not try very hard to get one. They were content with incorporating union on the terms they got. It took some time before Scotland's intolerable poverty was lifted, and then (from the mid-eighteenth century) it was largely due to economic forces the bargainers of 1706 did not understand.

Dicey was right that the Acts of 1707 brought fundamental change, although he and his followers have characterized it wrongly. We follow some of these changes in subsequent chapters. The Union made the Empire possible. It seemed to swallow Scottish politics up into English politics to make British politics. Actually, it never did that.

Ireland's incorporation: an 'excusable mistake'?

> I have long suspected the Union of 1800. There was a case for doing something: but this was like Pitt's Revolutionary War, a gigantic though excusable mistake (W. E. Gladstone, diary for 19.09.1885 in Matthew 1990: 403).

The Union of Great Britain with Ireland to form the United Kingdom was intended to be a bargain, like its predecessor; but one of the terms (Catholic emancipation) had to remain unspoken because of its bitter enemies in the Irish Parliament and on the throne. After the Irish Parliament had dissolved itself, King George III vetoed emancipation.

In Scotland, William III's succession saw the emergence of an assertive parliamentary system which strained the constitutional basis of a dual monarchy, and which, in turn, exposed the difficulties of reconciling the economic, military, and political interests of Scotland and England (and Wales). In Ireland, the Williamite succession led to a regal constitutional settlement which was, for the first century, much easier to manage from London. James II invaded Ireland, hoping to regain his throne with support from (especially Catholic) Irish people. After a campaign which defined the self-image of Ulster Protestants to this day, the Williamite forces resisted the siege of Londonderry and finally, led by William himself, defeated James decisively at the Battle of the Boyne on 12 July (1 July old style)[12] 1690. The military defeat of James II in Ireland led to the establishment of the Protestant (and constitutionally Anglican) ascendancy.

The eighteenth-century Irish Parliament and government were therefore closely tied in with the interests of the English court. The constitutional settlement of 1690 had established the control of a narrowly based Anglican ascendancy in Ireland. Against (the Dutch Reformed, religiously liberal) King William's desire for a conciliatory settlement, his military victory in Ireland was consolidated through the entrenchment of the Protestant (Anglican) ascendancy. The Irish administration was organized on the basis of the mutual interests of the Church of Ireland and the British government. Property law privileged Anglicans and deprived Catholics and (to a lesser extent) Protestant dissenters of rights of succession. They were given franchise rights in the Irish Parliament in 1793. If that Parliament had continued its independent path, their property rights might have been improved. But it was extinguished.

As under the US Constitution, there was a complete separation of powers between the Dublin Castle administration (purely an executive) and the Irish Parliament (purely a legislature). The Irish Parliament was weaker than the Scots Parliament had been. In 1690, only Anglicans were eligible to sit and vote in it. The largest denomination (Catholics) and the second-largest (Presbyterians, almost all in Ulster) were excluded. It did not control the executive. The monarch was not reliant on the Dublin Parliament for control of tax revenue, and there was no great challenge to the major trading interests of the London stock market. Until 1782, there was a common interest between the Crown and the Irish protestant ascendancy in maintaining a military presence in the interests of civil control and the prevention of foreign invasion, as well as a common interest in the continued sovereignty of an English-based monarch. By 1798 it was clear to Prime Minister Pitt the Younger and his inner circle that the divided government of Ireland could deliver neither security nor revenue. Pitt had wanted an economic union earlier, because he was a close reader of Adam Smith, but had been foiled by special interests.

The breakdown started with the grant of greater legislative independence to the bicameral Irish Parliament in 1782. The American War of Independence, whose ideology found particularly strong resonance amongst the non-conformist Irish in Ulster (Lecky 1902: 159–60; Stewart 1993: chapters 1–7), gave rise to the alarming Volunteer movement.[13] Conceding greater legislative autonomy was a concession to the Volunteers, and stability was enhanced by the control of John Beresford over the Dublin administration, based on a political grouping known as the 'friends of English government' (Johnston 1963: 72). The rival faction was those we have labelled 'country Whigs' suspicious of government and centralization. The leader of these country Whigs was Henry Grattan and the Parliament came to be known, to nineteenth-century Irish nationalists, as 'Grattan's parliament'.

In 1785, the youthful Pitt put forward his 'commercial propositions' for a free-trade zone, embracing Ireland and Britain, as Adam Smith had recently proposed in the *Wealth of Nations* (Hague 2004: 185–91; McLean 2006: 22–3). This would have repealed all discriminatory protectionist legislation hindering Irish economic development; both parties would have gained. But the British Commons voted them down under pressure for vested interests; there was no scheme acceptable to both the British and Irish Parliaments; and Pitt's attention moved elsewhere. But in October 1785 he wrote to Richard Lovell Edgeworth, the Irish author:

> An Union with Ireland with Great Britain will doubtless meet with strong opposition on your side of the water . . . [but] mature reflection may in the end convince your nation of its *equity*, and even of its *expediency*; for the fundamental principles of political and commercial connection seem to me to require an equal participation of burthens as of benefits, of expenses as of profits. (Reilly 1979: 161)

The next crisis came four years later, when George III first became too ill to function as king. As the Scottish Parliament's rejection of the Hanoverian succession had threatened Queen Anne's English advisors, so the Irish Parliament's proposal to appoint the Prince of Wales (the future George IV) as Regent in 1789 threatened the Pitt administration. The Prince of Wales was a bosom friend of Pitt's enemy Fox, and a Regent-controlled Parliament in either country would have immediately voted out Pitt and installed Fox. In London, Pitt successfully played for time until the king recovered. But the dynastic threat of Ireland remained.

A more pressing threat arose after 1793, when Britain declared war against revolutionary France. Catholic Ireland was an obvious security weakness to Protestant Britain. The French had supported James II up to the Boyne; and there was an opportunistic French naval raid on Carrickfergus in Protestant Ulster, in 1760 during the Seven Years' War (Stewart 1993: 9–19). The French government had an interest in exploiting widespread Irish (Catholic and Presbyterian) discontent. There were four military threats. First, the direct threat—realized in 1760 and 1798—of a French landing in Ireland to attack Britain from the west. Second, the Irish ports provided an important strategic base, extending British naval control over shipping routes (in particular) to the Americas. Third, the British army was dispersed around Ireland to cope with domestic unrest, such as that instigated by groups of agrarian protestors. Finally, as the international military commitments of the British increased, Ireland became an increasingly important recruiting ground for the British army. By the 1770s the enlistment of Catholics was a practical necessity. In 1774, Irish Catholics were first permitted to take an oath of allegiance to the Crown without violation of conscience (Beckett 1966: 214). At the start of the eighteenth century Irishmen comprised about 5 per cent of the rank and file of the army, whilst by the start of the nineteenth century the proportion may have been as much as a third (McDowell 1979: 60–2).

The crisis of Irish representation

In Protestant Ulster, where strong connections with the Presbyterian American settlers combined with sympathy with the complaint of 'taxation without representation', Protestant opinion was initially pro-American. However, the American alliance with the French in 1778 (and the capture of a British ship by the American privateer, Paul Jones, in Belfast Lough: Stewart 1993: xi–xii), combined with the dispersal of British troops in Ireland, exposed fears of a French invasion: 'The Presbyterians had sympathised with the Americans, but they hated and feared the French' (Beckett: 1966: 211).

In May 1798, British spies reported that Napoleon's fleet had left its port in Toulon for an unknown destination. Its target might well have been Ireland: Pitt started to plan for Union with two close colleagues, but did not yet tell most of his Cabinet (Jupp 2000). In fact the French fleet had sailed to Egypt, where it was routed by Nelson in August, but the threat level remained high. The Union was driven by security, not economics. The Act of Union with Scotland had contained numerous articles dealing with trading concessions, and the compensation due to Scotland for the acceptance of the English (and Welsh) national debt. The Act of Union with Ireland dealt with the subject in one Article (the seventh) containing no trading concessions, and a simple division of responsibility for the United Kingdom's national debt. Most non-agricultural economic activity in Ireland was in the hands of Presbyterians or Quakers, and therefore not represented in Irish politics.

It was impossible to fund the growing Irish national debt from inside Ireland. The basis of the Irish revenue reflected the monarchical basis of the Williamite succession in Ireland (rather than parliamentary basis, as in Scotland). The Irish administration was largely funded through taxes and duties which flowed automatically to the monarch (Johnston 1963: 96–7). These resources were insufficiently buoyant to cope with depression in the Irish economy (partly due to war with America), and between 1763 and 1773 the national debt almost doubled, approaching a million pounds (Beckett 1966: 206). A Dublin newspaper argued, in January 1775, that: 'by the same authority which the British Parliament assumes to tax America, it may also and with equal justice presume to tax Ireland without the consent or concurrence of the Irish parliament' (Beckett 1966: 206). Grattan hoped that the parliament would widen the popular basis of the Irish government, through the incorporation of the Catholic and Presbyterian middle classes. However, the legislature did not follow his reformist programme.

The war with France and the threat of rebellion fed on one another (Cullen 1968: 180). The national debt rose dramatically throughout the 1790s, as revenues remained static (Table 3.8).

To finance its debt, the Irish administration relied on the sale of government debentures to the public. Its success in maintaining payments without default had seen interest rates fall from 8 per cent in 1715 to 4.5 per cent in 1779. However, the failure to set a balanced budget in any year after 1770, and the increased expenditure associated with the rebellion, put new pressure on the system. The Irish banking system was in no position to finance such an expansion in government debt. A parliament of landowners gave little encouragement to banking. A Bank of Ireland was finally established in 1783 almost a century after the Bank of England, Bank of Scotland, and Royal Bank of Scotland, with Catholics contributing some 10 per cent of the total capital (Foster 1989: 205). However, the Bank still bore the imprint of the ascendancy parliament. Catholics and Quakers were debarred from the Directorate, discrimination which was 'regarded by Irish Catholics as an extension of the penal laws, and were a source of constant embarrassment to the Bank' (Hall 1949: 41). The Bank was too small to play a major role in financing the national debt. The government made a request for £300,000 in 1796, but was refused, and only given £150,000 in 1797 (Hall 1949: 64–5). The financial pressure on the government is shown in the interest rates paid on public loans in Britain and Ireland (McLean and McMillan 2005, their Table 3.7). Rates in

Ireland rose from 5.0 per cent in 1793 to a high of 8.2 per cent in 1798, while in Britain, even under wartime stresses, the interest rate on government debt was only 6.34 per cent. This forced the Irish government to turn to the London market, where rates were lower and capacity higher, and from 1798 an increasing proportion of the Irish national debt was financed this way. The fact that rates fell (both in London and Dublin) as the Union proceeded suggests that it was greeted favourably by the financial markets. The chaos in Irish public finances may not have been a major concern of the non-executive Dublin parliament. However, it was a key consideration both in Dublin Castle (seat of the Irish government) and in London. At Westminster the interests of both the government party and the British commercial sector were much more closely bound in to the system of representation.

The plan for Union drawn up by William Pitt and Lord Grenville in summer 1798 (Jupp 2000) and presented to his Cabinet in December after the defeat of a rebellion based in Country Wexford (Hague 2004: 436) was intended to be generous to the Irish, restricting exposure to the British national debt. Viscount Castlereagh wrote that 'the terms are considered as highly liberal, the proportional arrangements of the expenses having completely overset the argument on which the enemies of the measure had hitherto principally relied, viz., the extension of English debt and taxation to Ireland' (quoted in McCavery 2000: 355). Although the provisions for trade and the national debt were attacked by the opponents of the Union, particularly John Foster, and the demands for some protectionist measures for manufacturing conceded, the economic basis of the union was not a source of major division. Pitt was willing to buy a secure western frontier.

Furthermore, the economic provisions of the Union, unlike Pitt's commercial propositions, did not arouse the hostility of any significant political interest in Britain. Although protests from Yorkshire woollen manufacturers led to a demand for amendment of the economic article in the Act of Union in the House of Commons—providing 'the only spark of excitement in England on the Union'—it was easily defeated (Bolton 1966: 201).

Pitt and constitutional reform

Pitt himself was unusually secular for his era. But he was sensitive to religion as a badge of allegiance. He wrote in 1792 to the Lord Lieutenant:

> The idea of the present fermentation gradually bringing both [religious] parties [in Ireland] to think of a Union with this country has long been in my mind . . . I believe it, though itself not easy to be accomplished, to be the only solution for other and greater difficulties.

The admission of the Catholics to the . . . suffrage could not then be dangerous. The Protestant interest—in point of power, property, and Church establishment—would be secure, because the decided majority of the supreme Legislature would necessarily be Protestant; and the great ground of argument on the part of the Catholics would be done away, as, compared with the rest of the Empire, they would become a minority. (Pitt to Earl of Westmorland, 1792, quoted by Hague 2004: 435)

Except for its failure to discriminate between the two streams of Irish Protestantism, this cannot be faulted. Giving Catholics civil rights would remove their constitutional grievance. Bringing Ireland into the Union would protect Protestant interests better than the continuation of an Irish Parliament, because Catholics would always be in a minority in the Union parliament. To achieve Union on his terms, however, Pitt needed to convince three parties: the British and Irish Parliaments, and the King. This forced him to disguise his motives: To attach Catholic emancipation to the Union would have meant that it would not have passed through the House of Lords in Dublin, and such a measure might have struggled in the Lords in Westminster, although Pitt totally dominated the Commons there. However, his plans were defeated by a royal trump card.

The passage of the union

By the late 1790s, Fox and Grattan had absented themselves from the Westminster and Dublin Parliaments, removing the focus for any legislative opposition. The core of the Dublin Castle government: the lord lieutenant, Lord (Charles) Cornwallis, and chief secretary, Viscount Castlereagh (Robert Stewart), wanted parliamentary union accompanied by Catholic emancipation. However, Lord Clare, the leader of the Irish House of Lords, was an ardent supporter of a legislative union but would not countenance further concessions to the Catholics, whilst John Foster, the speaker of the Irish House of Commons, opposed the government on both counts.

Irish politicians divided in two dimensions on the Union (Table 3.9). A politician's stance on the Union was not correlated with his stance on Catholic emancipation. There were significant players in each of the four groupings of Table 3.9. This meant that both the pro- and the anti-Union coalitions were fragile. As in Scotland, the last Irish Parliament could vote first against Union and then for it without paradox.

The debate about whether to include Catholic emancipation along with Parliamentary Union caused ructions within the Dublin administration, with William Elliot, the under secretary to the military department, threatening to resign his position. However, the debate also shows the consideration which was given to Lord Clare, as leader of the House of Lords in Dublin. In a bicameral parliament, he had a significant influence over one of the blocking options against Union. Gaining Clare's conformity was deemed important enough to induce the Unionists to stop talking in public about Catholic emancipation. However, Foster saw his role in upholding the authority of Grattan's Parliament, and was not to be persuaded to support its abolition, especially by such a 'damn silly fellow' as Cornwallis (Geoghegan 1999: 43). This is an interesting contrast with the unicameral Scottish Parliament, in which the influence of the Lords was incorporated with that of the Commons. Whilst the majority of the Lords were in favour of a parliamentary union, the Irish case highlights a special interest given to the leader of the Lords, who controlled a veto player in the union game.

The Irish House of Commons and the Act of Union

How could the Irish Parliament, which had gained its extended powers only in 1782, be persuaded to vote itself out of existence in 1800, having refused to in 1799? To answer this, we repeated, as far as the data permitted, the analysis of vote switching that was offered for the 1706 Scottish Parliament earlier (McLean and McMillan 2005, their Tables 3.8 to 3.10).

Our analysis of the flow of votes suggests that the government succeeded in its attempts to stop the issue of Catholic rights and representation polarizing the political situation in such a way as to favour the opponents of Union. Secondly, it indicates that there was a core of the pro-Union support, comprising some one-third of the MPs who voted on each of the issues, within the Irish House of Commons who had been opposed to concessions directed at the Catholic population. Whilst supporting the administration's view that the two issues should be treated separately, it suggests that if the intention of Pitt and Cornwallis to treat Union and Catholic emancipation as dual strategies for Irish constitutional reform had been made explicit, then greater opposition could have been expected.

After the defeat of the Union measures in 1799 the government offered compensation for those borough constituencies which were to be abolished in the event of a legislative union, as the parliamentary representation of the Irish was rationalized and reduced. The original scheme planned by Pitt and Grenville was based on 150 Irish members in the Westminster House of Commons, but this total was reduced to 100 by the time that the proposals for Union were announced. Even this figure was too large for some. Lord Sheffield worried that 'I do not think that any of our country gentlemen would venture into parliament if they were to meet 100 Paddies' (quoted in Geoghegan 2003: 130). The provision for borough compensation may have persuaded of the patrons of the borough constituencies to support the government, but evidence in terms of the shifting of the vote is limited. Of the ten members from borough constituencies recorded as having switched from the anti-Union to pro-Union positions between 1799 and 1800, six came from boroughs which were due to be abolished, and hence receive compensation, and four from boroughs which were to retain their representation. Since three-quarters of the borough seats were to be abolished, this proportion is relatively low. Of the borough MPs who abstained in 1799 and then voted in 1800, the proportion voting in favour of Union from seats to be abolished (twenty-five members, out of thirty-four supporters of the Union, or 73.5 per cent) was very similar to those from seats to be abolished voting against the Union (seventeen out of twenty-four opponents, or 70.8 per cent). This suggests that the direct effect of the offer of borough compensation was extremely marginal.

Whereas the Scottish Union involved little change in the basis of the representation, the Irish Union changed the basis of representation towards a more popular mode of election. The seats abolished were the rottenest boroughs (all Scottish burghs were basically rotten). Given that religious discrimination in the choice of electorate had been removed in 1793, this gave the Catholics a certain leverage in county constituencies (although their influence could still be constrained in borough constituencies). The plan for Union focused on the size of Irish representation in a united Westminster Parliament; there was no challenge to the assumption that the greatest reduction in the number of Irish legislators would be through the abolition of the rottenest boroughs.

Table 3.8 Irish national debt, 1794–1801.

Year ending 25 March	£
1794	2,874,267
1795	4,002,452
1796	4,477,098
1797	6,537,467
1798	10,134,675
1799	15,806,824
1800	23,100,785
1801*	28,541,157

*9 months to 5 January.
Source: Hall (1949: 63).

Table 3.9 The bi-dimensionality of Irish politicians' attitudes, c. 1799.

		Catholic emancipation	
		For	Against
	For	Cornwallis. 'Both will help public order'	Clare. 'Union will preserve Ascendancy'
Union			
	Against	Grattan. 'Preserve independence of country Whigs from government'	Foster. 'Union will break Ascendancy'

My précis of politicians' positions, from *ODNB* online; Cullen (2000: 222). 'The alliance against Union was one of reckless elements on both sides, an improbable combination of a confederacy of Whigs under the leadership of Grattan, Ponsonby and others who had self-destructed in 1797, and of a hard-line group of loyalists such as Foster and Downshire who put the domestic circumstances of Irish protestants ahead of either conciliation of rebels or the interests of Britain'.

King George says no

The Union was thus needed, in Pitt's view, for four linked reasons: to secure Britain's western frontier during the French wars; to overcome the crisis of public finance, especially in Ireland but also in Britain; to reap the gains of free trade; and to increase the legitimacy of the British state in Ireland. The Union of 1800 reconciled the Presbyterians. It failed to reconcile the Catholics. A group of politicians less far-sighted than Pitt fatally damaged it.

Pitt dominated the Commons but not the Lords. Most of his own Cabinet were in the Lords. Some of them rejected the idea of any concessions to Catholics. They leaked Pitt's plan to its most obdurate opponent, the temporarily sane King George III. The king had long given clear signals of his opposition to Catholic emancipation, which he described as 'beyond the decision of any Cabinet of ministers'. In September 1800, Pitt called his Lord Chancellor, Lord Loughborough, to a Cabinet meeting to discuss 'the great question on the general state of the Catholics' (both quoted in Hague 2004: 465). Loughborough was on holiday in Weymouth with the king, and promptly showed him this letter. The king exploded, in public, saying to Pitt's closest ally Henry Dundas in the hearing of the Irish Secretary Lord Camden:

> What is the Question which you are all about to force upon me? What is this Catholic Emancipation . . . that you are going to throw at my Head. . . . ? I will tell you, that I shall look on every Man as my personal Enemy, who proposes that Question to me . . . I hope All my Friends will not desert me. (George III's words at a levee, 28.01.01, as recalled by Camden in 1804, quoted by Hague 2004: 468)

The king thought that concessions to Catholicism were inconsistent with the coronation oath that the 1689–1707 settlement required him to take. This royal indignation over Ireland was to be repeated by some of his successors, for instance when Queen Victoria attempted to block Gladstone from the Prime Ministership in 1892, and when George V seemed more disposed to listen to His Majesty's Opposition than to His Majesty's Government in 1912–14 over Irish Home Rule.

Pitt responded with a magnificent memorandum (quoted by Hague 2004: 470–1), as did George V's Prime Minister H. H. Asquith, equally magnificently, in the same circumstances in 1913 (Appendix to Chapter 12). Each prime minister pointed out that he must resign if the king maintained his attitude. In 1913 this was sufficient to persuade the king and his advisers to back down. In 1801 it was not. The king vetoed Catholic emancipation, and Pitt resigned in February 1801. The king had made Pitt's position totally impossible. His action ensured that the Union with Ireland was illegitimate in the eyes of the majority of the Irish population from the outset. Catholic Emancipation came in 1829 with great rancour, but proved inadequate to save Ireland for the Union. The king's veto in 1801 was the first great tragedy of Union. The failure of the unelected parts of the British government to accept Irish Home Rule from 1893 to 1914 was to be the second.

4

Why Should We Be Beggars with the Ballot in Our Hand?

Iain McLean and Jennifer Nou

This and the following three chapters consider the next existential crisis of Union, a century after George III's veto. As in 1801, the unelected parts of Parliament vetoed policies that had won the majority votes in the elected part, the House of Commons. Parliament was and is 'in the mouths of lawyers', as Dicey 1885/1915: 37–8) insists, a tricameral legislature. The three houses are the monarch, the Lords, and the Commons. The first two of these are unelected. They were both dominated for long periods by supporters of one party. When the opposite party formed a majority government, therefore, there was potential for conflict between the chambers. The British Constitution has no established procedure for handling such conflict: for instance, no provision for a conference between the houses; no procedure for a special majority to override a veto. Better-thought-through constitutions such as that of the United States have written procedures for conflicts among the chambers. The President is (in the mouths of political scientists) a chamber of the US legislature, and the Constitution specifies when he may veto legislation and when and how his veto may be overridden. That is why the constitutional crisis of 1909–14, to be described now, remains vital for the understanding of the weakness of the British Constitution.

A Liberal campaign song for the January 1910 General Election, to be sung to the tune 'Marching through Georgia', sets the scene. It is a good tune, though the Liberals who borrowed it probably did not know that General Sherman's march through Georgia in 1864 was as murderous for some as it was liberating for others.

> Sound the call for freedom, boys, and sound it far and wide,
> March along to victory for God is on our side,
> While the voice of Nature thunders o'er the rising tide,
> 'God gave the land to the people!'

Chorus
The land, the land, 'twas God who made the land,
The land, the land, the ground on which we stand,
Why should we be beggars with the ballot in our hand?
God made the land for the people.

Hark, the sound is spreading from the East and from the West,
Why should we work hard and let the landlords take the best?
Make them pay their taxes on the land just like the rest,
The land was meant for the people.

Chorus

Clear the way for liberty, the land must all be free,
Liberals will not falter from the fight, tho' stern it be,
'Til the flag we love so well will fly from sea to sea
O'er the land that is free for the people.

Chorus

The army now is marching on, the battle to begin.
The standard now is raised on high to face the battle din,
We'll never cease from fighting 'til victory we win,
And the land is free for the people.

Chorus

(This version from http://www.liberator.org.uk/article.asp?id=22403892, accessed 04.05.2005.)

This chapter and the next describe the successful obstruction of the elected Liberal governments of the United Kingdom by the unelected House of Lords and the unelected kings Edward VII and George V, between 1906 and 1914. In this chapter, we examine Chancellor of the Exchequer David Lloyd George's attempt to introduce land value taxation and the factors which led to its demise. In the next, we examine the Unionist coup d'état over Ireland.

Normally, the United Kingdom is a paradigm case of a low-*n* veto-player regime, which should mean (but in this case did not) that the elected government gets its way. Lloyd George introduced land value taxation in the UK Budget of 1909, but the land taxes then introduced yielded a trivial amount of revenue. Lloyd George's attempt to broaden the land tax base and increase its yield, in the 1914 Budget, also failed. We consider three possible explanations of this failure, namely incompetence, impracticability, and veto plays. We argue that the third of these is the most parsimonious—it explains the most with the least.

The concepts of 'veto players' and 'veto games' were introduced in Chapter 2. Tsebelis (1995, 2002) claims that they come in two varieties: institutional and partisan. An institutional veto player is one who has the legal power to block such proposals. Such a player may be an individual (the US President) or a chamber (the UK House of Lords). And the veto may be unconditional (the US President's at the end of a session of Congress, when there is no time to override it; the House of Lords on all non-monetary matters before 1911). Or it may be conditional (the US President when his veto may be overridden; the House of Lords since 1911, when it remains a veto player on non-monetary matters in the last year of a parliament but not otherwise; however, its powers of delay remain politically significant). A partisan veto player is a party (or other) group that may block a proposal so long as the group coheres. A governing party with over half of the seats in a chamber is a unique partisan veto player over all proposals that are carried if a simple majority votes for it. More than one party may be a veto player in a chamber where no party holds half the seats, or where more than a simple majority of those present is required to pass a measure.

The status quo is stable if it is relatively hard to upset. The more veto players there are in a political system, or the larger the qualified majority required for a proposal to pass, the more stable is the status quo. Equivalently, as either the number of veto players or the qualified majority threshold rises, the win set of the status quo diminishes, and the core, or the uncovered set of the game, gets bigger.

Recent extensions of the Tsebelis framework due to Persson and Tabellini (2002, 2005), Hallerberg (2004), Hallerberg and Maier (2004) and others draw substantive implications for fiscal policy from regime structure, and in particular from the number of veto players. Persson and Tabellini argue that proportional and majoritarian regimes differ systematically. Both deductively and by cross-sectional statistical analysis of data from 85 democracies (as classed by the well-known Freedom House indices—latest at: http://www.freedomhouse.org/uploads/FIWAllScores.xls), they show that majoritarian regimes are more fiscally responsible than proportional regimes; whereas proportional regimes spend more on redistributive welfare payments than do majoritarian regimes.

They may overstate their case, as they have not proved the direction of causation. It could be that a regime whose citizens value consensus, public services, and social insurance relatively highly also values, and chooses, a proportional electoral system; and the 85 countries span a wide range of continents and GDP per head levels.

The idea behind this work is that a proportional regime must involve a larger, and more stable, ruling coalition than a majoritarian regime. Therefore, more clients (veto players) have to be satisfied for this stability to continue. However, veto players can make an unexpected appearance in a majoritarian regime. In a Tsebelian framework, the United Kingdom is a paradigm low-*n* veto-player regime. We should expect it to be a regime with high fiscal discipline. Six features of its modern constitution, familiar to all beginning political science students of the United Kingdom, combine to produce this by ensuring that normally there is no veto player apart from the governing party and its ministers. They are:

- *Sovereignty of Parliament.* As classically enunciated by Dicey in 1885:

  Parliament means, in the mouth of a lawyer, . . . the King, the House of Lords, and the House of Commons; these three bodies acting together . . . constitute Parliament. (Dicey 1885/1915: 37–8)

- *The simple-majority single-ballot system favours the two-party system* (Duverger 1954: 217). This is what W. H. Riker renamed 'Duverger's Law', distinguishing it from Duverger's hypothesis that proportional representation tended to favour multipartyism. The Hypothesis is falsifiable, and in some circumstances false. The Law is securely grounded, providing that its antecedent conditions are correctly stated. In accordance with Duverger's Law, if local and regional parties are set aside, nationwide competition for votes under the United Kingdom's plurality electoral system will generally produce a single-party majority in the Commons, and hence no rival partisan veto players there. However, local and regional parties cannot be set aside. In particular, the problem of aggregating from two-partyism in each constituency to two-partyism in a country as a whole is complex (Cox 1997: 23–8; Chhibber and Kollman 2004). Where (as in Britain in 1910) there is a powerful regional party (the Irish Party), two-party competition in each constituency is consistent with a three-party system in the House of Commons.

- *Upper house unelected, and does not obstruct government programme.* The House of Lords is entirely unelected. Until 1958, when provision was first made for life peerages, membership was only by inheritance of a peerage, or by becoming a senior bishop or law lord. The convention that the Lords does not obstruct the manifesto measures of a government with a Commons majority was codified in 1945 as the 'Salisbury–Addison convention', after the Conservative and Labour leaders in the Lords at that time. Salisbury–Addison is discussed in depth in Chapter 12. Before 1945, the Conservatives, who had controlled the Lords since the time of Pitt the Younger, often vetoed non-financial legislation of Liberal governments.

- *Civil service code: loyalty is to ministers.* The modern civil service emerged in the mid-nineteenth century. Under the celebrated Northcote–Trevelyan reforms of the 1850s, entry was by merit in a competitive examination, and promotion was due to ability, not to patronage.

However, the loyalty of civil servants is to their ministers and the government of the day. If the government changes political complexion, the loyalty of civil servants transfers to the new administration. There are only a trivial number of political appointees in the UK administration (currently restricted to two special advisers per Secretary of State, with a slightly larger number for the Prime Minister and the Chancellor of the Exchequer). These political appointees are not on civil service contracts, and are not supposed to give orders to permanent civil servants.

- *House of Commons control over finance.* Since King Charles I was forced to call Parliament in 1640 to vote supply for his war against the Scots who had rebelled against his religious policies, it has been accepted that 'supply'— that is, voting for public expenditure and for the taxes to pay for it—was uniquely the function of the lower house of Parliament. The framers of the US Constitution, who were close students of British parliamentary procedure, carried this view over there (US Constitution Art. I: 7).

- *Monarchy purely ornamental.* Nothing is more basic to the unwritten constitution than that the monarch never vetoes legislation. As the children's section of the UK Parliament web site states:

  The Royal Assent is the Monarch's agreement to make a Bill into an Act of Parliament. The Monarch actually has the right to refuse Royal Assent but nowadays this does not happen—the Royal Assent is a formality. The last time that the Royal Assent was refused was in 1708, when Queen Anne refused her Assent to a Bill for settling the Militia in Scotland (http:// services.parliament.uk/education/online-resources/Glossary/Glossary.aspx? letter=r, accessed 26 March 2009).

In the following sections we show that during the years 1909–14 all six of these foundational assumptions about the British Constitution were violated. So far as we know, these are the only years in British history for which this is true. One would expect extensive political–scientific analysis of this phenomenon; but we have found almost none. It is of methodological importance because of veto games. It is of normative importance because the elected parts of government were stymied by the unelected parts. And it illustrates the effect of changes in the veto-player structure.

THE RISE AND FALL OF LAND VALUE
TAXATION 1909–20

Sovereignty of Parliament undermined. According to Diceyan constitutional theory of the last section, the United Kingdom is the paradigm low-veto-player regime, that is, Parliament is sovereign, and has the right to make or unmake any law whatsoever. However, in the three Parliaments elected at the General Elections of 1906, January 1910, and December 1910, the King-in-Parliament comprised two warring factions. In the policy areas where they were at war, each faction could veto laws; neither could make or unmake (i.e. repeal) them.

The 1906 General Election returned a strong Liberal majority in seats (Table 5.1). The Liberal Party held almost 60 per cent of the seats in the Commons. With the Labour and Irish Parties, it formed what contemporaries sometimes called the 'progressive forces'—jointly controlling over 75 per cent of the seats. However, it did not need their votes and therefore did not always promote their causes. The Liberals' Commons hegemony arose in part from the responsiveness of the system (showing Duverger's Law at work) and in part from an electoral bias in their favour, and still more in favour of the Irish Party.

Both 1910 General Elections were forced—the first by the House of Lords when they rejected the Budget of 1909, the second by King George V when he refused to create sufficient peers to enact the Parliament Bill without a second general election. These simple facts show that institutional veto players matter.

No longer single party majority. The results of the two 1910 elections were the same in aggregate, although there was much churning of individual seats. There was no longer a single-party majority. The Irish Party had become a partisan veto player in the Commons. The minimum-size winning coalition was Liberal + Irish. An alternative minimum winning coalition was Liberal + Conservative. The Labour Party remained a dummy: as in the 1906 Parliament it could neither make nor unmake any winning coalition.

Upper House of Parliament obstruction of government programme. In the 1906 Parliament, Lord Salisbury had gone and the Salisbury–Addison convention did not yet apply. Therefore, the House of Lords was free to operate as a *selective* institutional veto player. Most notably, it did not obstruct the Trade Disputes Act 1906. This was a Labour measure, adopted by Prime Minister Sir Henry Campbell-Bannerman when he abandoned his own ministers' bill in favour of a Labour one. By giving trade unions widespread legal immunities from tort actions, it readjusted property rights more radically, probably, than any preceding bill. However, the Lords did block numerous measures relating to the old centre–periphery political cleavage on such matters as school education, liquor licensing, and disestablishment of the minority Anglican Church of Wales. The Welsh nonconformist David Lloyd George, appointed

Chancellor of the Exchequer in 1908, explained the situation in the following Cabinet memorandum during the preparation of his Budget for 1909:

> The two objects sought...are: (1) To obtain a valuation of land in the United Kingdom, and (2) To raise a revenue which in the coming financial year would reach 500,000l., and which would afterwards gradually increase until it would produce something much more substantial. It is now clear that it would be impossible to secure the passage of a separate Valuation bill during the existence of the present Parliament, owing to the opposition of the Lords, and therefore the only possible chance which the Government have of redeeming their pledges in this respect is by incorporating proposals involving land valuation in a finance bill. On the other hand, it must be borne in mind that proposals for valuing land which do not form part of a provision for raising revenue in the financial year for which the Budget is introduced would probably be regarded as being outside the proper limits of a Finance Bill by the Speaker of the House of Commons.[1]

This is a particularly clear statement of the vetoes that Lloyd George must sidestep: one from the House of Lords, and one from the Speaker of the House of Commons. The former would veto any separate real-estate valuation bill, the latter would veto any such bill incorporated into a budget unless the budget also implemented any resulting land value taxes immediately. Lloyd George went on to state that he had confirmed with the Clerk of the House of Commons, Sir Courtenay Ilbert, that the Speaker would indeed veto a valuation provision in the budget if unaccompanied by a projected yield.

The Budget of 1909 was thus moulded from the outset by veto games. Its main thrust was to expand the United Kingdom's tax base to pay for two classes of public expenditure that were expected to grow fast, namely, defence and social security. Defence spending was growing fast because of a naval arms race which the opposition Unionists were loudly demanding. Social security spending could be expected to grow fast because of the first provisions for state old age pensions, in the 1908 Budget. These could in turn be explained by the shift of the median voter to one lower in the income distribution after the franchise extension of 1884.

Civil servants not entirely loyal to ministers. Its resistance was encouraged by Lloyd George's most senior official, the Permanent Secretary to the Treasury, Sir George Murray:

> The Government seem to me to be going straight on the rocks financially (and perhaps otherwise), and nobody will listen to me when I tell them so...I cannot believe that your House will swallow the Budget if the mature infant turns out to be anything like the embryo which I now contemplate daily with horror.[2]

So wrote Sir George to Lord Rosebery, whose private secretary he had once been. Rosebery was a former Liberal Prime Minister who felt himself stranded by the leftward movement of his former party. By 1909, he sat in the Lords as a cross-bencher. As the constitutional crisis grew, he was increasingly spoken of as a potential caretaker non-party Prime Minister. Although Murray later drew back from his encouragement to Rosebery to reject the Budget, his place was taken—for exactly opposite reasons—by his political master. As noted above, Lloyd George initially aimed to circumvent, not provoke, the House of Lords. But as talk of rejecting the Budget on behalf of the class interests of land grew, Lloyd George turned on the dukes in order to enrage them still further:

> Should 500 men, ordinary men chosen accidentally from among the unemployed, override the judgment—the deliberate judgment—of millions of people who are engaged in the industry which makes the wealth of the country? ... [W]ho ordained that a few should have the land of Britain as a perquisite; who made 10,000 people owners of the soil, and the rest of us trespassers in the land of our birth[?] (Speech at Newcastle upon Tyne, 09.10.09, quoted by Jenkins 1968: 94)

The King's secretary, Lord Knollys, requested Prime Minister H. H. Asquith 'not to pretend to the King that he liked Mr Lloyd George's speeches, for the King would not believe it, and it only irritated him' (Jenkins 1968: 95).

House of Commons control over finance undermined. The intention was to provoke the Lords to reject the Budget, which they duly did the following month. This forced a General Election which the trend of by-elections suggests would otherwise have been won by the Unionists.

With the Budget passed in April 1910, the parliamentary timetable was preordained for three years. The first Government move was to introduce legislation to restrict the veto power of the Lords. The Parliament Bill was introduced in April 1910, but because of, first, the death of Edward VII in May 1910, and then the new king George V's refusal to create the necessary new peers to force it through the House of Lords, it could not be enacted until after the Liberals and allies had won their third General Election in December 1910. It was enacted in August 1911. The Parliament Act 1911 confirms the pre-1909 understanding that the Lords may not amend a finance bill. It introduces the 'suspensory veto' that is still in force: a bill rejected by the Lords may nevertheless be enacted if the Commons pass it in three (since 1949 in two) successive sessions.

Monarchy not purely ornamental. The Act required a further general election because George V insisted that he would not create the peers required to swamp the bill's otherwise inevitable rejection in the Lords unless the Liberals and their allies won a further electoral mandate. He gave even that undertaking very grumpily and reluctantly. Knollys had falsely told the king that if he refused the undertaking (in which case the Asquith government would of course have resigned) the Unionist leader Balfour would refuse to take office. This had the effect of tricking the king into believing that he had no option. In fact, Balfour had signalled that he would take office in such a situation. By lying to his master, Knollys may have saved the British monarchy, but when George V found out the deception in 1913, he sacked Knollys (Jenkins 1968: 174–83; Bogdanor 1995: 116–19). If the king had followed his Unionist ideology, he would have intervened in politics on the side of the Unionists in summer 1910. He nearly did so on other occasions up to 1914. As detailed in Chapter 5, he was so angry with Irish Home Rule that he seriously contemplated either dismissing the Liberal government or vetoing the Home Rule Bill. Any of these vetoes would have raised the constitutional crisis to a higher level. By acting as a political partisan, the king would have undermined the standing of the monarchy.

The threat of creation was sufficient to persuade the Lords to enact the Parliament Bill in August 1911. The swamping of the Lords with Liberal peers was not required, so no Lord Baden-Powell, Lord Thomas Hardy, nor Lord Bertrand Russell were then created.[3] Thereupon, the partisan veto player the Irish Party was in a position to demand that Home Rule for Ireland should occupy essentially the whole Parliamentary timetable until 1914. The Government of Ireland Bill was bound to be (and was) rejected twice by the Lords without serious discussion or amendment. Therefore, it could not be enacted until 1914, by which time Ulster Protestants had created a private army to resist it with the connivance and perhaps the financial support of the Leader of His Majesty's loyal Opposition, Rt. Hon. Andrew Bonar Law. His Majesty himself was more loyal to his Opposition than to his Government. The Irish crisis is analysed in Chapter 5. For this and other reasons, Chancellor Lloyd George was unable to return to the subject of land taxation until his Budget of 1914.

By this time, in Avner Offer's words (1981: 368–9), 'two celebrated cases' in the courts had 'developed into serious reversals' for the 1910 land tax legislation: the more serious of the two emasculated Undeveloped Land Duty, the most productive (and most economically sound) of the land taxes. By the time Lloyd George introduced the 1914 Budget, the land valuation register enacted in 1910 was still incomplete. Treasury (as in 1909) and Inland Revenue (unlike in 1909) senior officials were unhelpful to their Chancellor. And the Liberals no longer held a single-party majority in the Commons. Lloyd George was now vulnerable to a revolt of landowning MPs in his own party. The revolt forced him to withdraw his site value rating proposals in June (Gilbert 1978; Offer 1981: 396–9). Within the month, Archduke Franz

Ferdinand had been assassinated in Sarajevo. An all-party coalition government was created in 1915, to be succeeded by a coalition between the Conservatives and a fraction of the Liberals under Lloyd George when war ended in 1918. In the wartime coalition, partisan domestic politics were muted; in the 1918 coalition, Prime Minister Lloyd George held relatively few seats and the Conservatives on their own held a majority. Unsurprisingly, all the 1909 and 1914 land taxation provisions had been repealed by 1920.

TWO EXPLANATIONS

Up to a point, the failure of land value taxation can be significantly explained by either individual missteps on the part of Lloyd George or the sheer impracticability of land taxes given the difficulties in site valuation. But Lloyd George and the Government also fell victim to veto plays.

Lloyd George was careless of details and made grand promises on the hoof. The grand promises were often electorally shrewd (not only in 1909–10 but also with his introduction of National Insurance in 1911) and accompanied by radical rhetoric. His officials either loved him or hated him. Murray began by loving him in a condescending way:

> I am leading quite a happy life with my Welsh Goat [this may be the earliest reference to Lloyd George as 'the Goat'], who feeds happily enough out of my hand at present. But I fear he will soon want something more stimulating . . . In his present humour he is a most engaging creature, full of graceful antics and the most unpractical notions. (Murray to Rosebery, 31.05.08, Rosebery MSS, National Library of Scotland, NLS MS 10049)

But he soon came to despise his Chancellor. For the 1909 Budget, therefore, Lloyd George relied on Sir Robert Chalmers, the chairman of the Board of Inland Revenue. Chalmers was as much an ideologue as Murray, but on the other side. When the Lords rejected the Budget, he was overheard saying 'I would like to festoon this room with their entrails' (Murray 1980: 80; see also Braithwaite 1957: 68). However, by 1913, Lloyd George's informality had alienated Chalmers too. He temporarily left the Treasury. This made Lloyd George more dependent on Edgar Harper, a land value taxation enthusiast whom Lloyd George had brought in from outside the Civil Service. This he was to repeat as a minister during the First World War, when he declared he wanted 'men of push and go', but with Harper he failed. Harper was a convinced land-taxer—a self-taught disciple of the American tax reformer Henry George (George 1882/1911).

Harper told the Royal Commission on Local Taxation that it was straight-forward to value land separately from the houses that stood on it. That was the key technical issue, as it would be with any attempt to restore land value taxation in the United Kingdom or any other regime today. The fundamental Georgeite—which is originally Ricardian—argument for the taxation of economic rent makes an intellectually impeccable case for land value taxation. The problems all lie in the implementation. In a 1908 Cabinet memorandum, Harper accurately pinpointed the key issue as being how to 'obtain substantial revenue from land which now escapes, wholly or partially, its share of existing burdens'—the main such category being (then as now) 'ripening building land'—in other words, land in transition from an earlier low-value use to the high-value use as housing land (Offer 1981: 245; 'Memorandum by Mr Edgar Harper on the Imposition of a National Tax on Land Values', 05.12.08, CAB 37/96 # 161). But neither he nor anybody else found a reliable way to value it for taxation. In Offer's withering summary (1981: 396–7), 'Valuation had turned out to be a white elephant, unsuitable for burden and bogged down in legal quicksands. Most of the blame lay with Harper. He had preached the project for many years, and was allowed, indeed, called in, to show his prowess . . . In retrospect Harper blamed everyone but himself.'

Incompetence and impracticality are thus part of the story. But over the introduction of National Insurance in 1911, Lloyd George behaved in exactly the same way and yet the scheme, which changed property rights but did not particularly attack the landed interest, got going successfully (Braithwaite 1957). It is not even sufficient (although it is necessary) to observe that the representatives of the landed interest (who always included the median member of the House of Lords, succession to which is usually synonymous with inheritance of land) had always been a veto player in British politics. In earlier crises, UK governments had shown that they could sideline landed interests when it really mattered for public order: for example, in a succession of Irish land acts in 1870, 1881, and 1903; and in the Crofters' Act 1886, which successfully headed off a Scottish Highland land agitation on Irish lines (McLean and McMillan 2005: 117–18, 222). All four of these Acts changed property rights to the benefit of tenants and the detriment of landowners. It might be argued that landowners in the periphery of the United Kingdom were marginal among landowners, but this is not so: they included Scottish dukes, and members of the Lords with large Irish interests such as the leading Unionist peers Lords Lansdowne and Midleton. However, in the 1903 Act, the landowners were generously compensated for the loss of their land. Prime Minister A. J. Balfour said that 'there is no measure with which I am more proud to have been connected'. By analysing the take-up of the loan stock that financed the deal, Offer argues that the cost of both the creation of the Irish peasantry and the compensation of their former landlords fell 'almost entirely [on] the shillings of British artisans'.[4]

What, then, made the veto power of the landed interest over land taxation so complete between 1906 and 1914, when it was not earlier or later? As hinted above, it was the fact that all seven elements of the Diceyan constitution were suspended at the same time: a suspension in which that fervent Unionist ideologue Professor Dicey took an active part, as we detail in the next two chapters.

In some cases the suspension was obvious to everybody at the time it happened. Nobody had challenged Commons supremacy over finance since the English Civil War of 1640–9, which was in large part fought over this issue. The Lords' challenge of 1909 was therefore revolutionary:

> The debate in the Lords began on November 23 [1909] . . . [A]s is so often the case when the House of Lords is engaged in reaching a peculiarly silly decision, there were many comments on the high level of the debate and on the enhancement it gave to the deliberative quality of the chamber. (Jenkins 1968: 100–1)

It could only have been sustained if the Unionists had won the January 1910 election: but their rejection of the Budget was sufficient to ensure, as Lloyd George saw but they did not, that they would not win that election. In other cases, the veto plays were known to political elites but not to the general public. This is particularly true of the royal veto threats between 1909 (by Edward VII) and 1913 (by George V over Ireland). Both kings signalled their reluctance to create peers in order to enact the programme of the elected government. That reluctance played a role in the first forced election and single-handedly caused the second. If either election had resulted in a Unionist victory, the royal veto would have been both effective and partisan. It is hardly surprising that monarchs of the era preferred the Unionists to the Liberals. The Unionists stood for land, church, and empire, all of them institutions in which the monarch had a material stake. Neither Edward VII nor George V was as shrill as their mother (grandmother) Victoria, whose passionate hatred of Gladstone, and naked attempts to manipulate in favour of Disraeli and then Salisbury, burst out in various undignified ways from 1874 onwards. But she was shielded, most notably by Gladstone himself, from the constitutional consequences of her partisanship. The stakes were higher from 1909 onwards.

Pervasive unionism took control of many other public servants. Sir George Murray's behaviour was an extraordinary breach of civil service neutrality, but his case was not the most extreme. That honour goes to (Sir) Henry Wilson, successively commandant of the army Staff College and director of military operations in the War Office during this period. In the Ulster crisis he helped to organize the paramilitary resistance against the military operations for which he was himself responsible, for instance by informing the paramilitary UVF of the planned deployment of British troops (Chapter 5).

The courts, too, were unusually activist in the cases mentioned above, that undermined the 1909 land valuation regime. Offer quotes the High Court judge who killed Undeveloped Land Duty in *Inland Revenue Commissioners v. Smyth* as saying artlessly in 1920, 'It is very difficult sometimes to be sure that you have put yourself into a thoroughly impartial position between two disputants, one of your own class and one not of your class'.[5]

Finally, the norm (as opposed to the legal doctrine) of parliamentary sovereignty received such a blow, largely at the hands of Professor Dicey himself, that its survival is truly miraculous. In order to justify their revolution, the Unionists had to appeal to a higher authority than Parliament. They found one in the people. The Lords resolution rejecting the Budget was carefully framed: 'that this House is not justified in giving its assent to the Bill until it has been submitted to the judgment of the country' (Motion by Lord Lansdowne, 10.11.09, quoted by Jenkins 1968: 95). From this the Unionists proceeded to full-blown advocacy of a referendum on Home Rule. The fullest intellectual case for the referendum appears in the long preface to the eighth edition of Dicey's *Law of the Constitution*, published in 1915. Here he commends it under the title of 'the people's veto'. He complains that the Parliament Act had nullified the 'wisdom and experience of the House of Lords' and that the referendum 'would be *strong* enough to curb the absolutism of a party possessed of a parliamentary majority'. Given Dicey's passionate opposition to Home Rule, it is not surprising that George V took up the theme, suggesting to Prime Minister Asquith in March 1914 'that the Home Rule Bill should be submitted to a Referendum especially now that the principle of this method was admitted for the Ulster counties to decide for or against exclusion' (Dicey 1885/1915: xc–cv, quoted at xcii and xcvii; stress in original. George V quoted in Bogdanor 1995: 128).

Unfortunately, this left the king and the Unionists in the position of demanding the referendum as a bulwark against Liberal or Irish tyranny, but never against Unionist or Conservative tyranny. Dicey's argument that the Parliament Act changed everything was hopelessly one-sided, as Asquith pointed out in a muscular memorandum to George V on the constitutional position of the Sovereign: 'When the two Houses are in agreement (as is always the case when there is a Conservative majority in the House of Commons), the Act is a dead letter' (Appendix to Chapter 12). He turned out to be wrong about the War Crimes Act 1991 but right about the general trend.

The elephant in the room was the Irish Party—the partisan veto player in the Parliaments of 1910–18. That party, although internally fissile, had totally dominated parliamentary representation in Ireland since the franchise extension of 1884. Its bloc of at least 80 seats gave it partisan veto power in the Parliaments of 1885–6, 1892–4, January–December 1910 and 1910–18. That is no disproof, but rather a confirmation, of Duverger's Law. Understood properly, Duverger's Law operates at district level, not at national level. In the Catholic five-sixths of Ireland (and the Scotland division of Liverpool), Duverger's Law delivered such hegemony to the Irish Party that many of its seats were uncontested (hence the apparent, but not real, over-representation shown in Table 5.1). Given that, all the responsiveness of the plurality electoral system was insufficient to deliver a single-party Commons majority in these four Parliaments. The Unionists were determined that Ireland must remain in the Union; but they overlooked the fact that as long as it remained in the Union, it would send a disaffected bloc of 80 MPs determined to weaken the Union and in a position to insist on their programme in every hung parliament. Despite their three election victories, Liberal and Irish Party voters remained beggars with the ballot in their hands. Land value tax, the subject of this chapter, was but one of several policies vetoed or delayed, because they threatened the material interest of the landowning class.

Thus, while the Lords' victory over the 1909 Budget was Pyrrhic, their victory over land taxes was real. The conventional, 'forward-marchish' view of British political history holds, in caricature, that the bad guys won in 1909; the People then intervened and the good guys won in 1911, putting the bad guys back in their red-padded box. Actually, the Lords, and the landed interest that they represented, did better than that. We return to this in Chapter 7. Meanwhile, we turn to the even bigger upset of Ireland.

5

The Curious Incident of the Guns
in the Night Time

Iain McLean and Tom Lubbock

The Curragh 'mutiny' and Larne gunrunning of spring 1914, which are the subjects of this chapter, made the elected UK government's Irish legislation unworkable. Some of the participants believed that the elected government was proposing a coup d'état against Ulster Protestants. It would be truer to say that Ulster Protestants and their allies, who included the king and the leader of His Majesty's Loyal Opposition, mounted a successful coup d'état against the elected government.

Dicey (1885/1915: 179–80) wrote:

> Foreign observers of English manners . . . have been far more struck than have Englishmen themselves with the fact that England is a country governed, as is scarcely any other part of Europe, under the rule of law.

If (as usual in Dicey) 'England' is deemed to include Wales, Scotland, and Ireland, in 1914 this England was not under the rule of law. The Government of Ireland Act 1914 was enacted in September 1914 under the procedures laid down by the Parliament Act 1911. The Parliament Act was itself endorsed by the king, the House of Lords, and the House of Commons. The 1914 Act was endorsed by the king and the House of Commons. It followed the correct procedures laid down by the 1911 Act for enactment without Lords' endorsement. However, by the time of its enactment, a Unionist coup d'état supported by the king had made it utterly unworkable and it was suspended as soon as it had been enacted. A. V. Dicey helped to plan the coup d'état. Parliament is usually sovereign, but a more elaborate theory is required when it is not.

Normatively, Diceyan parliamentary sovereignty dictates what constitutional actors (politicians, civil servants, judges, soldiers, kings, etc.) ought to do. But why? Is there something magical about the King-in-Parliament? For H. L. A. Hart (1961) a certificate of enactment by the King-in-Parliament provides a *rule of recognition*, whereby courts can judge whether such and such is valid law. For Major General Sir Charles Fergusson, discussed later, an officer 'must stick to the first principle, obedience to the King and constituted authority. If one lets go of that principle, one is all at sea, and can argue oneself into anything' (to his brother, 25.04.1914, in Beckett 1986: 340).

By the rule of law, 'every man, whatever be his rank or condition, is subject to the ordinary law of the realm and amenable to the jurisdiction of the ordinary tribunals' (Dicey 1885/1915, p. 189). This did not apply to Major General (later Field Marshal Sir) Henry Wilson nor to Major F. H. Crawford, to whom George V personally awarded a CBE at the state opening of the Northern Ireland Parliament in 1921 (McNeill 1922: 289). The Curragh 'mutiny'[1] and Larne gunrunning of spring 1914 jointly forced the elected UK government to suspend its laws. This chapter explains how and why this coup d'état succeeded.

THE CURRAGH

As noted in previous chapters, the UK General Election of December 1910 re-elected the Liberal administration of H. H. Asquith, which governed with the support of the Labour and Irish parties. The Liberals took all ministerial posts. Recall that both 1910 elections were forced on them by unelected veto players. In the Parliament of 1906–10 the Liberals on their own had a majority of seats, and need not have dissolved until the end of 1912. (The reduction of the maximum length of a Parliament from seven years to five was one of the provisions of the Parliament Act 1911.) However, the Lords' rejection of the 1909 Budget had forced the January election; and George V's refusal to create peers to enact the Parliament Bill without a third election forced the December election. It is important for what follows, therefore, to keep in mind that the governing alliance had won three consecutive General Elections.

The 'progressive alliance', as contemporaries called it, of Liberals, Irish Party, and Labour, held a substantial majority, both in seats and in votes, in the elected house (Table 5.1). Their majority in votes would have been higher had not almost all seats in Catholic Ireland been uncontested, so hegemonic was the Irish Party there. Referring forward to Table 11.1, on by-election trends through the Parliament of December 1910, we see that the position remained stable throughout the life of the Parliament. As usual, the Opposition made gains in early by-elections; as (not quite so) usual, the Government pulled these losses back towards the end.

Table 5.1 Seats, votes, and proportionality: UK general elections 1906–10.

Election	Lib		Con		Irish Nationalist		Lab		Prop/ality Index (Monroe)	Responsiveness	Bias to:
	Vote share (%)	Seat share (%)	Vote share (%)	Seat share (%)	Vote share (%)	Seat share (%)	Vote share (%)	Seat share (%)			
1906	48.98	59.70	43.05	23.43	0.62	12.39	5.86	4.48	61.37	1.35	L
1910J	43.03	41.04	46.75	40.75	1.90	12.24	7.58	5.97	80.91	0.96	L
1910D	43.82	40.60	46.26	40.60	2.52	12.54	7.10	6.27	81.33	0.97	L

Note: Monroe index adapted from B. L. Monroe, 'Disproportionality and malapportionment', *Electoral Studies* 1994, Eqn 15; responsiveness as between the two main parties only, the ratio of the gaining party's seat share to its vote share; bias as between the two main parties only, the one which would hold more seats if they had an equal number of votes; 'Con' columns include Liberal Unionists.

Sources: Summary statistics from F. W. S. Craig's *British Electoral Facts* 1989 Tables 1.18 to 1.20.

The two unelected houses—the Lords and the monarchy—were controlled by the opposition Unionists. As shown in the previous chapter, the Lords largely represented the landed interest, some of it in Ireland. Since 1885, the material interests of the land had been represented entirely by the Conservative and Unionist Party. Likewise those of the established Church of England. Its bishops had a vested interest in opposing the reduction of its privileges in Ireland and Wales, where it was in a small minority. They almost all voted against Home Rule and Welsh disestablishment.

Both kings' vetoes favoured the Unionists. If they had won either of the two forced General Elections, the programme of the government elected in 1906 would have been prematurely aborted. From 1910 to 1914, George V showed more sympathy to His Majesty's Unionist Opposition than to His Majesty's Liberal Government.

The Irish Party was pivotal in both the 1910 Parliaments (Table 5.1). It could make or unmake any governing coalition. The standard power index to measure this is known as the 'normalized Banzhaf' index (Felsenthal and Machover 1998, Chapter 3). This index measures the proportion of winning coalitions to which each party is crucial. A party is crucial to a coalition if adding it to a coalition turns the coalition from losing to winning, and removing it turns the coalition from winning to losing.

The 'seat share' columns of Table 5.1 show that in this sense, the Liberals, Conservatives, and Irish Party had equal power in the Parliaments of January and December 1910. Each, therefore, has a Banzhaf index of 1/3. The Labour Party was a dummy—there was no coalition to which it was crucial.

The Banzhaf index is a measure of *a priori* power. It treats all coalitions as equiprobable. A Liberal–Conservative or Conservative–Irish coalition is a priori as likely as a Liberal–Irish coalition. A Liberal–Conservative coalition was not out of the question. Chancellor Lloyd George had floated the idea in August 1910 but the Conservatives had turned it down. The ideologically closest pair of parties was the Liberals and the Irish. After being double-crossed by Lord Salisbury in 1885 (McLean 2001a: 84–5), the Irish Party was highly unlikely to seek a coalition with the Conservatives, who had become in turn more and more committed to Ulster (and more generally Irish) Unionism. 'If the GOM [Gladstone] goes for Home Rule, the Orange card would be the one to play,' said Salisbury's maverick Chancellor Randolph Churchill. And play it he did, as did the entire Conservative leadership.

Therefore, once the Parliament Act was enacted, the Irish Party was now in a position to insist on its programme of Home Rule (devolution) for Ireland. Its priorities ranked equally with the Liberals' (because their Banzhaf power was equal) and ahead of those of the weakest member of the alliance, the Labour Party. Furthermore, although bitterly resisted in both unelected chambers, it was common knowledge that Home Rule would require three parliamentary sessions and must therefore be started in 1912 to be sure of enactment before the 1915 General Election. It would, for sure, be enacted in 1914, provided that the king did not revive a veto last used in 1708 and that, as laid down in the Parliament Act, it was carried unaltered in three successive sessions of the Commons.

This three-session timetable gave the Ulster Unionists plenty of time to mobilize. The Parliament Act required the Bill to be presented *unaltered* each year: this gave them a handy but specious opportunity to say that the government was not listening. Protestants in Ulster had campaigned since 1886 under the slogans 'Home Rule is Rome Rule' and Randolph Churchill's 'Ulster will Fight and Ulster will be Right.' In 1912, the Ulster Covenant, modelled on the seventeenth-century Scottish Covenants, pledged its signatories to 'us[e] all means which may be found necessary to defeat the present conspiracy to set up a Home Rule Parliament in Ireland'. The Covenant, and a parallel women's declaration, attracted nearly half-a-million signatures (McNeill 1922: 124). A paramilitary organization, the Ulster Volunteer Force (UVF), was raised. Any two Justices of the Peace (JPs) could authorize paramilitary drilling in their area, so long as 'the object was to render citizens more efficient for the purpose of maintaining the constitution of the United Kingdom as now established and protecting their rights and liberties thereunder' (Stewart 1967: 69).

They were initially unarmed, but their leaders darkly threatened that 'all means' might in due course be 'found necessary'. They merely echoed the Leader of the Opposition, Andrew Bonar Law. Law, a Scots-Canadian Presbyterian, was the first non-Anglican and non-Englishman (with the possible exception of Disraeli) to lead the Conservative and Unionist Party when he unexpectedly became leader in 1911. In July 1912, Law made a set-piece speech at the Churchill family seat, Blenheim Palace, a location chosen to remind Unionists of Lord Randolph Churchill's Orange card and his son Winston's defection. Law described the Liberal government as 'a Revolutionary Committee which has seized upon despotic power by fraud'. This seems to imply as other Unionists did that the Parliament Act was in some sense fraudulent.[2] He went on to say:

> I repeat now with a full sense of the responsibility which attaches to my position, that, in my opinion, if such an attempt [viz. to include Ulster within the scope of Home Rule] is made, I can imagine no length of resistance to which Ulster can go in which I should not be prepared to

support them, and in which, in my belief, they would not be supported by the overwhelming majority of the British people. (Blake 1955: 130)

That seems crystal clear. In late 1913, Law considered using the Lords to block renewal of the Army (Annual) Act unless the government promised not to move against the Ulster paramilitaries. By tradition, going back to the English Revolution, a standing army could only continue in existence if annually approved by Parliament. To have held up the Army (Annual) Act would have been as revolutionary an act as the rejection of the 1909 Budget. It would have vetoed the Home Rule Bill. Scholars have long doubted the claim that army discipline depended on the annual Army Act (Fortescue 1914: 60; Strachan 1997: 47–51). However, the veto threat was credible because both sides believed it. Sir John Simon, the Attorney-General, circulated a Cabinet memo explaining that the Army (and Marines when not aboard Her Majesty's ships) could only be disciplined under the Army (Annual) Act, whereas the Navy, and marines aboard ship, had a permanent discipline act. John Seely, the Secretary for War, initialled his copy of this memo on 11 March (Nuffield College, Oxford, Mottistone (J. E. B. Seely) MSS, Box 16). However, the plan was apparently too strong meat for some of Law's own colleagues. Henry Wilson, the Director of Military Operations at the War Office, who was in closer contact with the insurgents than with his own superiors, initially opposed the move but came round to fervent support. But Law dropped it on 20 March, the day the Curragh revolt broke out (Blake 1955: 182; Wilson diary, Imperial War Museum HHW 1/23).[3]

The Army had both emotional and material interests in the Union and the Empire. The Curragh, Co. Kildare, in Ireland's horse country, was the main cavalry base of the British Army. All the leading soldiers in the 1914 events at the Curragh, bar one, had served in the Boer War (1899–1902). Following the old slogan 'England's difficulty is Ireland's opportunity', Irish Nationalist MPs had cheered Boer victories in the Commons. This was particularly galling for army officers, who largely believed that war against a virile rural Teutonic Protestant race was a mistake, but who felt bound (in 1902) not to criticize their political masters publicly (Surridge 1997). They, therefore, had reason to hate the Irish Party.

Although constitutional theory paid lip service to the dual control of the army, senior officers in 1914 did not believe it. Under dual control, the soldier's duty was to the Crown, but the government of the day was responsible for finance. However, books used in the Staff College revealed officers' contempt for politicians. One of them, *Stonewall Jackson and the American Civil War*, argued that the war (on both sides) went well when generals ran it, but badly when politicians ran it. The author of another, a *History of the*

British Army, declared that he was 'absolutely nauseated by their [politicians'] hollowness and cant' (Strachan 1997: 4–6). Army officers, therefore, tended to hate all politicians, but anti-Unionist politicians more than Unionist ones. The second most senior serving officer involved in the Curragh was Henry Wilson.[4] While Director of Military Operations at the War Office between 1910 and 1914, he did not disguise his contempt for the government he served; and passed on embarrassing information about government plans and potential army mutinies to Unionist politicians and the leaders of the UVF, including his next-door neighbour Sir Edward Carson.

Efforts to arm the paramilitaries began in 1913. Sir William Bull MP was political secretary to Walter Long, who had been the Unionists' Ireland spokesman. The gunrunning was a fiasco. Bull's unreliable brother-in-law, to whom he had foolishly delegated it, reported:

> [The police] say they have us all smoked in their jargon but the Government are scratching what to do the whole thing was given away by a case of Rifles breaking in half either at the Hamburg Docks or here. In 48 hours every port (i.e. Custom officials) was warned. (Churchill College, Cambridge. Bull MSS, 4/8, Capt H. P. Budden to Bull, 16.06.1913)

The government's inaction is indeed curious. In December 1913, however, they did prohibit the private import of arms to Ireland (Beckett 1986: 7). By then, intelligence reports told them that the Protestant paramilitaries numbered about 80,000, armed with about 4,000 rifles, 3,000 swords, and 400,000 ammunition rounds (Cabinet memo by Augustine Birrell, 05.03.1914, in Mottistone MSS Box 16). In early 1914, ministers decided to send military reinforcements to protect arms dumps around northern Ireland from paramilitary raids. The GOC (Ireland), Sir Arthur Paget, was summoned to London to be given those instructions. Some Unionists thought they were designed to incite the Ulster Volunteers to attack the military or police, in order that they could then be violently suppressed. Senior army officers were already worried that some officers might refuse to act against the Ulster Protestants. They, or Unionist politicians, had conveyed these anxieties or hopes to the king, who put them to Asquith (Appendix to Chapter 12). Paget asked the Secretary for War, John Seely, if he could permit officers domiciled in Ulster to 'disappear' for the duration of the operation. Seely had himself served in South Africa, and had complained to Joseph Chamberlain about being ordered to burn Boer farms. Chamberlain had replied, 'All you soldiers are what we call pro-Boer' (Surridge 1997). Therefore, Seely had reason to understand, if not to support, Army officers' unwillingness to coerce the equally Protestant Ulstermen. He agreed to Paget's request, but insisted that any other officer unwilling to obey orders must be dismissed.

On 20 March 1914, Paget returned to Ireland. He issued his ultimatum with very short notice. Officers who could not claim the Ulster domicile exception must resign 'and would be dismissed the service with loss of pensions. An answer must be given by 6 pm' (Notes by Lieutenant Colonel I. G. Hogg on the events of 20–23 March 1914, in Beckett 1986: 114). Brigadier General Hubert Gough passed on the ultimatum to his officers in the Third Cavalry Brigade at the Curragh camp in Co. Kildare the same afternoon. About sixty officers, including Gough himself, announced that they would resign. Gough and his allies immediately alerted their Unionist political contacts in London, who learnt before government ministers did what was going on.

The officer who did most to limit the fallout was Major General Sir Charles Fergusson, who commanded all the infantry forces in the northern half of Ireland—thus being junior to Paget but senior to Gough. Fergusson—the only army player in the story not to have served in South Africa—persuaded most of the would-be resigners he spoke to not to resign. He stressed soldiers' duty to the king and the likely reaction of enemies of the Empire to news of mass resignations in the army.

Gough was relieved of his command and summoned to London, where he parlayed with the Secretary of State. He made it clear to brother officers that, far from going in disgrace and under the shadow of court martial, he was going in search of written guarantees that the government would not coerce the Ulster Protestants (Major P. Howell [to C. Wigram, one of George V's equerries], Curragh, 22.03.14, in Beckett 1986: 103). He got them. The Cabinet stated that the whole affair was a 'misunderstanding', but that 'it is the duty of all soldiers to obey lawful commands', including those for the protection of public property and the support of the civil power. Seely then, on his own disastrous initiative, added two 'peccant paragraphs',[5] saying that the Government 'have no intention whatever of ... crush[ing] political opposition to the policy and principles of the Home Rule Bill'. Even this was not good enough for Gough, who had been coached and stiffened by Wilson. He demanded and got an assurance from Sir John French, the Chief of the Imperial General Staff, that this meant that 'the troops under our command will not be called upon to enforce the present Home Rule Bill on Ulster'. With this piece of paper he returned in triumph to the Curragh and his command. When Asquith discovered what Seely had done, he dismissed him, and French also resigned. Gough's undertaking could not practicably be revoked.[6]

Gough and his friends continued to brief Unionist politicians and journalists. The most remarkable briefer was Wilson. Dining with his neighbour Carson on 18 March, he agreed that 'the Lords must amend the Army Annual Act'. The following day, Carson stormed theatrically out of the Commons, saying that 'I go to my people.' Talk of creating a Provisional Government in Ulster was (at the time) a bluff, but a well-informed bluff. Wilson had just told Carson that the Army Act veto play might protect his private army. He then kept the Unionists up do date with the Curragh developments as they happened and before ministers got to hear of them. A comparable act would have been for a British Army general to have let the Provisional IRA know the weaknesses in a forthcoming British offensive against them. On 21 March, Wilson briefed Bonar Law on Gough's campaign, and produced a draft for Seely containing 'what the army would agree to'. He, thus, controlled both Gough's campaign (as a Unionist activist), and the government response to it (as Director of Military Operations). He told his diary that he was 'more than ever determined to resign, but I cannot think of a really good way of doing it'. He never did; remaining in his official capacity a government adviser, and in his unofficial capacity an adviser to Gough, Bonar Law (whom he saw daily at the height of the crisis), and the Ulster paramilitaries at the same time. He urged Sir John French to persist with his resignation. 'Sir John was charming to me and thanked me, etc', and took Wilson's advice. He later hesitated, but when he finally did resign, the non-resigning Wilson wrote:

> This is splendid. Rang up B.L. & told him & added that it was now his business to drive the wedge deep into the Cabinet by causing the down fall of Seely, Morley & Haldane. A good day's work.[7]

The majority of army officers whose reactions have been recorded sided with Gough. A minority did not. The most eloquent was Fergusson, who may have saved the army through his efforts to dissuade officers from resigning, even as the Director of Military Operations in London was doing the opposite. For Fergusson, 'all personal considerations invited me to do as Gough did'. However, '[w]ithout a united Army with strong discipline, nothing can save King and Country when the crisis comes. Therefore I will do nothing that will in any way weaken the discipline of the Army . . . I don't blame Gough & Co. They acted up to their opinions, but I hold them to be absolutely deluded and wrong.' For this he was roundly abused, not only by Goughite Unionists, but also by the king whose name he had used in order to save the British Army. A petulant series of messages from the king complained that he had known nothing of 'his' orders.[8] The British Army's effective strength was six infantry divisions plus one cavalry division. The king was not grateful, or even aware, that Fergusson had saved a seventh of his army from destruction.

LARNE

The Ulster Volunteers took Wilson's advice not to raid the arms depots in Northern Ireland. However, it was in their interest not to reveal to the UK government whether or not they were bluffing. Thanks to Wilson, the Protestant paramilitaries knew better what was going on in the UK security services than vice versa.

For several months after the Bull fiasco, the leaders of the UVF were uncertain whether to try again. The intercepted guns of 1913 had led to the proclamation against arms imports to Ireland and, probably, to the fateful orders of March to protect military depots. Major F. H. Crawford, a former Artillery officer who was acting as the UVF's director of Ordnance, urged the UVF to buy 30,000 rifles in Hamburg. The leaders of the UVF made bellicose noises, but were quite hesitant about Crawford's expedition, twice trying to call it off while he was on the high seas. Nevertheless Sir Edward Carson became the quartermaster for what became the Larne gunrunning. He had at least £90,000 subscribed by sympathizers in England, including Rudyard Kipling who paid £30,000 (Stewart 1967: 136). The most startling claim in the whole story is Crawford's statement, written in 1915, that on 27 March he

> called and saw Walter Long, MP. He sent his secretary to see Bonar Law. The latter when introduced to me said, with a twinkle in his eye, 'I have heard of you before, Mr Crawford'. I had a private letter from the Chief [Carson] . . . to him. I had to see WL about the finances of the business, and make my final arrangements for paying [a] very large cheque. (Fred Crawford, 'Diary of the gunrunning' in Public Record Office of Northern Ireland, PRONI D/1700/5/17/2/4)

The standard biographies state that Law did not know about the Larne gunrunning until after the event. However, in the Appendix to this chapter we show that Law likely knew that something was afoot. His apparent encouragement of Crawford is consistent with his behaviour at Blenheim, over the Army Act and over the Curragh.[9]

By mid-March, Crawford had enough money to buy his 30,000 rifles and 3 million ammunition rounds. Prices were high as Hamburg dealers were also supplying Mexicans for their civil war. The plan would also involve buying ships for cash at short notice, since no questions could be asked. On 16 March (four days before the Curragh), Crawford bought outright a Norwegian collier, SS *Fanny*. The *Fanny* was to pick up the rifles from a Hamburg lighter at Langeland, in Danish Baltic territorial waters. Danish customs officers spotted the transfer of cargo and came to investigate, demanding the papers of both vessels. They promised to return the next day. Crawford was caught.

> I went into my cabin and threw myself on my knees, and in simple language told God all about it: what this meant to Ulster, that there was nothing sordid in what we desired, that we wanted nothing selfishly. I pointed out all this to God, and thought of the old Psalm, 'O God our help in ages past, our hope for years to come'. (Ibid, quoting the opening of Psalm 90 in the *Scottish Metrical Psalter*[10])

God, or luck, helped. Both ships eloped in the night before Danish customs could return. Unfortunately, news of the arrest, with accurate guesses as to the *Fanny*'s cargo and destination, appeared in the English papers. The UVF tried to countermand Crawford's orders, but did not know where he was and had no radio. Having renamed and repainted the *Fanny*, Crawford sailed coastwise round Wales, where he put off at Tenby and went to Belfast to consult the UVF committee, and to London to get his large cheque. The UVF authorized him to buy another collier, the *Clydevalley*, in Glasgow for £4,500. The arms were transhipped at night off Wexford as the *Fanny* and *Clydevalley* were made fast together and 'steamed through the traffic with one set of lights' (Stewart 1967: 195). Crawford now renamed the *Clydevalley* the *Mountjoy II* and made for Belfast Lough.

The Ulster Volunteers had announced a training exercise centred on Larne, the ferry port in Protestant country near the mouth of Belfast Lough. On the night of 24–25 April 1914, they took total control of the port, cutting all telephone lines and blockading all roads out. The railway was also in Unionist hands, but for added security 600 Volunteers were assembled at Belfast York Road to prevent any attempt to send a troop train to Larne. A decoy ship was sent to Belfast, where it was intercepted by Customs. Meanwhile, the *Clydevalley* was unloaded by the Larne dockers, also known as the Larne Harbour section of the Volunteers. All Volunteers' motor cars in Co. Antrim had been ordered to arrive at Larne by 1 a.m. The only hitch was that the *Innismurray*, one of the two ships chosen for coastwise delivery of some of the guns, turned out to have a Nationalist captain. 'The saboteurs [*sic*] were replaced by a volunteer crew of more reliable politics,' relates Stewart, though he does not tell us how, nor what happened to the master and crew. The following description is from a police report in Asquith's papers:

> Mr Robinson said...that as Commanding Officer of the East Antrim Regiment [of the UVF] he had orders from Sir William Adair not to allow anyone to approach the harbour...I asked him if it was intended to prevent the police and Customs officers from going there in discharge of their duty and he said *It was*. I asked him would he prevent them by force

and he said he was prepared to do so and that he had 700 men there for that purpose if necessary.[11]

Belfast customs, when they spotted the other delivery ship tying up, 'were met by a determined U.V.F. guard' and did not get to see her cargo of rifles (Stewart 1967: 206–8). A Unionist pamphlet of August illustrates how, as each vehicle of the motor car corps left Larne with its cargo of rifles, a washerwoman daubed its licence plate with tar so as to obscure it, accompanied by a cry of 'There you go m'dear' (PRONI, Carson Papers, D1507/A/5/ 28). The only casualty of the night was a coastguard who had a fatal heart attack while cycling with a dispatch to a superior officer. Field Marshal Lord Roberts, who was staying with Carson when the success of the operation was confirmed, reportedly exclaimed 'Magnificent!' (McNeill 1922: 220).

WHY THE UNIONIST COUP SUCCEEDED

The primary definition of 'coup d'état' in the *Oxford English Dictionary* is 'a sudden and decisive stroke of state policy'. Both Curragh and Larne fit that description. They do not fit the secondary definition: '*spec.* a sudden and great change in the government carried out violently or illegally by the ruling power'. They were not violent, nor carried out by the ruling power. But at least the following were unlawful:

- At the Curragh:
  - Insubordination and perhaps sedition (Major General Wilson);
  - Insubordination (Brigadier-General Gough, for showing his 'undertaking' to all and sundry on return to Ireland in defiance of orders).
- At Larne:
  - Breach of the Royal Proclamation against importing arms to Ireland (Carson, Lord Milner, Crawford, Long, the officials of the UVF);
  - Sailing without papers and falsification of ships' identities (Crawford);
  - Disobeying an order of Danish customs (Crawford);
  - Disobedience of ships' lighting regulations (Crawford);
  - False imprisonment of the crew of the *Innismurray*;
  - Criminal damage to telephone lines;
  - Obstruction of police and customs (freely admitted—see earlier).[12]

After Larne, the government again considered prosecuting Carson, Adair, and Major Robert McCalmont (Unionist MP for East Antrim and commander of the Central Antrim UVF). However, advised by Irish Party leader John Redmond that a prosecution would be counterproductive, they did nothing.

The paramilitaries also behaved as if they were the revolutionary government of *Catholic* Ulster. According to an intelligence report:

> Great annoyance is caused to the Roman Catholic inhabitants of Co. Monaghan, who are in a large majority, by being challenged when walking along the roads at night by so-called sentries of the UVF . . . and being asked for passwords or countersigns. . . . [T]he continuance of this practice by the Ulster Volunteers is very dangerous as it may cause a serious outbreak at any moment. ('Further notes on the Movement in Ulster', circulated to Cabinet by A. Birrell, 05.03.1914. MS Mottistone Box 16)

How did so many Unionists persuade themselves to break a wide range of laws? The lead came from the top. Bonar Law and Carson made public statements of inflexible extremism. They were more flexible in private— Law, in particular, had three private meetings with Asquith—but their followers did not know that.

Bonar Law worked particularly hard on the king. Initially the king found Law prickly and uncomfortable company. However, he soon adopted Law's words as his own. In August 1913, the king wrote in his own hand to Asquith:

> Whatever I do I shall offend half the population. One alternative would certainly result in alienating the Ulster Protestants from me, and whatever happens the result must be detrimental to me personally and to the Crown in general.

He complained that the government was 'drifting', and asked Asquith to consult the Opposition in order to get an agreed settlement. A month later he went further. Responding to Asquith's claim that the Parliament Act had 'not affected the Constitutional position of the Sovereign', he replied:

> But the Preamble of the Bill stated an intention to create a new Second Chamber; that this could not be done immediately; meanwhile provision by the Bill would be made for restricting the powers of the House of Lords.
>
> Does not such an organic change in the Constitutional position of one of the Estates of the Realm also affect the relations of all three to one another; and the failure to replace it on an effective footing deprive the Sovereign of the assistance of the Second Chamber?

Going on to complain that the passage of the Home Rule Bill might lead to civil war, he complained:

> Do you propose to employ the army to suppress such disorders? . . . Will it be wise, will it be fair to the Sovereign as head of the Army, to subject the discipline, and indeed the loyalty, of his troops, to such a strain?[13]

The handwriting was the king's, but the arguments were Bonar Law's. More precisely, they were arguments that Law had assembled from a number of Unionists, including Professor A. V. Dicey and Field Marshal Lord Roberts. The two main contentions were:

- The Constitution had been in abeyance since 1911.
- In the event of civil war, the loyalties of the armed forces to the Ministers of the Crown were dissolved.

A summary of the Unionist constitutional arguments is given in Table 5.2. They appealed to the king, who urged Asquith to compromise: to discuss his proposals with the Unionists; to propose the temporary exclusion of Ulster from Home Rule; to call a general election; to consider a scheme for federalism, with 'Home Rule All Round' for England, Scotland, and Wales as well. He seriously considered either dissolving the Parliament or refusing Royal Assent to the Government of Ireland Act.

Asquith was equally forthright. The king undoubtedly had the right to dismiss the government and dissolve the Parliament, but the last one to do so was William IV in 1834, 'one of the least wise of British monarchs'. The Tories, whom William favoured, lost the election, and he was stuck again with the Whigs whom he had tried to oust. As to Ireland, Asquith swept aside the king's speculations that most Irishmen were no longer interested in Home Rule and that the Catholic Church did not want it. Asquith did not take the Unionist arguments for a forced dissolution seriously. Nor, unfortunately, did his administration call the Ulster paramilitaries' bluff until it was no longer a bluff. As a consequence, the Government of Ireland Act 1914 was unworkable from the moment it received Royal Assent. A Suspensory Act delayed the operation of both Irish Home Rule and Welsh disestablishment until the end of the war. When it ended, the Welsh got their wish but the Irish did not.

Thus, the leaders of His Majesty's Loyal Opposition encouraged armed rebellion against His Majesty's Government. Only one source that we have found directly implicates Bonar Law in Larne; but there is no doubt about Sir William Bull MP, Sir Edward Carson MP, Captain James Craig (later Lord Craigavon), Lord Milner, Captain Fred Crawford CBE, Major Robert McCalmont MP, Major General (later Field Marshal Sir) Henry Wilson, or Field Marshal Lord Roberts. A selection from the copious evidence that links the leaders of Unionism to the armed conspiracy in Ulster is given in Table 5.3.

Table 5.2 Unionist constitutional arguments 1911–14.

Argument	Source	Example of use	Effect
'The Constitution is in suspense because of the 1911 Preamble'	Lord Lansdowne, Unionist leader in H of L	*A Revolutionary Committee . . . has seized upon despotic power by fraud. . . . In our opposition to them we shall not be . . . bound by the restraints which would influence us in an ordinary Constitutional struggle. We shall take the means, whatever means seem to us effective, to deprive them of the despotic power which they have usurped. . . . [T]here are things stronger than Parliamentary majorities. . . .* Bonar Law at Blenheim 29.07.12, in Blake, *Unknown PM*, p.130. Stated as fact by George V in his memo to Asquith 22.09.13.	Forced GE; royal veto of GoI Act (see next row); armed insurrection in Ulster all ok.
The King may veto the GoI Bill	Bonar Law	*They may say that your assent is a purely formal act and the prerogative of veto is dead. That was true as long as there was a buffer between you and the House of Commons, but they have destroyed that buffer and its true no longer.* Law to King 4.5.12, according to A. Chamberlain. Blake, *Unknown PM:* 133	Govt would resign after veto, therefore forced GE.
Fundamental constitutional change should be put to a referendum	Dicey	*[T]he referendum judiciously used may, at any rate in the case of England, by checking the omnipotence of partisanship, revive faith in that parliamentary government which has been the glory of English constitutional history.* Dicey, *Law of the Constitution* 8th edn p. c.	Repeal of Parliament Act and non-implementation of GoI Act.

The people hate Home Rule	Bonar Law, Dicey, and many others	[T]he present Bill … is opposed by practically the whole of the House of Lords; by one third of the House of Commons; by half the population of England … Ibid. [NB Unionists always say England, never the	Referendum should be held, perhaps only in GB.
Lords may amend the Army (Annual) Act	Lord Hugh Cecil, Unionist frontbencher and intellectual	Would 'compel the government to refer the question of Home Rule to the people … [H of Lords had] the right to insist that before the standing army is used to establish Home Rule in Ireland against the will of a large section of the Irish population, it should at least be certain that the electorate approve of Home Rule and of such use of the King's armed forces. Memo, 5.6.13 in G. Boyce and A, O'Day ed, *The Ulster Crisis*, (Basingstoke: Palgrave, 2006): 58.	Forced referendum on GoI Bill and/ or forced GE. Govt believed the threat credible, see Atty-Gen. Cabinet memo March 1914.
The Irish aren't interested in Home Rule, therefore there is no point in forcing it down the throats of Protestant Ulster	Bonar Law, ?Lord Midleton (southern Irish Unionist leader) and/or Lansdowne	*But is the demand for Home Rule in Ireland as earnest and as National today as it was, for instance, in the days of Parnell? Has not the Land Purchase Policy settled the agrarian trouble, which was the chief motive of the Home Rule agitation? I am assured by resident Landowners in the South and West of Ireland that their tenants, while ostensibly favourable to Home Rule, are no longer enthusiastic about it. … The hierarchy of the Church of Rome is indifferent and probably at heart would be glad not to come under the power of an Irish Parliament.* George V to Asquith, 22.9.13, in Appendix to Chapter 12.	No disorder in nationalist Ireland if Govt drop the GoI Bill.

(*continued*)

Table 5.2 (Continued)

Argument	Source	Example of use	Effect
If civil war is pending, the Army is released from its duty to uphold the civil power	Bonar Law, Lord Roberts, Milner	*United Kingdom, when promoting this argument].* *It is a soldier's duty to obey, but if and when Civil War breaks out no ordinary rules will apply. In that case a soldier will reflect that by joining the Army he has not ceased to be a citizen, and if he fights in such a quarrel he will fight on the side he believes to be right.* Draft letter to press by Roberts, approved by Law and Carson to be issued in event of Army orders against Protestant paramilitaries, 27.1.14, in Blake, *Unknown PM*: 178.	

Table 5.3 The Unionist coup d'état 1913–14.

Source	Date	Author	Document	Comment
Churchill College Bull MSS 4/8	4.6.13	FT Bigham, CID, Scotland Yard	Capt Budden [WB's bro-in-law] is Organising officer of the National Reserve of the Hammersmith District. . . . W J Silcock [is] . . . proprietor of the premises where the cases are stored . . . intimate friends, together with Sir William Bull . . . members of the same Political Association (Conservative & Unionist).	File marked 'This material opened and returned to file on instructions of Cabinet Office April 2004'. Bull was political secretary to Walter Long.
Churchill College Bull MSS 4/8	16.6.13	H. P. Budden to Sir W Bull	The members of the political side of Scotland Yard in this case are Irwin of course as chief McBrien Riley & Parker they say they have us all smoked in their jargon but the Government are scratching what to do the whole thing was given away by a case of Rifles breaking in half either at the Hamburg Docks or here in 48 hours every port (i. e., Custom officials) was warned.	As above
IWM HHW 1/23	23.3.14	Henry Wilson	I went to B.L. at 9.10 am. Told him that I was going to claim equal treatment with Hubert [Gough] & that I felt confident the whole G.S. would follow me; told him Hubert had been in to breakfast & we had determined our plan of campaign which was that any proposals made must be in writing & must state that he would not be called on to imploy his troops and coerce Ulster to accept the present H.R. bill.	
IWM HHW 1/23	26.3.14	Henry Wilson	Talk with Bonar Law and Milner after breakfast. It seems to me Johnny French must resign, but the rest of us must stand fast unless the Government take action against Hubert. Wired him again to	At least one Divisional Commander—Fergusson, who was in Ireland trying to contain the effects of the Curragh—cannot have been there.

(continued)

Table 5.3 (Continued)

Source	Date	Author	Document	Comment
			keep absolutely quiet. Sir John [French] sent for us three Directors at 1 o'c and told us he had resigned, but Seely would not accept. Directly after, all Cs in C and Divisional Commanders came into the CIGS's room and told him the army was unanimous in its determination not to fight Ulster. This is superb. At 3 o'c Sir John sent for me to talk things over. He told me the Cabinet are all opposed to his going and were trying to find some way out of it. I told him that he and Ewart must stick to their resignations…	
IWM HHW 1/23	29.3.14	Henry Wilson	I lunched at Bonar Law's house, only Carson there fresh back from Belfast. We talked about the situation in all its bearings. Carson told me of … the visits of all officers of the *Pathfinder* to him, and of the petty officers, of the friendship between the Navy and the Ulster boys, and of the signalling practice that goes on between the two, and of how excellent the Ulster men are.	HMS *Pathfinder* had been sent to the Ulster coast to aid with operations to protect arms depots. Her Captain had written to his Rear-Admiral to say 'I have no intention of going against Ulster'. Beckett 1986: 284.
Bonar Law MSS 32/1/ 65	22.3.14	Lord Stamfordham to BL	My dear Bonar Law, Many thanks for the copy of your letter of today to the Prime Minister, which the King has read with interest. Indeed this is a most serious disaster to the Army—worse than a defeat at the hands of an enemy—nothing to compare with it has happened in the history of our country—the facts as to what actually happened are not yet positively known. If the Govt will not	The king's secretary gives political advice to the Leader of the Opposition, suggesting a way around the problem of Fermanagh and Tyrone and their inconvenient nationalist majorities.

			have Referendum on the liberal terms you offered—could you not press for exclusion of 6 counties without referendum—(by this means you wd avoid certain zones) and for an unlimited period—and increase the subsidy from the English treasury to say 5 millions. Worth the money! Yrs very truly, Stamfordham [but 'though I am a believer in the referendum', doesn't think it should be forced this time because Asquith would control the wording and timing]
Bonar Law MSS 32/1/75	28.3.14	AV Dicey to BL	The plain truth is that at the present crisis it is absolutely essential that we should either get rid of the Government or ensure an appeal to the people by way of a dissolution or a referendum before the Home Rule Bill passes into law.
PRONI D/1700	July 1915, refers to 27.3.14	Fred Crawford diary	Arrived in London. Called and saw Mr Walter Long, MP. He sent his secretary to see Bonar Law. The latter when introduced to me said, with a twinkle in his eye, 'I have heard of you before, Mr Crawford'. I had a private letter from the Chief, whom I left in Belfast, to him. I had to see WL about the finances of the business, and make my final arrangements for paying [a] very large cheque.

IMPLICATIONS OF CURRAGH AND LARNE FOR CONSTITUTIONAL THEORY: POSITIVE THEORY

In 1914, the Unionist leaders, including Professor Dicey, observed neither the rule of law nor parliamentary sovereignty. Because they regarded the 1911 Parliament Act as somehow fraudulent, they were prepared to take extreme steps, some of them illegal, to prevent the enactment of Home Rule. In normal times, the elected government can use its control of parliament to enact whatever it likes. Parliamentary sovereignty, as subsumed in veto player theory, then says that the elected government may override all vetoes, including any purported vetoes in the shape of attempts to entrench earlier Acts. With few veto players, the winset of the status quo comprises any points to which the elected government might choose to go. With more veto players, the winset of the status quo contracts to the set of points that no veto player regards as inferior to the status quo.

What then upset the supremacy of the elected UK government between 1909 and 1914? At one level the answer is easy. The House of Lords exercised a veto in 1909. Though that veto was modified by the Parliament Act, it was not eliminated. The three sessions needed to enact the Government of Ireland Act (spring 1912–autumn 1914) were the three sessions needed to turn the Ulster Volunteers from bluff to credible threat. Both kings—Edward VII and George V—vetoed their Liberal governments. Their actions increased the power of the Opposition and decreased that of the government. If defeated in even one of the forced 1910 general elections, the programme of the Liberals and their allies would have been aborted. Some public servants abandoned, or never showed, loyalty to their elected superiors. Chapter 4 showed that the Permanent Secretary to the Treasury encouraged Lord Rosebery to reject the 1909 Budget. His actions were mild compared to (Sir) Henry Wilson's.

...NORMATIVE THEORY

At a purely formal level, parliamentary sovereignty supplies Hart's 'rule of recognition'. Judges are to recognize that parliament is sovereign in one of two senses—either the sense in which each parliament individually is sovereign, so that any parliament may override any law of its predecessors, or a broader sense in which 'parliament', as a continuing institution, can occasionally bind itself in constitutional statutes such as the Parliament Act 1911. Yet, in 1914, the Unionist leadership, including Dicey, disowned that theory. The Parliament

Act 1911 had turned the elected government into a 'Revolutionary Committee', they said, as they formed a counter-revolutionary committee of their own.

The Unionists' alternative theory of sovereignty was a badly formulated appeal to the people. The Home Rule Bill must either be stopped outright or be put to the people, who, they were totally confident, would reject it. This idea underlies everything: the Army Act ploy, Curragh, Larne, the intense pressure on the king either to dismiss the government or to veto Home Rule. This is discussed more fully in the next two chapters.

But how could they be sure that they represented the people? Asquith told the king:

> The Parliament Act . . . has not affected . . . the constitutional position of the Sovereign. It deals only with differences between the two Houses. When the two Houses are in agreement (as is always the case when there is a Conservative majority in the House of Commons), the Act is a dead letter. When they differ, it provides that, after a considerable interval, the thrice repeated decision of the Commons shall prevail, without the necessity for a dissolution of Parliament. (Appendix to Chapter 12)

The people had voted for a Liberal, or Liberal-led, government in three general elections in a row. Even in Ulster, the Liberals and Nationalists held seventeen seats to the Unionists' sixteen. Table 5.4 gives more details.

The Unionists did have a grievance, but not one that we have seen expressed: gerrymandering. The Irish constituencies had not been redistributed in 1885, unlike those in Britain. It is clear that this was bipartisan, in order to let the sleeping Nationalist dog lie, and that the leaders of both British parties at the time, Gladstone and Salisbury, concurred. Salisbury could have used the Lords' veto to force an Irish redistribution and reduction in seats had he thought it desirable.

But Salisbury's inaction harmed the Ulster Protestants. Constituencies in Ulster had become very unequal in population by 1914, so that the Liberals and Nationalists won more seats, with fewer votes, than the Unionists. Nevertheless, Table 5.4 gives the lie to any conception of a homogeneous Protestant Unionist Ulster.

DISCUSSION: OBSERVABLE IMPLICATIONS

We have required an extensive narrative to justify our contention that the events of spring 1914 constituted a successful coup against the elected government of the United Kingdom. We have done this because with

Table 5.4 Religion and politics in Ulster 1914.

Home Rule Ulster Constituency	RC population 1911	Non RC population 1911	Total population
S Armagh	23,511	11,050	34,561
W Cavan	38,011	9,170	47,181
E Cavan	36,177	7,713	43,890
N Donegal	33,503	7,560	41,063
W Donegal	42,085	4,166	46,251
E Donegal	24,657	14,983	39,640
S Donegal	32,698	8,768	41,466
S Down	24,441	21,232	45,673
S Fermanagh	18,948	11,743	30,691
N Monaghan	24,354	12,204	36,558
S Monaghan	28,987	5,850	34,837
N Tyrone	20,144	16,622	36,766
Mid Tyrone	22,308	13,277	35,585
E Tyrone	20,561	16,933	37,494
W Belfast	36,577	30,340	66,917
Newry Town	9,183	3,270	12,453
Londonderry City	22,978	17,821	40,799
Subtotal Home Rule seats	459,123	212,702	671,825
Unionist Ulster			
N Antrim	10,629	32,915	43,544
Mid Antrim	9,575	33,377	42,952
E Antrim	6,627	48,524	55,151
S Antrim	12,526	36,486	49,012
N Armagh	13,616	31,854	45,470
Mid Armagh	17,000	22,538	39,538
N Down	7,166	52,850	60,016
E Down	16,539	31,114	47,653
W Down	7,651	35,083	42,734
N Derry	18,505	34,452	52,957
S Derry	22,953	23,912	46,865
N Fermanagh	15,801	15,319	31,120
S Tyrone	15,922	16,670	32,592
E Belfast	25,018	111,080	136,098
S Belfast	13,265	67,715	80,980
N Belfast	18,218	81,847	100,065
Subtotal Unionist seats	231,011	675,736	906,747
TOTAL	690,134	888,438	1,578,572

Source: George Philp & Co., *Political Map of Ulster in 1912*, Mottistone Papers, incorporating religious data from 1911 Census; authors' calculations to take account of Londonderry City by-election 30.01.13 (Lib. gain from Con.).

few exceptions the historiography of the period is so bland.[14] The standard work on the UK monarchy and the constitution argues that the two kings ought to have refused even more firmly than they did Asquith's requests for the creation of peers, and that on Ulster in 1914 'the king's judgement was superior to that of his prime minister'.[15] How an eminent political scientist, using essentially the same evidence base as us, can reach these conclusions eludes us.

The purpose of this chapter is analytic as well as descriptive. Descriptively, we have shown that four unelected veto players enabled the coup to succeed. These veto roles, played by varying people, were the median member of the House of Lords, the monarchy, the set of army officers prepared to mutiny or resign rather than obey orders, and the Ulster Protestant paramilitaries. The leaders of the Commons Opposition, not themselves veto players, supplied ammunition (literally in the case of Larne) for all four.

How then has the belief that the United Kingdom is a low-n veto-player regime, with a large win set over the status quo, become so persistent in modern political science?[16] First, we argue, because the veto power of the post-1911, pre-1999 House of Lords has been ignored or mischaracterized. For all that period, the median Lord was a Conservative, as he had been since the late eighteenth century. He always held a potential veto in the last two years (after 1949, in the last year) of a parliament. Towards the end of a parliament, it is common knowledge that there is insufficient time for the government to legislate without the Lords under the terms of the Parliament Acts. Even nearer the start of a parliament, time is always scarce, so that the median peer, though not a formal veto player, may be in a position to block potential legislation that is not high on the government's agenda.

How have political scientists managed to miss this (to us) glaringly obvious fact? First, as Asquith told George V, because the veto power is not evident in periods of Conservative government, when the median peer is close in issue space to the median MP. Therefore, scope for it arose only in the periods 1911–15, 1924, 1929–31, 1945–51, 1964–70, 1974–9, and 1997–9. The period since 1999 is discussed in Chapter 11. Since 1945 it has been modified by the 'Salisbury–Addison convention', whereby the Conservative leaders of the Lords undertook not to veto the manifesto commitments of the elected government. This convention and its collapse, after 1999, are also discussed in Chapter 11. But as Salisbury–Addison is merely a convention, it does not restrict the median peer's formal veto power. That there were not constant vetoes of government legislation in the parliaments just listed merely reflects parliamentarians' common knowledge of the veto power.

Table 5.5 Veto plays by UK monarchs.

Monarch	Reigned	Example veto play	Veto play successful?
Elizabeth II and I	1952–	None known	
George VI	1936–52	None known	
Edward VIII	1936	Attempted marriage contrary to ministers' wishes	No
George V	1910–36	Threat to dissolve Parliament or withhold Royal Assent from Government of Ireland Bill, 1913–14	Partial
Edward VII	1901–10	Refusal to create peers without second general election 1909–10	Yes
Victoria	1837–1901	Attempts to prevent Gladstone from becoming Prime Minister, 1886 and 1892	No
William IV	1830–7	Dismissal of PM Lord Melbourne, 1834	Yes
George IV	1820–30	Delay and attempted veto of Catholic emancipation 1828–9	No
George III	1760–1820	Veto of Catholic Emancipation in Ireland 1801	Yes

Sources: *Oxford Dictionary of National Biography*; C. Matthew, *Gladstone 1809–1898* (Oxford: OUP 1997); I. McLean and A. McMillan, *State of the Union* (Oxford, OUP, 2005); V. Bogdanor, *The Monarchy and the Constitution*; R. Jenkins, *Asquith*.

That the monarchy is not regarded as an active veto player, is an overgeneralization from the behaviour of the last two monarchs in the series, George VI and Elizabeth II and I, who have indeed never threatened vetoes, as constitutional theory says they should not. Table 5.5, which is not exhaustive, lists attempted and successful veto plays by the last ten monarchs of the United Kingdom. All of them (except Edward VIII, who failed), vetoed or attempted to veto radical, rather than conservative, actions and/or governments. A future monarch with strong conservative opinions might revive the trend.

The whole army was not behind the contingent mutineers of the Curragh; but enough of its senior officers were behind them to veto the deployment of troops to Ulster in support of the civil power. Others in the drama, especially Paget and Seely, made unforced blunders which made matters worse. But the Gough–Wilson faction in the army vetoed the policy of the elected government. Nothing remotely comparable has happened in the

British Army since 1914, but other democracies have been deposed in military coups since then.

Finally, the intransigence of Ulster Protestantism owes something to Calvinist theology. Whether it be Fred Crawford asking God to save him from arrest by the Danes, or more tragically the march of the UVF, transformed into the Thirty-sixth (Ulster) Division, straight into German lines on 1 July 1916, shouting as they went 'No Surrender' and 'Remember 1690' (Stewart 1967: 239), Calvinists' certainty that God is on their side is a source of both strength and weakness. On 1 and 2 July 1916, the Thirty-sixth Ulster Division lost 5,500 troops, killed, wounded, and missing. This exceeds the total toll of violent deaths in Northern Ireland from 1968 to date. Calvinism remains a strand of Ulster Protestantism.[17]

Of these vetoes, that of Ulster Protestants (outside Ulster) and the Army are now dead; that of the monarch is at least sleeping. That of the House of Lords remained in full force until 1999. Further research could usefully examine the constraints it imposed on non-Conservative UK governments from 1911 to 1999.

Appendix to Chapter 5.
How Much Did
Bonar Law Know About the
Larne Gunrunning?

Letters from and to Ronald McNeill
MP, 21.12.1921. Law MSS, Parliamentary
Archives, BL 107/1/107 and 107/4/18

My dear Bonar,

I don't know whether I told you that I am writing a book on the Ulster resistance to Home Rule; but I have just now been reading for it a MS of Fred Crawford's, the gun-runner. I see he says that just on the eve of the voyage of the "Fanny" James Craig told him

"that Bonar Law & Walter Long would like to meet me before I went, so I saw both these statesmen & they wished me God speed & a successful issue"

I should like to know whether you have any objection to my publishing this statement that you were privy to, & wished well to, the gunrunning, or whether you would prefer not to have your name mentioned. I will of course do as you wish about it. Yours ever, Ronald McNeill.

My dear Ronald,

It is difficult looking back so far to feel sure that one's memory is accurate but my recollection is that I did not know of the gunrunning till after it had taken place & that Carson told me that he had deliberately refrained from letting me know about it because he thought it better that in my position I shd not have any responsibility for it.

You had better ask Carson [?word illegible, perh. 'now'] whether or not his recollection tallies with mine. I do not remember seeing Mr Crawford, but I saw at different times with Carson a number of our supporters in Belfast & very likely Mr Crawford may have been one of them.

All this however is very immaterial. I took full responsibility at the time for all that was done & have never thought since that I was wrong in doing so. Yours sincerely [unsigned, BL's file copy].

Although Law does not explicitly corroborate Crawford's claim, he concedes that he may have met Crawford; he does not deny the outline of the story: he explains that Carson was deliberately keeping him in the dark, and he claims full responsibility for his actions in 1914. It is hard to believe that he did not guess where the very large sums of money being raised in Britain for the Ulster Protestants were going.

Law had served for over four years as Deputy Prime Minister to Lloyd George. In March 1921 he had retired through illhealth. By December he had returned to politics in order to protect Protestant Ulster in Lloyd George's Irish settlement. Ulster Protestants and their allies, including McNeill, denounced the Sinn Fein delegates who had signed a treaty with Lloyd George on 6 December as rebels and murderers. It hardly suited Law's purposes to admit that he had encouraged rebellion on the opposite side. That he was willing to go so far in his reply to McNeill is eloquent. He could have simply said No. His letter has a tone, as our French teacher used to tell us, of *Qui s'excuse, s'accuse.*

6

The Contradictions of Professor Dicey

[N]either the Act of Union with Scotland nor the Dentists Act, 1878, has more claim than the other to be considered a supreme law. Each embodies the will of the sovereign legislative power; each can be legally altered or repealed by Parliament; neither tests the validity of the other. Should the Dentists Act, 1878, unfortunately contradict the terms of the Act of Union, the Act of Union would be *pro tanto* repealed ... The one fundamental dogma of English [*sic*] constitutional law is the absolute legislative sovereignty or despotism of the King in Parliament. (Dicey 1885/1915: 141)

No work that I have ever read brings out in a more distinct and emphatic manner ... the absolute supremacy of Parliament [than Dicey's *Law of the Constitution*]. (W. E. Gladstone, introducing the Government of Ireland Bill 1886, House of Commons 09.04.1886. In Matthew 1999: 469)

I am absolutely certain that nothing but great energy ... will avert this calamity [viz, Home Rule for Ireland]. I do most earnestly implore you, and every influential unionist, to put in the forefront of our claims the demand for a dissolution before the third session of the bill has begun. I know you will think that I am on the point of unionism a fanatic; it is a case in which a good deal more fanaticism would do a great deal of good. (A. V. Dicey to Walter Long, MP. 16.04.1913. Long MSS, British Library add mss 62406)

The statesmen of 1707, though giving full sovereign power to the Parliament of Great Britain, clearly believed in the possibility of creating an absolutely sovereign legislature which should yet be bound by unalterable laws ... [T]he enactment of laws which are described as unchangeable, immutable, or the like, is not necessarily futile. The declaration contained in the Act for Securing the Protestant religion and Presbyterian Church government within the Kingdom of Scotland, which is embodied in the Act of Union ... is not unmeaning. (Dicey and Rait 1920: 252–3)

A. V. Dicey was guilty of a simple contradiction in believing both that the Acts of Union 1707 were fundamental, and that they preserved the English tradition of parliamentary sovereignty. This has been challenged (Bogdanor 2007: 2008).[1] Nevertheless, this chapter aims to show that:

- Dicey is indeed guilty of contradiction;
- from a contradiction anything follows;
- his passionate political views led him into dubious places;
- Dicey's first position is untenable and unrealistic;
- his second and third positions can be rescued but only by better arguments for popular sovereignty or entrenchment than Dicey ever offered.

We follow H. L. A. Hart's useful distinction between two versions of the doctrine of parliamentary sovereignty. Hart writes:

> [O]lder constitutional theorists wrote as if it was a logical necessity that there should be a legislature which was sovereign, in the sense that it is free, at every moment of its existence as a continuing body, not only from legal limitations imposed *ab extra*, but also from its own prior legislation . . . [A]nother principle . . . might equally well, perhaps better, deserve the name of 'sovereignty'. This is the principle that Parliament should *not* be incapable of limiting irrevocably the legislative competence of its successors but, on the contrary, should have this wider self-limiting power. Parliament would at least once in its history be capable of exercising an even larger sphere of legislative competence than the accepted established doctrine allows to it. (Hart 1961: 145; see also Young 2006)

Hart calls the former conception '*continuing* omnipotence' and the latter '*self-embracing* omnipotence' (his italics). Which form of parliamentary sovereignty applies is an empirical question; 'the presently [in 1961] accepted rule is one of continuing sovereignty, so that Parliament cannot protect its statutes from repeal'.

DICEY'S THREE DOCTRINES OF SOVEREIGNTY

Obviously, Dicey was one of the 'older constitutional theorists' in Hart's sights. In his 1885 text, as republished seven times up to 1915, his comparison of the scope of the Act of Union 1707 and the Dentists Act 1878 is an assertive statement of continuing omnipotence. Introducing the Government of Ireland Bill 1886 (better known as the first 'Home Rule' Bill), W. E. Gladstone praised Dicey's recently published text, which he had been studying assiduously as he prepared his Irish legislation.

According to Dicey's text, the Parliament was fully entitled to amend the Act of Union 1800 by granting a limited measure of devolution to Ireland. As we have seen, the 1886 bill failed. The Second (1893) and Third (1912) Home

Rule Bills were carried in the elected house of the Parliament but defeated in one of the unelected houses, the House of Lords. Under the provisions of the Parliament Act 1911, the 1912 Bill became the Government of Ireland Act 1914 without Lords' consent. However, Dicey passionately tried to block it, as our third introductory quotation shows. He wrote that there might be 'acts of oppression on the part of a democracy, no less than of a king, which justify resistance to the law, or, in other words, rebellion'; the 1912 Bill lacked 'constitutional authority' (Dicey 1913: 114) because it had not been confirmed in a general election. However, the governing Liberals had won three successive general elections, the last two of them (January and December 1910) forced by the Lords' rejection of the 1909 Budget and the refusal of two successive kings to overturn Lords' vetoes without a general election. Dicey's claim that the government lacked constitutional authority for the Government of Ireland Act makes no Diceyan sense.

Dicey was reportedly furious at Gladstone's use of his name to justify the 1886 bill. He published four critiques of Home Rule, each more strident than the previous: *England's Case Against Home Rule* (1886), *Unionist Delusions* (1887), *A Leap in the Dark* (1893, republished 1911), and *A Fool's Paradise* (1913). In *The Verdict* (1890), Dicey claimed that commissioners investigating rural intimidation in Ireland under Parnell had proved that the Land League and its leaders were guilty of treason, sedition, and criminal conspiracy. In the long introduction to the eighth edition of *The Law of the Constitution* (1915), Dicey called for a referendum on contentious constitutional legislation. Finally, his *Thoughts on the Scottish Union* (1920), written with the Historiographer-Royal for Scotland, revisited the 1707 Act of Union in a calmer tone of voice.

In these seven books, plus his numerous letters to Unionist politicians, Dicey moved from the doctrine of continuing omnipotence first to an ill-expressed doctrine of popular sovereignty, and then towards self-embracing omnipotence. Gladstone had skewered him in 1886. Under continuing omnipotence, the Act of Union 1800 had no entrenched status. Therefore, the Parliament had the unfettered power to pass a Government of Ireland Act, as it finally did in 1914. Dicey very badly wanted the Parliament not to pass a Government of Ireland Act, so he repudiated continuing omnipotence. The increased strength of party discipline meant that his 1885 version of self-correcting unitary democracy did not preserve popular sovereignty in the manner in which he wished.

At the peak of his fury he abandoned parliamentary sovereignty altogether. In *A Leap in the Dark*, he states (without evidence) that in 1893 the 'hereditary House of Lords, and not the newly elected House of

Commons, truly represented the will of the nation' (Dicey 1893/1911: xvii) by overwhelmingly rejecting the second Home Rule Bill. In *A Fool's Paradise* and letters to Unionist frontbenchers such as Walter Long, who may have been the paymaster of Larne, this blossoms into a complete confidence that Dicey and his friends represent the will of the nation. There are things stronger than parliamentary majorities, according to Bonar Law in his notorious Blenheim speech in July 1912 (Blake 1955: 130). Dicey agreed, calling for a referendum or a dissolution to prove that the will of the nation was what he said it was, and giving his authority to other ploys, such as an appeal to George V to veto the Home Rule Bill.

In *A Fool's Paradise*, Dicey observes that there are 40 million people in Great Britain and 4 million in Ireland, of whom a million are Unionists. (The actual Irish numbers, from the 1911 Census, are: total population 4,390,219, of whom 3,238,656 [73 per cent] were stated by the person returning the forms to be Roman Catholics. Great Britain's population in 1911 was just under 41 million.) As an 'old . . . Benthamite', he declares that he prefers the welfare of the 40 million to that of the 3 million. This seems to imply that his much-touted referendum was not to take place in Ireland, or at least that if the UK majority in such a referendum was in favour of Home Rule while the Great Britain majority was against, the latter should prevail. If Home Rule were enacted and Unionist demands for a dissolution or a referendum ignored, the Act would:

> in the eyes of every Unionist, lack moral authority. The question will at once arise whether revolution, achieved by intrigue or fraud, may not be reversed or arrested . . . A combination of discordant parties is attempting to drive through Parliament, without an appeal to the electors, a policy which has been twice deliberately rejected by the electorate of the United Kingdom . . . Every loyal citizen of the United Kingdom ought in general, and as a paramount duty, to obey the law of the land, or, in other words, the clearly and indubitably expressed will of the nation. But . . . such obedience can be due only when a law is the clear and undoubted expression of the will of the nation.

When Dicey says that Home Rule has been 'twice deliberately rejected by the electorate of the United Kingdom' he must be referring to the General Elections of 1886 and 1895.[2] But the second of those was not fought on Home Rule, which the outgoing Liberals had dropped on Gladstone's retirement. If every general election were nevertheless treated as a referendum on Home Rule, then the Home Rule coalition had won four general elections since 1886 to the Unionist coalition's three. He goes on to cite with approval 'the old Whig doctrine that oppression, and especially resistance to the will of the nation, might justify what was technically conspiracy or rebellion' (Dicey 1913: 44, 112–14, 126 respectively). These were weighty and carefully chosen words, when his party leader had stated at Blenheim the previous year 'I can imagine no length of resistance to which Ulster can go in which I should not be prepared to support them' (Bonar Law 29.07.12, in Blake 1955: 130).

Dicey firmly refuses to answer two obvious questions:

1. What if the forced general election he was demanding produced a fourth Home Rule majority in a row? 'My reply is this . . . I will not try to give an opinion on a case which has not yet arisen and may probably never arise'.
2. 'What are the limits within which the tyranny either of a king or of a democracy justifies civil war is not an inquiry on which I will enter' (Dicey 1913: 114; 127).

By 1913, therefore, Dicey has moved away from parliamentary sovereignty altogether to a belief in popular sovereignty (which underpins American and, arguably, Scottish constitutionalism). So extreme is his position in 1913 that he believes that people are obliged to obey the law only if it reflects the 'the clearly and indubitably expressed will of the nation'. This may surprise public lawyers: not least because modern lawyers are unlikely to read the eighth edition of Dicey (1885/1915) in which his fury is laid bare. Subsequent editors suppressed the embarrassing eighth edition preface.

Dicey's total confidence that the will of the nation was what he said was never tested by either a dissolution or a referendum. But the nation included— as Dicey insisted it must include—nationalist Ireland, which would have voted unanimously for Home Rule in a referendum as it had done in seven general elections in a row. So it is not clear how Dicey 'knew' that the nation opposed Home Rule. We have quoted two alarming hints. The first is that the will of (at least nationalist) Ireland should not count towards the will of the nation. The second is that rebellion against a 'democracy' in the name of the 'will of the nation' might be justified. Dicey's position in 1913–14 was 'Parliament is sovereign, unless the elected house does something I deeply deplore, in which case the will of the people—which is what I say it is—is sovereign'. Thus Dicey contradicted himself. In the eighth edition of *Law and the Constitution* he argues both that Parliament ought always to be treated as sovereign (e.g. at p. 141) and that it sometimes ought not to be (e.g. at page xcix). From a contradiction anything follows. This contradictory text lacks authority.

Constitutional commentators do not seem to regard Dicey's anti-Home Rule polemics, his letters to Unionist politicians, and the embarrassing introduction to the eighth edition of *Law and the Constitution* as 'really' part of his writings. But he wrote them; he published most of them; he called his opponents 'fools' in the title of one of them; so why is it unfair or inappropriate to read them together, and thence to argue that his oeuvre is contradictory?

Bogdanor (2008), in a riposte to an earlier version of this chapter, is more subtle. He argues that we confused four doctrines of Dicey's, which he characterizes thus:

1. The legal doctrine that Parliament is sovereign.
2. The political doctrine that the unity of the United Kingdom is best preserved by maintaining the unitary state, federalism being unsuitable.
3. The political doctrine that there is no stable *via media* such as 'Home Rule' or 'devolution' lying between the unitary state and federalism.
4. The moral doctrine that there are certain things which a sovereign Parliament ought not to do.

According to Bogdanor, Dicey's constitutional writings, including Dicey (1885/1915), are about (1); his polemical writings are about (2–4); therefore, Bogdanor argues, there is no inconsistency. Dicey was (rightly, Bogdanor implies) furious at Mr Gladstone for making the same mistake as me when in his speech introducing the Home Rule Bill of 1886 he cited Dicey with approval for the opinion that the Parliament was entitled to grant devolution to Ireland.

In favour of Bogdanor's interpretation, Dicey repeatedly and eloquently states in the main text (not the introduction) of *The Law and the Constitution* that his task is to 'state what are the laws which form part of the constitution, to arrange them in their order, to explain their meaning, and to exhibit where possible their logical connection' (Dicey 1885/1915: 31). He distinguishes this from history and politics. He describes his task as analytic, not normative.

Parliamentary sovereignty on this interpretation is concerned with the status of Acts after their enactment. Up to September 1914 it has nothing to say about the Government of Ireland Bills because none of them is an Act. Therefore, it is argued, there is no inconsistency in Professor Dicey being (in his own phrase) a 'fanatic' opponent of Home Rule and an upholder of parliamentary supremacy at the same time. In the most limited reading of parliamentary sovereignty, it is simply an instruction to the courts not to inquire into how an Act of Parliament was passed. Famous cases in which judges decided to keep out of that thicket were *Edinburgh and Dalkeith Railway* v. *Wauchope* in 1842 and *Ex parte Canon Selwyn* in 1872. Wauchope complained that the Parliament had failed to follow correct procedures in passing the railway's private Act. Canon Selwyn complained that the Queen was wrong to give royal assent to the disestablishment of the Church of Ireland as it contradicted her coronation oath, and that the courts should intervene. In both cases the courts declined: their job was merely to examine the 'roll of Parliament' to confirm that the Acts complained of had been duly passed and had received Royal Assent.

Did Mr Gladstone, then, get Dicey completely wrong? If I err with Mr Gladstone, I am in good company. But I fail to see where the error lies. At the most trivial level, if (what I do not accept) the main text of Dicey (1885/ 1915) is merely a footnote to *Wauchope* and *Ex parte Selwyn*, what about the hundred-page preface to the same work, in which Dicey shares his fierce Unionism with his readers? Given that, as I have just shown, it contradicts the main text, which are we to believe?

Consider the range of actions that Dicey is prepared to endorse in order to prevent the Government of Ireland Bill becoming law. He calls for a referendum, arguing that since the 1911 Act Parliament has degenerated into an elective dictatorship of the Commons only. For the same reason he is willing to endorse almost anything the Ulster Unionists are threatening to do on the grounds that this corrupted 'Parliament' is opposed to the 'will of the people'. In an earlier book (Dicey 1890) he claims that the Irish Party under Parnell has been guilty of sedition and criminal conspiracy; yet he is prepared to endorse comparable actions when undertaken by Unionists.

The distinction he vigorously makes between the analytical and the normative is untenable. His analysis has normative implications. For instance his chapter on the Army (Part II, ch. IX) concludes that Army discipline depends on the annual renewal of the Army Act. Other experts, then and since, have disputed this, but the Liberal Cabinet believed it. And it implies that if His Majesty's Loyal Opposition block the renewal of the Army Act, they will leave His Majesty without an army until their wishes are granted.

Even if we do read the doctrine of parliamentary sovereignty as purely formal, we are not out of the woods. For, as Bogdanor goes on to say, in 1920 Dicey and Rait set out the doctrine that Hart would later call self-embracing omnipotence. This concession empties the doctrine of parliamentary sovereignty, if it is to be treated as purely formal, of any content, because it acknowledges that Parliament can indeed, in a 'not unmeaning' way, claim to bind its successors.

The Treaty and Acts of Union of 1706/7 embodied (as Dicey had already conceded, but then ignored, in 1885) a true treaty between two parliaments, only one of which had a tradition of parliamentary sovereignty. That treaty was then embodied in two Acts, one in the last Scottish Parliament and one in the last English Parliament. These three documents created a new Parliament. They (purport to) entrench constitutional protections, notably for the respective national churches of Scotland and England. The Scottish entrenchment, as recited and re-enacted in the English Act, states:

And her Majesty with advice and consent aforesaid expressly provides and declares that the foresaid true Protestant religion contained in the above mentioned confession of faith with the form and purity of worship presently in use within this Church and its Presbyterian Church government and discipline (that is to say) the government of the Church by kirk sessions presbyteries provincial synods and general assemblies all established by the foresaid Acts of Parliament pursuant to the claim of right shall remain and continue unalterable and that the said Presbyterian government shall be the only government of the Church within the kingdom of Scotland.[3]

Dicey and Rait argue that the draftsmen of the Treaty and Acts 'clearly believed in the possibility of creating an absolutely sovereign legislature which should yet be bound by unalterable laws' (Dicey and Rait 1920: 253). Dicey thus has three doctrines of sovereignty. In 1885 (Dicey I) he endorses continuing omnipotence of Parliament. In 1913 (Dicey II) he expounds a form of popular sovereignty. In 1920 (Dicey III) he and Rait expound self-embracing omnipotence of Parliament. Two questions then follow for each of these doctrines. Is it a correct description of the actions of United Kingdom judges and legislators for (some of) the period since 1707? And is it an attractive (or at least a coherent) normative doctrine?

WHICH DOCTRINES ARE DEFENSIBLE?

Recall that Hart states that in 1961 'the presently accepted rule is one of continuing sovereignty, so that Parliament cannot protect its statutes from repeal'. In 1712, after a Tory General Election victory, Parliament passed the Patronage Act (10 Anne, Chapter 12), which Dicey and Rait (1920: 280) call 'the chief and almost the only example of an Act of the British Parliament passed in violation of the Act of Union'. The Act gave lay patrons the right to present ministers to Scottish parishes. It led to endless disputes and secessions in the Scottish churches, culminating in the Disruption of 1843 (for the best legal treatment of which see Rodger 2008), and was repealed in 1874.

However, in stating that in 1961 the 'presently accepted rule is one of continuing sovereignty', Hart seems to have overlooked the Church of Scotland Act 1921 (10 & 11 Geo V. c.29). Parliament there bound itself to recognize the doctrines of the Church of Scotland (the 'Declaratory Articles', drafted by the Kirk and published as a schedule to the 1921 Act) as trumping attempts to override them. By s.1 of the Act:

> The Declaratory Articles are lawful articles, and the constitution of the Church of Scotland in matters spiritual is as therein set forth, and no limitation of the liberty, rights and powers in matters spiritual therein set forth shall be derived from any statute or law affecting the Church of Scotland in matters spiritual at present in force, it being hereby declared that in all questions of construction the Declaratory Articles shall prevail, and that all such statutes and laws shall be construed in conformity therewith and in subordination thereto, and all such statutes and laws in so far as they are inconsistent with the Declaratory Articles are hereby repealed and declared to be of no effect.

The Parliament, thus, promised not to repeat what it had done in 1712. In 1921, as in 1707, the Parliament was willing to be bound by a form of words drafted not by itself but under the authority of the General Assembly of the Church of Scotland. It has shown no inclination to break these fetters. It is true that on its face the 1921 Act expressly repeals only past Acts inconsistent with the Declaratory Articles; unlike the Act of Union it does not attempt to entrench them against future legislation. Behaviourally this may be a distinction without a difference. The Declaratory Articles remain important in current litigation as defining the area of spiritual independence of the Church of Scotland. Where they draw that line was determined by the courts in 2005, in an important case to which we recur later.

Before Hart, Lord President Cooper had attempted to subvert continuing omnipotence in *MacCormick* v. *Lord Advocate*, 1953 S.C. 395. MacCormick's case (that the naming of Queen Elizabeth as Elizabeth II in Scotland was unlawful under the Act of Union) was dismissed. But Cooper continued:

> The principle of the unlimited sovereignty of Parliament is a distinctively English principle which has no counterpart in Scottish constitutional law. It derives its origin from Coke and Blackstone, and was widely popularised during the nineteenth century by Bagehot and Dicey, the latter having stated the doctrine in its classic form in his Law of the Constitution. Considering that the Union legislation extinguished the Parliaments of Scotland and England and replaced them by a new Parliament, I have difficulty in seeing why it should have been supposed that the new Parliament of Great Britain must inherit all the peculiar characteristics of the English Parliament but none of the Scottish Parliament, as if all that happened in 1707 was that Scottish representatives were admitted to the Parliament of England. That is not what was done. Further, the Treaty and the associated legislation, by which the Parliament of Great Britain was brought into being as the successor of the separate Parliaments of Scotland and England, contain some clauses which expressly reserve to the Parliament of Great Britain powers of subsequent modification, and other clauses which either contain no such power or emphatically exclude subsequent alteration by

declarations that the provision shall be fundamental and unalterable in all time coming, or declarations of a like effect. I have never been able to understand how it is possible to reconcile with elementary canons of construction the adoption by the English constitutional theorists of the same attitude to these markedly different types of provisions (*MacCormick v. Lord Advocate* [1953] S.C. 396, 411).

It is true that Cooper's remarks are what lawyers call 'obiter', i.e. in passing. They do not bind later judges. It has been suggested that Cooper felt safe to say these revolutionary things just *because* nothing hung on them: Mac-Cormick had lost on other grounds. The Scottish courts have resisted any temptation to strike down UK Acts on Cooperian grounds. Nevertheless, Cooper's attack on Dicey I seems unanswerable (see also MacCormick 1998). At least in relation to Scotland, Dicey I is neither descriptively correct nor normatively defensible.

Undoubtedly, Cooper's words were in the ears of those who drafted the Scottish Constitutional Convention's Claim of Right in 1989: 'We, gathered as the Scottish Constitutional Convention, do hereby acknowledge the *sovereign right of the Scottish people* to determine the form of Government best suited to their needs' (Claim of Right 1989; my emphasis). One of the drafters of the Claim was Neil MacCormick, Regius Professor of Law at Edinburgh University and son of the petitioner in *MacCormick* v. *Lord Advocate*. MacCormick and his colleagues were pointedly claiming that in Scotland sovereignty rests with the people, not with Parliament (Maccormick 1998). This claim has not been tested in a court, but is in any case a normative claim as much as, or more than, a legal claim.

Furthermore, since Hart wrote, a number of statutes have been seen as privileged. These include the European Communities Act 1972 and the three devolution statutes—to Scotland, Wales, and Northern Ireland—of 1998. In *R. v. Secretary of State for Transport, ex parte Factortame Ltd and Others (No. 2)* [1991] 1. A.C. 603, the Law Lords held that the Merchant Shipping Act 1988 was inconsistent with the 1972 and 1986 Acts governing the UK's membership of the European Union—and that the later, not the earlier, Act should give way. Lord Bridge's fig leaf is:

> If the supremacy within the European Community of Community law over the national law of member states was not always inherent in the E.E.C. Treaty (Cmnd 5179-II), it was certainly well established in the jurisprudence of the European Court of Justice long before the United Kingdom joined the Community. Thus, whatever limitation of its sovereignty Parliament accepted when it enacted the European Communities Act 1972 was entirely voluntary...[W]hen decisions of the European Court of Justice have exposed areas of United Kingdom statute law which failed to implement

Council directives, Parliament has always loyally accepted the obligation to make appropriate and prompt amendments (*R. v. Secretary of State for Transport, ex parte Factortame Ltd and Others (No. 2)* [1991] 1. A.C. 603 at 658–9).

The UK courts now hold that Parliament may bind its successors in certain respects. The recent *Jackson* judgment (*R. (Jackson and others) v. Attorney General.* [2006] 1 A.C. 262; see also Young 2006) reinforces this. In *Jackson*, which turned on the validity of the Parliament Act 1949 and thence on the exact meaning of the Parliament Act 1911, several of the judges joined in an opinion that the section of the 1911 Act which forbids the House of Commons from extending its life without Lords' consent is itself entrenched. It could not, as the appellants in *Jackson* had claimed, be altered in two stages, first by amending the 1911 Act to remove that restriction and then by enacting a prolongation of Parliament, both without Lords' consent. As to Parliamentary sovereignty, Lord Steyn said:

> We do not in the United Kingdom have an uncontrolled constitution as the Attorney General implausibly asserts. In the European context the second *Factortame* decision [1991] 1 AC 603 made that clear. The settlement contained in the Scotland Act 1998 also point[s] to a divided sovereignty. Moreover, the European Convention on Human Rights as incorporated into our law by the Human Rights Act 1998, created a new legal order. One must not assimilate the European Convention on Human Rights with multilateral treaties of the traditional type. Instead it is a legal order in which the United Kingdom assumes obligations to protect fundamental rights, not in relation to other states, but towards all individuals within its jurisdiction. The classic account given by Dicey of the doctrine of the supremacy of Parliament, pure and absolute as it was, can now be seen to be out of place in the modern United Kingdom (302).

And Lord Hope of Craighead (a Scottish judge) said:

> Step by step, gradually but surely, the English principle of the absolute legislative sovereignty of Parliament which Dicey derived from Coke and Blackstone is being qualified . . . It has been suggested that some of the provisions of the Acts of Union of 1707 (6 Anne c 11) (Scot c 7) are so fundamental that they lie beyond Parliament's power to legislate. Lord President Cooper in *MacCormick v Lord Advocate* 1953 SC 396, 411, 412 reserved his opinion on the question whether the provisions in article XIX of the Treaty of Union which purport to preserve the Court of Session and the laws relating to private right which are administered in Scotland are fundamental law which Parliament is not free to alter. Nevertheless by expressing himself as he did he went further than *Dicey, The Law of the Constitution*, 10th edition (1959), page 82 was prepared to go when he said

simply that it would be rash of Parliament to abolish Scots law courts and assimilate the law of Scotland to that of England (3034).

The Law Lords therefore (or at least some of them) are willing to accept that some statutes may be deemed to be entrenched and that to that extent parliamentary sovereignty is not absolute. The relevance of *Factortame*, the Act of Union, and human rights law to this claim are all discussed further in later chapters.

What is it about a statute that gives it a claim to entrenchment? There seem to be three categories:

1. a statute that embodies an agreement previously reached in a treaty (e.g. the Acts of Union 1706/7; the European Communities Act 1972; and perhaps the Human Rights Act 1998);
2. a statute that (purports to) amend the rule of recognition for future statutes (e.g. the Parliament Act 1911);
3. a statute that has been endorsed by referendum (e.g. the Scotland Act 1998; Government of Wales Act 1998; Northern Ireland Act 1998).

The Act of Union 1800, which Dicey held inviolable, does not qualify under any of those criteria. Although the Irish and British administrations agreed terms on which the Irish Parliament voted for its own abolition, that agreement was then dishonoured, because King George III ruled that widening Catholic civil rights violated his Coronation Oath. In his opposition to Irish Home Rule, Dicey could not argue by analogy from the 1706/7 Acts to that of 1800. That is perhaps why he formulated his arguments in terms of popular sovereignty. Unfortunately, as we have seen, they were extremely weak. He asserted both that the elected House of Commons did not represent the will of the people and that the unelected House of Lords could force an election to verify the will of the people. Dicey got George V to adopt his views. Prime Minister Asquith squashed them:

> The Parliament Act was not intended in any way to affect, and it is submitted has not affected, the Constitutional position of the Sovereign. It deals only with differences between the two Houses. When the two Houses are in agreement (as is always the case when there is a Conservative majority in the House of Commons), the Act is a dead letter.
>
> The demand . . . for a[n immediate] General Election . . . is open to objections of the most formidable character. (1) If such an election resulted in a majority for the Government, and the consequent passing of the Irish Bill next session, the recalcitrance of North-East Ulster would not in any way be affected. Sir E. Carson, and his friends have told the world, with obvious sincerity, that their objections to Home Rule have nothing

to do with the question whether it is approved or disapproved by the British electorate . . . (2) If such an election resulted in a Government defeat, the circumstances are such that neither in Ireland nor in Great Britain would it be accepted as a verdict adverse to Home Rule . . . .even when the bye-elections have gone against the Government, the attempt (wherever made) to arouse interest and resentment by pushing to the forefront the case against Home Rule and the supposed wrongs of Ulster, has met with no success. The General Election would be fought, as the bye-elections have been, not predominantly on Home Rule, but on the Insurance Act, the Marconi contract, and a score of other 'issues' which happened for the moment to preoccupy public attention. (3) The concession of the demand for a General Election, at this stage, would be in the teeth of the intentions of the Parliament Act. (Appendix to Chapter 12)

It is not difficult to construct a better argument than Dicey's for popular sovereignty. In 1787, the United States Framers did exactly that, in setting the criteria for ratification (minimum of nine states) and amendment of the US Constitution into the Constitution itself. Several states had already had ratifying conventions for their state constitutions, and more would follow. The Commonwealth of Australia followed the same path a century later.

Popular sovereignty has been an undercurrent of Scottish constitutionalism for a long time. It is implied, but not expressed, by Lord Cooper in *Mac-Cormick*. For if the Parliament is not sovereign in Scotland, the people are. So said the Claim of Right and subsequent Scottish Constitutional Convention (1989). These were of course unofficial bodies, but the Scotland Act follows the recommendations of the Scottish Constitutional Convention. A constitutional statute which is subject to a referendum, as were all three of the devolution statutes in 1997/8, is a small step towards popular sovereignty. But it leaves open the question 'Who are the people'? Dicey did not want the people of Ireland to vote in his proposed referendum on Irish Home Rule. But the people of England did not get a vote on the devolution statutes of the 1990s, which maybe they should have done.

Popular sovereignty implies an elected legislature. Dicey's claim that the elected Commons did not represent the people, but the unelected Lords did, was absurd. But no less absurd claims were made in the Commons and Lords debates on Lords reform in March 2007. An elected legislature is a necessary, but not sufficient condition for any claim that ultimate sovereignty lies with the people. The implications of this are the main theme of this book.

7

Causes and Consequences of the Unionist Coup d'État

CAUSES

What then possessed the Unionists to assert so fervently between 1909 and 1914 that they, and not the elected government, represented the people? In relation to the Budget, the Unionist peers initially argued that as it had not been put to the people they were justified in resisting it. That argument, and the peers' resistance, collapsed temporarily after the January 1910 election. But after the failure of the Unionist–Liberal talks in the summer and autumn of 1910 (for which see Jenkins 1968, ch. IX), it revived in full force. In Chapter 4, we showed that the Lords were still able to veto the land taxes proposed by the elected government's chancellor. All the evidence of the last three chapters also shows that the Unionists and the king did not accept the legitimacy of the Parliament Act.

To explain the first phase of the constitutional crisis (from Budget to Parliament Act), it is probably sufficient to fall back on the vulgar Marxism introduced earlier. The Budget and the Parliament Bill felt like threats to the vital interests of the landed class, and to a lesser degree those of the Church of England, whose own material interests were largely invested in land (Peterson and McLean 2007; on the landed interest more generally, Offer 1981; Adonis 1993).

Karl Marx himself was as clear and eloquent on class in Britain as any subsequent Marxist. Explaining the 1852 election to readers in the United States, he wrote:

> Whigs, Free Traders and Peelites coalesced to oppose the Tories. It was between this coalition on one side, and the Tories on the other, that the real electoral battle was fought . . . Opposed to . . . entire official England, were the Chartists . . . The fatal year, 1846, with its repeal of the Corn Laws, and the shout of distress which this repeal forced from the Tories, proved that they were enthusiasts for nothing but the rent of land . . . The year 1846 brought to light in its nakedness the *substantial class interest* which forms

the *real base* of the Tory party . . . They are distinguished from the other Bourgeois, in the same way as the rent of land is distinguished from commercial and industrial profit. Rent of land is conservative, profit is progressive; rent of land is national, profit is cosmopolitical; rent of land believes in the State church, profit is a dissenter by birth. The repeal of the Corn Laws of 1846 merely recognized an already accomplished fact, a change long since enacted in the elements of British civil society, viz., the subordination of the landed interest under the moneyed interest, of property under commerce, of agriculture under manufacturing industry, of the country under the city. Could this fact be doubted since the country population stands, in England, to the towns' population in the proportion of one to three? (Marx 1852: 351–3).

For Marx, Repeal of the Corn Laws in 1846 marked the triumph of the bourgeoisie over the landed class. The proletariat, represented by the Chartists, were waiting in the wings. His analysis is brilliant but fatally undermined by his failure to think about the House of Lords and its veto. In 1846 the Lords, under the Duke of Wellington, withheld their veto over the revolutionary change in property rights introduced by Corn Law repeal. From the 1880s, under Lord Salisbury and his successors, the Lords became a much more active veto player on behalf of their class interest (Chapter 11). Salisbury knew when it was prudent to give in—for instance over the Irish Church in 1868 and over redistribution and electoral reform in 1884–5 (see, generally, Adonis 1993: ch. 5). His successors lacked his subtlety, hence the constitutional crisis.

It is customary to say that the Lords 'lost' the constitutional battle in 1911. In one sense that is obviously true. But they won some battles in the class war; and in others, they staged a retreat so slow that the triumph of the bourgeoisie over the landed interest came not, as Marx believed, in 1846, but in 1918. In Chapter 4 we saw that that was true of land tax. The Lords had not resisted some measures of the 'new liberalism', notably the Trades Disputes Act 1906, which gave legal privileges to trade unions beyond anything the Chartists could have dreamt of. Nor did they resist whisky duties. Their resistance to 'supertax' (i.e. progressive income tax) was crushed by their overreach in 1909. But on the land and the church which (if we accept Marx's analysis) was tied to the material interest of land, they continued to resist. The intended beneficiaries of Welsh disestablishment did not get their money until the 1940s, and then at a fraction of the rate intended in the Welsh Church Act 1914 (Peterson and Mclean 2007). Adonis (1993: ch. 4) also shows that from 1850 to 1914 the private bill procedure, which adjusted property rights in order to allow railways, tramways, and waterworks to be built, was tightly controlled by a succession of four Unionist peers who doughtily protected the private interests of existing real estate holders.

But as we have seen, the coup d'état came in the final phase of the Lords' resistance, over Ireland. Why were the Unionists so passionate about Ireland? A Marxist answer takes us some of the way: Irish landowners were disproportionately represented among Unionist peers. However, this explanation does not get us far for two reasons: (*a*) Salisbury realized, for reasons of public order, that the Liberals' Irish Land Bill of 1881 was one where the Tory peers must abandon their protection of landed property rights (Adonis 1993: 128); (*b*) although Southern Irish landlords (especially Lords Lansdowne and Midleton) remained powerful in the Unionist leadership in the Lords through the coup d'état, their material interest had been largely extinguished by the Unionists' own Irish Land Act of 1903. As we saw above, the coup d'état was staged on behalf of (largely Presbyterian) Ulster Protestants, not of Church of Ireland Ascendancy landowners.

The roots of the coup d'état therefore lie in empire and (rather oddly) an appeal to the people. As to empire, Salisbury told the Lords in 1889: 'We are engaged upon an enterprise of momentous importance, that of keeping unimpaired the unity of an Empire which has never been divided yet' (speech in Lords, 21.02.89, quoted by Adonis 1993: 129: Salisbury seems to have overlooked American independence). Irish nationalism must be resisted because if Ireland broke away, who knows where might be next? The new colonies and protectorates in the tropics that were being rapidly added to the empire? The Boer colonies in South Africa? Above all, the jewel in the crown, India?

Imperialism was widely popular because it provided jobs for Britons in many different parts of the class structure. Younger sons of peers could go out and govern New South Wales, or serve abroad in the British or Indian Army. Professionals excluded from the UK hierarchy, perhaps because they were not Oxford or Cambridge graduates, had vast opportunities in the Empire, for instance as doctors, administrators, railway and marine engineers. Scots were particularly prominent in this stratum. The Empire also offered emigration opportunities for the working class. Numerous studies have tracked the popular support for imperialism in this period (cf. McKenzie and Silver 1968; Powell 1977; Pugh 1985).

The dark side of Empire was contempt for 'the lesser breeds without the Law', as Rudyard Kipling called them. By that phrase Kipling did not actually mean black Africans and Asians. He meant inferior Europeans. The inferior Europeans closest at hand were the Irish—the majority Irish that is, namely the Catholic, mostly rural, population devastated in the famine of the 1840s and then spread about the cities of Britain and America. Lord Salisbury compared Irish people to Hottentots[1] (Cecil 1921, vol. 3: 302; for the context see Chapter 11). Dicey (1886: 89–90) stated that the English were

> ripe for Protestantism at a time when the people of Ireland had hardly risen to the level of Roman Catholicism.

For Salisbury and Dicey, as for many others, the Irish (and Catholicism) were lower on the evolutionary ladder than the English (and Protestantism). 'Paddy' was a stereotype beloved of 'Mr Punch' and other cartoonists (Foster 1995). The Protestant Irish, on the other hand, were regarded as 'grim, dogged, determined "ghazis" with good leaders and a certain amount of discipline', in the words of George V's equerry in 1914 (Chapter 12).

Add this to the referendal concept of democracy being advanced by Dicey (Chapter 6) and Salisbury (Chapter 11) and you get the two versions of the ideology which drove the 1914 coup.

- Version 1: The Liberal Government is riding roughshod over the people and has refused to put its policy before them. Therefore, the people are entitled to resist.
- Version 2: The people of Ulster are being denied a say in something that vitally affects them.

The difficulty with Version 1 is that when Unionists counted the people, the people of Ireland did not count. The difficulty with Version 2 is that when Unionists counted the people of Ulster, the Nationalist people of Ulster did not count. We have already given examples of this myopia: here are a few more. In 1912, Bonar Law told a Catholic correspondent that 'the population there [in Ulster] is homogeneous' (Law to Lady N. Crichton Stuart, 10.07.1912, quoted by Blake 1955: 126). Table 5.4 was compiled from the 1911 census and was published by a commercial map-maker, and was therefore available to all at the time. The copy we use is itself a historic document. It is the copy on which Secretary of War Seely scribbled the names and locations of the arms dumps he asked Sir Arthur Paget to order the army to protect (Chapter 5). Seely knew which dumps were in Protestant, and which in Catholic, territory (copy in Mottistone Papers, Nuffield College, Oxford).

Table 5.4 shows that Irish nationalists were simply invisible to Unionist eyes. Dicey stated that, as an 'old Benthamite', he put the welfare of the 40 million British ahead of that of the 3 million nationalist Irish (Dicey 1913, p. ix). He did not want the nationalist Irish to have a vote in the referendum he was demanding. And yet, Unionists insisted, they must forever remain citizens of the United Kingdom. Dicey's theory of popular sovereignty fails.

Dicey's equally eminent colleague Sir William Anson, Warden of All Souls College, Oxford, and author of those constitutional textbooks of the day not written by Dicey, was a former Liberal candidate who had become a Liberal Unionist. His Version 2 statement similarly shows complete unawareness of the data in Table 5.4. Writing to *The Times* after the Curragh, he says:

> A body of good and loyal citizens find that they are about to be driven outside the pale of the Constitution . . . If the Covenanters meet [that] with armed resistance, I for one believe, *with a conviction which no results of a Referendum or a General Election can alter,* that they are justified in their resistance. . . . [T]he cession of Ulster to the Nationalists . . . in face of the determined opposition of the men who have made the prosperity of Ulster, is an outrage which takes us outside the accustomed bounds of political obligation . . . Ministers know that the passing of the Home Rule Bill will be the equivalent of a declaration of war (Anson 1914; my emphasis).

Anson, at the time MP for Oxford University and tutor on the constitution to the Prince of Wales (later Edward VIII), is thus even more extreme than Dicey or Law. For him, the right of Ulster Protestants to rebel trumps any referendum in the United Kingdom as a whole, or election majority. Versions 1 and 2 of the coup ideology were inconsistent.

One problem with Dicey's (or anybody else's) referendum is: in what territory? After the Curragh, the king's secretary, Lord Stamfordham, wrote helpfully to Bonar Law:

> If the Govt will not have referendum on the liberal terms you offered— could you not press for exclusion of 6 counties without referendum—(by these means you wd avoid certain zones) and for an unlimited period—and increase the subsidy from the English treasury to say 5 millions. Worth the money! (Stamfordham to Bonar Law, 22.03.14. Parliamentary Archives, Bonar Law MSS 72/1/65).

The constitutional implications of a letter from the King's secretary to the leader of the Opposition, advising him how best to resist His Majesty's Government, are interesting. This practical suggestion from one fervent Unionist to another presages what happened. The six counties of Northern Ireland were indeed excluded from the rest of Ireland without a referendum. The subsidy from the British Treasury has continued to flow. And 'certain zones' were avoided. By that delicate phrase, Stamfordham probably means the nationalist districts within Northern Ireland, especially in Fermanagh, Tyrone, Derry City, west Belfast, and southern Armagh, which would have inconveniently voted the wrong way in any referendum.

The Unionist theory of popular sovereignty thus had the following flaws:

1. It ignored the fact that the electorate had voted three times in a row for the Home Rule coalition, at least the second and third times in the full knowledge that voting for it would lead to a Home Rule Bill.

2. It ignored the one representative argument that was readily to hand: namely that Ireland was malapportioned. The number of seats assigned to Ireland was left at 105 in 1884–5, presumably because neither Gladstone nor Salisbury wanted to incur Irish wrath.[2] Boundaries within Ireland had not been redrawn since 1885; Ireland as a whole was now overrepresented. The population of Catholic Ireland was declining, at least relatively: whereas that of Protestant Ireland was increasing. Furthermore, the Protestant population was inefficiently lumped (from the point of view of maximizing seats). Unionists held their seats by huge majorities; Nationalists by smaller ones (Table 5.4).Therefore, Nationalists held a majority of seats in Ulster.

3. It assumed, without evidence, that 'the people' would vote down Home Rule in a referendum; and that they would vote Unionist in a General Election. There is no evidence to support either hypothesis in the trend of by-election results. The Unionists had done well in 1911 and 1912 (as Oppositions usually do in mid-term); but as the date for the general election that was due by autumn 1915 at latest approached, the parties were back where they had been in December 1910 (see Table 11.1).

4. It was unclear as to which people should vote in any such referendum. (*a*) The people of the whole United Kingdom? (*b*) The people of Great Britain? (*c*) The people of Ireland? (*d*) The people of Ulster? (*e*) The people of predominantly Protestant Ulster? (*f*) The people of predominantly Catholic Ulster? How groups (*a*) and (*b*) would have voted is unknown, but there is no convincing evidence that they would have rejected Home Rule. They had voted three times in a row for a pro-Home Rule coalition of parties. Group (*c*) would have overwhelmingly supported it. Group (*d*) would have narrowly rejected it. Group (*e*) would have overwhelmingly rejected it. Group (*f*) would have overwhelmingly supported it.

A non-contradictory theory of popular sovereignty therefore requires at least that the legislature be elected and that the coalition which can command a majority there is entitled to have its programme enacted until the next general election. It may also involve the referendum, but who should vote in such a referendum is not always clear. These remain current issues, as we shall see.

CONSEQUENCES

It is worth starting with the fact that the Unionists' attempted coup d'état has rarely been recognized as such (Bayly 2000). And yet, Sir Henry Wilson, Director of Military Operations at the War Office, told the Ulster Protestant paramilitaries where British troops were about to be deployed against them. It is certain that Bonar Law, the Leader of the Opposition, encouraged the paramilitary revolt; it is likely, although not certain, that he was complicit in financing it (Jackson [2003: 133, 327]; Appendix to Chapter 5). The most surprising fact about this evidence is how little it seems to have upset the conventional narrative of the wisdom, flexibility, etc., of the unwritten British Constitution. Two successive kings imposed conditions on their Liberal Governments that helped to force elections which the Unionists might have won. The second king apparently came close to either dismissing the Liberal Government or refusing Royal Assent to the Government of Ireland Act in 1913–14. By comparison, the behaviour of Sir George Murray in 1908–9 is relatively mild. The Unionists' inconsistent demands simultaneously to treat Ireland as an indissoluble part of the Union and to ignore the votes of Ireland's elected MPs led to the coup d'état attempt of 1914. George V, Bonar Law, Sir Henry Wilson, and even Sir George Murray may not have viewed their conduct as an attempt to unseat the elected government without recourse to an election: but such it undoubtedly was. If the Irish Party was invisible to Unionists, they could discount the mere parliamentary majority against them. Hence the sudden increase in the number of veto players in British politics from 1906 to 1914.

But one looks in vain for any sign of surprise in much of the modern historical literature, let alone in most of the few political scientists and constitutional lawyers who consider these events. Because the best-known statement of the gravity of the constitutional crisis is shrill and unbalanced (Dangerfield 1936; but cf. Ensor 1936: 473–9), the idea that either there was no crisis or that if there was one it was provoked by the Liberals has gained ground by default. Bogdanor (1995: 309), in his text on the UK monarchy, concludes that the United Kingdom is one of 'a small number of favoured nations' in which constitutional monarchy 'far from undermining democracy . . . serves to sustain and strengthen democratic institutions'. It is hard to see how he reaches this conclusion in the face of his copious evidence about (especially) George V and his advisers between 1910 and 1914. From the same evidence base I reach opposite conclusions.

This myopia arises from failure to understand how sharply the veto game of British politics changed for the period this chapter discusses. Historians, and some political scientists, have failed to appreciate that the Irish Party was a partisan veto player for the periods stated (and that the Labour Party never was until 1923). The institutional veto plays of the Lords have been under-estimated, partly because detailed evidence has not been understood in a veto game context (e.g., that the threat of their veto forced the 1909 Budget to be written in an impracticable way), partly because the range of policies that Liberal Governments did not even try to implement before 1911 is not fully considered. (Think about Welsh disestablishment, which an overwhelming majority of MPs for Wales had been demanding since 1868). The institutional veto plays of successive monarchs have been inexplicably understated, despite the ample evidence of them that this book draws on.

Did the veto game structure affect the winset of the status quo in British politics? Yes, profoundly, and in ways which remain to be mapped carefully although historians have been writing about them for centuries. As a first rough structure we suggest the following (for England only). Until 1640 the monarch was the unique domestic veto player. From 1640 to 1689 a 'long revolution' occurred. During those years of civil war, restoration, and deposition of James II, it was established (so all constitutional actors believed) that the monarch was no longer an institutional veto player. Each House of Parliament was a full veto player except on financial matters, where the House of Commons was the unique institutional veto player. The pattern of partisan veto players depended on party structure in the Commons. Party structure in the Lords was invariant after about 1815. The Lords were always Conservative, but successive Conservative leaders in the Lords could decide to use or withhold their veto power (Chapter 11). The crisis of 1909–11 shook these beliefs. It is normal to say that after 1911 it was established that the House of Commons was the unique institutional veto player. But this state-ment needs qualification. First of all, the leaders of the Opposition, the king, and the House of Lords did not accept this from 1911 to 1914. Secondly, except in the last year or two of a Parliament, the House of Lords retains its practical veto on non-financial matters.

This suggests a stable core to British politics throughout the long nine-teenth century, given that the optima of the median peer and the median MP would not be particularly close. The House of Lords was by construction almost exclusively a landed house. The House of Commons contained repre-sentatives of capital—especially finance capital but later also industrial capital—from the eighteenth century. Representatives of Labour never joined a governing coalition directly until 1915, although sometimes (as with the Trades Disputes Act 1906) the representatives of land and capital would combine to enact a pro-Labour measure for electoral reasons or reasons of preserving social order. Apart from such concessions, the 'contract line', as game theorists call it, for policy embraced the points acceptable to the median representative of land and the median representative of capital. That modern Marxist story explains why Marx was wrong about 1846.

From 1914 to 1999 the influence of land did not simply vanish. It stalled the redistribution enacted by the Welsh disestablishment bill for three decades. It continued to block land taxation and serious discussion of church establishment. However, the main consequence of the coup d'état was for Ireland, and especially Northern Ireland.

Probably, neither the Commons nor the Lords realized at the time of their bargaining in 1911 what effects 2.(4) of the Act as enacted would have:

> (4) A Bill shall be deemed to be the same Bill as a former Bill sent up to the House of Lords in the preceding session if, when it is sent up to the House of Lords, it is identical with the former Bill or contains only such alterations as are certified by the Speaker of the House of Commons to be necessary owing to the time which has elapsed since the date of the former Bill, or to represent any amendments which have been made by the House of Lords in the former Bill in the preceding session. (Parliament Act 1911 2(4))

The subsection has a proviso that amendments can nevertheless be made if the Lords agree to them. But in the Home Rule bargaining game of 1912–14, this proviso was irrelevant. The Lords had an incentive to oppose rather than to amend the bill each time they encountered it. They did. This ensured that the bill, when finally enacted in spring 1914, would be as bad as it possibly could be (from the median Lord's standpoint). The median Lord *wanted* the Act to be as bad as it possibly could, so that he could say that it coerced Ulster, had not been submitted to the people, violated the Constitution, and did all the other terrible things that we have copiously documented them as saying.

With the wisdom of hindsight, of course, Asquith and colleagues should have included some opt-out for Protestant Ulster when they introduced the bill in 1912. The Liberal backbencher Thomas Agar-Robartes proposed an opt-out for the four most Protestant counties when the bill had its first run through the Commons (Jackson 2003: 122). Of course that would have led to a furious row with the pivotal Irish Party, which would nevertheless have accepted a Home Rule Bill with an opt-out rather than no Home Rule Bill. In 1912, however, Asquith and colleagues did not know that the new leadership of the Opposition would be willing to threaten a paramilitary coup against the Bill. Sheer convenience may have driven them to reject the Agar–Robartes Amendment. For instance, the bill already required revenue collection to be split between Britain and Ireland. Splitting it three ways would have increased the transaction costs of Home Rule still more. Section 2(4) of the Parliament Act locked them into submitting an identical bill to the Lords three times, even when it had become obvious that its failure to allow Protestant Ulster an opt-out was likely to lead to paramilitary resistance. This suited the Opposition and (at least in the short run) the Ulster Protestants. It did not suit the peace and good government of Ireland. I roundly reject the claim that the tragedy was largely or even substantially the fault of Asquith's myopia (see e.g. Jalland 1980).

During and after the First World War, the Irish Party collapsed in favour of Sinn Fein, which promised to boycott the Westminster Parliament and declare itself the provisional government of Ireland. There were numerous reasons for this switch, including the bloody suppression of the Easter Rising in 1916 and the attempt to extend conscription to Ireland in 1918. But the failure of the Irish Party to get by constitutional means the object for which it had been formed, after returning huge nationalist majorities to Westminster in every Parliament since 1885, undoubtedly contributed. As Asquith told George V in response to the latter's complaints about likely disorder in Ulster:

> On the other hand, if the Bill is rejected or indefinitely postponed, or some inadequate and disappointing substitute put forward in its place, the prospect is, in my opinion, much more grave. The attainment of Home Rule has for more than 30 years been the political (as distinguished from the agrarian) ideal of four-fifths of the Irish people. Whatever happens in other parts of the United Kingdom, at successive general elections, the Irish representation in Parliament never varies. For the last 8 years they have had with them a substantial majority of the elected representatives of Great Britain. The Parliament of 1906 was debarred by election pledges from dealing with the matter legislatively, but during its lifetime, in 1908, the House of Commons affirmed by an overwhelming majority a resolution in favour of the principle. In the present Parliament, the Government of Ireland Bill has passed that House in two successive sessions, with British majorities which showed no sign of diminution from first to last. If it had been taken up by a Conservative Government, it would more than a year ago have been the law of the land. It is the confident expectation of the vast bulk of the Irish people that it will become law next year.
>
> If the ship, after so many stormy voyages, were now to be wrecked in sight of port, it is difficult to overrate the shock, or its consequences. They would extend into every department of political, social, agrarian and domestic life. It is not too much to say that Ireland would become ungovernable—unless by the application of forces and methods which would offend the conscience of Great Britain, and arouse the deepest resentment in all the self-governing Dominions of the Crown. (Appendix to Chapter 12)

Asquith's prediction was borne out to the letter between 1918 and 1921. The Sinn Fein members elected in the UK General Election of 1918 refused to take their seats, but constituted themselves as the First Dail of (what became) the Irish Free State. Three years of guerrilla war, which had exactly the reputational consequences for Britain that Asquith had predicted, led to a truce in summer 1921 and a treaty in December of that year (McLean 2001*a*: chapter 7). The treaty was ratified in both countries and the Irish Free State came into existence, without the six counties of present-day Northern Ireland. However, the large minority of the Second Dail who did not accept the Treaty terms rebelled, and a civil war ensued, won by the pro-Treaty faction.

Meanwhile the British Coalition government had drafted what became the Government of Ireland Act 1920. Prime Minister Lloyd George, by this time more or less a prisoner of the Unionists who held an absolute majority of seats in the Commons (and with no Irish allies left in the House), allowed the Unionists, in the shape of Walter Long, to draft the bill. Long had certainly been complicit in the Larne gun-running (unless Crawford was a complete fantasist): but for that very reason, he could prevent a Unionist revolt in either house of Parliament over the terms of the bill.

The Government of Ireland Act (1920 c.67) provided for a Parliament for each of Southern Ireland and Northern Ireland, with a Council of Ireland overarching them. However, as in 1918, the Sinn Fein members elected to the Parliament of Southern Ireland refused to take their seats there, and constituted themselves as the Second Dail. The Council of Ireland also fell, leaving only Northern Ireland with that Home Rule that Carson and Crawford had brought 30,000 rifles to Larne to resist. Northern Ireland was temporarily defined to comprise the six north-eastern counties of Ireland, four of which were majority Protestant and two of which (Fermanagh and Tyrone) were majority Catholic. The three most Catholic counties of pre-1920 Ulster, namely, Cavan, Monaghan, and Donegal (Table 5.4) were assigned to Southern Ireland and became part of the Irish Free State (since 1949 the Republic of Ireland).

An essential part of Lloyd George's game plan to get the treaty through three parliaments and three executives, in none of which he controlled a majority, was a Boundary Commission (McLean 2001*a*: chapter 7). Irish negotiators understood it to be a body that would squeeze the Protestant North to a size that would become economically unviable and force it to come into the Free State. Ulster Unionists understood it to be a body which protected the integrity of Northern Ireland. When the Commission reported in 1925, it was much closer to the Unionist than to the Free State expectations. It would have moved (on 1911 Census figures) 31,319 people from Northern Ireland to the Free State, and 7,594 the other way. It would have moved 32,673 people the 'right' way (Catholics into the Free State plus non-Catholics out of it), and 6,240 people the 'wrong' way (Catholics into Northern Ireland plus non-Catholics out of it). (Hand 1969, my calculations from tables in text). However, before the report was published, its Unionist member had leaked it to the hard-right *Morning Post*. This led to the resignation of the Free State member, and to the later agreement of all parties to leave the boundary as defined in the 1920 Act and to suppress the report, which was not published until 1969 (Hand 1969; Blake 1995).

The leak to the *Morning Post* led to a strategic difference among Ulster Unionists. The leaker, J. R. Fisher, had seen the boundary in military terms:

> With North Monaghan *in* Ulster and South Armagh *out*, we should have a solid ethnographic and strategic frontier to the South, and a hostile 'Afghanistan' on our north-west frontier [i.e., Co. Donegal] would be placed in safe keeping. (Fisher 1922, in Gwynn 1950: 215–6; stress in original)

The leakee, James Craig, Prime Minister of Northern Ireland, saw it in primordial terms: 'no surrender', which had been the slogan of militant Ulster Protestantism since 1689. Craig won the intra-Unionist argument, though Fisher had been more perceptive. South Armagh has always been (from an Ulster Protestant perspective) the most troublesome part of Northern Ireland and the heartland of paramilitary republicanism.

When Michael Collins, one of the Irish delegation at the Treaty talks, noted of his conversation with Lloyd George that the latter 'remarked that I myself pointed out on a previous occasion that the North would be forced economically to come in', he was half right.[3] If Northern Ireland had been reduced to its Protestant core *and if* it had been fiscally responsible in the way envisaged in all four Home Rule statutes, it would probably have been fiscally unviable. Neither condition applied. The 1920 Act assigned the revenue from most tax collected in Ireland to the Irish governments (s.22). It followed all its predecessors in envisaging that (Northern) Ireland would then pay back an 'imperial contribution' to the UK Treasury as its contribution to paying for reserved services. These arrangements never worked. Northern Ireland's assigned tax receipts never covered even the cost of local services. The 'imperial contribution' flowed the other way, from HM Treasury to Northern Ireland (Mitchell 2006). It kept Northern Ireland in the Empire. Whatever might be the right fiscal arrangements for devolution (to be discussed below), the 1920 Act did not get them right: presumably, therefore, neither would the 1886, 1893, or 1912 provisions if they had been brought into force.

What was the human cost of the Unionist coup d'état? That is unknowable. We do not know how much blood would have been shed in Ulster if the 1914 Act had proceeded unhindered by the First World War, and/or if an opt-out for Protestant Ulster had been negotiated. We do know how much blood was shed in the Anglo–Irish guerrilla war between 1918 and 1921; and in Northern Ireland and elsewhere as a result of paramilitary violence and state response to it between 1968 and 1998. The death toll in the first has been estimated at about 1,400; in the second, at 3,524 for the years 1969–2001 (Hopkinson 2002; data compiled by Malcolm Sutton at http://cain.ulst.ac.uk/sutton/tables/Year.html). We also know that in 1930 George V said to Prime Minister Ramsay MacDonald:

> What fools we were not to have accepted Gladstone's Home Rule Bill. The empire now would not have had the Irish Free state giving us so much trouble and pulling us to pieces. (Rose 1983: 240)

Part III

The Erosion of Diceyan Ideology

8

The Impact of UK Devolution

This chapter is not a history of devolution to Scotland, Wales, and Northern Ireland within the United Kingdom. Millions of words have been written about that, some of them by me with co-authors (especially McLean and McMillan 2005). Rather, it aims to explain *why* devolution has occurred, and what that implies for the traditional constitution of the United Kingdom.

SCOTLAND: A DIGESTED HISTORY, DIGESTED

The settlement of 1707 was successively unpopular, popular, ignored, and questioned. As noted above, it was wildly unpopular at enactment, if the riots and petitions are anything to go by. There were three Jacobite rebellions in 1708, 1715, and 1745–6. The second and third of these led to the last pitched battles on the British soil. On the other side, the Union was equally unpopular with strict Presbyterians. But as the two groups opposed to Union had nothing in common with one another, the Union survived. The Jacobites could win or draw a battle (Sheriffmuir in 1715; Prestonpans in 1745), but not a war. Bonnie Prince Charlie set up his court in the Palace of Holyroodhouse. After Prestonpans he invaded England, but fizzled out at Derby, not noted for either its Jacobites or its Presbyterians. Within twenty years Scotland had experienced the huge economic, social, and cultural surge known as the Scottish Enlightenment. It has spread its tentacles all over the world, as detailed in various places in this book.

The integration of the Scottish economy with England's produced far bigger advantages, per head, to the Scots than to the English. By opening the British Empire to them it created jobs, above all, for those trained in skills and professions where Scots training was better than English. Scots doctors, engineers (both graduates and technicians), Presbyterian ministers, and people who, if they had not been barred by religion or lack of cash, might have gone to Oxford or Cambridge,[1] sustained both the general staff and the NCOs of the British Empire.

As for Presbyterian suspicion of Union, Scots who cared about church and state could get angry, with good reason, at the way the main Scottish churches were treated by the UK Parliament and the Law Lords. In 1904 the Law Lords handed the property of about 1,100 ministers and parishes of the United Free Church to a splinter group of about 24 ministers, on the grounds that the latter's theology was sounder (Rodger 2008: 98–108). However, Scots not concerned about church and state were untroubled. The settlement of 1921–25 removed church and state as a ground for Scottish devolution.

The decline of the British Empire also did not immediately lead to demands for devolution. Rather, the rise of the Labour Party and the collapse of the capital-goods industries of the Empire such as shipbuilding and locomotive construction, between 1931 and 1960, threw attention on the United Kingdom as a social insurance device. However inadequate the dole, it was more than an independent Scotland could have afforded. The same was true of the collapse of the coal industry in Wales and of shipbuilding in Northern Ireland. When unemployment is structural rather than (or as well as) cyclical, then social insurance can damp the shock in the worst-affected areas. Imbued in the politics of industry, depression, unemployment, and social welfare, the Labour Party had abandoned its Home Rule origins in both Scotland and Wales by 1929. It did not return until 1974, and then for very different reasons.

The Conservatives were the party of what we have called 'primordial Unionism' (McLean and McMillan 2005: 122–34). The Union was to be upheld *because it was there*. Officially named the *Conservative and Unionist Party* until recently, in Scotland it was in fact the *Unionist Party* pure and simple for many decades. The Union in question was that with Ireland, not with Scotland; but unionism was a general principle. If you let Ireland go, which part of the Empire would go next? Canada? India? Scotland?

Administrative and some financial devolution to Scotland dates back to the 1880s, as a by-product of attempts to keep Ireland in the Union (for a comprehensive history see Mitchell 2003). Administrative devolution meant that all the main functions of government in Scotland, except social protection, have been run from Scotland, by Scottish civil servants as part of a unified Civil Service across Great Britain.[2] Financial devolution means that many of those functions are financed out of general UK-wide taxation, from the proceeds of which a block grant is made over to the Scottish civil service.

In the years of administrative devolution, both Scotland and (Northern) Ireland have done very well. In previous writing I have argued that this arises from the credible threat that Scotland and Ireland (later Northern Ireland) pose to the Union. When there was any threat to their generous public spending, the relevant Secretary of State could always argue in Cabinet that any cut would fuel nationalist resentment and imperil the Union. Hence the block grant has in recent years given Scotland and Northern Ireland (but not Wales) more to spend per head than an assessment of relative needs would give them. Perhaps because that is common knowledge in the world of public finance (although it is not often shared with the Scottish electorate), there has only been one interdepartmental needs assessment in modern times (HM Treasury 1979; McLean, Lodge, and Schmuecker 2008).

The Scottish National Party (SNP) dates back to 1928 (McLean 1969). In its early decades it expounded cultural rather than economic nationalism. It won a parliamentary by-election in 1945, during the wartime truce between the main parties, but promptly lost the seat again at the 1945 general election. It first became electorally competitive in the mid-1960s, when the Wilson Labour government of 1964–70 encountered deep political and economic difficulty. It subsided in 1970, winning just one seat in that year's general election. But the discovery of oil in the North Sea then enabled the SNP to claim, as it has ever since, that *It's Scotland's oil.* For the first time that gave it a credibility beyond the ranks of cultural nationalists and the temporarily disgruntled.

Elsewhere (e.g. in McLean and McMillan 2005, Chapter 7) we have told the story of the shotgun conversion of the Labour Party to devolution in the summer of 1974. Misreading opinion polls to say that the Scots wanted independence or devolution (read more carefully, they show that if offered more public spending the Scots would accept it), Wilson forced the unwilling Scottish Labour Party to say that it wanted devolution. There was no devolution in the Labour Party itself. The Conservatives also flirted with devolution, from 1968 to 1979. The SNP reached its Westminster high-water mark in the general election of October 1974, when it beat the Conservatives into third place, winning 30 per cent of the Scottish vote. Because its vote was evenly distributed around Scotland this translated into only 11 of the 72 Scottish seats (15 per cent). This even distribution, as was common knowledge, would turn from curse to blessing if their vote advanced only a few percentage points. At about 35 per cent of the vote, the SNP would win a majority of seats in Scotland under the first-past-the-post electoral system for the UK Parliament. It would then be in a position to open talks on independence. The Wilson (later Callaghan) Labour government of 1974–9 therefore made a devolution scheme for Scotland and Wales its flagship policy. Flagships are especially vulnerable to enemy fire. This one sank in February 1977, victim of a 'Geordie revolt'. Labour MPs from the north-east of England complained that devolution would only further entrench Scotland's spending advantage, compared to their region which was as poor as Scotland but received considerably less public expenditure per head.[3] Labour proceeded with separate referenda on devolution for Scotland and Wales. In Wales the proposal was heavily defeated; in Scotland it narrowly passed but Labour were unable to implement it because of another backbench revolt. However the SNP, after peaking in 1975, had sunk again in the polls. In March 1979 the Callaghan government lost a confidence vote on the collapse of its policy. In the ensuing general election, Margaret Thatcher, described by a colleague as 'the most Unionist politician in Downing Street since the war' (Young 1990: 465) swept to power, and immediately ditched Scottish devolution.

And nothing happened. There were no riots in the streets of Edinburgh. It seemed that the demand for devolution had been broad but not deep. Not till after Margaret Thatcher's third successive general election victory in 1987 did the devolutionist forces stir in Scotland. Rather suddenly, they noticed that a Government which held only ten seats in Scotland—one fewer than the SNP had won in October 1974—could implement deeply unpopular policies there, such as the poll tax, which was piloted in Scotland a year ahead of England and Wales.

When devolution revived in 1988–9 it was in the hands of cultural nationalists. They called their manifesto, significantly, a Claim of Right. This title had more resonance than most people noticed. In 1689 the Scottish Parliament had enacted a Claim of Right Act deposing James VII in favour of William III. It stated in the preamble:

> Wheras King James the Seventh . . . Did By the advyce of wicked and evill Counsellers Invade the fundamentall Constitution of this Kingdome And altered it from a legall limited monarchy to ane Arbitrary Despotick power.

As part of the contract to make William the Parliament-chosen monarch of Scotland, the Act goes on to list certain basic civil liberties. Announcing that William and his wife Mary had promised to honour those civil liberties, the Act continues:

> Haveing therfor ane entire confidence that his said Majesty the King of England will perfect the Delyverance so far advanced by him and will still preserve them from violation of their Rights which they have here asserted and from all other attempts upon their Religion lawes and liberties,

> The said Estates of the Kingdome of Scotland Doe resolve that William and Mary King and Queen of England France and Ireland Be and be Declared King and Queen of Scotland (Claim of Right Act 1689, at http://www.rahbarnes.demon.co.uk/clai1689.htm).

As with the English Convention Parliaments of 1660 and 1689, and the US Constitutional Convention of 1787, the constitutional status of the Convention Parliament which enacted the Claim of Right is itself unclear. It purported to legitimate itself by saying that James VII had never taken the required oath. But the plain political fact was that it had deposed one king and invited another to take office on terms it laid down, which the incoming king agreed.[4]

In whose name did these revolutionary conventions act? The Americans were unambiguous, choosing the wording 'We the people of the United States ... do ordain and establish this Constitution'. In both England and Scotland the idea that Parliament was acting for the People was in the air; in neither was it explicit. In England, the dangerous radicalism of Thomas Rainborough was associated with the regime that the Convention of 1660 was called to abolish. John Locke developed the doctrine that the king governed by the consent of the people, which James II (VII) had forfeited. But he did not publish that doctrine until 1690. So the English did not use Putney (Rainborough) language in 1689 either. Therefore, the Scots came closer than the English, in 1689, to stating that they were acting in the name of the people. In their covering letter to William asking him to accept the crown of Scotland on the terms offered, the Scottish Convention Parliament referred to the 'petition or claim of right of the subjects of this Kingdom'.

Three centuries later, the promoters of the new Claim of Right were unambiguous. 'We acknowledge the sovereign right of the Scottish people to determine the form of Government best suited to their needs', they said. The Claim of Right served as the preamble to the report of the Scottish Constitutional Convention. This convention was a private initiative supported by the Labour and Liberal Democrat parties in Scotland, various civil society organizations and churches. Its chair was an Episcopal clergyman. The Conservatives and Scottish Nationalists stayed out. Nevertheless, the constitution drafted by the Convention became, with few alterations, the Scotland Act 1998 after a two-pronged referendum of 1997. In this referendum, the Scottish electorate voted strongly for an elected parliament and (by a smaller margin) for it to have powers to tax. Donald Dewar, who became Scotland's first First Minister, repeated a phrase from John Smith (Tony Blair's predecessor as UK Labour leader) when he described a Scottish Parliament as 'the settled will of the Scottish people'.

The Scotland Act does some things well and some things badly. On the whole, the things that the Constitutional Convention discussed have turned out well. The Scottish Parliament has more open and inclusive procedures than Westminster. It has enacted some things that were long overdue, including the abolition of the feudal system in Scotland and general access to unenclosed moors and mountains. These may overshadow the Parliament's timidity in the face of cultural conservatives over the abolition of a ban on 'promoting homosexuality' in schools, and over the institution of civil partnerships. The latter were among the surprisingly many devolved matters which the Parliament has remitted back for Westminster to deal with, under what has become known as the 'Sewel Convention'.[5] The day-to-day operations of the Parliament are explained, and the differences from Westminster noted, in Calman (2008).

The weakest parts of the Scottish devolution settlement are the parts the Constitutional Convention did not consider. These are representation and finance. How many MPs from Scotland should continue to sit in the UK Parliament? What powers should they have? What should a government do about the anomaly that Scottish MPs may vote on English matters which are devolved in Scotland, such as top-up fees at English universities? This conundrum is now known as the 'West Lothian Question'.

The Scottish Parliament is essentially financed by block grant from UK tax receipts, under what has become known as the 'Barnett Formula'. Its supposed inventor, the former Labour minister Lord (Joel) Barnett, was formerly proud of the fame it brought him, but has recently become a fierce critic, one of many. As finance and representation are headaches for the relations between the United Kingdom and all three devolved territories, we consider them in a separate, later, section of this chapter.

The first two Scottish Parliaments (1999–2003 and 2003–07) were governed by coalition Labour-Liberal Democrat administrations. The third (2007–11) is governed by a minority Scottish National Party administration. It retains a Unionist majority, and in 2008 the three main Unionist parties in the Parliament (Conservative, Labour, and Liberal Democrat) combined to set up the (Calman) Commission on the future of Scottish devolution. To date, it has produced an interim report (Calman 2008), as has the Independent Expert Group on finance that it created, of which I am a member (Muscatelli 2008). I draw on these reports in what follows.

NORTHERN IRELAND: A DIGESTED HISTORY, DIGESTED

In the earlier chapters we saw how Northern Ireland came into existence. Protestant Unionists in the north-east of Ireland raised a private army to oppose Home Rule. And in 1920 they ended up with Home Rule. But it was Home Rule on Unionist terms, for Unionists. The 1920 Act envisaged the governments of northern and southern Ireland coming together as a federation under a devolved government of Ireland. Any possibility of this was dispelled by election results in the south, and by the Treaty of 1921, in which the United Kingdom recognized the independence of the Irish Free State (now the Republic of Ireland).

Some actors from previous chapters took up their positions in Northern Ireland Protestant civil society. Fred Crawford the gunrunner received his Commander of the Order of the British Empire (CBE) personally at the hands of George V at the opening of the grand parliament building at Stormont, east Belfast, in 1921 (McNeill 1922: Chapter XXIV). This seems an odd reward for Crawford's numerous breaches of the British and Danish law.[6] James Craig became the first Prime Minister of Northern Ireland, serving until his death in 1940. He abolished proportional representation for Stormont elections in 1929 in defiance of the UK government. The latter complained that PR, and the associated protection of the Catholic minority in Northern Ireland, was a fundamental part of the devolution settlement. Furthermore, it was not within the powers delegated to the Stormont parliament to change the electoral system. Against this Craig had, and used, a credible threat. If the UK government blocked the abolition of PR, he told them, he would simply call a Northern Ireland general election, at which he would be returned with an even larger electoral majority and re-present the proposal. Faced with this, the UK government backed down.

In 1934, when Eamon de Valera had recently become prime minister of the Irish Free State and had promised to base a revised constitution on Catholic social teaching, Craig said in Stormont, 'All I boast of is that we are a Protestant parliament and a Protestant state.' The permanent minority status of Catholics was unstable. The state, and almost all local authorities, was permanently in Unionist hands, assisted by gerrymandering of local government boundaries and the abolition of PR for Stormont. At various times, Irish nationalist paramilitaries, under the changeable banner of the Irish Republican Army (IRA), threatened the state. As J. R. Fisher had predicted (Chapter 7), they were at their strongest in solidly Catholic south Armagh, close to the boundary with the south. However, they did not pose a credible military threat until 1968. The so-called Troubles that then broke out claimed about 3,500 lives in the following thirty years. To give this number some perspective, note that about 5,000 men of the thirth-sixth Ulster Division— the former Protestant paramilitaries of 1912–14—died in the first ten days of the Somme in 1916.

The Stormont government responded to the Troubles by interning suspected Catholic paramilitaries without trial. They largely got the wrong people, whom they successfully converted into paramilitaries. On refusing to cede control of internment to the UK government in 1972, the old Stormont was prorogued, never to reconvene. The UK government then began a thirty-five-year struggle to bring peace and restore devolved government to Northern Ireland. These objectives were hard to reconcile. Since Protestant-Unionists still formed the majority of the population, their parties would dominate any restored local democracy. Several times the UK government tried and failed to impose political cohabitation on Northern Ireland. They designed constitutions that required governments to be cross-community coalitions. They finally, at the time of writing, seem to have succeeded in 2007, when a coalition government led by the two extreme parties—the Protestant-Unionist Democratic Unionists and the Catholic-nationalist Sinn Fein—warily got to work. However, there have been numerous suspensions of devolved government in Northern Ireland, and there may be more.

In the days of the British Empire, British constitutional writers talked of bringing 'responsible government' to their colonies. They never brought it to the nearest one. The financial arrangements for Stormont were based on those that Gladstone had dreamt up in 1886 for a devolved Ireland. Most domestic responsibilities would be devolved to the Home Rule Parliament. So would responsibility to collect taxes in Ireland. There are two main ways to devolve tax-raising power: 'assignment' and devolution proper. Under assignment, the proceeds of certain taxes (such as income tax or land taxes) are handed over to the subnational government, and it must pay for the services it provides out of them. If the subnational government's area is richer than average, it may be required to make an 'Imperial Contribution' as Gladstone and his successors called it. An Imperial contribution would pay for the services that were provided to Ireland by the UK ('Imperial') Parliament, such as defence, foreign policy, and the collection of customs. If it were poorer than average, it would have to receive equalization payments if it was to provide the same level of services as the rest of the country.

Under tax devolution, the subnational government has all the above powers, but also the power to vary tax rates or tax bases. A tax rate is self-explanatory. A tax base is just anything that may be the subject of taxation. For instance, the United Kingdom has a relatively narrow tax base for the main expenditure tax (VAT) because food, house-building, and children's clothes are excluded from the tax base. A subnational government with devolved tax powers might, for instance, have the power to broaden or narrow the VAT tax base. The concepts in these two paragraphs are explained more fully in Muscatelli (2008).

Northern Ireland was created with the forms of tax devolution but the reality of utter dependency. Tax rates and tax bases marched in step with those in Great Britain, yielding revenue that was miserably insufficient even to fund domestic services, let alone to pay an Imperial Contribution. In his authoritative treatment, James Mitchell (2006) echoes Bagehot by calling the financial relationship between Westminster and Stormont 'undignified and inefficient'. As Mitchell summarizes:

> what transpired was the opposite of that which had been intended by the 1920 [Government of Ireland] Act. Instead of Stormont having sources for raising revenue from which it funded services (a revenue-based system), Stormont's expenditure determined levels of income as agreed with the Treasury (an expenditure-based system)...a system which encouraged dependency on the centre and discouraged financial responsibility (Mitchell 2006: 58).

For this there were two reasons. One was structural unemployment. Like Scotland and Wales, Northern Ireland was badly hit by the Great Depression. The skills which had built the *Titanic* in 1912 were less in demand. Therefore the UK welfare state came to function as a social insurance mechanism. Secondly, and even more important in my view, Northern Ireland posed a credible threat to the Union. Its large Catholic minority, frozen out of power and public resources, had no reason to support the state. Perhaps the offer of the UK level rather than (the then much lower) Irish level of social protection deferred the revolt until 1968, but in retrospect it is hard to see how a permanent minority can have been expected to remain quiescent forever.

After the Troubles broke out, the United Kingdom moved sharply away from the primordial Unionism of 1912–14, leaving the local majority of Northern Ireland Unionists potentially isolated. They had credible threats of their own. For instance, they defeated the first power-sharing executive created in 1973 by means of a strike that shut down power and transport in 1974 (for documentation see http://cain.ulst.ac.uk/events/uwc/index.html). Optimists then predicted that with the accession of both the United Kingdom and Ireland to the European Union (EU) in 1973, the old issues would fade away. In the long run, the optimists may yet prove to be right. Effective Anglo-Irish cooperation began in 1985, but nothing substantial happened for a further decade. It took very hard diplomacy through the last years of UK Conservative government and the first year of Tony Blair's premiership, matched by equal commitment from the Irish government and from centrist politicians in Northern Ireland, to produce the Belfast ('Good Friday') Agreement of 1998. This set up a new assembly and the government of Northern Ireland, with compulsory cohabitation. The party that gains the largest number of seats in the Assembly supplies the First Minister; the next largest supplies the Deputy First Minister. Given the demography of Northern Ireland, this implies a Protestant, Unionist, First Minister and a Catholic, nationalist, Deputy First Minister. At the same time, the government of Ireland promised to hold a referendum on removing the irredentist clauses from its constitution that had laid a claim over the territory of Northern Ireland. The required referenda passed overwhelmingly in the Republic of Ireland and comfortably among both communities in Northern Ireland (although more narrowly among Protestants than among Catholics). Although there have been several suspensions of devolution since then, an uneasy sort-of-calm has settled over cohabitation at the time of writing.

AND TO A LESSER EXTENT WALES

Of the three non-English parts of the United Kingdom, Wales has always posed the least credible threat to the Union. Unlike Ireland and Scotland, it never elected a separatist MP until 1966. The nationalist party Plaid Cymru ('Party of Wales') is a party more of cultural than of economic protest. It is strong-to-hegemonic in Welsh-speaking Wales, and its voters are much more likely to be Welsh-speaking than Welsh voters as a whole (McLean and McMillan 2005, Tables 8.14 to 8.18). But its strength there is its weakness in the rest of Wales. Fewer than 30 per cent of Welsh inhabitants speak Welsh (Table 8.1). As a language party it has been quite successful. Policies inspired by threat or reality of Plaid voting in Welsh-speaking Wales have reversed a long decline in the proportion of the population who speak the language. But Plaid Cymru is weak in Anglophone Wales. It is not credible to believe that it could win the majority of seats in Wales, either in the National Assembly or at Westminster.

Table 8.1 Knowledge of Welsh.

	All people aged 3 and over	People aged 3 and over: Some knowledge of Welsh (%)	People aged 3 and over: No knowledge of Welsh (%)
Wales/Cymru	2,805,701	28.43	71.57
North Wales	602,898	39.46	60.54
Mid and West Wales	511,300	48.38	51.61
South Wales West	487,064	23.45	76.56
South Wales Central	616,999	18.06	81.94
South Wales East	587,440	14.78	85.22

Source: 2001 Census, Crown copyright 2003

Accordingly, devolution to Wales is more limited. Visit any machine-readable text on UK devolution, type 'and to a lesser extent Wales' into an internet search engine, and there is a good chance that you will score at least one hit. From Tudor until Victorian times, Wales was administratively inseparable from England. When recognizably modern boundaries, of administrative counties and parliamentary constituencies, were created in the late nineteenth century, it was even uncertain whether the county of Monmouth was part of Wales. The administrative phrase 'Wales and Monmouthshire' which was in regular use from then until the 1960s, suggests that it was not, which might surprise the people of Blaenau Gwent.

A promise to create a Welsh Office appeared in the Labour Party's 1964 manifesto, where it attracted little attention even in Wales. Nevertheless, a Welsh Office headed by a Secretary of State for Wales came into existence when Labour won the general election. The Aberfan disaster of October 1966 showed graphically how weak was the most junior Secretary of State (McLean and Johnes 2000). At Aberfan, 144 people, mostly children in school, were killed when a colliery waste tip slid down a mountainside and into the school and the village. But South Wales was impregnably Labour; therefore a Labour government could ignore its interests, and the Conservative opposition could not hope to win a seat there. It posed no credible threat to either party. Therefore, the interests of the coal industry trumped those of Wales. After the disaster, Ministers protected the National Coal Board from the consequences of its criminal negligence. To add insult to injury, the Charity Commission intervened in the affairs of the disaster fund when it should not have done (obstructing the construction of a memorial and flat-rate payments to bereaved families) and failed to intervene when it should have done. The Labour government improperly took £150,000 from the charitable disaster fund towards the costs of removing the remaining tips from the mountainside. Removing dangerous tips was the responsibility of the organization that had put them there. Not until Wales had got devolution was this wrong righted. The £150,000 was repaid to the disaster fund at par by Ron Davies, the first post-devolution Secretary of State. The chapter was not closed until 2007, when the National Assembly for Wales repaid the £1.5 million that represented the true value, in current pounds, of the money taken in 1968 plus accrued interest forgone (McLean 2009).

Plaid Cymru won its first Westminster seat a few months before Aberfan, in the Welsh-speaking constituency of Carmarthen. Although it got a respectable vote in by-elections in the south Wales Valleys and won some council seats, it failed to break out. Therefore, the second Wilson administration's offer of devolution to Wales in 1974 was, as usual, an afterthought. Scotland engaged Harold Wilson's statecraft; Wales did not. To the many enemies of the devolution flagship, the Welsh mast was the easiest target. It was blown off in the February 1977 defeat mentioned earlier. Scotland and Wales were then split into two vessels. As with Scotland, the Government of Wales Act 1978 was enacted subject to a referendum. In that referendum, the Welsh electorate rejected devolution by a margin of eighty to twenty. The 'No' campaign managed to persuade the electorate that devolution would create a privileged class of Welsh speakers. Not coincidentally, the proportion of the population who spoke Welsh bottomed at 19 per cent in the 1981 Census.[7]

The second revival of devolution was again driven from Scotland, as described above. Once again, separate referenda took place, this time before legislation. In Wales, the outcome in 1997 was agonizingly close for the devolutionists, with *No* ahead all night until the last area reported, which was one of the rural Welsh-speaking areas tipping the overall result to a squeak of a *Yes* (McLean 2001*b*, Table 1). Although the Welsh-speaking/ Anglophone division persisted, it was much weaker, and support for devolution was much higher in both parts of Wales than in 1979.

Although the majority for devolution could not have been narrower, it set a path for the government of Wales that is unlikely to be retraced. Once a National Assembly came into existence, all the interests and lobbies moved from London to Cardiff. Because in all three devolved territories, the national assembly was elected by proportional representation, the most Unionist party—the Conservatives—won seats in Scotland and Wales that they would not have won otherwise. Everybody expected the National Assembly to be dominated by Labour, even with proportional representation. In fact it has not been. Labour governed, either as a minority administration or in coalition with the Liberal Democrats, in the first two sessions of the National Assembly (1999–2003 and 2003–7). In the third Assembly, elected in 2007, Labour failed to gain a majority, and after some haggling, went into a coalition with Plaid Cymru. Plaid thus entered government for the first time. Nationalists therefore share power in all three devolved administrations elected in 2007.

THE WICKED ISSUES: FINANCE AND REPRESENTATION

Finance and representation were the two issues that most troubled Mr Gladstone in 1886. They cause Mr Brown and Mr Cameron no less trouble in 2009. All three devolved administrations are financed on an expenditure, not revenue, basis. Scotland has a trivial power to vary the standard rate of income tax up or down by 3p in the pound. This is called the Scottish Variable

Rate of tax (SVR). It was authorized by referendum in 1998. But it has never been used. Apart from SVR, the only tax base that the devolved administrations control is real estate. They levy business rates and council tax (domestic rates in Northern Ireland).

Real estate—land and property—is a very suitable subject for tax devolution. According to the theory of fiscal federalism (Oates 1972; Muscatelli 2008), the less mobile a tax base, the more suitable it is to devolve to subnational government. People, and companies, can easily move or hide. Land cannot move, nor, in the short run, can the buildings on it. A naïve public finance specialist might therefore expect that the governments of Scotland, Wales, and Northern Ireland would be vigorously growing their real-estate tax base; ensuring vigorous economic growth and encouraging house-building and commercial developments in high-value locations; and taxing land and property to pay for domestic services.

They have done the opposite. Northern Ireland has resisted Treasury pressure to increase domestic rates for decades. The minority Scottish government announced in 2008 that it would abolish Council Tax. (It had to abandon this promise in 2009). In Wales, there has been a revaluation of houses for Council Tax, but this left so many scars that Welsh politicians do not want to go anywhere near the issue. Whenever there is a change in relative tax liability, those who suffer scream; those who benefit keep silent. Council Tax has now become seriously regressive throughout the United Kingdom, so that it is a much more substantial burden on the poor than on the rich. This could be addressed by increasing the bands, or turning it into a true land value tax, levied at a constant rate on the capital value of each property.

Why do the devolved administrations (DAs in Treasury-speak) make such a weak tax effort? Because they can. Essentially, all of their funds come by block grant from Westminster under the notorious 'Barnett Formula'. In Northern Ireland and Scotland, the block grant has been so generous that their administrations have never had to make much tax effort. In Wales, this is not so, but after the bruising experience of Council Tax revaluation there is as yet no sign that the National Assembly wants to revisit land and property taxation.

In the 1970s (actually before Joel Barnett became a minister),[8] the Treasury devised a new formula for block grant to replace the 'Goschen proportion' that had existed since 1888. Under Goschen, some tax revenues were assigned to Ireland, Scotland, and England (which then included Wales) in the proportions 9:11:80. Times changed; most of Ireland left the Union in 1921; and Scotland's population steadily declined to less than 11/80ths of that of England and Wales. But in annual bargaining, Scottish officials could always insist on at least 11/91 of the Great Britain share of spending on any programme. If circumstances such as remoteness or poor health could be argued, they were on top of that. Therefore public spending per head in Scotland on every domestic service was above that in England and Wales. There was no political devolution to Scotland from 1888 to 1997, but there was administrative devolution. Scotland always had a Secretary (titled Secretary of State from 1926: Mitchell 2003: 182–8). The Secretary of State for Scotland could always argue in Cabinet for Scotland to have at least the Goschen proportion of any spending programme and, where possible, more. Like Northern Ireland, Scotland possessed a credible threat against the Union.

With devolution in the air in the 1970s, Treasury officials renewed a ninety-year old struggle to cut Scotland down to size. They devised two weapons: the Barnett Formula and a needs assessment. Barnett was intended to serve two purposes. The first was to substitute a single block for the previous service-by-service appropriations for Scotland. This reduced transaction costs and scope for bargaining. The low transaction costs are nowadays put forward as one argument (the only credible argument) for retaining the Barnett regime (HM Government Scotland Office 2008). The second was to design a formula with the property that in the long run spending per head would become equal in all the territories it covered. This is because Barnett assigns *increments* in expenditure each year in proportion to population, leaving the 1970s baseline untouched. In the long run, the increments should swamp the baseline, leading to equal expenditure per head. By 1980, Barnett was applied to all three (what are now) DAs, with England as a reference category. Therefore, by 2008, if Barnett were the whole story, expenditure per head should be imperceptibly different from equal. It is not. Scotland gets more per head than Wales, even though Wales is poorer. This confirms that credible threats do more work than equalizing formulas to determine the allocations.

Moreover, equal spending per head is the wrong target even in principle. Wales and Northern Ireland are poor; Scotland has a cold climate, a long indented coastline, and numerous inhabited offshore islands. A needs-based allocation would give each of the three more spending per head than England. But how much more? This was the aim of the other branch of Treasury policy: to determine the relative spending needs of the four countries of the Unites States. The exercise was famously bad-tempered, and documents issued to me in 2005 in a Freedom of Information request proved that the Treasury and the Scottish Office remained un-reconciled on the question of how much greater were Scotland's health needs per head than England's. The Treasury published meagre results in 1979 (Table 8.2).

Table 8.2 The Needs Assessment 1979 (data relate to 1976–7).

	England	Scotland	Wales	Northern Ireland
Needs per head for devolved services	100	116	109	131
Expenditure per head on devolved services	100	122	106	135

Source: HM Treasury (1979)

Thus Scotland and Ireland were more generously funded than they 'needed' to be for the services that were then proposed for devolution; Wales more meanly. Applying the convergent Barnett Formula would therefore have had perverse effects for Wales.

It seems that the Treasury intended to let Barnett operate, for Scotland and Northern Ireland, until their spending had come down to their respective 'needs', whereupon a needs formula would be substituted. This has never happened. The Needs Assessment did not appear until after the Conservatives had won the 1979 general election. As noted above, Margaret Thatcher immediately scrapped any talk of, or plans for, devolution. The Treasury made a unilateral needs assessment in 1984, which was bitterly resisted by the Scottish Office, as has been revealed in a 2008 Freedom of Information request.[9]

The Scottish Constitutional Convention had every incentive to let that sleeping dog lie, and did. Therefore, Barnett survived to become embedded in the devolution White Papers (although not the succeeding Acts) in 1997. Defenders of the *status quo* may fairly say that Barnett was the deal on which the Scots and Welsh were invited to vote; they voted for devolution on the assumption that Barnett would continue; and that therefore it should.

But that line has become more and more difficult to sustain. By the end of 2008 three official inquiries into Barnett had started. One was the Scottish Calman Commission. One was a House of Lords Select Committee, initiated on a motion from Lord Barnett himself. The third is the Independent Commission on Funding and Finance for Wales, announced in 2008 as an outcome of the 2007 coalition agreement between Labour and Plaid Cymru.[10] This book is not the right place for a technical discussion of the post-Barnett options (for which see McLean 2005; McLean, Lodge, and Schmuecker 2008; Muscatelli 2008), but I hope this section has shown that the United Kingdom is not in constitutional equilibrium on devolution finance.

Nor is it on representation. When Mr Gladstone sat down to think about Westminster representation for Ireland after Home Rule, he came to various conclusions which are as valid now as then. The first was that Ireland could not be excluded altogether, as he had originally proposed: for that would mean taxation without representation for Ireland. The second was that the 'in and out solution' that he toyed with in 1893 would not work either. The 'in and out solution' has recently been revived under the guise of 'English votes on English laws'.

Under either name it would solve the West Lothian Question (WLQ) as follows. MPs for a territory with devolved government would be excluded from speaking or voting on bills that did not affect their constituency. In the most refined version of the proposal, put forward by the Conservative Party's Democracy Task Force in summer 2008, such MPs would be barred from speaking or voting on the *committee* stage of such business, while remaining free to vote on the principles (Second and Third Reading). Their thought is that such MPs would exercise voluntary restraint in the case where an English-only Committee on the bill has modified it before it comes up for Third Reading, and would not simply reinstate an earlier version.

How frequent is the WLQ in practice? Here it is necessary to be precise. A government with a UK Commons majority often does not have a majority in one or other part of the country. Wales has never returned a Conservative majority of MPs since 1868, but has been governed by the Conservatives (alone or in coalition) for most of the time since then. Since the 1950s, the same has been true of Scotland. It was true of Ireland throughout the nineteenth century, and of Northern Ireland since the divorce between the Conservatives and the Ulster Unionists in 1972. This does not mean that the WLQ occurs constantly. What I have defined elsewhere as the 'true' WLQ occurs only when MPs from Not-X determine policy affecting *only* X, when the majority of MPs from X voted in a different way. The principal instances of the true WLQ are then:

- (where X = Ireland): Irish Coercion Acts in the nineteenth century
- (where X = Wales): the Welsh Church Act—blocked until 1920;
    Liverpool Corporation Act 1957 (flooding a Welsh valley and destroying a village for Liverpool's water supply: Butt Philip 1975: 297)
- (where X = Scotland): Abolition of Domestic Rates (etc.) Scotland Act 1987 (i.e. poll tax. Butler, Adonis and Travers 1994: 102)
- (where X = NI): Prorogation of Stormont 1972

- (where X = England): Prayer Book Measure 1927, 1928
  Four votes in 2004, two on top-up fees and two on foundation hospitals

Since devolution, the first four cases have become impossible in practice. Whatever the statutes say (to be considered in a moment), the UK Parliament could not legislate on a matter affecting only Scotland, Wales, or Northern Ireland. So the WLQ has, since devolution, become exclusively an English question.

How worried should the English be about the WLQ? A current jibe is 'The solution to the WLQ is a large Conservative majority.' A government (of any party) with a large majority should have not difficulty in enacting legislation applying to all parts of its territory. (The constraints on the Liberals in 1906 and Labour in 1945 came from the unelected house). The narrower the majority of the elected government, the more conspicuous the WLQ becomes. It becomes truly toxic in the event that one party has a majority in England, and the opposite party has a majority in the United Kingdom. The pattern of centre-periphery politics since the 1860s determines that, in the United Kingdom, that should read 'when the Conservatives have a majority in England, and Labour, alone or in coalition, has a majority in the UK'. If we treat Labour as the successor to the Gladstonian Liberals, then that situation has arisen in the Parliaments elected in 1885, 1892, 1910J, 1910D, 1923, 1929, 1950, 1964, 1974F, and 1974O. If we then treat the general election of 1868 as the first with a wide enough franchise to make the exercise meaningful, we may ask how probable is the troublesome WLQ for England.

The first step is to calculate the ten parliaments listed as a proportion of all parliaments since 1868. The answer is 0.29. But the *prevalence* of the English WLQ is lower than its *incidence*. Twenty-nine per cent of general elections have given rise to it, but it is a problem for less than 29 per cent of the time, because these have typically been short parliaments. Rounding the duration of parliaments to the nearest whole year, the English WLQ has prevailed for twenty-five years since 1868, a prevalence of 0.18. The shortness of the parliaments is endogenous. A government that does not command a majority in the country that accounts for 85 per cent of the UK population is likely to be a weak and short-lived government.

Note also that four of the ten cases are before the secession of most of Ireland. Furthermore, Ireland was, as noted in earlier chapters, seriously over-represented before 1918. This gave the Unionists their sense of primordial grievance during the parliament of December 1910, by far the longest-lasting in the series.

These descriptive statistics help us to revisit 'English votes on English laws'. Mr Gladstone dropped the idea for two reasons, each sufficient to kill it. The first was that it was impossible to determine which laws were English and which were not. The second was that it was impossible for two governments to coexist in a single legislature.

The first issue is at the heart of the Democracy Taskforce solution. For this scheme to work, the Speaker would have to issue a territorial extent certificate not merely for each bill, but for each clause of a bill. Formally, the territorial extent of Bills and Acts is already stated, as 'Scotland', 'England & Wales', 'Wales', 'Great Britain', etc. But the reality is too complicated for the current formulas, which would become unworkable in a parliament such as that of 1892 or 1950. For the party battle would then be displaced from the substance of a bill to its territorial extent. The most controversial Act of the Parliament of 1950 was perhaps the nationalization of iron and steel. If 'English votes on English laws' had been in force, the Conservatives would have insisted that nationalization of assets in England was an English matter, for English MPs only to vote on. Either they would have failed, to the detriment of the authority of the Speaker; or they would have succeeded, in which case there would have been two governments in that Parliament. The UK (Labour) government would have controlled votes on defence, foreign policy, and perhaps taxation and social protection. But it would have lost every controversial vote on an 'English law', and hence could not have controlled health, education, housing, or transport policy in 85 per cent of the country.

The Barnett Formula could give rise to similar issues. Scots, Welsh, and Irish MPs can currently insist that there is no such thing as a 'purely English' piece of legislation: or, at least, that if there is such a thing, neither English university top-up fees nor foundation hospitals are cases in point. For any increase or cut in English public expenditure carries, under Barnett, a corresponding increase or cut in Scottish, Welsh, and Northern Ireland public expenditure, *pro rata* to their populations. Therefore the constituents of a Scottish MP have a legitimate interest in the funding of the English NHS.

If 'English votes on English laws' are impracticable, have we reached an impasse? Public opinion both in Scotland and in England favours Scots MPs being barred from voting on English matters (data monitored by John Curtice, reported in Hazell 2008*b*: 78). It seems fair, but impracticable. However, a rough substitute is available, and it has been tried before. That is to reduce the numbers, but *not* the powers, of MPs from territories with devolved governments. This would involve two steps: reducing them *to* their population share, and then reducing them *below* it.

Scotland and Wales have been overrepresented in the UK Parliament since 1922. Ireland was overrepresented from the Famine of 1846–8 (which sharply reduced Ireland's absolute population, and therefore reduced her population share by even more) until the creation of the Irish Free State in 1921. We have discussed the reasons for, and extent of, this overrepresentation elsewhere (McLean 1995; McLean and McMillan 2005). Once again, it is a story of credible threats. Although all three territories lost population share due to economic decline, politicians who wanted to sustain the Union did not want to give separatists an extra grievance by cutting the territories' representation at Westminster.

However, in the case of Northern Ireland, the UK government of the day took the opposite line. Because in 1920 Northern Ireland got the Home Rule its leaders had been resisting, as a *quid pro quo* its representation at Westminster was reduced to about 2/3 of its population share—from about eighteen territorial seats to twelve. This policy was probably designed in order to cut the numbers of Westminster MPs from *southern* Ireland, who had posed such a threat to the Union since 1880. But with Irish independence, those seats never came into existence. I have found no record of resentment in Northern Ireland at its under-representation at Westminster, which lasted until the October 1974 parliament inclusive. The majority community had its Protestant Parliament. The minority community was impotent anyhow. Any visibility it got at Westminster would be imperceptibly different with four MPs or with two.

The situation at the general election of 2005 is shown in Table 8.3.

By 2005, Wales was considerably over-represented. Scotland, although it had lost some seats following devolution, was slightly over-represented. So was Northern Ireland, in proportion to its relative electorate, although not in proportion to population. (This disparity probably arises because Northern Ireland has an unusually young population structure). Thus the first move in this solution to the WLQ would be to introduce parity of representation for the four nations of the United Kingdom. Holding the size of the Commons constant, this gives the numbers in the second-last column of Table 8.3. At parity, Scotland would have 56 seats; Wales 33; and Northern Ireland 15. The second move would be to repeat the calculations made in 1920 for Ireland. Giving each territory with devolution 2/3 its proportionate assignment of Commons seats produces the final column of Table 8.3. Scotland then gets 38 seats; Wales 22; and Northern Ireland 10. Scotland and Wales, at least, might be allowed an extra seat or at most two to allow for their difficult geographies and dispersed rural electorates. But even in Scotland and Wales, most of the electorate is urban.

This solution not only sidesteps Mr Gladstone's insoluble dilemma, but has independent merits. It shows that devolution comes at a price, but a price which public opinion seems to regard as fair. If devolution to the English regions, stalled since it was rejected in a referendum in the North-east in 2004,

Table 8.3 Population, electorate, and seats in the House of Commons, nations of the United Kingdom, 2005

Territory	Population (thousands)	Population ratio	Electorate (thousands)	Electorate ratio	Seats	Compared to population	Compared to electorate	Seats at electoral parity	Seats with DAs at 2/3
England	50,431.7	83.8	37,043.6	83.8	528	0.98	0.98	541	541
Scotland	5,094.8	8.5	3,857.9	8.7	59	1.08	1.05	56	38
Wales	2,958.6	4.9	2,233.5	5.1	40	1.26	1.23	33	22
Northern Ireland	1,724.4	2.9	1,045.5	2.4	18	0.97	1.18	15	10
United Kingdom	60,209.5	100.0	44,180.5	100.0	645	—	—	645	611

Note: Population: mid-year estimates, electoral: 2004 electorate (in force at GE 2005).

Source: Office for National Statistics; author's calculations.

returns to the policy agenda, the same deal could be offered. If accepted, the size of the House of Commons, which is unusually large by international standards, could be reduced.

Most subtly, the probability of being pivotal is not a linear function of bloc size. Suppose, to simplify, that all MPs from each non-English territory voted as a territorial bloc, as the eighty-five-strong Irish Party did from 1885 until 1918. A bloc of (say) 40, one might expect, would be half as likely to be pivotal as one of 80. However, in general this is not so (Felsenthal and Machover 1998). Although much would depend on the particular configurations of all the parties involved, a bloc of 40 would probably be pivotal *less* than half as often as a bloc of 80. Illustratively, there has probably been no occasion since 1920 when the ten or a dozen Northern Irish Unionist MPs have held the balance of power in the Commons *on their own*. There have been pivotal votes, to be sure. But in a hung parliament such as those of 1974–9, *everybody* may be pivotal. Prime Minister Callaghan's desperate search for votes to avoid losing a motion of no confidence in March 1979 caused a cascade of presents. The three Welsh Nationalists got silicosis compensation. The Ulster Unionists 'openly offered their votes for the speedy installation of a gas pipeline' to Northern Ireland (Butler and Kavanagh 1980: 126). In most matters, however, the interests of Protestant/Unionist and of Catholic/Nationalist legislators are opposed. Thus, given that there is no prospect of the return of an eighty-five-strong territorial bloc to the Commons, in most situations either no territorial bloc is pivotal or every territorial bloc is pivotal. This perhaps takes the sting out of the WLQ.

SOVEREIGNTY IN A DEVOLVED UNITED KINGDOM

The form of the devolution statutes is defiantly Diceyan. The Government of Ireland Act 1920 states at s.75:

> Notwithstanding the establishment of the Parliaments of Southern and Northern Ireland, or the Parliament of Ireland, or anything contained in this Act, the supreme authority of the Parliament of the United Kingdom shall remain unaffected and undiminished over all persons, matters, and things in Ireland and every part thereof.

The Scotland Act 1998 states at s.28 (7):

> (7) This section does not affect the power of the Parliament of the United Kingdom to make laws for Scotland.

The Act makes provision for reference to the Judicial Committee of the Privy Council to determine disputes as to whether the Scottish Parliament has passed an Act that is *ultra vires*: that is, outwith its powers.

In the usual 'lesser extent' mode, the Government of Wales Act 1998 sets the National Assembly up as a sort of biggish local authority, where the preservation of Parliamentary supremacy is so fundamental that the act does not have to mention it at all. That model having proved unworkable, the Government of Wales Act 2006 aligns the National Assembly more closely with the Scottish Parliament, and contains at s.93 (5) the same saving as for Scotland and (Northern) Ireland:

> (5) This Part does not affect the power of the Parliament of the United Kingdom to make laws for Wales.

However, form and reality diverge. A veto player—credible threat perspective is more insightful than a Diceyan one. As already noted, when James Craig promised to abolish proportional representation for elections to Stormont (which is prescribed in the 1920 Act at s.14), the British government was unable to stop him. At his back, he had the credible threat of calling a Northern Ireland general election, being re-elected with as large a majority as he already had, or larger, and simply re-presenting the proposal as often as he had to until the British government backed down. Similar issues are currently arising in Scotland, although without the sectarian tinge of Northern Ireland in the 1920s. The SNP minority government has announced:

> The Scottish Government is committed to bringing forward a referendum bill in 2010, offering the options of enhanced devolution and independence—but it will be the people of Scotland who decide Scotland's constitutional future.[11]

But these are explicitly reserved matters under the Scotland Act 1998. The Scottish Parliament has no power to decide them. Now listen to the dog that has not barked. The UK Government has *not* said that the Scottish Government's proposal is unconstitutional or *ultra vires*. It undoubtedly is. But it does not serve the UK Government's interest to make the point. For this would merely enhance the minority Scottish government's standing in Scotland, just as Craig's actions in 1929 did in Northern Ireland. In practice, if the Scottish people wish to secede from the United Kingdom, no UK government is likely to stop them, although it may require more than one referendum. In the case of Northern Ireland, explicit guarantees have been given, for example in the Northern Ireland Constitution Act 1973, and more comprehensively in the Belfast Agreement and Northern Ireland Act of 1998, that if the majority of voters in Northern Ireland vote to join the Irish Republic, the United

Kingdom will not impede them. The 1973 Act did not repeal the 1920 Act in full; however, the 1998 Act has. Therefore s.75 has gone beyond recall.

But it was used just once. In March 1972 the UK government demanded that the Northern Ireland government should hand over its powers of internment, which it exercised by virtue of a Stormont Act (the Civil Authorities [Special Powers] Act [Northern Ireland] 1922). The Northern Ireland Government refused and resigned en bloc. The United Kingdom then instituted direct rule under the Northern Ireland (Temporary Provisions) Act 1972, which passed all its stages within a week of the UK government's proroguing of Stormont. Why was Northern Ireland Prime Minister Brian Faulkner not credible as Craig and Carson had been? Because the forces that had maintained Protestant ascendancy no longer could do so. Faulkner's government depended on the British Army, which had entered Northern Ireland in 1969 to maintain public order. There was no new Curragh mutiny in 1969; nobody questioned the right of the UK government to send troops in support of the civil power, nor the duty of the troops to go. In retrospect it seems inevitable that the UK government, responsible for soldiers who were being killed, would take direct control. The Stormont government had lost its credible threat.

The same point can be made in lawyers' rather than political scientists' language. In his authoritative account, Christopher McCrudden contrasts what he sees as British constitutional 'pragmatism' with the more 'ideologically driven constitutional approach' of the UK (and Irish) governments in relation to Northern Ireland. In the former tradition, 'authoritative constitutional structures are thought to *evolve*; they are seldom *made*' (2007: 228–9). By contrast, the constitution of (Northern) Ireland has been formally determined in successive statutes of 1914, 1920, 1972, 1973, and 1998. All of these constitutions since 1920 have incorporated some rights protection. The local majority have been given various assurances that the United Kingdom will not unconditionally walk away from Northern Ireland. But the local minority have also been given constitutional assurances. Some of these have turned out to be paper tigers, such as the guarantee of proportional representation in the 1920 Act. But the same Act contains a remarkable section (not discussed by McCrudden, although it would have helped his argument; but see also Calvert 1968; Hadfield 1989).

> 5.—(1) In the exercise of their power to make laws under this Act neither the Parliament of Southern Ireland nor the Parliament of Northern Ireland shall make a law so as either directly or indirectly to establish or endow any religion, or prohibit or restrict the free exercise thereof, or give a preference, privilege, or advantage, or impose any disability or disadvantage, on

account of religious belief or religious or ecclesiastical status, or make any religious belief or religious ceremony a condition of the validity of any marriage, or affect prejudicially the right of any child to attend a school receiving public money without attending the religious instruction at that school, or alter the constitution of any religious body except where the alteration is approved on behalf of the religious body by the governing body thereof, or divert from any religious denomination the fabric of cathedral churches, or, except for the purpose of roads, railways, lighting, water, or drainage works, or other works of public utility upon payment of compensation, any other property, or take any property without compensation.

The opening words of this section are clearly drawn from the First Amendment to the US Constitution: *Congress shall make no law respecting an establishment of religion, or prohibiting the free exercise thereof.* The section shows that from the beginning the UK Parliament has been prepared to entrench rights protection in the devolved constitutions it has enacted. The trend has continued. The Northern Ireland constitution now contains elaborate provisions for forced consociation: controversial proposals require cross-community support. None of the devolved assemblies may act in a way that contravenes the European Convention on Human Rights (Lester and Beattie 2007: 82).

Could the UK Parliament bind itself in the ways that it has bound the parliaments of Northern Ireland, Scotland, and Wales? That is the subject at the heart of this book, to which I return in the final section. Next, however, I consider the erosions of parliamentary sovereignty due to two distinct European bodies: the EU and the Council of Europe.

9

The European Union and Other Supranational Entanglements

This chapter and the next explain how two supranational bodies, each with an attendant court, have eroded parliamentary sovereignty—perhaps sovereignty of any kind—in the United Kingdom. This chapter deals with the European Union (EU) and its court—the European Court of Justice. Chapter 10 deals with the Council of Europe and *its* court—the European Court of Human Rights. The two sets of bodies are frequently confused by many people, ranging from undergraduates to Eurosceptic newspapers and columnists. So we start with basic facts, similarities, and differences.

The EU (then known as the European Communities) originally comprised six member states not including the United Kingdom. The United Kingdom joined in 1973. It now comprises twenty-seven member states including the United Kingdom. It has developed a body of Community law which is overseen by the European Court of Justice (ECJ) sitting in Luxembourg. It originated in the early 1950s as a set of three intergovernmental bodies—the European Coal and Steel Community (1950); EURATOM (European Atomic Energy Commission, 1955); and the European Economic Community (EEC, 1958). The three bodies merged, and formed what is now the EU. For simplicity, in this chapter I use the label EU anachronistically to denote whatever the body was called at the relevant time (successively, in English, the European Economic Community; European Community; European Union). The EU's governing bodies are its Commission (an executive); its Council of Ministers (an intergovernmental body), and its Parliament (EP), first elected in 1979 as successor to an earlier unelected European Assembly.

The Council of Europe is older. It was created in 1949 by ten founding member states including the United Kingdom. It now has forty-seven member states across the whole of Europe, including most of the European countries that are not EU member states. The Council of Europe created the European Convention on Human Rights in 1950 and the European Court of Human Rights (ECtHR) in 1959. The ECtHR sits in Strasbourg.

Some of the confusion is understandable. Both bodies' web sites[1] resonate with generic Europeanness, their English-language versions being in a language which is not quite English. Both of them use yellow stars as a logo. To a first-time visitor they are probably as indistinguishable as the Judean People's Front and the People's Front of Judea. The EP, an organ of the EU, also sits sometimes in Strasbourg, the home of the ECtHR, which is not an EU body.

The Second World War was swiftly followed by the 'iron curtain', east of which the Soviet Union dominated the nominally independent 'people's democracies'. The last of these to fall under complete Communist domination was Czechoslovakia, after the death (perhaps murder) of the last non-Communist minister there, Jan Masaryk, in March 1948.

The states of Western Europe and North America therefore decided to create three organizations to protect (their conception of) democracy and human rights from any revival of Nazism or spread of Soviet Communism. One of those, NATO (the North Atlantic Treaty Organization), is not discussed in this book because it has remained an intergovernmental military organization with no powers give instructions to its member states. The other two have become in part supranational organizations.

The distinction between an intergovernmental and a supranational organization is, at least in principle, clear-cut. An intergovernmental organization, as the name implies, is created by governments and can act only if, and insofar as, its member state governments allow it to. The word is first attested, according to the *Oxford English Dictionary* (OED), in 1927, in the era of the League of Nations. The League was undoubtedly an intergovernmental (and not a supranational) organization, a restriction that hastened its downfall. A supranational organization does have powers over governments. The first usage of 'supranational' picked up by the *OED* is in 1908, but two of the early defining quotations are of particular interest. In 1924, John Reith, first chairman of the BBC, described it as a word 'coined, I believe, by Lord Cecil to indicate that which is above not only nationality, but something more even than international'. Lord Robert Cecil was president of the League of Nations Union, a pressure group which tried, but failed, to make the League of Nations supranational (Ceadel 2004). And in 1950, Winston Churchill, then Leader of the Opposition, gave his reasons for refusing to support UK membership of the ECSC as follows:

> I would add, to make my answer quite clear to the right hon. and learned
> Gentleman, that if he asked me, 'Would you agree to a supranational

authority which has the power to tell Great Britain not to cut any more coal or make any more steel, but to grow tomatoes instead?' I should say, without hesitation, the answer is 'No'. (HC Deb 27 June 1950 vol 476 cc2104–59 quoted at 2147)

The speakers in that debate, on the Schuman Plan which created a supranational High Authority for the ECSC, were more aware of intergovernmental and supranational power than either the White Paper or the debates on the UK's successful application to join the EU in 1972.

A HISTORY OF UK ACCESSION

Thus, from the outset, the institutions that became the EU had both intergovernmental and supranational components—and some British politicians recognized this fact when considering whether to join. The idea behind the Schuman Plan was explicitly to create a supranational authority over coal and steel in the Ruhr so as to prevent any repetition of the Franco-German hostilities which had marked the slide into the Second World War (Gillingham 2003: 22–30). The ECSC came to nothing. Jean Monnet, the actual author of the Schuman Plan, had failed to realize that neither was any longer a commanding height of the European economy. Coal and steel no longer mattered enough to start a European war. But the principle of a supranational High Authority was embedded in all the EU institutions, with the aim of achieving economic, political, and more recently environmental goals that were (in the view of the Commission) beyond the capacity of national governments.

There has been a long and fruitless academic debate on whether the EU should be regarded as primarily intergovernmental or primarily supranational (but see Moravcsik 1998; McLean 2003). It is inextricably both. The Council of Ministers, comprising ministers from every member state, is explicitly intergovernmental. The Commission (successor to Monnet's 'High Authority') is explicitly supranational. The Court—the ECJ—aggressively took supranational authority to itself in a series of cases which UK politicians had not yet noticed in 1972, as will be discussed below. The Parliament is more supranational than the Council of Ministers, but less supranational than the Commission. As the Commission, Parliament, and Council of Ministers have mutual vetoes in certain circumstances, the win set of the status quo consists, at most, of points on the contract curve joining them (Tsebelis 2002: chapter 11). An example of an effective veto is known, in the curious language of eurocracy, as the 'Luxembourg Compromise'. The Luxembourg Compromise is a compromise in the same sense that the Russian invasion of Georgia in 2008 is a peacekeeping mission. In 1965, the French government of General de Gaulle boycotted the Council of Ministers in protest against what he regarded as the overreaching supranationalism of the Commission, which had proposed that decisions on farm support should be taken by qualified majority votes. The French agreed to refill their empty chair in Luxembourg in 1966, on condition that:

> Where, in the case of decisions which may be taken by majority vote on a proposal of the Commission, very important interests of one or more partners are at stake, the Members of the Council will endeavour, within a reasonable time, to reach solutions which can be adopted by all the Members of the Council while respecting their mutual interests and those of the Community.[2]

This comes from the EU's official definition of the phrase 'Luxembourg Compromise'. We will see shortly how the Compromise has held up.

Neither Clement Attlee's Labour government (1945–51) nor their Conservative successors under Winston Churchill or Anthony Eden (1951–7) were interested in applying for membership of the Communities. The next Conservative Prime Minister, Harold Macmillan, made the first application in 1961, but it was vetoed by de Gaulle. Labour's leader, Hugh Gaitskell, opposed the Macmillan application. But both parties contained substantial pro- and anti-EU factions. Labour Prime Minister Harold Wilson made a second application in 1967, to the annoyance of many of his followers. De Gaulle, still in office, vetoed it again. But he resigned in 1969. This cleared the way for the UK Conservative government elected under Edward Heath in 1970 to make a third attempt.

All three applications crosscut UK party lines. Wilson had applied in the teeth of hostility from much of the Labour Party, especially but not only on the left. When Heath applied, the official line of the Labour Opposition was arrived at tortuously: to 'oppose . . . entry into the Common Market on the terms negotiated by the Conservative government' (resolution of Labour Party National Executive 28.07.1971, quoted in Butler and Kitzinger 1976: 16). The idea of a referendum on the terms was born at the same time. It appealed to anti-marketeers in both main parties, who suspected, rightly, that the median member of the public was more hostile to the EU than was the median MP.

The Commons debates on the European Communities Bill were thus highly unusual in Westminster two-party terms. The Heath government had a fairly small overall majority, holding 330 of the 630 seats in the

Commons after the General Election. This number, however, included eight Ulster Unionists who were to defect during the Parliament. Although their defection was for other reasons, they were anti-marketeers. The fate of the bill therefore rested in the hands of the two groups of rebels: Conservative anti-marketeers and Labour pro-marketeers. The latter group were led by Roy Jenkins, deputy leader of the Labour Party, and they outnumbered the former. The principle of entry was therefore carried by 356 votes to 244 (and by a huge majority in the unelected House of Lords). At a late moment, Heath was persuaded to allow Conservative MPs a free vote. His allies assumed that this would persuade Opposition leader Harold Wilson to do the same, so that an unwhipped majority of MPs would be seen to have voted in favour of entry. The result, in partisan terms, was even better for Heath: Labour refused to remove its party whip, and yet sixty-nine Labour MPs including the deputy leader defied it, outweighing the thirty Conservatives who voted against (Jenkins 1992: chapter 17–18; Campbell 1993: chapter 20). The only whip imposed had been against entry; but the majority in favour of entry comfortably exceeded the Government's normal majority. Heath went home and 'played Bach's First Prelude and Fugue for the Well-Tempered Clavier' (E. Heath quoted in Campbell 1993: 405). The prelude is easy; the fugue is unexpectedly difficult for a piece in the key of C major. The detailed passage of the bill in early 1972 was bloodier for Heath, but thanks to the silent collusion of the Labour pro-marketeers, the government lost no votes on the Bill, which was enacted. However, Labour whipped its members to vote for an unsuccessful amendment calling for a referendum moved by two Conservative anti-marketeers, Neil Marten and Enoch Powell.

THE MISSING DISCUSSION OF SOVEREIGNTY

On the legal and constitution aspects of membership, the White Paper explaining the United Kingdom's intention to apply and the ensuing parliamentary debates were therefore a whole pack of dogs that didn't bark. Pro-marketeers, in all parties, did not want to talk about sovereignty at all, as it was their most vulnerable point with the Eurosceptic British public. Labour anti-marketeers were not interested in the issue. They cared more, in Wilson's words, about 'the unacceptable burdens arising out of the Common Agricultural Policy, the blows to the Commonwealth, and any threats to our essential regional policies' (quoted in Butler and Kitzinger 1976: 17). Therefore, only the smallest of the four groups, the Conservative anti-marketeers, raised the issue, and their case suffered from the ambiguous position of their leading member.

During the 1967 application, the Labour Government had issued a White Paper *Legal and Constitutional Implications of United Kingdom Membership of the European Communities* (Cmnd 3301: 1967). This document explained that the body with the power to issue directives was the Council of Ministers, operating normally by qualified majority voting, but mentioning the Luxembourg Compromise (Cmnd 3301 paragraph 14). It explained the jurisdiction of the ECJ and continued

> If this country became a member of the European Communities it would be accepting Community law...A substantial body of legislation would be required to enable us to accept the law...The Community law having direct internal effect is designed to take precedence over the domestic law of the Member States. From this it follows that the legislation of the Parliament of the United Kingdom giving effect to that law would have to do so in such a way as to override existing law so far as inconsistent with it. (Cmnd 3301 paragraphs 18–34, quoted at 20 and 23)

The White Paper introducing the third application was remarkably concise on these matters. They were condensed to a single paragraph in a section headed 'The Political Case'. The material part says:

> The Community system rests on the original consent, and ultimately on the continuing consent, of member states and hence of national Parliaments. The English and Scottish legal systems will remain intact. Certain provisions of the treaties and instruments made under them, concerned with economic, commercial, and closely related matters, will be included in our law. The common law will remain the basis of our legal system, and our courts will continue to operate as they do at present. In certain cases however they would need to refer points of Community law to the European Court of Justice. (Cmnd 4715: paragraph 31)

In the opening debate the key Conservative anti-Market speech came from the most intellectually eminent, but most isolated, of the group, Enoch Powell. Called as the last speaker before the Opposition and Government winding-up speeches, he said: 'I do not think the fact that this involves a cession—and a growing cession—of Parliament's sovereignty can be disputed', and went on to cite the *previous* government's White Paper, Cmnd 3301, as his authority. He went on:

> What we are asked for in this House and in this country is an intention, an irrevocable decision, gradually to part with the sovereignty of this House and to commit ourselves to the merger of this nation and its destinies with the rest of the Community...

Winding up, Heath did not mention Powell (whom he detested) by name, but said:

If sovereignty exists to be used and to be of value, it must be effective. We have to make a judgment whether this is the most advantageous way of using our country's sovereignty. Sovereignty belongs to all of us, and to make that judgment we must look at the way in which the Community has actually worked during these last 12 years. In joining, we are making a commitment which involves our sovereignty, but we are also gaining an opportunity. (HC Deb 28 October 1971 vol 823 cc2076–217 quoted at 2186, 2187, and 2211)

The battle was not over for either Heath or Powell. When the Bill which became the European Communities Act 1972 was introduced, Powell grew fiercer:

For this House, lacking the necessary authority either out-of-doors or indoors, legislatively to give away the independence and sovereignty of this House now and for the future is an unthinkable act. Even if there were not those outside to whom we have to render account, the very stones of this place would cry out against us if we dared such a thing. (HC Deb 17 February 1972 vol 831 cc629–761 quoted at 707)

Nevertheless, the bill passed all its stages in July 1972 and the United Kingdom joined the EU in 1973.

Many lawyers since 1972 have commented on the wording of the Act. The sections on sovereignty are oblique.

2.—(1)   All such rights, powers, liabilities, obligations and restrictions from time to time created or arising by or under the Treaties, and all such remedies and procedures from time to time provided for by or under the Treaties, as in accordance with the Treaties are without further enactment to be given legal effect or used in the United Kingdom shall be recognised and available in law, and be enforced, allowed and followed accordingly; and the expression 'enforceable Community right' and similar expressions shall be read as referring to one to which this subsection applies.

(2)   Subject to Schedule 2 to this Act, at any time after its passing Her Majesty may by Order in Council, and any designated Minister or department may by regulations, make provision—

(*a*)   for the purpose of implementing any Community obligation of the United Kingdom, or enabling any such obligation to be implemented, or of enabling any rights enjoyed or to be enjoyed by the United Kingdom under or by virtue of the Treaties to be exercised; or

(*b*)   for the purpose of dealing with matters arising out of or related to any such obligation or rights or the coming into force, or the operation from time to time, of subsection (1) above;

and in the exercise of any statutory power or duty, including any power to give directions or to legislate by means of orders, rules, regulations or other subordinate instrument, the person entrusted with the power or duty may have regard to the objects of the Communities and to any such obligation or rights as aforesaid. . . .

(4) The provision that may be made under subsection (2) above includes, subject to Schedule 2 to this Act, any such provision (of any such extent) as might be made by Act of Parliament, and any enactment passed or to be passed, other than one contained in this Part of this Act, shall be construed and have effect subject to the foregoing provisions of this section; but, except as may be provided by any Act passed after this Act, Schedule 2 shall have effect in connection with the powers conferred by this and the following sections of this Act to make Orders in Council and regulations.

Section 2(1) gives Community law immediate effect in the United Kingdom, in terms that even non-lawyers can understand. It was probably a lawyer who first coined the phrase 'the devil is in the details'—in this case in Section 2(4). Complete with its circular references to other parts and schedules of the statute, this is incomprehensible at first reading; but it is the subsection that both the ECJ and the UK courts have now used to strike down UK primary legislation.

Accession day was 1 January 1973, which the Heath government declared to be the start of a 'Festival of Europe'. It made small grants available to local groups wishing to celebrate. Opera North, Newcastle-upon-Tyne, used one of these grants to mount a spectacular performance of Purcell's *Faery Queen*, whose relevance to Europe was not immediately obvious. However, the Heath government fell in February 1974, to be replaced by a minority Labour government under Wilson, whose party was as deeply split as ever on EU membership. It therefore implemented its earlier promise to renegotiate the terms of entry, and hold a national referendum on the result. This enabled Ministers to campaign on opposite sides of the issue. Collective responsibility was suspended.

In March 1975, Wilson announced that the Government (meaning, in this case, a majority of Government ministers) recommended that the 'British people [should] vote for staying in the Community'. His statement went through the seven points of renegotiation which the Labour manifesto had announced, and declared that he was satisfied on all seven. The matters covered by the 1972 Act s.2 were not among the seven (Cmnd 5999).

In the referendum campaign, each household in the country was sent three leaflets. One was a Government statement recommending a *Yes* vote, and the other two were from the omnibus campaign coalitions: from Britain in Europe, also recommending a *Yes*, and from the National Referendum Campaign recommending a *No*. The theory and practice of manifesto analysis (Riker 1996; Budge et al. 2001) leads us to expect that these documents would talk past one another, each emphasizing the popular and ignoring the unpopular parts of its case. Therefore, one would expect the two *Yes* documents to say little or nothing about sovereignty and the *No* document to say a lot. This is only partly true. The Britain in Europe document says nothing about sovereignty, as predicted. The National Referendum Campaign document has a paragraph which now reads strangely:

> The real aim of the Market is, of course, to become one single country in which Britain would be reduced to a mere province. The plan is to have a Common Market Parliament by 1978 or shortly thereafter. Laws would be passed by that Parliament which would be binding on our country. No Parliament elected by the British people could change those laws (National Referendum Campaign 1975).

By concentrating on the European Parliament and ignoring the ECJ and the effect of the 1972 Act, the No campaigners threw away not just the ace of trumps but their entire trump suit. The EP has never threatened sovereignty (in the Diceyan sense). The ECJ and the UK courts have destroyed it.

It is, surprisingly, the government statement that says most about sovereignty issues, in a somewhat defensive tone. Under the heading 'Will Parliament Lose its Power?' it lists four facts, or 'facts':

> Fact no. 1. is that in the modern world even the Super Powers like America and Russia do not have complete freedom of action . . .

> Fact no. 2. No important new policy can be decided in Brussels or anywhere else without the consent of a British Minister answerable to a British Government and British Parliament . . .

> Fact no. 3. The British Parliament in Westminster retains the final right to repeal the Act which took us into the Market . . .

> Fact no. 4. On 9 April, 1975, the House of Commons voted by 396 to 170 in favour of staying in on the new terms. (HM Government 1975: 11–12).

For Fact no. 2 to be true, the Luxembourg Compromise would have to apply to every 'important new policy'. In other words, every such policy must be decided by unanimity, not by qualified majority vote, in the Council of Ministers.

Like the Unionists in 1912 (but with better evidence), the anti-marketeers in 1975 believed that the people were on their side. Most polls since 1961 had shown a majority of British public opinion to be against the EU (Butler and

Kitzinger 1976: chapter 10, Table 1). How then did the 1975 referendum go in favour of staying in by two to one?[3] Part of the answer lies with a *status quo* bias. By 1975, the consequences of being an EU member seemed to be clear (even though the legal consequences were very generally unknown). The consequences of leaving were not at all clear. *Always keep a hold of Nurse, For fear of finding something worse.*

For most people, most of the time since discussions of EU membership began, Europe has been a low-salience issue. Most people have little information on it and don't care very much either way. There are a few very intense partisans on each side, but most people, most of the time, have too little information on which to base an opinion. This often works to the sceptics' advantage. If a newspaper says that 'Europe' has forced the United Kingdom to rename Bombay Mix or to allow vultures to attack livestock, members of the public will readily assume that they are against 'Europe'. This is such a recurrent problem for the EU and its supporters that its Press Office maintains a standing list of Euro-myths.[4]

But in 1975 the low salience of 'Europe' worked, for once, in the opposite direction. Faced with a decision about which they were bombarded with contradictory claims and felt that they had no access to unbiased information, it seems that voters took an informational short cut. What politicians were urging a *Yes*, and what politicians were urging a *No*? Table 9.1 summarizes the results.

Table 9.1 shows that the politicians advocating a *Yes* vote were widely liked and those advocating a *No* vote were widely disliked. In April, when this poll was taken on behalf of the *Yes* organization Britain in Europe, few people knew the position on Europe of most of the politicians on the list. But the results were (as people did not say in 1975) a no-brainer for the *Yes* campaign. They only had to tell the public that Tony Benn, Enoch Powell, Ian Paisley, and Hugh Scanlon of the engineers' trade union were all urging a *No* in order for the result to fall into their lap, as it duly did on 5 June.

Table 9.1 shows that those urging *Yes* were centrists. Those urging *No* were extremists. Two of the latter (Enoch Powell and Ian Paisley) were of the far right (although different far rights). The rest were of the hard left. Voters who approved of Enoch Powell would not approve of Tony Benn, and vice versa. Therefore, voters from the right and left received conflicting signals; voters in the centre received a consistent signal.

The only *No* advocate with a positive rating was Powell. But nobody, in 1972 or 1975, was indifferent about Enoch Powell. His rating of +2 almost certainly included roughly equal numbers who loved him and who hated him. In 1968, Heath had dismissed him from the Shadow Cabinet for a racist speech. His popularity soared. He may, although an outcast, have helped

Table 9.1 The UK referendum on Europe 1975: public perceptions of *Yes* and *No* advocates

	Supporters				Opponents		
	Known?	EEC position correctly perceived?	Net rating		Known?	EEC position correctly perceived?	Net rating
Harold Wilson	97	75	+15	Enoch Powell	92	50	+2
Edward Heath	94	78	+21	Ian Paisley	83	18	−59
Jeremy Thorpe	91	46	+29	Tony Benn	81	32	−15
William Whitelaw	83	52	+25	Michael Foot	79	33	−9
Roy Jenkins	82	39	+25	Hugh Scanlon	75	25	−17
Reginald Maudling	79	43	+12	Jack Jones	74	22	−5
Mean rating			21.17				−17.17

Sources: Harris Poll for Britain in Europe, 1–5 April 1975, reported in Butler and Kitzinger (1976, Chapter 10, table 9); my calculations. Most familiar six on each side (from list of 20) shown.

Heath to his narrow victory in 1970. In February 1974, he urged voters to vote Labour in protest against Heath's negotiation of entry to Europe. He may have helped Wilson to his narrow victory (for the calculations see McLean 2001a, Appendix to chapter 5).

Furthermore, Powell exactly repeated Dicey's error of 1912. Powell, like Dicey, was passionate about parliamentary sovereignty. When parliament seemed about to do something they passionately detested, Powell, like Dicey, called for a referendum. But you cannot at the same time believe wholeheartedly in parliamentary sovereignty and believe wholeheartedly in the referendum. If either Powell or Dicey had felt able to come out in favour of 'us the people'—in favour of popular sovereignty—they would have been rescued from contradiction. But this would have revealed that parliamentary sovereignty, whatever its value as a *legal* doctrine, has none as an *ethical* doctrine.

Powell misplayed his hand for another reason also. In 1963, the threat to Parliamentary sovereignty had already been stated in an ECJ judgment that all public lawyers now hold to be the *Marbury* v. *Madison* of that court.[5] In the *Van Gend en Loos* case of 1963, the Court ruled (in the English version):

> The European Economic Community constitutes a new legal order of international law for the benefit of which the states have limited their sovereign rights, albeit within limited fields, and the subjects of which comprise not only the member states but also their nationals. Independently of the legislation of member states, community law not only imposes obligations on individuals but is also intended to confer upon them rights which become part of their legal heritage. These rights arise not only where they are expressly granted by the treaty but also by reason of obligations which the treaty imposes in a clearly defined way upon individuals as well as upon the member states and upon the institutions of the Community.

By joining the EU, the United Kingdom was signing up to this judgment.[6] Between 1971 and 1975, some of the *Yes* advocates, including Ministers and Parliamentary draftsmen, knew this but held their peace in Parliament. Once the 1972 Act was in the bag, the junior minister Geoffrey Howe was remarkably frank in a speech later published in an academic journal:

> Consider for a moment the key provision, to be found in Section 2 (4) of the Act [section then quoted] . . . What the Act seeks to do . . . is to enjoin our courts, in their interpretation of future legislation, to give full effect to the concept of 'enforceable Community rights' which, as defined in Section 2 (1) (and the treaties) contains the element of supremacy. (Howe 1973: 7)

Immediately before this passage, Howe praises the Parliamentary draftsmen for their ingenuity in drafting the wording of s.2 in order to reconcile the supremacy of Community law with the Diceyan tradition. It seems that the draftsmen even outwitted Enoch Powell. The phrase 'Van Gend' appears in *Hansard* online a total of thirteen times.[7] Disregarding one mention of the company that was not about its lawsuit gives twelve mentions, six of which were in the 1972 debates. On each occasion in the Commons, the Solicitor-General (the same Geoffrey Howe) fended off the attacks of the two Conservative MPs who persistently raised the issue, Powell and Sir Derek Walker-Smith. Powell and Walker-Smith had the logic but not the numbers on their side.

Howe's lecture correctly anticipated the next flashpoint, which would occur when he was a senior minister in the Conservative administration of Margaret Thatcher (1979–90). If the Common Market was to be an effective common market, it must enforce open market rules on all member states (Howe 1973: 2). It was this that had provoked de Gaulle's walkout, and therefore the Luxembourg Compromise. De Gaulle had walked out in order to prevent a qualified majority of member states from voting in the Council of Ministers to reduce the market-distorting protection received by French farmers. Qualified-majority therefore enters, centre stage.

Votes in the Council of Ministers are cast in member state blocs. Each member state has a bloc of votes that is roughly proportionate to the square root of its population.[8] A proposal gains *qualified-majority* approval if the number of votes in its favour passes the current threshold, which has hovered between 67 and 70 per cent of the weighted votes in the Council, changing slightly as the thresholds are reset at each enlargement of the EU. A proposal gets *unanimity* approval, obviously, only if every single member state supports it at the Council. The Luxembourg Compromise prescribed the unanimity rule for everything that any member state claimed affected its vital interests.

To British Conservatives and other (confusingly but correctly labelled) economic liberals, the point of the EC/EU was to create an internal market without trade, regulatory, or tariff barriers, so that intra-Community trade would grow and protection for sub-Community economic interests would disappear. For them, the EU treaties are a matter of jurisdictional integration exactly like the Acts of Union of 1707. However, unlike 1707, the Treaty of Rome does not create a single state. True, the Commission could impose internal free trade by relying on the *Van Gend* principle to insist that Community free-trading regulations trumped Member State protectionist rules. But in the 1980s both the Commission and a number of Member State governments decided that economic integration was going too slowly, because under the Luxembourg Compromise it remained at the mercy of French farmers and other single-country protectionist lobbies.

The next cession of British sovereignty was initiated by the Single European Act of 1986 and completed by the Maastricht Treaty of 1991. The three main actors were a very ill-matched trio: Prime Minister Margaret Thatcher; UK EU Commissioner Lord Cockfield,[9] and Commission President Jacques Delors. Two of the three (Thatcher and Cockfield) were economic liberals who believed, in principle (Cockfield in practice), in removing barriers to the single market. Two of the three (Cockfield and Delors) believed in the reinvigoration of the EU, although Delors 'was no friend of economic or political liberalism' (Gillingham 2003: 160).

When Mrs Thatcher sent Cockfield to Brussels as UK Commissioner in 1984, it was probably in order to get rid of an intransigent minister who had been proved right too often for his own good. The obituaries portray a slow-moving, slow-talking, fiercely intelligent man of remorseless humourless logic. She thought she had sent a fellow Eurosceptic to Brussels and was horrified when she found that, as she put it, he had 'gone native'. Cockfield's view was that it was his mission to extend to the EU the economic liberalism and deregulation that Thatcher had inaugurated in the United Kingdom. He therefore produced a White Paper listing nearly 300 moves to dismantle non-tariff barriers impeding a free internal market, with a date for implementation beside each. Although Delors's economics was light years away from Cockfield's (see e.g. Gillingham 2003: 160–1), they shared a vision of re-energizing the EU. For Cockfield, this was instrumental—a means to the end of extending the single market. For Delors, it was primordial—a more powerful EU was an end in itself.

The Single European Act (SEA: so named rather confusingly) is not an Act of the UK (or any other) parliament, but an EU treaty drafted by Cockfield. It was adopted by each Member State in 1986 and came into force in 1987. The main provision relevant to this chapter is that it extended qualified majority voting (QMV) to measures that would help to implement the single European market. In other words, it would remove all single-nation vetoes—French, British, and any other—on market-integration measures approved by a qualified majority of member states in the Council of Ministers. In those matters, it therefore superseded the Luxembourg Compromise and invalidated Fact 2 put forward by the Wilson government in 1975 (see above).

Because the SEA was a constitutional treaty ratified by the United Kingdom, the Thatcher government decided to enact a UK statute to confirm it. This was the European Communities (Amendment) Act 1986 c.58, whose preamble announces its purpose as:

> An Act to amend the European Communities Act 1972 so as to include in the definition of 'the Treaties' and 'the Community Treaties' certain provisions of the Single European Act signed at Luxembourg and The Hague on 17th and 28th February 1986 and extend certain provisions relating to the European Court to any court attached thereto; and to amend references to the Assembly of the European Communities and approve the Single European Act.

The UK Act itself was very brief. But it had the effect of approving a new Article 100a of the Treaties of European Union, which extended QMV to single-market measures. As in 1950 and 1971–2, therefore, the question arises: did the House of Commons know what it was doing when it enacted the 1986 Act?

The most relevant debate is on a guillotine motion on 1 July 1986. Since 1975, Euroscepticism had strengthened considerably in the Conservative Party, and it no longer depended on Enoch Powell (still in the Commons, but as Ulster Unionist MP for South Down). Labour anti-marketeers were also more effective. The veteran anti-EU Labour MP Peter Shore made a much more telling speech than in 1972:

> What is special about the Bill is that it gives legislative effect to a treaty concluded with other nations—the member states of the EEC—and upon whose institutions it confers additional legislative powers. Once passed, this

measure cannot be repealed by a subsequent Parliament, unless that Parliament is prepared to tear up the underlying treaty itself—a special dimension of difficulty which I do not believe many Conservative Members have even given serious thought to.

Moreover, it is a Bill that directly affects the power of Parliament . . . The powers of the United Kingdom Parliament will be weakened in two principal ways: first, because, as a result of amendments to the Rome treaty, qualified majority voting in the Council of Ministers will be substituted for unanimity voting in five important articles of the Rome treaty and, secondly, because it introduces the new so-called "co-operation" procedure between the European Assembly and the Council of Ministers which will remove the national veto from a wide range of Council decisions and permit the Council to reject amendments by the European Assembly only if the Council itself is unanimous . . .

The veto power in the Council of Ministers has been the central defence of British national interests. During the referendum campaign in 1975, the then Government, supported by the Conservative Opposition, sought to comfort the sceptical British electorate with this categorical statement—I quote from the document "Britain's New Deal in Europe"—no important new policy can be decided in Brussels or anywhere else without the consent of a British Minister answerable to a British Government and British Parliament.

To this onslaught the minister, Lynda Chalker, blandly appealed to the Luxembourg Compromise:

Its role is in no way changed by the Single European Act. In any case, it is not the Luxembourg compromise on which we have relied to safeguard our interests. Where we need to retain unanimity we have done so, and where we need national safeguards we have secured them, too.

Why then, in the face of better-informed concerns about sovereignty than in 1972, did the guillotine motion carry comfortably and the Bill proceed rapidly to enactment? Because the Conservatives had a large majority sufficient to overwhelm their own doubters and the entire Opposition. Enoch Powell, quoting his fellow Parliamentary outrider Denis Skinner (the hard-left Labour member for Bolsover), drew attention to the oddity of Mrs Thatcher's position:

The hon. Member for Bolsover (Mr. Skinner), in a speech which delighted the House last Friday, drew attention to a curious anomaly which had engaged his notice, namely, that the Prime Minister was, to all appearances, strongly opposed to the step which we are invited to embody in United Kingdom legislation. The Prime Minister had stated publicly and repeatedly that no such treaty was necessary, and that for the purposes and interests of the United Kingdom in the Common Market no such legislation as this to embody that treaty would be called for. Nevertheless, the hon. Member for Bolsover pointed out, she went along and signed. (HC Deb 01 July 1986 vol 100 cc930–82 quoted at 937, 974, 945)

The oddity of her position is stressed by Lord Cockfield after she had cast him into outer darkness. He seemed particularly pained not to have been invited to the 1992 celebrations inaugurating the single market which he had created. Here, albeit yoked together from disparate points in his account, is his digested view of Mrs Thatcher:

> The publication of the White Paper marked the first days in the deterioration of my relations with the Prime Minister . . . [T]he most powerful support I enjoyed in the Community was the Prime Minister's hostility . . . [D]espite Mrs Thatcher's efforts we did get [qualified] majority voting and as a result we have now seen the successful completion of the Internal Market Programme . . . Her support of . . . the Single Market . . . was largely based on a misunderstanding. (quoted in Cockfield 1994: 55, 59, 64, 135. For the 1992 disinvitation see page 93)

After she had been re-elected with a reduced but still substantial majority, the Merchant Shipping Bill 1988 contained clauses that would prevent Spanish fishing companies from what was called 'quota-hopping'. Fish stocks all round the EU were dwindling because of a classic 'tragedy of the Commons'—every fishing boat was overfishing and contributing to stock declines—*even though fishermen knew that stocks were declining through overfishing*. Nevertheless, it was in the interest of each boat to overfish—a skipper who unilaterally declined to overfish would be a sucker and would soon be out of business.

This is one of the issues that a supranational body is better equipped to handle than a national government because the scale of the tragedy is supranational, and fish do not observe national boundaries. Nevertheless, EU quotas limiting catches were deeply unpopular with fishing lobbies, which in the United Kingdom were concentrated in a small number of marginal seats, notably in Cornwall and Devon. These fishermen were enraged by the fact that Spanish fishing companies were buying up British boats to catch not fish but quotas, a practice that Adam Smith had noticed two centuries earlier.[10] The Merchant Shipping Act 1988 c.12, as finally enacted, required at s.14 that:

(1) Subject to subsections (3) and (4), a fishing vessel shall only be eligible to be registered as a British fishing vessel if—

(a) the vessel is British-owned;

(b) the vessel is managed, and its operations are directed and controlled, from within the United Kingdom; and

(c) any charterer, manager or operator of the vessel is a qualified person or company.

Even in the Parliamentary debates, the Government was warned that this was probably unlawful under European law (HL Deb 24 November 1987 vol 490 cc 553–94, speech of Lord Parry at 575). It introduced one of those non-tariff barriers that Mrs Thatcher's man in Europe, Lord Cockfield, was devoting his energies to removing. Cockfield was himself removed by non-reappointment in 1989. Like other politicians, it seemed that Mrs Thatcher was in favour of removing non-tariff barriers except when a key interest group (key, in this case, because Falmouth and St Ives were marginal Conservative seats) wanted them. In this she was identical to General de Gaulle.

THE COURTS STEP IN

However, unlike General de Gaulle, she had to contend with two things: qualified majority rule in the Council of Ministers on market-opening measures, and the ECJ. The latter attacked first. We have already referred to the *Factortame* litigation (Chapter 6). The aggrieved Spanish companies, one of which was called Factortame, went to court. Initially, the UK courts referred to the ECJ the question whether an 'overriding principle of Community law' entitled the Spanish companies to seek compensation for the losses they would incur if the 1988 Act was enforced against them. The ECJ duly said that it did. The result was *Factortame* (*no. 2*), in which the House of Lords granted the injunction sought by the Spaniards against removing their ships from the register of British fishing vessels.

But this required, for the first time since 1707, the clear 'disapplication' of a statute enacted by Parliament. Let us have another look at what I earlier described as 'Lord Bridge's fig-leaf'.

> If the supremacy within the European Community of Community law over the national law of member states was not always inherent in the E.E.C. Treaty (Cmnd 5179-II), it was certainly well established in the jurisprudence of the European Court of Justice long before the United Kingdom joined the Community. Thus, whatever limitation of its sovereignty Parliament accepted when it enacted the European Communities Act 1972 was entirely voluntary ... [W]hen decisions of the European Court of Justice have

exposed areas of United Kingdom statute law which failed to implement
Council directives, Parliament has always loyally accepted the obligation to
make appropriate and prompt amendments. (*R. v. Secretary of State for
Transport*, ex parte Factortame Ltd and Others (No. 2) [1991] 1. A.C. 603 at
658–9)

This may be good law; but it is bad history, as my survey of the 1971–2 debates
shows. Parliament 'voluntarily' accepted limitation of its sovereignty only
because two crusty Conservative backbenchers (Walker-Smith and Powell)
were too isolated, even or especially in their own party, to get Parliament to
take their concerns seriously.

The other EU case recognized by all public lawyers as raising profound
constitutional questions is *Thoburn* v. *Sunderland City Council*, [2002] 3
WLR 247. Thoburn was one of a number of self-styled 'metric martyrs'. He
was a greengrocer in Sunderland who had been fined for failing to weigh
bananas by the kilo, as required by an EU directive implemented by various
UK regulations. His counsel argued that the UK Weights and Measures Act
1985, which consolidated previous law on the subject, implicitly repealed s.2
of the European Communities Act 1972 in relation to the retention of pounds
and yards. The 1985 Act restated earlier statutes affirming that imperial
weights and measures continued to be valid in the United Kingdom. Thus,
exactly as Dicey argued that the Dentists Act 1878 might have partly repealed
the Acts of Union 1706/7, so Thoburn's counsel argued that the 1985 Act
partly repealed the 1972 one, and therefore that directives implemented
by post-1985 statutory instruments, purporting to make metric measure-
ments primary, were invalid.

The courts would have none of this. The key judgment was delivered by Sir
John Laws, a judge who already had a reputation as a constitutionalist. He could
have used similar reasoning to that of Bridge in *Factortame* to the effect the EU
law overrode any UK law to the contrary. Actually, he did something quite
different. He discovered a principle of the common law according to which, he
said, constitutional statutes must be treated differently to ordinary ones:

> We should recognise a hierarchy of Acts of Parliament: as it were "ordinary"
> statutes and "constitutional" statutes. The two categories must be distin-
> guished on a principled basis. In my opinion a constitutional statute is one
> which (a) conditions the legal relationship between citizen and state in
> some general, overarching manner, or (b) enlarges or diminishes the scope
> of what we would now regard as fundamental constitutional rights. (a) and
> (b) are of necessity closely related: it is difficult to think of an instance of (a)
> that is not also an instance of (b). The special status of constitutional
> statutes follows the special status of constitutional rights. Examples
> are Magna Carta 1297 (25 Edw 1), the Bill of Rights 1689 (1 Will & Mary

sess 2 c 2), the Union with Scotland Act 1706 (6 Anne c 11), the Reform Acts
which distributed and enlarged the franchise (Representation of the People
Acts 1832 (2 & 3 Will 4 c 45), 1867 (30 & 31 Vict c 102) and 1884 (48 & 49
Vict c 3)), the Human Rights Act 1998, the Scotland Act 1998 and the
Government of Wales Act 1998. The 1972 [European Communities] Act
clearly belongs in this family . . . The 1972 Act is, *by force of the common law,*
a constitutional statute. Ordinary statutes may be impliedly repealed. Constitutional statutes may not . . . This development of the common law regarding constitutional rights, and as I would say constitutional statutes, is
highly beneficial. It gives us most of the benefits of a written constitution, in
which fundamental rights are accorded special respect. But it preserves the
sovereignty of the legislature and the flexibility of our uncodified constitution. (*Thoburn* v. *Sunderland City Council,* [2002] 3 WLR 247, Laws LJ
quoted at paragraphs 62–4 my emphasis)

Some commentators have heartily disapproved of Laws's reasoning, regarding
it as judicial law-making. But it has been emulated in non-EU cases including
the hunting case *Jackson* mentioned in Chapter 6.

Between them, Bridge and Laws have killed parliamentary sovereignty in
relation to the EU. What should go in its place? I can only return to this
question at the end of this book, but have already dropped broad hints that we
need some conception of popular sovereignty. For all the twists and turns,
incompetence and misinformation, that this chapter has chronicled, Parliament did ratify the United Kingdom's treaties of accession to the EU and
subsequent amending treaties including the Single European Act. The accession was ratified by a two-thirds majority of the voters in the only UK
nationwide referendum. Parliament undoubtedly could legislate to leave the
EU, as it could legislate to change the shape of the United Kingdom by ceding
Scotland or Northern Ireland. At the end of this book I will try to imagine
how 'our, the people's' constitution might deal with those matters.

10

Human Rights

As already noted, the Council of Europe antedates the European Union. In 1945, the United Kingdom was the hegemonic Western European power. France had been liberated only in 1944; Italy, the Low Countries, and Germany in 1945. The towering British politician of the day was Winston Churchill. Pushed into opposition by the UK General Election of July 1945, he transferred some of his energy to rebuilding Europe. In 1946, at Zurich, he called for a 'United States of Europe' although he refused to become involved in writing the constitution of these united states (Crowson 2007: 15). Nevertheless, ten Western European governments formed the Council of Europe in 1949. The inaugural members were five of the six that were to form the European Communities shortly afterwards (not Germany, still emerging from multi-power occupation), plus the United Kingdom, Ireland, Norway, Sweden, and Denmark. The UK government did not ratify the accession treaty, but the initial months of the Council were discussed at an adjournment debate in November 1949, at which Foreign Secretary Ernest Bevin made it clear that the UK Government were not willing to let the Council acquire any supranational powers (HC Deb 17 November 1949 vol 469 cc2202–338).

The future EU member states soon became dissatisfied with the limited scope of the Council. Their progress towards what became the EU has already been discussed. But the Council of Europe did not close down. One of its first acts was to draft a European Convention on Human Rights. The chair of the committee that produced it was Sir David Maxwell Fyfe, a British Conservative former minister who had been the deputy (but *de facto* chief) British prosecutor in the Nuremburg trials of German Nazi war criminals. His Labour counterpart, Sir Hartley Shawcross, had brought Fyfe to Nuremburg to show that prosecution of Nazi war crimes was bipartisan in the United Kingdom.

The Convention was one of many instruments designed to ensure that Nazism could never rise again in Europe. As the status of the Nuremburg Tribunal was (and is) disputed, it made sense that the Convention should acquire a Commission to explore and a Court to try violations of human rights. The Convention was ratified by twelve governments including (in 1951) the United Kingdom. It entered into force in 1953 on receiving the requisite number of ratifications. In the 1950 Commons debate the Conservative spokesman Duncan Sandys (son-in-law of Winston Churchill), contrasting the European Convention with the non-binding UN Declaration of Human Rights, said:

> It was felt at Strasbourg that what at present would not be feasible on a worldwide scale is none the less possible and necessary within the circle of the Western European democracies. The European Convention of Human Rights, which was signed in Rome the other day by the Under-Secretary of State for Foreign Affairs on behalf of this country, is a very different thing from the United Nations declaration. In the first place, it is confined to a very small number of vital and fundamental rights, which are the foundation of our Western way of life. Nor is it not just a declaration. It is a binding treaty which imposes the obligation on all the signatory States, to assure to their citizens the rights which it contains. What perhaps is the most novel and important feature of this Convention is the provision for the setting up of a European Court of Human Rights, to which cases of alleged infringement of the Convention can be referred for adjudication. (HC Deb 13 November 1950 vol 480 cc1391–504 quoted at 1412)

He urged the Labour government to sign up to the Court's jurisdiction. Bevin was unwilling to do so on the spot. In fact, the United Kingdom has accepted the jurisdiction of the Court in stages. Initially, only member states had access to the court. The United Kingdom permitted individual access to the Commission in 1966 (as an executive act, without parliamentary discussion or ratification: Lester and Beattie 2007: 63). However, from then until the UK Human Rights Act 1998 came into force, in 2000, aggrieved individuals had to trek to Strasbourg to claim a violation of their human rights. Not many did or could.

AN EIGHTEENTH-CENTURY SECESSION

To understand the format of human rights protection in the United Kingdom, and the policy options open to a future government, it is useful to understand how the movement for human rights, originating in seventeenth-century England, flowed after 1787 into two distinct streams.

Many of the leaders of the American Revolution were lawyers, trained in the United Kingdom (often in Scotland) or in American universities where they were taught by Scots. Of the Framers of the US Constitution and Bill of Rights, Thomas Jefferson, James Wilson, and James Madison are all cases in point. Wilson was educated in Scotland, and both Madison and Jefferson were taught by Scots professors. After 1707, it was natural for Scottish intellectuals to be 'country' or 'opposition' Whigs. They were Whigs because they appreciated the liberation from both hellfire and Jacobite rebellion that the Union had brought them (McLean 2006). But they were country Whigs because they tended to suspect the Court, the London government, and its business managers.

The ideology of country Whiggery was well defined by the 1770s, mixing history and myth. According to the mythical part, freeborn Englishmen had been crushed by the Norman yoke in 1066. They had started to re-establish their rights with Magna Carta in 1215, but did not start to regain them in earnest until the seventeenth century. Then, first the common lawyers and later Parliament stood up for the freeborn English against Stuart absolutism. The first expression of this as a *democratic* ideal was by Col. Thomas Rainborough and the Levellers in the Putney Debates of 1647 ('the poorest hee that is in England hath a life to live as the greatest hee': Sharp 1998: 103). But Rainborough was unknown to the American revolutionaries. He was only rediscovered in 1890. Therefore, its best-known formulation was by John Locke, whose *Second Treatise of Government*, published in 1690, is now known to have been written *before* the revolution of 1688, which it sought to justify by arguing that government existed only by consent, which James II had forfeited.

The American revolutionaries took their legal and political philosophy from this country Whig tradition. Its most eloquent exponent was Thomas Jefferson. In the last letter he ever wrote, the sick Jefferson excused himself from attending the 4 July 1826 celebrations in Washington DC (he was actually to die on that day), but wrote as his testament to the Mayor of Washington:

> May it [the Declaration of Independence] be to the world, what I believe it will be (to some parts sooner, to others later, but finally to all,) the signal of arousing men to burst the chains under which monkish ignorance and superstition had persuaded them to bind themselves, and to assume the blessings and security of self-government. That form which we have substituted, restores the free right to the unbounded exercise of reason and freedom of opinion. All eyes are opened, or opening, to the rights of man. The general spread of the light of science has already laid open to every view the palpable truth, that the mass of mankind has not been born with saddles on their backs, nor a favored few booted and spurred, ready to ride them legitimately, by the grace of God. (TJ to Roger C. Weightman, 24.06.1826 in Peterson 1984: 1517)

Douglass Adair (1974: 192–202) has proved that the striking image of 'saddles on their backs' comes from the dying speech of Col. Richard Rumbold, a former Parliamentarian executed for rebellion against James II in 1685. Although he did not know it, Jefferson was at only one remove from Rainborough. Rumbold had been a supporter of the Levellers.

The dominant country Whig ideology among the American Framers therefore led them in 1787 to write a constitution that was distinctly suspicious of the executive, incorporating a number of individual rights against the government: for instance restricting the scope of impeachment; giving the monopoly of supply to the lower house of Congress; protecting habeas corpus; and outlawing bills of attainder and *ex post facto* [retrospective] laws (US Constitution I.3; I.7; I.9). It was not enough for the country Whigs of several states, nor for Thomas Jefferson, by then in Paris as American Minister: 'I will now add what I do not like. First the omission of a bill of rights providing clearly & without the aid of sophisms for freedom of religion, freedom of the press, protection against standing armies, restriction against monopolies, the eternal & unremitting force of the habeas corpus laws, and trials by jury in all matters of fact' (TJ to James Madison, 20.12.1787 in Peterson 1984: 915–16). Several state conventions signalled that they would not ratify the Constitution unless a Bill of Rights were added, containing among others the items listed by Jefferson. It was done. Madison was the floor manager of what became the Bill of Rights, namely, the first ten amendments of the Constitution, ratified together in 1791. The Bill of Rights entrenched further individual rights against the state: for instance, freedom of speech and religion (First Amendment); the right to bear arms (Second Amendment); no searches without warrant (Fourth Amendment); a right against self-incrimination (Fifth Amendment); and a ban on 'cruel and unusual punishments' (Eighth Amendment: a phrase lifted direct from the English Bill of Rights Act 1689).

In France, too, human rights were enshrined in the *Declaration of the Rights of Man and the Citizen* promulgated in 1789, and now incorporated into the preamble of the Constitution of the Fifth Republic. Elsewhere, I have pointed out how the fingerprints of Thomas Jefferson are all over this document (McLean 2004). This is rarely acknowledged by either American scholars (who do not read French) or French scholars (unwilling to admit that an American helped to draft their sacred document) but can easily be traced through the letters of the disloyal American Minister in Paris: disloyal, that is, to the regime of Louis XVI to which he was accredited.

Thus, country Whig ideology flowed into both the American and French declarations of human rights. The American declaration has always been entrenched in the Constitution. The French declaration was not entrenched until 1971, when the *Conseil constitutionnel* decided for the first time that the rights it set out were justiciable (Stone Sweet 2000).

By the 1790s, anything popular in France (or even the United States) was anathema to most politicians and thinkers in the United Kingdom. Britain was at war with France for most of the time from 1792 to 1815. The bloody course of the French Revolution led to an understandably hostile reaction to the Enlightenment. Neither the US nor the French declarations of rights had much intellectual support, even though both of them had developed from English and Scottish thought. Legal positivism came to dominate lawyers' thinking about the British constitution. A landmark in this was Jeremy Bentham's dismissal of rights in *Anarchical Fallacies*, a savage attack on the 1791 version of the French declaration of the rights of man—and hence, indirectly, on Jefferson. '*Natural rights* is simple nonsense: natural and imprescriptible rights, rhetorical nonsense—nonsense upon stilts' (Bowring 1843: 501). His follower John Austin applied Benthamite positivism in *The Province of Jurisprudence Determined* (1832/1861). For legal positivists, there was necessarily a single sovereign: 'Supreme power limited by positive law, is a flat contradiction in terms', said Austin (1832: 225).

Until very recently, British legal thinking was almost all conducted in the shadow of Bentham and Austin. Dicey came to throw an even deeper shadow of his own. As noted in various places in this book, Dicey still has his followers. So does Bentham—the most eminent modern Benthamite probably being Professor John Griffith, for whom 'the constitution is what happens' (quoted in King 2007: 4). For a socio-legal scholar like Griffith, the 'constitution' is simply the result of fights between elected politicians and unelected judges. Griffith is on the side of the politicians because he distrusts the class composition of the judicial bench. Even Dicey's most biting critic among English constitutional lawyers, Sir Ivor Jennings, still sailed down the other branch of the seventeenth-century Whig stream—call it the 'court' branch.

'Court' and 'country' were the main party labels in mid-eighteenth-century Britain. After the Jacobite rebellions, no politician dared to call himself a Tory. They were all Whigs. They all celebrated the parliamentary revolt against Charles I and the Glorious Revolution. Country Whigs in Scotland and America read the tradition as one of constraints on rulers who violated fundamental rights. Court Whigs read it differently. For them, what happened in 1688–9 is that Parliament inherited all the prerogative powers of the Crown. The monarch (both branches of Whigs agreed) reigned only by consent of the two Parliaments that had separately invited William III to be the monarch, and the post-Union parliament which finally confirmed the Hanoverian succession. Therefore (court Whigs continued), the royal prerogative is exercised by ministers on behalf of the Crown. When the monarch becomes involved, he acts only on the advice of his ministers (see, once again, Asquith's letters to George V). But the everyday exercise of the prerogative, to get things done, does not even require reference to the monarch. Sir Ivor Jennings was therefore a comfortably a court Whig for the wartime and post-war governments which vastly expanded executive power. It was all done in the name of the Crown.

Beginning, perhaps, with Asquith, court Whigs added that they represented the elected house of Parliament, and therefore the people. When the Crown (i.e. ministers) used its prerogative, it was acting (i.e. they were acting) ultimately in the name of the people. In this perspective, entrenched rights are counter-majoritarian. What right have unelected judges got to strike down the acts of elected ministers?

A rights culture did not return to UK constitutional thinking, therefore, until it arrived by the backdoor route of opening individual access to the European Court of Human Rights. Since then, there has been a human rights revolution in the UK constitution: cheered by some, deplored by others.

THE ROAD TO AND FROM THE HUMAN RIGHTS ACT

The narrative that follows depends heavily on Lester and Beattie (2007). This authoritative source is co-authored by one of the people who has done most to bring human rights into the British constitution, and explains why and how the legislation has taken the (to a non-lawyer) unexpected form that it has.

When the Wilson Labour government allowed individual access to the European Court of Human Rights, it may have seemed a small decision. The human rights court had decided only two cases, because hardly any states had yet accepted its jurisdiction. After 1966, it started to find against all three branches of UK government—legislative, executive, and judicial. For instance, the Commonwealth Immigrants Act 1968 was held to have breached the Convention rights of British Asian passport holders from East Africa; the Home Secretary was held to have breached the Convention rights of prisoners; and the Law Lords were held to have breached the right of free expression in a judgment preventing the *Sunday Times* from publishing articles about thalidomide, a wonder drug that had gone disastrously wrong (Lester and Beattie 2007: 64).

A few lawyers headed by Antony (Lord) Lester started to lobby for incorporation of the ECHR into UK law as early as the 1960s. Home Secretary Roy Jenkins published a consultation paper on it in 1976;[1] the Liberal and Labour parties had adopted it as policy by 1993. In 1994, Lord Lester introduced the first bill to incorporate the ECHR into UK law. This bill would have taken the same route as the ECJ had by then enforced in relation to EU law. However, advised by senior judges that, although they supported the principle of incorporation, another attack on parliamentary sovereignty was likely to fail, Lester introduced a second bill modelled on an earlier New Zealand statute requiring judges to interpret legislation in a way that was compatible with Convention rights, whenever possible. The New Zealand Bill of Rights Act 1990 states at s.4:

> No court shall, in relation to any enactment (whether passed before or after the commencement of the Bill of Rights):
>
> (a) Hold any provision of the enactment to be impliedly repealed or revoked, or to be in any way invalid or ineffective; or
>
> (b) Decline to apply any provision of the enactment by reason only that the provision is inconsistent with any provision of this Bill of Rights. (quoted in Lester and Beattie 2007: 67 note 28)

Lester's 1996 bill failed, but his approach was adopted by the incoming Labour government in 1997, when he again became a government adviser. Labour prepared its ground on the assumption that it might need a coalition with the Liberal Democrats, the party most in favour of incorporation. The parliamentary arithmetic of 1997, however, meant that Labour went it alone. Introducing the Bill which became the Human Rights Act 1998, the Lord Chancellor, Lord Irvine of Lairg, said:

> I look forward especially to the contribution today of the noble Lord, Lord Lester of Herne Hill. His major role in the development of the anti-discrimination legislation of the 1970s under the future Lord Jenkins of Hillhead is well known. I should also acknowledge from this position, as did the White Paper,[2] that he has perhaps for 30 years been a tireless campaigner for legislation on human rights. His has not been a silent but an eloquent vigil, and his day has now almost arrived...

> This Bill will bring human rights home. People will be able to argue for their rights and claim their remedies under the convention in any court or tribunal in the United Kingdom. Our courts will develop human rights throughout society. A culture of awareness of human rights will develop. Before Second Reading of any Bill the responsible Minister will make a statement that the Bill is or is not compatible with convention rights...

> Our critics say the Bill will cede powers to Europe, will politicise the judiciary and will diminish parliamentary sovereignty. We are not ceding new powers to Europe. The United Kingdom already accepts that

Strasbourg rulings bind. Next, the Bill is carefully drafted and designed to respect our traditional understanding of the separation of powers. It does so intellectually convincingly and, if I may express my high regard for the parliamentary draftsman, elegantly.

The design of the Bill is to give the courts as much space as possible to protect human rights, short of a power to set aside or ignore Acts of Parliament. In the very rare cases where the higher courts will find it impossible to read and give effect to any statute in a way which is compatible with convention rights, they will be able to make a declaration of incompatibility. Then it is for Parliament to decide whether there should be remedial legislation. Parliament may, not must, and generally will, legislate. (HL Deb 03 November 1997 vol 582 cc1227–312 quoted at 1227–8)

Since the passage of the Human Rights Act 1998, all except one of the main legal systems that derived from seventeenth-century England have incorporated human rights and to some extent restricted parliamentary sovereignty. The United States did so in 1791. Canada did so in 1982, when it enacted the Canada Charter of Rights and Freedoms as part of the process of patriating the Canadian constitution. Human rights are therefore entrenched unless the federal or a provincial government uses the 'notwithstanding clause' (s.33 of the Charter) to override some of the protected rights for a maximum of five years. This preserves at least a shadow of parliamentary sovereignty. It has been used a handful of times by provincial governments, and never to date by the federal government. India enacted some 'fundamental rights' into Part III of its Constitution in 1950. The then Attorney General of India explained in 2004 that all pre-independence constitution drafts drafted either by Indians or by their British sympathizers had included rights protection. The (British) Simon Commission of 1930 had dismissed the idea. Therefore, it was natural for India to adopt entrenched rights at independence (Sorabjee 2004). India also created a Human Rights Commission in 1993.[3] The South African Constitution of 1996 incorporates a bill of rights, which states at s.39(2), 'When interpreting any legislation, and when developing the common law or customary law, every court, tribunal or forum must promote the spirit, purport and objects of the Bill of Rights.' The Republic of Ireland incorporated the ECHR into domestic law by its European Convention on Human Rights Act 2003. This Act is modelled on the UK statute, and provides for declarations of incompatibility on similar lines. The only Anglophone common-law legal system that descends from the Glorious Revolution but has not enacted a bill of Rights at federal level is Australia. There was discussion at the time of Federation of incorporation of a US-style bill of rights, but this did not prevail. Recently, the states of Victoria and ACT have adopted Bills of Rights at state level (*Justice* 2007).

Of these Anglophone systems, therefore, the United States has the strongest entrenchment; Canada the next strongest; and the others try to reconcile the principles of entrenched rights and of parliamentary sovereignty in various ways—very similar ways in New Zealand, the United Kingdom, and Ireland, which copied one another's statutes.

Young (2009: 2) argues that the format of the act 'facilitates inter-institutional dialogue between the legislature and the courts'. What form has that dialogue taken? Not all states that have signed the ECHR are required to adopt all of its clauses and protocols. The Convention and those of its Protocols currently (autumn 2008) ratified by the United Kingdom are in the Appendix to this chapter. Some of the rights they confer are unqualified, for example, the prohibition of torture in Article 2 and of slavery in Article 3. Others are qualified by wording such as the typical sub-paragraph 2 of Article 9 on freedom of religion:

> 2. Freedom to manifest one's religion or beliefs shall be subject only to such limitations as are prescribed by law and are necessary in a democratic society in the interests of public safety, for the protection of public order, health or morals, or for the protection of the rights and freedoms of others.

Freedom of religion is absolute; freedom to manifest one's religion is qualified. Thus, several UK (and other) attempts to use Article 9 to overturn school and employment dress codes to allow religious observers to wear, variously, a jilbab, niqab, or 'purity ring'[4] have failed because the freedom to manifest one's religion or beliefs is not unqualified.

Section 3 of the Human Rights Act 1998 states:

> So far as it is possible to do so, primary legislation and subordinate legislation must be read and given effect in a way which is compatible with the Convention rights.

Where a court decides that it is not possible to do so, it may issue a declaration of incompatibility (Table 10.1). These procedures constitute the mechanism by which Parliament and the courts display what Young and other lawyers call 'comity' to one another: 'Comity between the legislature and the courts not only furthers stability, but instigates a form of checks and balances between the legislature and the courts' (Young 2009: 172). By 'comity' she means respectful collaboration: a mutual recognition by each that the other is better placed to do dome of the things in their joint territory. The Canadian lawyer Janet Hiebert (1996, 2002) has explored this in her studies of the relationship between the Canadian Parliament and courts in the interpretation of the weakly entrenched *Canadian Charter of Rights and Freedoms*. The Charter itself defers to the legislature in two places. Section

33 allows a legislature to pass time-limited laws 'notwithstanding' an avowed incompatibility with Charter rights. Section 1 states:

> The Canadian Charter of Rights and Freedoms guarantees the rights and freedoms set out in it subject only to such reasonable limits prescribed by law as can be demonstrably justified in a free and democratic society.

When a law seemed to conflict with a Charter right, Canadian judges therefore had to decide how far to defer to the legislature's view of what is reasonable. They have recognized that it may be dangerous to impose their view of reasonability over the legislature's.

Returning to the equivalent UK problem with Convention rights, Young states, 'although courts can interpret legislation to achieve compatibility, they cannot question or overturn legislation that is incompatible with Convention rights' (2009: 4). The Ministry of Justice has tabulated all the declarations in force as at January 2009 (Table 10.1).

Table 10.1 shows that of the fifteen declarations in force, six concerned immigration, asylum, or terrorism issues; three concerned mental health; two the rights of convicted criminals; and four the personal rights of small (and unpopular) groups of citizens such as social workers and those convicted of attempted buggery in Northern Ireland. This encapsulates the political problem of human rights. The humans whose rights are likeliest to be violated are those with whom the median voter has little sympathy. Probably the only case in Table 10.1 of which this is not true is #6, which led to the Human

Table 10.1 Declarations of incompatibility with the European Convention on Human Rights issued by UK courts since entry into force of the Human Rights Act 1998.

	Subject	Date D of I issued	Statute declared incompatible with ECHR	Result to Jan. 2009
1	Mental health— discharge from hospital	28.03.01	Mental Health Act 1983 s.72, s.73	Amended
2	'attempted buggery'— N. Ireland	15.01.02	Offences against the Person act 1861 s.62	Repealed
3	Penalties on carriers unknowingly transporting clandestine entrants to the United Kingdom	22.02.02	Immigration and Asylum Act 1999 Part II	Amended

4	Sec. of State's power to set minimum life tariff	25.11.02	Crime (Sentences) Act 1997 s.29	Repealed
5	Discretionary life prisoner—access to court	19.12.02	Mental Health Act 1983 s.74	Amended
6	Deceased father's name not allowable on birth certificate	28.02.03	Human Fertilisation and Embryology Act 1990 s. 28(6)(b)	Amended
7	Validity of marriage of post-op. ♂-to-♀ transsexual	10.04.03	Matrimonial Causes Act 1973 s.11(c)	Amended
8	Designation of abusive adoptive father as 'nearest relative' of mental patient	16.04.03	Mental Health Act 1983 s.26, s.29	Amended
9	Detention of foreign nationals: derogation from ECHR Article 5 (1)	16.12.04	Anti-Terrorism, Crime and Security Act 2001 s.23	Derogation quashed; section replaced
10	Disregarding dependent children subject to immigration control in determining eligibility for social housing	14.10.05	Housing Act 1996 s.185(4)	Amended; relevant Schedule not yet in force
11	As #10 but with respect to pregnant wife	28.03.06	As #10	As #10
12	Anti-sham marriage procedures for persons subject to immigration control	10.04.06; 16.06.06	Asylum and Immigration (Treatment of Claimants, etc.) Act 2004 s.19(3)	Scope of DoI restricted by higher court. 'The Government is considering how to rectify the [remaining] incompatibility'
13	Listing care workers as unsuitable to work with vulnerable adults	21.01.09 (date of reinstatement of DoI by Lords)	Care Standards Act 2000 s.82(4)(b)	'The Government is considering how to rectify the incompatibility'
14	Early release provisions for prisoners that discriminate by national origin	13.12.06	Criminal Justice Act 1991 s.46(1) and 50(2)	Amended
15	Blanket ban on convicted prisoners voting in	24.01.07	Representation of the People Act 1983 s.3(1)	'The Government is currently engaged in a process of consultation

(*continued*)

Table 10.1 (Continued)

Subject	Date D of I issued	Statute declared incompatible with ECHR	Result to Jan. 2009
Parliamentary elections			on how to respond . . . so as to provide the public debate on this issue that had been identified as lacking'.

Sources: http://www.dca.gov.uk/peoples-rights/human-rights/pdf/decl-incompat-tabl.pdfhttp://www.dca.gov.uk/ peoples-rights/human-rights/pdf/decl-incompat-tabl.pdf accessed 30 October, 2008; Ministry of Justice 2009. My précis of subject descriptions. Disregards two declarations in respect of provisions (discriminating against widowers) that had already been repealed, seven declarations issued but overturned by a higher court, and two under appeal at the time of the most recent list.

Fertilisation and Embryology (Deceased Fathers) Act 2003. One would have to have a heart of stone not to think that Act a good deed in a wicked world.

Another monitor is the refreshingly bad-tempered annual reports of the Joint Committee [of the two houses of Parliament] on Human Rights and the Government responses (latest at JCHR 2008 and Ministry of Justice 2009). These discuss both the DoIs and individual judgments against the UK at the Strasbourg court. In its latest report, the Joint Committee waspishly notes that:

> In our previous reports, we have drawn attention to a number of cases where significant delay in implementation has tarnished the otherwise good record of the United Kingdom in responding to the judgments of the European Court of Human Rights. For the most part, these cases have been legally straightforward, but politically difficult. (Joint Committee on Human Rights 2008: paragraph 4.62)

This encapsulates the political problem of human rights. Usually, they are the rights of the deeply unpopular. In Chapter 14, I will return to the vexed question of what an eminent US Supreme Court Justice, Harlan Stone, called 'discrete and insular minorities' that might need special protection from majoritarian legislatures.

Comity requires separation of powers. Paeans to the general wonderfulness of the British Constitution since (and including) Bagehot have enjoyed pointing out that Montesquieu got Britain wrong. The efficient secret of government in Britain was the fusion, not the separation, of executive and legislature. But Bagehot's praise cannot be extended to the fusion of government and judiciary. The position of Lord Chancellor, who until 2005 straddled all three branches, became intolerably anomalous in the human rights era. The Lord Chancellor simultaneously presided over a house of the legislature (the Lords); directed the judiciary; and was a senior member of the executive as a Cabinet Minister.[5] The Constitutional Reform Act 2005 ends these anomalies, although the circumstances of its introduction were extremely messy. It makes comity possible by fully separating the executive from the judiciary.

A BRITISH BILL OF RIGHTS?

The 1998 Act has not been incorporated into the hearts and minds of the British people. At the time of writing, the policy of the Conservative Party is to repeal it and replace it by a British Bill of Rights.[6] Human rights lawyers and civil libertarians have been sceptical about this policy. Unless accompanied by withdrawal from the ECHR, the effect of such a repeal would merely be to restore the situation as it was between 1966 and 1998, namely, that UK citizens who felt their human rights had been violated could go to Strasbourg for a remedy. It is unlikely that it would lead UK judges to change their recent practice of taking into account the human rights implications of the cases before them. And if British Conservatives did withdraw from the ECHR, they would be abandoning an institution created by British Conservatives in the shadow of Nazism and communism.

But if bad law, the Conservatives' proposal is good politics. Other parties are making similar noises about a British Bill of Rights—although the other parties' bills would add to, rather than subtract from, the ECHR rights. For human rights to be entrenched, there has to be a sort of magical transformation of the sort that has occurred in the United States and Canada. Those countries' entrenched protections of human rights (respectively the Constitution and Bill of Rights, and the Canada Charter of Rights and Freedoms) are overwhelmingly popular. But there is no reason to suppose that the marginal people whose rights they directly protect, including migrants, criminals, and those with unusual sexual tastes, are any more popular in those countries than elsewhere. The magical transformation is that people, seemingly, love their constitutions without knowing what is in them.

The legal NGO *Justice* recently published a weighty report on how a British Bill of Rights might be enacted, and how it might go beyond the ECHR (Justice 2007). Unusually for an NGO report, it can be reached directly from the web page of the Ministry of Justice. In devastatingly polite footnotes, it reveals the incoherence of Conservative policy (although Conservative lawyers served on it). The public lawyers and constitutionally minded political scientists who served on the *Justice* committee were clear that a British Bill of Rights could only add to, not subtract from, ECHR rights. A Bill of Rights drafted nowadays would differ from that of 1950. For instance, a modern bill would be unlikely to permit the 'lawful detention of persons for the prevention of the spreading of infectious diseases, of persons of unsound mind, alcoholics or drug addicts or vagrants', as the 1950 document does. As *Justice* crisply says, a modern code would not imprison people 'merely for what they are rather than for what they have done'.[7] It might also add rights not to suffer discrimination on grounds of sexual orientation; and restrictions on surveillance.

This book is not about futurology. But I nevertheless predict that the rapid rise of human rights jurisprudence in the United Kingdom is unlikely to be reversed under a government of any political complexion. In Chapter 14, I will return to the question: if rights are to be entrenched, should it be by the indirect 'interpret consistently with Convention, failing which declare incompatibility' route studied in this chapter, or by the direct disapplication of statute, as studied in the EU cases discussed in Chapter 9?

Appendix to Chapter 10

European Convention on Human Rights and Protocols Adopted by the United Kingdom as of 2008

Articles of the European Convention on Human Rights and Protocols given further effect by the United Kingdom under Schedule 1 of the Human Rights Act 1998. List as of 2008.

Part I

THE CONVENTION

Rights and Freedoms

Article 2

Right to life

1. Everyone's right to life shall be protected by law. (No one shall be deprived of his life intentionally save in the execution of a sentence of a court following his conviction of a crime for which this penalty is provided by law). [this sentence superseded by Thirteenth Protocol, see below]
2. Deprivation of life shall not be regarded as inflicted in contravention of this Article when it results from the use of force which is no more than absolutely necessary:
(a) in defence of any person from unlawful violence
(b) in order to effect a lawful arrest or to prevent the escape of a person lawfully detained
(c) in action lawfully taken for the purpose of quelling a riot or insurrection.

Article 3

Prohibition of torture

No one shall be subjected to torture or to inhuman or degrading treatment or punishment.

Article 4

Prohibition of slavery and forced labour

1. No one shall be held in slavery or servitude.
2. No one shall be required to perform forced or compulsory labour.
3. For the purpose of this Article the term 'forced or compulsory labour' shall not include:
(a) any work required to be done in the ordinary course of detention imposed according to the provisions of Article 5 of this Convention or during conditional release from such detention

(b) any service of a military character or, in case of conscientious objectors in countries where they are recognised, service exacted instead of compulsory military service

(c) any service exacted in case of an emergency or calamity threatening the life or well-being of the community

(d) any work or service which forms part of normal civic obligations.

Article 5
Right to liberty and security

1. Everyone has the right to liberty and security of person. No one shall be deprived of his liberty save in the following cases and in accordance with a procedure prescribed by law:

(a) the lawful detention of a person after conviction by a competent court

(b) the lawful arrest or detention of a person for non-compliance with the lawful order of a court or in order to secure the fulfilment of any obligation prescribed by law

(c) the lawful arrest or detention of a person effected for the purpose of bringing him before the competent legal authority on reasonable suspicion of having committed an offence or when it is reasonably considered necessary to prevent his committing an offence or fleeing after having done so

(d) the detention of a minor by lawful order for the purpose of educational supervision or his lawful detention for the purpose of bringing him before the competent legal authority

(e) the lawful detention of persons for the prevention of the spreading of infectious diseases, of persons of unsound mind, alcoholics or drug addicts or vagrants

(f) the lawful arrest or detention of a person to prevent his effecting an unauthorised entry into the country or of a person against whom action is being taken with a view to deportation or extradition.

2. Everyone who is arrested shall be informed promptly, in a language which he understands, of the reasons for his arrest and of any charge against him.

3. Everyone arrested or detained in accordance with the provisions of paragraph 1(c) of this Article shall be brought promptly before a judge or other officer authorised by law to exercise judicial power and shall be entitled to trial within a reasonable time or to release pending trial. Release may be conditioned by guarantees to appear for trial.

4. Everyone who is deprived of his liberty by arrest or detention shall be entitled to take proceedings by which the lawfulness of his detention shall be decided speedily by a court and his release ordered if the detention is not lawful.

5. Everyone who has been the victim of arrest or detention in contravention of the provisions of this Article shall have an enforceable right to compensation.

Article 6
Right to a fair trial

1. In the determination of his civil rights and obligations or of any criminal charge against him, everyone is entitled to a fair and public hearing within a reasonable time by an independent and impartial tribunal established by law. Judgment shall be pronounced publicly but the press and public may be excluded from all or part of the trial in the interest of morals, public order or national security in a democratic society, where the interests of juveniles or the protection of the private life of the parties so require, or to the extent strictly necessary in the opinion of the court in special circumstances where publicity would prejudice the interests of justice.

2. Everyone charged with a criminal offence shall be presumed innocent until proved guilty according to law.

3. Everyone charged with a criminal offence has the following minimum rights:

(a) to be informed promptly, in a language which he understands and in detail, of the nature and cause of the accusation against him

(b) to have adequate time and facilities for the preparation of his defence

(c) to defend himself in person or through legal assistance of his own choosing or, if he has not sufficient means to pay for legal assistance, to be given it free when the interests of justice so require

(d) to examine or have examined witnesses against him and to obtain the attendance and examination of witnesses on his behalf under the same conditions as witnesses against him

(e) to have the free assistance of an interpreter if he cannot understand or speak the language used in court.

Article 7
No punishment without law

1. No one shall be held guilty of any criminal offence on account of any act or omission which did not constitute a criminal offence under national or international law at the time when it was committed. Nor shall a heavier penalty be imposed than the one that was applicable at the time the criminal offence was committed.

2. This Article shall not prejudice the trial and punishment of any person for any act or omission which, at the time when it was committed, was criminal according to the general principles of law recognised by civilised nations.

Article 8
Right to respect for private and family life

1. Everyone has the right to respect for his private and family life, his home and his correspondence.

2. There shall be no interference by a public authority with the exercise of this right except such as is in accordance with the law and is necessary in a democratic society in the interests of national security, public safety or the economic well-being of the country, for the prevention of disorder or crime, for the protection of health or morals, or for the protection of the rights and freedoms of others.

Article 9
Freedom of thought, conscience and religion

1. Everyone has the right to freedom of thought, conscience and religion. This right includes freedom to change his religion or belief and freedom, either alone or in community with others and in public or private, to manifest his religion or belief, in worship, teaching, practice and observance.
2. Freedom to manifest one's religion or beliefs shall be subject only to such limitations as are prescribed by law and are necessary in a democratic society in the interests of public safety, for the protection of public order, health or morals, or for the protection of the rights and freedoms of others.

Article 10
Freedom of expression

1. Everyone has the right to freedom of expression. This right shall include freedom to hold opinions and to receive and impart information and ideas without interference by public authority and regardless of frontiers. This Article shall not prevent States from requiring the licensing of broadcasting, television or cinema enterprises.
2. The exercise of these freedoms, since it carries with it duties and responsibilities, may be subject to such formalities, conditions, restrictions or penalties as are prescribed by law and are necessary in a democratic society, in the interests of national security, territorial integrity or public safety, for the prevention of disorder or crime, for the protection of health or morals, for the protection of the reputation or rights of others, for preventing the disclosure of information received in confidence, or for maintaining the authority and impartiality of the judiciary.

Article 11
Freedom of assembly and association

1. Everyone has the right to freedom of peaceful assembly and to freedom of association with others, including the right to form and to join trade unions for the protection of his interests.
2. No restrictions shall be placed on the exercise of these rights other than such as are prescribed by law and are necessary in a democratic society in the interests of national security or public safety, for the prevention of disorder or crime, for the

protection of health or morals or for the protection of the rights and freedoms of others. This Article shall not prevent the imposition of lawful restrictions on the exercise of these rights by members of the armed forces, of the police or of the administration of the State.

Article 12

Right to marry

Men and women of marriageable age have the right to marry and to found a family, according to the national laws governing the exercise of this right.

Article 14

Prohibition of discrimination

The enjoyment of the rights and freedoms set forth in this Convention shall be secured without discrimination on any ground such as sex, race, colour, language, religion, political or other opinion, national or social origin, association with a national minority, property, birth or other status.

Article 16

Restrictions on political activity of aliens

Nothing in Articles 10, 11 and 14 shall be regarded as preventing the High Contracting Parties from imposing restrictions on the political activity of aliens.

Article 17

Prohibition of abuse of rights

Nothing in this Convention may be interpreted as implying for any State, group or person any right to engage in any activity or perform any act aimed at the destruction of any of the rights and freedoms set forth herein or at their limitation to a greater extent than is provided for in the Convention.

Article 18

Limitation on use of restrictions on rights

The restrictions permitted under this Convention to the said rights and freedoms shall not be applied for any purpose other than those for which they have been prescribed.

PART II

THE FIRST PROTOCOL

Article 1

Protection of property

Every natural or legal person is entitled to the peaceful enjoyment of his possessions. No one shall be deprived of his possessions except in the public interest and subject to the conditions provided for by law and by the general principles of international law.

The preceding provisions shall not, however, in any way impair the right of a State to enforce such laws as it deems necessary to control the use of property in accordance with the general interest or to secure the payment of taxes or other contributions or penalties.

Article 2
Right to education
No person shall be denied the right to education. In the exercise of any functions which it assumes in relation to education and to teaching, the State shall respect the right of parents to ensure such education and teaching in conformity with their own religious and philosophical convictions.

Article 3
Right to free elections
The High Contracting Parties undertake to hold free elections at reasonable intervals by secret ballot, under conditions which will ensure the free expression of the opinion of the people in the choice of the legislature.

ARTICLE 1 OF THE THIRTEENTH PROTOCOL

Abolition of the death penalty
The death penalty shall be abolished. No one shall be condemned to such penalty or executed.

Part IV

Things to Leave Out of a Written Constitution

11

Unelected Houses

LORD MOUNTARARAT. This comes of women interfering in politics. It so happens that if there is an institution in Great Britain which is not susceptible of any improvement at all, it is the House of Peers!

SONG—LORD MOUNTARARAT

When Britain really ruled the waves –
(In good Queen Bess's time)
The House of Peers made no pretence
To intellectual eminence,
Or scholarship sublime;
Yet Britain won her proudest bays
In good Queen Bess's glorious days!
When Wellington licked Bonaparte,
As every child can tell,
The House of Peers throughout the war
Did nothing in particular
And did it very well.
Yet Britain set the world ablaze
In good King George's glorious days.
And while the House of Peers withholds
Its legislative hand,
And noble statesmen do not itch
To interfere in matters which
They do not understand,
As bright will shine Great Britain's rays
As in King George's glorious days.

(Gilbert 1882, Lord Mountararat's Song, Act II)

AN UNELECTED UPPER HOUSE

The United Kingdom's Parliament, in the mouth of a lawyer (to quote Dicey 1885: 37 one more time) comprises three chambers. Two of them are unelected: the House of Lords and the monarch. This and the next chapter discuss how these two chambers might be reshaped if parliamentary sovereignty were to be replaced by a conception based on popular sovereignty.

The English parliament was bicameral from high medieval times, except for a brief period under Cromwell, when it was first unicameral and then zero-cameral. Under feudalism, barons were deemed to hold their land from the king on condition that they performed military service when required. They passed the same reciprocal obligations on to their tenants. As the Royal Commission on the Reform of the House of Lords explains:

> With its origins in the medieval royal practice of summoning the great landowners (both lay and ecclesiastical) to offer counsel and provide resources, the House of Lords pre-dates the House of Commons by some centuries and it was long the pre-eminent House of Parliament. The House of Commons' power over financial resources was evident as early as the 14th century, and it asserted its sole privilege in financial matters from the 17th century onwards. (Wakeham 2000*a*, 2.1)

Note: 'both lay and ecclesiastical'. Medieval bishops sat in the Lords primarily because they owned land, not because they were spiritual advisers.

Perhaps because feudalism was less developed in Scotland, where some land tenure remained 'allodial' (freehold) and there was no Norman Conquest, the Scottish Parliament before 1707 was unicameral. The Irish Parliament before 1800 was bicameral. At the two Unions, Scotland and Ireland were assigned a number of 'representative peers' (sixteen for Scotland and twenty-eight for Ireland), to be chosen, indeed, by their peers, to sit in the enlarged House of Lords. For Ireland, this system ended with independence in 1922; for Scotland, it ended in 1963. From then until 1999, all Scottish peers could sit in the House of Lords.

As already noted in the Introduction, some of the officers of Cromwell's army debated representation in Putney Church in October 1647. The 'Levellers' had produced a document called 'An agreement of the people for a firm and present peace upon grounds of common right and freedom'.

> *Commissary-General Henry Ireton:* . . . It is said they [MPs] are to be distributed according to the number of inhabitants. This does make me think that the meaning is that every man that is an inhabitant is to be equally considered, and to have an equal voice in the election of representers . . . and if that be the meaning then I have something to say against it.
>
> *Maximilian Petty:* We judge that all inhabitants that have not lost their birthright should have an equal voice in elections.
>
> *Colonel Thomas Rainborough:* I desired that those that had engaged in it might be included. For really I think that the poorest he that is in England has a life to live as the greatest he; and therefore truly, sir, I think it's clear

that every man that is to live under a government ought first by his own consent to put himself under that government; and I do think that the poorest man in England is not at all bound in a strict sense to that government that he has not had a voice to put himself under. (Sharp 1998: 102–3)

Colonel Rainborough's ideas were reformulated by John Locke and the American revolutionaries. But in their native land, after the restoration of the monarchy in 1660, General Ireton's views overrode Colonel Rainborough's at least until the 'Great' Reform Act of 1832. The nineteenth-century reform acts forced the issues raised at Putney back on to the political agenda. However, the renewed Putney debate beginning in 1831 did not take the form of calls for an elected Lords or monarchy. Rather, the argument went as follows: given that one house of Parliament was elected (by a broadening franchise as the century wore on), ought not the unelected house, and the monarchy, to defer to it? The idea that the Commons held the primacy over supply, in particular, already familiar to Rainborough and his contemporaries, was imported into the US and Australian Constitutions, was challenged in 1909, and was finally reaffirmed in 1911.

The constitutional crisis of 1832 was resolved by the Lords' and King William IV's surrender to the Commons, where the Whigs under Earl Grey had a huge majority. Threatened with the mass creation of peers, and civil disturbance in the streets, Tory peers abstained on the final voting and the Reform Act became law. As in 1911, no peers were actually created. The next constitutional crisis blew up only a dozen years later. The Duke of Wellington, who had been an unsuccessful Prime Minister as the Reform Bill crisis was brewing, discovered as leader of the Lords in the 1840s a deftness he had earlier lacked. The Tory Prime Minister Sir Robert Peel (1841–6) deeply offended many of his own supporters, twice. In 1845 he proposed an enhanced grant to the Roman Catholic seminary at Maynooth, County Kildare, Ireland. This was anathema to what were called the Ultras—politicians who believed ardently in Protestant supremacy. They were stronger in the Lords than in the Commons. How could Wellington prevent them from defeating the government?

After pretending not to hear an interruption from the Ultra Duke of Newcastle, who demanded that the proposal be dropped as being inconsistent with the Act of Succession, Wellington went on:

There can be no doubt of the absolute necessity of finding some means of educating the Roman Catholic priests for the service of the Roman Catholic mission in Ireland. It was stated at the time this institution was founded, that the population of Ireland was 3,000,000. It has advanced to the amount of 8,175,000—it was so in the year 1841, and probably it is now 8,500,000; and of that number, about the seven-eights are to be considered as Roman Catholics; and there can be no doubt whatsoever, whatever the numbers may be, that a very large proportion of the people in Ireland are Roman Catholics—that we cannot avoid their being Roman Catholics—and that we must find the means of providing them with ecclesiastics capable of administering to them the rites of the Roman Catholic Church—that we must have these ecclesiastics educated at home, or we must consent to and encourage the sending them abroad. (*HL Deb 02 June 1845 vol 80 cc1160–1174*)

On the even greater 'betrayal' of Repeal of the Corn Laws the following year, to which Wellington was personally opposed, he went further:

My Lords, in the month of December last, I felt myself bound, by my duty to my Sovereign, not to withhold my assistance from the Government—not to decline to resume my seat in Her Majesty's Councils—not to refuse to give my assistance to the Government of my right hon. Friend (Sir R. Peel)—knowing as I did, at the time, that my right hon. Friend could not do otherwise than propose to Parliament a measure of this description . . . I am in Her Majesty's service—bound to Her Majesty and to the Sovereigns of this country by considerations of gratitude of which it is not necessary that I should say more to your Lordships . . . This measure, my Lords, was recommended by the Speech from the Throne, and it has been passed by a majority of the House of Commons, consisting of more than half the Members of that House . . . *We know by the Votes that it has been passed by a majority of the House of Commons; we know that is recommended by the Crown; and we know that, if we should reject this Bill, it is a Bill which has been agreed to by the other two branches of the Legislature; and that the House of Lords stands alone in rejecting this measure. Now that, my Lords, is a situation in which I beg to remind your Lordships, I have frequently stated you ought not to stand; it is a position in which you cannot stand, because you are entirely powerless; without the House of Commons and the Crown, the House of Lords can do nothing.* (HL Deb 28 May 1846 vol 86 cc1401–05. My emphasis.)

Thus Wellington in the 1840s claimed that if the House of Lords was isolated—on the opposite side to the Crown and the Commons—it ought not to press its opposition. It was not what he had said or thought earlier. Also, it could be objected (and was—for an example, see McLean 2001*a*: 54) that Wellington's line left the Lords with nothing to do. That might have been good, as Gilbert's Lord Mountararat was to observe in 1882. But the alternative carried an opposite risk.

Consider some vulgar Marxist analysis of class interests. Until 1958 there were only three ways to become a member of the House of Lords: to become a bishop, or a senior judge, or (the overwhelmingly predominant route) to inherit a title. Titles go, by the rules of succession, to the eldest son of the previous title-holder. So, generally, did landed estates in the British Isles, despite the protests of Adam Smith, Thomas Jefferson, and many other thinkers of the Enlightenment that there was neither economic nor moral basis for this practice, known as 'primogeniture'. The economic effect of primogeniture was that landed estates were not often split up, but went to a sole inheritor from generation to generation. Therefore the House of Lords became, not merely a landed house, but a house comprising, on average, the wealthiest landowners in the United Kingdom.

The Industrial Revolution changed this less than might be expected. True, it shifted economic activity to cities and mining villages: But they, too, sit on land, and land was usually owned by a large landowner. The traditional aristocracy cornered substantial income streams from mining (e.g. the Earls of Bute and the Marquesses of Londonderry) and urban development (e.g. the Dukes of Devonshire and Westminster). It follows that the interests of the class most likely to be found in the House of Lords were overwhelmingly landed. We saw earlier what this caused them to do to the 1909 Budget.

Wellington's policy of ensuring that the House of Peers withheld its legislative hand was continued by his immediate successors. It was changed by Lord Cranborne, later the third Marquess of Salisbury, a leading Conservative peer from 1868, Tory leader from 1880, and Prime Minister four times between 1885 and 1902. Salisbury's first action was a managed retreat, over the disestablishment of the Anglican Church in Ireland. The Liberals had made it a prominent campaign issue in the 1868 general election, which they won. Before that election, the Liberals had won a Commons vote on the issue, but Salisbury had directly argued against the Wellington doctrine.

> My Lords, it occurs to me to ask the noble Earl whether he has considered for what purpose this House exists, and whether he would be willing to go through the humiliation of being a mere echo and supple tool of the other House in order to secure for himself the luxury of mock legislation? I agree with my noble Friend the noble Earl (the Earl of Derby) below me that it were better not to be than submit to such a slavery. ...[O]n these rare and great occasions, on which the national mind has fully declared itself, I do not doubt your Lordships would yield to the opinion of the country— otherwise the machinery of Government could not be carried on. But there is an enormous step between that and being the mere echo of the House of Commons. (HL Deb 26 June 1868 vol 193 c.89)

However, after the general election Salisbury recognized, against his personal interests and tastes as a high Tory, that the Liberal government now had the right to pursue Irish disestablishment. He echoed his own 'mere echo' speech, this time saying:

> If we do merely echo the House of Commons, the sooner we disappear the better. The object of the existence of a second House of Parliament is to supply the omissions and correct the defects which occur in the proceedings of the first. But it is perfectly true that there may be occasions in our history in which the decision of the House of Commons and the decision of the nation must be taken as practically the same. (HL Deb 17 June 1869 vol 197 cc83–4HL Deb 17 June 1869 vol 197 cc18–118)

Irish disestablishment was such a case, as it was the specific platform on which the Liberals under Gladstone had gone to the country and won.

Salisbury therefore sought an alternative basis for Lords' resistance. By 1872 he had found it:

> The plan which I prefer is frankly to acknowledge that the nation is our Master, though the House of Commons is not, and to yield our opinion only when the judgement of the nation has been challenged at the polls and decidedly expressed. This doctrine, it seems to me, has the advantage of being: (1) Theoretically sound. (2) Popular. (3) Safe against agitation, and (4) so rarely applicable as practically to place little fetter upon our independence. (Salisbury to Lord Carnarvon, 20.02.1872, in Cecil 1921–32, vol. 2, 25–6)

Salisbury had thus neatly moved from accepting Commons supremacy when the general election had conferred a mandate, to accepting it *only* when a general election had called a mandate. In his typically clear and cynical way, he thought this would arise 'so rarely as practically to place little fetter upon our independence'. But, the vulgar Marxist may note, class conflict in the Parliament intensified after 1868. As the franchise extended in 1867 and 1884, so the economic interest of the median voter moved further down the income distribution. Increasingly the Conservatives became the party of capital as well as the party of land. Gladstone, as socially conservative as he was politically radical, continued to respect the monarchy and the Whig aristocracy, which did not reciprocate. More and more Whig peers became Tories, including peers created or advanced by Gladstone himself; and the flow became a flood after Gladstone became converted to the cause of Irish Home Rule in 1885.

As Liberalism moved left, Salisbury's Conservatism became more and more reactionary, using that word non-emotively. His own colleagues wondered whether he was pushing the Lords too far. W. S. Gilbert, who poured his satirical scorn equally on all parties, may have been implying this in his most political libretto, *Iolanthe* (1882)—notably when he has Lord Mountararat sing (to Sullivan's magnificent music) his paean to the uselessness of the House of Peers. The sublime pairing of Sullivan's big tunes and Gilbert's mordant satire has two other peaks: the Sentry's Song, also in *Iolanthe* ('every boy and every gal/That's born into the world alive/Is either a little Liberal/ Or else a little Conservative'), and the Boatswain's Song in *HMS Pinafore* ('But, in spite of all temptations/To belong to other nations/He remains an Englishman').

However, any confrontation between the houses was delayed by the Liberal split of 1886 over Irish Home Rule. The partisan effect of the split was to weaken the Liberals in both houses. In the Commons they had a bare majority in the Parliament of 1892–5, dependent on the Irish Party and insufficient to lead a 'Peers against the People' appeal against the Lords' rejection of the second Irish Home Rule Bill by 419 to 41. That rejection had in turn become inevitable because by 1893 almost all the Whig peers had become Unionists (the name the Conservatives and their Liberal Unionist allies took between 1887 and 1914).

Salisbury's own views about Irish Catholics were pungent:

> You would not confide free representative institutions to the Hottentots, for instance... When you come to narrow it down you will find that this,— which is called self-government but is really government by the majority,— works admirably when it is confided to people who are of Teutonic race, but that it does not work so well when people of other races are called upon to join it. (Speech at St James' Hall, 15.05.1886, in Cecil 1921–32, 3:302; See Bentley 2001: 235.)

After his death, this attitude—shared by many of his successors—combined with his doctrine of the mandate to give the Unionists the unshakeable assurance, discussed in earlier chapters, that they and not the elected house of Parliament represented the will of the people.

This proposition was never tested in a general election. Therefore, the only evidence bearing on it is the trend of by-elections in the Parliament of 1910–14. Figure 11.1 shows the trend, where the variations in individual by-election results are smoothed by grouping the by-elections into two-month periods.

Throughout the constitutional crisis, Unionists insisted that they represented the voice of the people; that the Liberals had no mandate for Irish Home Rule; and that therefore the conditions for Lords' deference to the Commons were not met. Dicey wrote to Bonar Law, proposing:

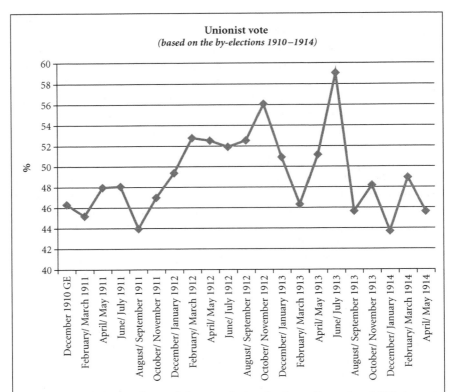

Figure 11.1 Unionist share of the vote in by-elections, December 1910–August 1914 (grouped).

(*Source*: Our calculations from Craig 1974. By-elections in Ireland excluded.)

The National Insurance Act 1911 was enacted on 6 December, having been widely discussed during the year. Its sections were gradually brought into operation during 1912.

The Marconi 'scandal' broke in summer 1912 in the shape of allegations that government ministers including Lloyd George had benefited from insider trading in the shares of the Marconi wireless company. It ended with a parliamentary select committee report in June 1913 which divided on party lines. The majority cleared Lloyd George and his colleagues of wrongdoing.

The Irish constitutional crisis became gradually more acute during 1913 and 1914. The Curragh 'mutiny' took place on 20.03.14; the Larne gunrunning on 24–25.04.14.

1. the presentation of petitions for a dissolution;
2. the constant holding of meetings in favour of it;
3. the clamour of it at every contested election;
4. the subordination of every other object to the obtaining of a dissolution; and
5. the gaining if possible of contested elections. (A. V. Dicey to A. Bonar Law 28.03,13, BLP 29/2/45, cited by Smith 1993: 165)

Liberals, including Prime Minister Asquith, insisted that the December 1910 election *was* acknowledged by both sides to be about Home Rule; that there was no evidence that the country had rejected the Liberals; and that were a general election to be called, it might be dominated not by Home Rule but by 'the Insurance Act, the Marconi contract, and a score of other "issues" which happened for the moment to preoccupy public attention' (Asquith to George V, [19].09.1913, Appendix to Chapter 12).

Figure 11.1 enables us to test these claims. The overall picture is that following a mid-term loss of popularity (normal in the United Kingdom, and observed in almost every parliament since democracy began), the Liberals and allies were in the same position at the outbreak of war in August 1914 as they had occupied at the December 1910 general election. The dates of the Insurance Act and the Marconi 'scandal' are given in the source notes to Figure 11.1. There appears to be a correlation between the Insurance Bill/Act being under discussion and relative Liberal success; between Marconi being under discussion and relative Unionist success; and between the increased Unionist militancy over Ireland and a sharp reversal of Unionist fortunes. As far as they go, the data vindicate Asquith and do not support the Unionists' claims to represent the people. Dicey's proposed strategy was doomed. Therefore he and Law were forced to suggest undemocratic means of halting Home Rule, via the Lords, the king, the Army, and the paramilitaries.

After the cataclysmic events of 1909–14, proponents of Salisbury's mandate theory went quiet for three decades. The Labour governments of 1924 and 1929–31 were both minority governments, so it was difficult to frame disputes between the houses as 'peers against people' arguments. However, the issue returned in full force with the results of the 1945 general election, which returned a Labour government in the Commons with a majority of 156 over all other parties put together. In the Lords, Labour was, in the words of Viscount Addison, Leader of the House, 'but a tiny atoll in the vast ocean of Tory reaction' (quoted by Morgan and Morgan 1980: 252).

The Conservative leader in the House of Lords was Lord Cranborne, grandson of the third Marquess of Salisbury, and later to become fifth Marquess. He had a good relationship with Addison (who was much older and had first been a minister in 1914) and was, initially, much more accommodating than his grandfather. In the 1945 debate on the King's speech introducing the Labour government's nationalization programme in the Lords, he said:

> Whatever our personal views, we should frankly recognize that these proposals were put before the country at the recent General Election and that the people of this country, with full knowledge of these proposals, returned the Labour Party to power. The Government may, therefore, I think, fairly claim that they have a mandate to introduce these proposals. I believe that it would be constitutionally wrong, when the country has so recently expressed its view, for this House to oppose proposals which have been definitely put before the electorate. (HL Deb 16 August 1945 vol 137 c47)

Although hedged about with qualifications, this is much milder, and more deferential to the elected house, than his grandfather's views. It is this which is generally now called the 'Salisbury' or 'Salisbury–Addison' convention. As a convention, it has no written form except Cranborne's speech, and in books and articles which discuss this, including a helpful House of Lords Library Note (Dymond and Deadman 2006). It is generally interpreted to imply that the Lords do not vote on second or third reading against a government manifesto bill, and that they do not agree to 'wrecking amendments' to such a bill.

Relations worsened later in the 1945–51 government. On his side, Addison pointed out that the doctrine could not cover issues which came up during the lifetime of the government, such as Indian independence. On his, Cranborne (now the 5th Marquess of Salisbury) complained that what became the 1949 Parliament Act did not come under the terms of his 1945 statement. The Parliament Bill was itself introduced because ministers anticipated that the Conservatives would claim that the bill for iron and steel nationalization was not covered by the terms of the agreement, and that time would run out in the 1945 Parliament before iron and steel nationalization could be carried without Lords' consent under the terms of the 1911 Act. The 1949 Act therefore reduced the time required for a bill to be presented without Lords' consent from two full sessions to one.

The parties never reached full agreement on whether the 1949 bill was itself covered by either the Salisbury–Addison convention or the Parliament Act (*Parliament Bill: Agreed Statement* 1948; Morris-Jones 1948). The Parliament Act 1949 was in the end enacted under the procedures of the 1911 Act without Lords' consent. A recent Law Lords' judgment has rejected the contention that the 1949 Act was itself not validly carried under the terms of the 1911 Act (*R.* [on the application of Jackson] v. *Att.-Gen.* [2005] UKHL 56; [2006] I. A.C. 262).

One more reform to the unelected House was significant before we move on to the modern situation. Legislation in 1958 enabled life peers to be created. This had several consequences:

1. It reduced the Conservative predominance in the Lords, as all parties nominated their supporters (including retired MPs and ministers) for life peerages.
2. An informal convention grew up that party leaders in the Commons could nominate new partisan life peers in rough proportion to their strengths (in seats, not in votes) in the Commons. Thus it arose that all the main parties (and also some minor parties, including Ulster Unionists) had a cadre of working peers, most of those being life peers.
3. By 1997 the majority of members of the House of Lords were life peers.

DEVELOPMENTS SINCE 1997

The changes that have taken place in the House of Lords since 1997 are as great as any since the seventeenth century, with the sole exception of the Parliament Act 1911. The Labour manifesto for the 1997 election promised to 'end the hereditary principle in the House of Lords'. It went on:

> As an initial, self-contained reform, not dependent on further reform in the future, the right of hereditary peers to sit and vote in the House of Lords will be ended by statute. This will be the first stage in a process of reform to make the House of Lords more democratic and representative. The legislative powers of the House of Lords will remain unaltered.
>
> The system of appointment of life peers to the House of Lords will be reviewed. Our objective will be to ensure that over time party appointees as life peers more accurately reflect the proportion of votes cast at the previous general election. We are committed to maintaining an independent cross-bench presence of life peers. No one political party should seek a majority in the House of Lords.
>
> A committee of both Houses of Parliament will be appointed to undertake a wide-ranging review of possible further change and then to bring forward proposals for reform.
>
> We have no plans to replace the monarchy. (Labour Party 1997)

If anything was covered by the Salisbury–Addison convention, therefore, the House of Lords Act 1999, was designed to end the right of hereditary peers to sit and vote in the Lords. It passed the Lords without serious trouble, except that, in a backstairs deal between 10 Downing Street and Lord Cranborne (the Conservative leader in the Lords, grandson of the Cranborne/Salisbury of 1945, and great-great-grandson of the Prime Minister), ninety-two hereditary peers were to remain until the second phase of reform had been completed. Lord Cranborne was sacked by his leader, William Hague, for this, but the hereditaries do remain. Some of them have started to claim that they are the most legitimate members of the house, because they have been elected by their peers.

Although the victorious party's manifesto had spoken of making the upper house 'more democratic and representative', Prime Minister Tony Blair dragged his feet, with the mostly silent connivance of many of his colleagues. As Leader of the Opposition, Blair had said in the John Smith Memorial Lecture in 1996 that 'Labour has always supported an elected upper house.' Strictly, this did not imply that *he* favoured an elected upper house. It was also not true (Dorey 2008). It soon became clear, on his election as Prime Minister, that he did not support an elected upper house, and the Smith Memorial Lecture, with its potentially embarrassing statement, disappeared from sight. (Literally, a thorough Google search has failed to find any trace of it.)

The Labour government appointed a Royal Commission on the Reform of the House of Lords, chaired by Lord Wakeham, a former Conservative Cabinet Minister. The Committee reported in 2000. It recommended an upper house of about 550 members. Only a minority of those should be elected, however. The Royal Commission presented three models: under one, there would be 65 elected members; under the second, favoured by 'a substantial majority of the Commission' (Wakeham 2000*b*: 13), there would be 87 under the third, there would be 195 elected members.

The Labour Party's evidence to Wakeham had attempted to square the circle of calling for a 'representative' upper house without actually calling for it to be elected.

> The reformed House of Lords must be fully representative—it should fairly represent political opinion in the country, it should be representative of the different interests in the country (such as business, labour, education, science and the arts), and it should be representative of the people as a whole... [R]eform of the House of Lords should address questions such as the age, gender, and ethnic composition of its membership, and how fairer representation can best be secured. (Labour Party 1999, paragraph 5.5)

It would thus fall to a proposed independent Appointments Commission to ensure that the new upper house would be 'representative' in this microcosmic, and functionalist, sense. The Wakeham Commission went further. Containing as it did a bishop who was a member of the House of Lords, it managed to persuade itself that 16 Church of England bishops should remain in the reformed upper house. It recognized that there were other faith communities in the United Kingdom, and suggested that a further 15 religious representatives should be appointed: five to represent other Christian denominations in England; five religious representatives from Scotland, Wales, and Northern Ireland; and five to represent non-Christian faiths (Wakeham 2000a, Recommendations 109–10.)

This pair of recommendations was so problematic that it cast a bright light on the whole murky concept of non-democratic representativeness, as proposed in the Labour Party's evidence. Dealing first with religious representation, and working up from the smallest issue:

1. Would Northern Ireland have one faith representative, or two? In population terms it would be entitled to only one; but the idea that two confessional communities of comparable size, with a 300-year history of sectarian conflict, might be comfortable with a single representative of faith was absurd.

2. Where did Wakeham get its numbers on the comparative size of faith communities? They were at odds with other data sources, and the 2001 Census later confirmed that Wakeham's numbers were wrong. McLean and Linsley (2004, Table 2), using National Statistics data that were available at the time of the Wakeham Report, showed that to scale up from Wakeham's proposed 16 Church of England bishops would have required 77 representatives of faith communities in total. This issue is discussed in Chapter 13.

3. Did guaranteed representation for people of faith not also imply guaranteed representation for people of no faith?

4. How could non-democratic representation cope with multiple criteria? For instance, a high proportion of those 77 faith representatives would have to be female, to comply with the suggestion that the new upper house should have a more equal gender balance, given that all 16 of the Church of England bishops would be male.

5. Microcosmic representation by the multiple criteria proposed in the Labour Party's evidence would be difficult, if not impossible. An Appointments Commission would have to secure an unelected house that was nevertheless simultaneously representative by age, gender, region, political opinion, ethnicity, and sector of the economy. This would require the UK population to be disaggregated into groups some of which are so small that the Appointments Commission would struggle to fund suitable candidates.

The Labour Party's evidence and Wakeham's recommendations on religious representation therefore fulfil an intellectually useful role. They show that representation without democracy is unachievable. If a replacement for the House of Lords is to represent the people, it must be elected by the people.

This was, of course, exactly what many politicians in governing parties most feared. Labour politicians feared it most, because the House of Lords, overwhelmingly Conservative until 1999, had caused governments of the left far more trouble than governments of the right. A natural reaction is therefore unicameralism—the belief that there should be only one chamber of Parliament. But unicameralism allied to the United Kingdom's electoral system and the tradition of parliamentary sovereignty is a triply toxic brew. The electoral system typically exaggerates the lead of the largest single party; that in itself may aid rather than hamper parliamentary sovereignty. However, in UK conditions it is also possible that the winner in terms of votes is not the winner in terms of seats. This happened after the general elections of 1951 and February 1974. The direction of bias varies from time to time, but under current conditions it favours Labour. It would be possible for Labour to win a plurality—perhaps even a majority—of Commons seats while coming second to the Conservatives in votes. When the equivalent situation arose in the United States after the Presidential Election of 1876, it came close to reigniting the Civil War: peace was maintained though a grubby bargain such that the Democrats would not press their claim to the presidency, which they had won on the popular vote, on condition that the incoming Republican administration allowed the white Democrats to regain control of state governments throughout the Confederacy.

It is no surprise, therefore, that the Conservative politician Lord Hailsham (1976) called this triple toxicity 'elective dictatorship' when in opposition. Once the Conservatives were returned to government in 1979, however, Hailsham managed to live with it again, confirming the wisdom of Asquith's statement to George V in 1913: *When the two Houses are in agreement (as is always the case when there is a Conservative majority in the House of Commons), the [Parliament] Act is a dead letter.*

Labour politicians worried more, and with good reason, about the wrecking potential of the Lords: held in check essentially only by a speech in the Lords by Lord Cranborne in 1945. One response is abolition of the Lords. This made the Labour manifesto in 1983, (Labour Party 1983, in *The Times* 1983: 307), the year of Labour's worst general election defeat. After that, it did not resurface as an overt aim of Labour leaders. The process was more subtle. For as long as the Lords remained an unelected house with hugely disproportionate Conservative tendencies, for so long the Salisbury Convention remained secure and a Labour government could expect to get most of its legislation through. Any threat by the Lords to use their formal powers would meet the response: 'We are the elected house. You have no legitimacy.' An elected, or largely elected, Lords would destroy this equilibrium. Thus, Tony Blair and the Labour leadership were led into the intellectual contortions just described.

But they failed to control subsequent events, even though they held commanding leads in the Parliaments of 1997 and 2001, and a still substantial lead in the Parliament of 2005. The idea of an unelected upper house has been more and more laughed out of court since 1999. A succession of Green Papers, White Papers, and reports from academics and think tanks has left the Wakeham Report dead in the water. In 1997 the Liberal Democrats were calling for a predominantly elected upper house (as they had, after all, been doing since 1911). Perhaps more surprisingly, the Conservatives joined them for the 2001 election. They had appointed a commission under Lord Mackay of Clashfern, a former Lord Chancellor (and, as may be relevant, a Scottish independent Presbyterian). The Mackay Commission reported in 1999 ('In the light of the quickening pace of progress towards Lords reform, the Constitutional Commission has decided to report early,' their report opens. (Mackay 1999, Executive Summary: 1). They threw into the debate on upper house reform a number of ideas that have stayed there. Most importantly, they recommended that Senators should serve a single non-renewable term of three parliaments (with provision that if a parliament was exceptionally short, like that of February to October 1974, a resolution of both Houses could allow upper house members to serve for a fourth parliament (Mackay 1999, paragraph 44). That was a neat solution to four classic problems at once.

1. Unicameralists, open and covert, have always worried that an upper house elected at different times to the Commons would claim greater legitimacy. It is a sociological law that the government of the day, in all democracies, is unpopular at mid-term. The Parliament of 1910 provides an example (Figure 11.1). Therefore in a typical election that does not coincide with the election to the lower house, the current opposition will do well. It will then be tempted to claim that it represents the true voice of the people.

2. On the other hand, if elections to the two houses *do* coincide, then, in the words of the anti-reform Conservative peer and former minister Geoffrey Howe (Lord Howe of Aberavon), the upper house might be 'clones of the clowns in the Commons' (*Hansard*, Lords, 10.01.2002, c.699). His views echo Salisbury's 'mere echo' of over a century earlier and they seem to be widely shared in the Lords, judging by their votes on their own reform. They would be especially clone-like if elected by the same electoral system as the Commons.

3. If the real locus of power is the Commons, then the upper house would risk being a refuge for failed and would-be Commons politicians. However, the long non-renewable terms proposed by Mackay and his colleagues would eliminate this risk.

Table 11.1 Mackay Commission models for a partly elected upper house.

	Model A	Model B
Appointed members	150	45
Members elected by devolved administrations and English regions	99	
Members elected from UK-wide party lists in proportion to the votes cast for the parties in the general election	99	
Members elected by thirds from eighty, six-member constituencies		480
Life members	100	
Ex officio members	2	
	450	525

Source: Mackay Commission.

4. Relatedly, the long fixed term would weaken the power of the party whips over their party members in the upper house. They would not face re-election, and could therefore not be threatened with deselection.

Unlike Wakeham the following year, Mackay and his colleagues were prepared to consider a predominantly, but not wholly, elected house. They offered two options (Table 11.1).

Under either of Mackay's options, more than half of the reformed upper house would be elected. Under what I have listed as Model A, 249 of its 450 members would be elected, either directly or indirectly. Under 'Model B', all but 45 of its 545 members would be directly elected. The appointed members would mostly be appointed for their expertise, but some could be political appointees, including (in Model B) government ministers.

The weakest part of the Mackay report (in my view) was its proposals on electoral system. All three electoral systems proposed (indirect election, election by party list, and election in two-member districts) suffer from serious flaws, which seem to have been replicated in later Conservative thinking. However, that apart, the Mackay Commission report is perhaps the most intellectually distinguished proposal for upper house reform since 1997. The Conservative manifesto for 2001, although it did not mention the Mackay Commission report, called for a 'substantial elected element' in the upper house.

In the 2001–5 Parliament, both houses voted on options for Lords reform. A series of reports and parliamentary motions had called for a higher elected proportion than in Wakeham (for details see McLean, Spirling, and Russell 2003). The houses appointed a joint committee which came up with various reform options from a wholly appointed to a wholly elected upper house. In 2003, the unelected Lords voted by a substantial majority for an unelected Lords. The story in the Commons was more complicated. In a series of

Table 11.2 Votes in the House of Commons (including tellers) on Lords reform, 4 February 2003.

	Abolish	Elect zero	Elect 20%	Elect 40%	Elect 50%	Elect 60%	Elect 80%	Elect all
Aye	174	247	0	0	0	255	283	274
Did not vote	29	23	0	0	0	22	26	30
No	392	325	595	595	595	318	286	291
Majority	−218	−78	−595	−595	−595	−63	−3	−17

Base: All who cast at least one vote; *n* = 595.

Source: Division lists in *Hansard* (online version) for 4 February 2003.

Table 11.3 House of Lords reform: main party statements in the general election of 2005.

Party	Statement
Conservative	We will seek cross-party consensus for a substantially elected House of Lords.
Labour	In our next term, we will complete the reform of the House of Lords so that it is a modern and effective revising Chamber....[A] reformed Upper Chamber must be effective, legitimate and more representative without challenging the primacy of the House of Commons.
Liberal Democrat	Reform of the House of Lords has been botched by Labour, leaving it unelected and even more in the patronage of the Prime Minister. We will replace it with a predominantly elected second chamber.

Note: The manifestos of the three next largest parties in the 2005 Parliament (SNP, DUP, and Plaid Cymru) made no mention of Lords reform.

Source: Party websites; BBC Election 2005 site.

free votes, the Commons managed to contradict themselves. They voted against all eight options on offer, thus retaining the status quo. But the status quo was an all-appointed Lords, which they had opposed by 325 votes to 247 (Table 11.2).

Elsewhere (McLean, Spirling, and Russell 2003) we have analysed the combination of confusion and strategic voting that seems to have led to this result. It was no doubt pleasing to Prime Minister Blair and the Labour Party whips, most of whom were organizing (in these supposedly free votes) to try to ensure the defeat of proposals for an elected upper house. Prime Minister Blair's declared objection was that he did not like a 'hybrid' (part elected, part appointed) upper house, although that was precisely what the Royal Commission had proposed, and various Green and White Papers put out by his government had endorsed.

Nevertheless, the parties continued to edge towards election. The statements made by the three main parties in their 2005 general election manifestos are given in Table 11.3.

Labour still want a 'representative' upper house without committing themselves to an elected one. However, both the main opposition parties are now calling for a 'substantially' or 'predominantly' elected upper house. In 2007 both houses revisited the issue, again on free votes. The minister responsible (Jack Straw) proposed unsuccessfully to use a voting procedure designed to preclude a repetition of the contradictory outcome of the 2003 vote. The government issued a White Paper saying that it favoured a 50 per cent elected upper house. Once again, the unelected Lords voted by a substantial majority for an unelected Lords. However, the Commons as a whole, this time, produced a non-contradictory result (Table 11.4).

Table 11.4 shows that in 2007 the Commons voted by 338 to 226 for a 100 per cent elected upper house, and by 306 to 269 for an 80 per cent elected house. The government's preferred option did very badly, going down to heavy defeat and supported by a majority of MPs in none of the main parties. The party breakdown in the table shows that Liberal Democrats were the only main party to vote as a block—against unelected options and in favour of the maximally elected ones. Conservative MPs, despite their 2005 manifesto, voted by narrow pluralities against the maximally elected options. As a group, they did what the whole Commons had done in 2003: contradictorily voting for a bicameral parliament and then voting against all the compositions offered for the reformed upper house. Labour MPs voted most heavily for an all-elected house, and against the other composition options offered. The naive interpretation is that they were almost as thoroughgoing democrats as the Liberal Democrats. The more sophisticated interpretation, supported by careful analysis of the data (Constitution Unit 2007; Russell 2009), is that a number of Labour unicameralists voted strategically in favour of 'all-elected' in the hope of quietly wrecking reform.

Further cross-party talks ensued. In July 2008, the Government issued a White Paper stating the results of these talks and the Government position on the issues (Ministry of Justice 2008). The headline message of this White Paper was that Lords reform would not proceed before the general election due in 2009 or 2010. This caused most of the UK media either to ignore the White Paper altogether or to treat it dismissively. This was myopic. The veto power of the Lords remains in full force during the last year or two of the Parliament. The Parliament of 2005 had reached that point by July 2008. The Lords had voted twice by large margins against becoming an elected house and it was therefore utterly predictable that any Lords reform bill in the 2005 Parliament would be vetoed by the Lords. There would not then be time to enact it on Commons votes only, under the Parliament Act 1949, before the dissolution of the 2005 Parliament. The statement that no Lords reform

Table 11.4 Divisions in the House of Commons on Lords reform 2007, by party.

Division	65 Bicameral		66 Fully Apptd		67 50% elect		68 60% elect		69 80% elect		70 100% elect		71 rmve hereds (amend)		72 rmve heredits	
	Aye	No	Aye	No	Aye	No	Aye	No	Aye	No	Aye	No	Aye	No	Aye	No
Party Con	182	1	80	103	26	155	42	139	80	98	57	126	174	8	16	112
Lab	169	155	117	201	129	189	135	184	159	164	212	98	5	311	307	0
LibDem	60	0	0	61	0	63	0	60	62	0	59	0	63	0	60	0
SNP	6	0	0	6	0	6	0	6	3	0	6	0	0	6	6	0
PC	3	0	3	0	0	3	0	3	3	0	3	0	0	3	3	0
UU	1	0	1	0	0	1	0	0	0	0	0	0	0	0	0	0
Ind/Other	2	1	3	0	1	2	2	1	2	1	1	2	1	2	1	1
Total	423	157	204	371	156	419	179	393	306	269	338	226	243	330	393	113
χ^2	168.88		48.01		71.19		56.72		72.04		119.45		519.78		422.4	
p-value	<0.01		<0.01		<0.01		<0.01		<0.01		<0.01		<0.01		<0.01	

would be attempted in that Parliament was therefore a simple recognition of political reality.

The tone and content of this widely ignored White Paper are more interesting. In tone, it is by turn accommodating and threatening. It is accommodating (on the surface) when it notes that 'All three main parties included pledges in their 2005 manifestos in favour of further reform of the Lords'. It is threatening in a 1911ish way when it states:

> [T]he House of Commons voted by a margin of 113 for a wholly elected House of Lords. The Commons also backed, by a margin of 38, a mainly elected second chamber based on 80% elected and 20% appointed. It voted by a majority of 280 to remove the remaining hereditary Peers. The House of Lords voted by a majority of 240 for a fully appointed House. It rejected the options of a wholly or 80% elected second chamber (respectively by majorities of 204 and 222). Given the difference of view between the two chambers, the Government said that it would look at how best to deliver a mainly or wholly elected second chamber in accordance with the wishes of the House of Commons, which is the primary chamber in the UK legislature. . . . The Convenor of the Crossbench Peers expressed concern in the talks that the basis on which they were proceeding ignored the outcome of the free votes in the House of Lords. The Convenor continues to believe that this is unacceptable and that therefore any use of the term 'consensus' in the White Paper is inappropriate. (Ministry of Justice 2008, 1.5–1.6)

Despite the Convenor of the Crossbench Peers' disapproval, I take this White Paper as the latest proposal on the table at the time of drafting this chapter. The next section therefore analyses its proposals. How far does it go, and how far should constitutional designers go, towards making the upper house of the United Kingdom, a house of the people?

THE 2008 WHITE PAPER

Before proceeding to detailed analysis, the reader may object: *This particular White Paper is merely the latest of a string of proposals since 1911, none of which has got anywhere. Why is it worth analysing this one in any depth?* To which I reply as follows: *I make no special claims for the brilliance of this document. It merely happens to be the one on the table at a time when the status quo has become unsustainable through the collapse of the Salisbury–Addison convention and the greater assertiveness of the post-1999 House of Lords.* The two points are linked.

The Liberal Democrats in the Lords, who are now one of the pivotal parties, have announced that they no longer intend to abide by the Salisbury–Addison

Table 11.5 Outcome of government proposals initially defeated in Lords, 1999–2005.

Code	Frequency		% of total
1	Government win	95	41.7
2	Government wins more than Lords	41	18.0
3	Government and Lords meet halfway	16	7.0
4	Lords wins more than the Government	34	14.9
5	Lords win	42	18.4
Total	Total	228	100.0

Source: Russell and Sciara (2007).

convention (Liberal Democrats 2006). The Joint Committee on Conventions agreed that the convention had 'evolved', that it was impossible to define a 'manifesto bill' in sufficiently precise language to allow the convention to operate smoothly, and that the convention should be renamed the 'Government Bill Convention' (Joint Committee on Conventions 2006, Chapter 3). We seem to be once again in the world of Sidney Low: *We live under a system of unwritten understandings. Unfortunately, the understandings are not always understood.* If those who will have to operate the convention in future do not know what it says, do not know what bills are covered by it, and do not know what it is called, then it is safe to assume that the convention has ceased to be a binding constraint.

More broadly, the House of Lords has become much more assertive since the removal of most of the hereditary peers. Russell and Sciara (2007) found that the Labour government had been defeated 283 times in the Lords between 1999 and 2005. Of course, the Government reversed many of these defeats by insisting on its position, in which case the Lords usually, but not always, gives way. The next move is to eliminate double-counting: If a proposal shuttles between the houses and is defeated in the Lords more than once, it would be wrong to count it more than once. This reduces the 283 defeats to 228 government *proposals* defeated in the Lords in this period. Russell and Sciara examined the final outcome of these proposals (Table 11.5), and classified each on a five-point scale ranging from government victory to 'Lords win' (i.e. a victory for the Lords' original position).

Table 11.5 shows that the Lords won about 40 per cent of these ping-pong matches. Not just on minor issues, either (Table 11.6). If the five outcomes are collapsed to two, then the rate of Lords' 'wins' on what the authors class as 'high-' and 'medium-significance' issues is higher than on minor issues.

As always in conditional veto games, the 'rule of anticipated reactions' is in play. In summer 2008, it was common knowledge that the government's

Table 11.6 Policy significance of government defeats in Lords, 1999–2005.

Policy significance	Outcome			
Govt win	Lords win		Total	% Lords win
Minor policy	23	9	32	28.1
Medium significance policy	53	42	95	44.2
Significant policy	62	39	101	38.6
Total	138	90	228	39.5

Source: Russell and Sciara (2007).

detention proposals for terrorist suspects were unlikely to be passed in the Lords. The Government's persistence with them through autumn 2008 must therefore have been a game play: The government wanted to establish a reputation for being tough and may not have minded if the proposals are lost. After fierce criticism in the Lords, and from unlikely places including the police and a retired head of the secret Intelligence Service, the government withdrew its plans in late 2008. It had run out of time (as everybody knew) to force them through using the Parliament Acts.

Another sceptical reaction to the White Paper's proposals for an elected upper house is, *Do the people actually want one?* The candid answer, from the same research team as the above, is, *Not intensely.* Russell (2007) reports the results of roughly parallel surveys of peers and of the general public in autumn 2007. Respondents were asked which from a list of characteristics they regarded as 'very important' determinants of the legitimacy of the House of Lords. Respondents were allowed to choose more than one of the options offered as 'very important'. The options offered were a mixture of what the Lords do, and how they are appointed. The histograms in Figure 11.2 compare peers' and public's reactions.

Top of the list, for both groups, comes 'Trust in the appointments process' (the fieldwork was done during one of the periodic eruptions of 'cash for peerages' allegations in British politics). Next most important among composition options, for the public, comes 'Presence of experts' (peers agree), followed by 'Acting in accordance with public opinion' (peers disagree) and only then by 'Addition of members elected by the public' (peers again disagree).

Would not an unelected house do, then, providing that the appointments process is satisfactory and the house contains experts? No, for reasons already discussed. Such a house could not 'act in accordance with public opinion' unless it knew what public opinion was. Historically, the House of Lords has not been good at that. Only an elected house can be sensitive to public

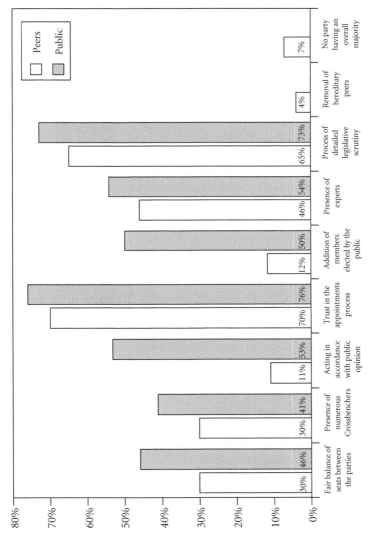

Figure 11.2 Peers' and public views on factors considered 'very important' to Lords' legitimacy, October 2007. (*Source:* Russell 2007. Source of Peers' survey: Constitution Unit. Source of public survey: IPSOS-MORI. The last two options were not put to the public sample. 'Don't know' response [c. 10%] excluded from public sample.)

opinion. It is a fundamental premise of this book that 'we the people' cannot elect a government unless we elect all the branches of it.

Nevertheless, I share the wide consensus among specialists that the re-formed upper house should have some appointed members—probably, as supported by the House of Commons in 2007 and nearly in 2003, a house which is 80 per cent elected and 20 per cent appointed. What options to achieve this does the White Paper offer? Can they be improved upon?

On appointment, the White Paper contains some consensus proposals and some on which there was no cross-party consensus. There was a consensus that the 20 per cent of appointed members should all be appointed by an Appointments Committee working from published criteria, and that there should be no party-political appointments. Such appointees would serve the same single long non-renewable term as the elected members, and after a transition period they too would be appointed in thirds with over-lapping terms. The Government proposes further consultation on whether a government should be able to propose names to serve in the upper house for the purpose of acting as ministers. Government representatives wanted to retain Church of England bishops (over and above that 20 per cent). The Liberal Democrats dissented.

On methods of election of the 80 or 100 per cent of elected members, the party representatives divided. All parties agreed that the 'representative basis for elected members of the reformed second chamber should be different from that for members of the House of Commons' (Ministry of Justice 2008, 3.3). They should be elected by thirds, at general elections, for a single long, non-renewable term of three parliaments. The White Paper adopts the Mackay Commission proposal that in the event of a short parliament, there would be what it calls a 'rider' to allow members to serve for one more parliament. At the end of the term, they should be ineligible to run for the Commons for five years. The Government proposes consultation on the mirror requirement, that ex-MPs should be ineligible to run for the new house for five years. This seems an obvious consistency requirement, which only those with vested interests could oppose.

The reformed upper house should be smaller than the Lords—the Conservatives proposed a size of between 250 and 300 members. To achieve election by thirds, members must be elected in multi-member districts with district magnitudes all a multiple of 3—hence the size of the elected member-ship must also be divisible by 3. This could be a binding constraint, because Northern Ireland, the smallest devolved unit in the United Kingdom, could not be sensibly combined with any other part for electoral purposes. Northern Ireland contains about 2.5 per cent (1/40) of the UK electorate (ONS 2007). For illustration, therefore, a 300-member, 80-per-cent-elected house would have 240 elected members, of which Northern Ireland would have six, with two up for election on each occasion. This quick calculation suggests that the house should be no smaller than 300 strong.

Quite a lot of the 2008 White Paper is given over to reporting the results of modelling elections to an elected upper house back to 1966. The modelling assumed that the house size would be about 450 (with therefore either about 120 or about 150 seats to fill at each election); and that votes would have been cast for the parties in the same proportions as at the accompanying general election. It modelled four electoral systems: plurality (favoured by the Conservatives), Alternative Vote (AV), Single Transferable Vote (STV) (favoured by the Liberals), and a list system. Under plurality or AV each district would have three members, with one up for election each time. Under STV or list systems, district magnitudes must be bigger. They need not all be the same size. In the White Paper exercise, the modelled STV constituencies were the same size, with 18 members each (therefore six to fill each time). This equality was achieved at a cost—it left Northern Ireland over-represented and Wales (which has 5 per cent of the UK electorate) under-represented, with 4.17 per cent of the seats each. This would not go down well. In reality, there would be no need for STV constituencies to be of the same magnitude. They are of varying magnitude in the Republic of Ireland, the legislature that has used STV for the longest continuous time. The modelled list seats used the United Kingdom's 12 standard regions as districts, with between three (Northern Ireland) and 20 (South-East) senators to be elected in each round.

The modelling exercise shows (as it was no doubt intended to) that neither plurality nor AV is suitable for delivering an upper house in which no party has an overall majority. These systems exaggerate the lead in votes of the modal party into a greater lead in seats. Therefore, even with staggered elections they would have led (on the modelling assumptions used) to one party having an overall majority for a substantial proportion of the time since 1966. These systems can therefore be discarded.

The choice therefore lies between STV and a list system. The choice between those is not as crucial as dedicated proponents of each system claim, so long as two side constraints are satisfied: unequal district magnitudes, and any list system to be an open list system. I discuss these constraints first.

Unequal district magnitudes: The United Kingdom's 12 standard regions have unequal populations (Table 11.7). The South-East is the largest and Northern Ireland is the smallest.

Some federal systems give an equal number of seats in their upper house to each State or province. The United States and Australia have two and 12 Senators per State, respectively, regardless of population. These constitutional rules are understandable, given that both federations began from previously

Table 11.7 Electorate of the 12 standard regions of the United Kingdom, with illustrative numbers of Senators for each in an elected upper house, electing by thirds.

Country	Region	Electorate December 2007	Seats to be filled at each 1/3 election	Total seats
England		38,594,720	84	252
	North-East	1,963,352	4	12
	North-West	5,254,594	11	33
	Yorks. and the Humber	3,828,927	8	24
	East Midlands	3,357,919	7	21
	West Midlands	4,106,389	9	27
	East	4,292,194	9	27
	London	5,483,584	12	36
	South-East	6,295,985	14	42
	South-West	4,011,776	9	27
Wales		2,273,586	5	15
Scotland		3,926,262	9	27
Northern Ireland		1,125,935	2	6
United Kingdom		45,920,503	99	297

Note: Seats per territory derived by simple rounding. For a real election, Sainte-Laguë apportionment should be used (see text).

Source: ONS; author's calculations.

independent states deciding to come together. They obviously privilege people, and interests, in the more thinly populated units: Alaska shooters and Tasmanian environmentalists can influence national decisions out of proportion to their population shares. There is no case for a similar rule in the United Kingdom, even with respect to Scotland, Wales, and Northern Ireland (just imagine the Scots reaction to Northern Ireland having as many senators as Scotland); and absolutely none for the English regions, none of which except London has an elected body of its own.

Therefore, if the standard regions are the units for elections to the upper house (as they already are for elections to the European Parliament), they must have varying numbers of Senators, though each number should be divisible by 3 if the house is to be elected by thirds. Table 11.7 gives illustrative numbers for a house of 297, with 99 senators to be elected at each election. I have chosen these numbers for ease of rounding. Table 11.7 derives the entitlement for each region by simple rounding. An actual election system would not use simple rounding. It would use what is known in Europe as the Sainte-Laguë method and in the United States as the Webster method of apportionment—both of Senators to each region and (if a list system is used) of seats to each party within each region. The present system for European Parliament uses this method to assign seats to regions but not to assign seats to parties in each region. However, the Electoral Commission has accepted the case made by a consortium of academics including me that Sainte-Laguë, alias Webster, is the only fair system to use for both tasks. The reasons are mathematical and too complicated to explain in a general book like this, but see Balinski and Young (2001) and Electoral Commission (2003, 2007).

Table 11.7 also suggest that if the electoral system for the upper house is to be STV, the standard regions should again be the basic building blocks. The range of district sizes would be between two and 14 at each election. A two-member district is too small for STV to work at its best (so may be Northern Ireland Senators should be elected by halves every six years, instead of by thirds every four years), but a 14-member district is not too large. However, if policy-makers were uncomfortable with districts of 12 and 14, it would be easy to cut the large electoral areas into half.

The fundamental number in all these calculations is the so-called (Droop) quota Q, which is a simple function of District Magnitude (number of seats to be filled M, when the total of votes cast is V:

$$ Q = \left\lceil \frac{V}{M+1} \right\rceil $$

where the symbol $\lceil\ \rceil$ means 'the whole number next above'. Thus in a ten-member seat in which 10,000 votes had been cast, the quota Q would be 910—the exact fraction is 909.09 recurring, and the next number above that is 910. In this situation, any party which could get 910 votes is guaranteed one seat, and in total as many seats as it can get multiples of 910. Only ten blocks of at least 910 votes can fit into a vote total of 10,000. This procedure operates whether the electoral system is STV or party list. It has the effect that small parties can more easily win seats in large districts. If (say) the Greens got a uniform 10 per cent of the upper house vote and the British National Party (BNP) got a uniform 5 per cent, then, on the numbers given in Table 11.7 and with region-wide constituencies, the Greens would win a seat each in North-West, London, and South-East (and would come within a whisker in the three, nine-member districts of West Midlands, East Midlands, and Scotland), whereas the BNP would win no seats. If districts were made smaller, then the thresholds for winning a seat would be correspondingly higher. These calculations suggest that an explicit threshold rule is unnecessary.

However, it is necessary that the people should choose their Senators. STV was invented to give electors maximal control over those they elect. Closed party list systems, where each party names a ranked list, voters cast a single vote for one party, and the parties win seats in proportion to their share of those votes, do not give electors maximal control. A candidate's chances depend on their rank in the party's list more than on the people's votes. Each party will win as many seats as it has Droop quotas. Candidates ranked above this cutline are certain to win; those ranked below are certain to lose. It is essential to the consensus conception of the upper house as a deliberative assembly that parties should not be able to discipline their members by electoral threats. The non-renewable nature of Senate places largely secures this. But a party may still put those it regards as most reliable—whom outsiders might regard as its 'hacks'—at the top of its lists, and mavericks lower. The people should be allowed a say in that matter, either through an open-list system (where votes can vote for an individual candidate rather than that candidate's party, if they wish) or through STV.

Thus a consensus for upper-house reform is emerging. Senators should be:

1. Largely (say 80 per cent) elected.
2. Elected for a fixed non-renewable term of three parliaments.
3. Elected by thirds at general elections, with an override provision in the event of a short Parliament.
4. Elected in fairly large districts, say the United Kingdom's 12 standard regions, which are the constituencies for European Parliament elections.
5. Ineligible to move directly between the Senate and the Commons.
6. If appointed, should be appointed by a non-partisan, probably statutory, commission working to published criteria and in line with the standard arrangements for making public appointments.
7. Subject to the same ethics rules as appointees or elected members of other public bodies.

These rules, between them, would ensure that We the People elected two of the three branches of the Parliament, by different electoral systems and to serve under different conditions which would ensure the political primacy of the Commons. The powers of the Upper House would not change; the Commons monopoly of Supply would continue. In the next chapter we proceed to see whether, and if so how, the People could choose the third house of Parliament, namely the monarch.

12

Monarchs

Every democracy needs a head of state. Most of the time, her duties are purely ceremonial—opening events, presiding at military parades, receiving other countries' heads of state, and so on. However, once in a blue moon, she matters. She matters when her state is under internal or external attack. At these times, her actions may boost or damage democracy. I am not aware of a systematic survey of the performance of heads of state at times of threats to their democracy. It would be nice to know whether monarchs (and their nominees) are better or worse at protecting democracy than elected heads of state. In the simplest 2 × 2 classification, Table 12.1 suggests that none of the four cells has been empty in the twentieth century. It is possible to find a monarch who did well (Juan Carlos of Spain), a 'monarch' who did badly (Sir John Kerr of Australia), an elected head of state who did well (T. G. Masaryk of Czechoslovakia), and an elected head of state who did badly (Paul Hindenburg of Germany).

This chapter, therefore, proceeds as follows. First, I explore the role of head of state. Then, I examine how well the British monarchy has filled that role, concluding that on the whole an elected head of state would fill it better. Next, I discuss mechanisms of election, and finally, the disposal of the current 'royal prerogative' powers.

WHAT IS A HEAD OF STATE FOR?

Here are three definitions of the role of head of state, from the constitutions of France, Germany, and the United States.

France:
Le président de la République veille au respect de la Constitution. Il assure, par son arbitrage, le fonctionnement régulier des pouvoirs publics ainsi que la continuité de l'État. Il est le garant de l'indépendance nationale, de l'intégrité du territoire et du respect des traités.

Table 12.1 Unelected versus elected heads of state in C20: protecting versus damaging democracy.

	Protected democracy			Damaged democracy		
	Country	Year	Event	Country	Year	Event
Unelected head of state	Spain	1981	King Juan Carlos refuses to support military coup plotters who had invaded parliament	Australia	1975	Governor-General dismisses Prime Minister; appoints opposition leader PM
Elected head of state	Czechoslovakia	1918–20	President Tomáš Garrigue Masaryk persuades victorious Allies to recognize Czechoslovak independence	Germany	1933	President Hindenburg finally invites Hitler to form a government (having earlier resisted), believing that his allies can keep Hitler in check

Sources: Colomer (1995); Whitlam (1979); Kerr (1979); Galligan (1995); various encyclopaedias

The President of the Republic attends to the protection of the Constitution. Through his arbitration he ensures the regular functioning of public authorities and the continuity of the state. He is the guarantor of national independence, of territorial integrity and of respect for treaties.

Germany:
On assuming his office, the Federal President shall take the following oath before the assembled Members of the Bundestag and the Bundesrat: 'I swear that I will dedicate my efforts to the well-being of the German people, promote their welfare, protect them from harm, uphold and defend the Basic Law and the laws of the Federation, perform my duties conscientiously, and do justice to all. So help me God.' The oath may also be taken without religious affirmation.

The United States

Before he enter on the Execution of his Office, he shall take the following Oath or Affirmation: 'I do solemnly swear (or affirm) that I will faithfully execute the Office of President of the United States, and will to the best of my Ability, preserve, protect, and defend the Constitution of the United States'.[1]

Thus, there is a consensus that the core duty of the president is to protect the constitution from internal and external attack. There are executive and non-executive presidents. The former (as in France and the United States) combine the roles of head of state and head of government. The latter (as in the United Kingdom and Germany) do not. No constitutional reformer known to me has proposed that the United Kingdom should adopt a 'strong president' system where the roles are combined, so I do not discuss that option further.

The task, therefore, is to see what tasks a non-executive head of state has in the United Kingdom; whether the UK monarchs have performed them, on average, well or badly; to explore whether a non-hereditary head of state might be expected to do better; and to discuss how a non-hereditary head of state might be chosen.

External attack is the easiest to discuss and the hardest to say much about. We would all like our head of state to be a universally respected person who stands up for the nation in its darkest hours. However, this neither tells us what the head of state should do, nor helps adjudicate between kings and presidents. In 1940, both King Leopold III of the Belgians and President Pétain of France (not directly elected, but chosen by the elected government) surrendered to the German invaders. Leopold may simply have been facing reality according to his lights; Pétain went on to head the Vichy puppet government and was convicted of treason after the liberation of France. Leopold's unconditional surrender was against the wishes of his cabinet. He was excluded from Belgium at its liberation and abdicated in 1951. King George VI and Queen Elizabeth stayed in London throughout the war, an action which probably restored the British monarchy to a pinnacle of popular affection. But these diverse histories do not enable us to judge whether kings or presidents are better at resisting overwhelming force.

What about internal attacks on the constitution? A nation which has judicial review does not need the head of state to *veille au respect de la Constitution*. The constitutional court does that. The United States has had judicial review since the Supreme Court gave itself the power to review the constitutionality of legislation in *Marbury* v. *Madison* (1803); Germany since the adoption of the Basic Law in 1949; and France since the *Conseil Constitutionnel* decided in 1971 that it could rule on the constitutionality of legislation—see Stone Sweet (2000). In France, the *Conseil Constitutionnel* is now entrenched, as Charles de Gaulle would be appalled to discover were he to return to Colombey-les-deux-églises. The United Kingdom is very slowly and haltingly finding its way to a judicial review regime. In the worst constitutional crisis in British history since 1707, namely the Home Rule crisis of 1912–14, the Opposition persistently accused the government of behaving unconstitutionally. They persuaded enough people to believe them, including some of the king's advisers and most of the army officers at the Curragh, that they did indeed induce a constitutional crisis.

The first duty of the UK head of state is therefore to prevent any possibility of the repetition of 1912–14. The second is to fill any gaps in the UK's parliamentary government. All the UK constitutional textbooks dwell at length on the role of the monarch in appointing a prime minister, and accepting (or refusing) the prime minister's request to dissolve Parliament. The current state of play is summarized in the leading authority, namely Bogdanor (1995), to which readers are referred.

Most of the discussion of the head of state's role in these matters is intellectually unsatisfactory. This is not to attack Bogdanor, who merely follows the style of all his predecessors, when he uses the letters of George III, Queen Victoria, and A. V. Dicey, and previous constitutional texts (not to mention the mid-Victorian journalist Walter Bagehot), to define what the British Constitution is. An anonymous letter to *The Times* saying that some matters about the king's prerogative may not be discussed in public was quoted above. The circularity of this is only too evident when we learn from Bogdanor (1995: 41) that:

> It is known, indeed, that George V, George VI, Elizabeth II, and the Prince of Wales have all studied [Bagehot's] *The English Constitution.*

Presumably, therefore, they have absorbed Bagehot's distinction between the 'dignified' and 'efficient' parts of the Constitution; decided that they belong in the former; but understand that they have the right to be consulted, the right to advise, and the right to warn. How do they know that they have these rights? Because a journalist said so, in a book published in 1865. Intellectually, this is on the level of the Bellman in Lewis Carroll's *Hunting of the Snark.*[2]

Therefore, it is time to apply some social science to these hallowed questions. The head of state must be politically neutral, yet must sometimes intervene when politicians fail to take a decision. This creates a backward induction game. If it is common knowledge that the head of state will intervene when politicians fail to, the politicians have an incentive to duck difficult decisions and to play brinkmanship games. The existence of a monarch therefore creates a moral hazard. On this, consider the Australian constitutional crisis of 1975 (Table 12.1).

Australia is one of the Commonwealth states whose sovereign is the monarch of the United Kingdom. Elizabeth II is the 'head of the Commonwealth', but only for those Commonwealth states which so choose, and in each of them a Governor General acts for her. The Governor General is now invariably a national of the state, appointed on the recommendation of its prime or first minister. Therefore, although any proposal to abolish the monarchy in the United Kingdom should, as a courtesy, involve consultation with those Commonwealth countries which have the UK monarch as their nominal head of state, no deep constitutional principle is involved either in the United Kingdom or in any of those countries. Therefore, I do not discuss the question of Commonwealth consent to abolition of the monarchy in the United Kingdom further in this chapter.

In 1975, Australia had divided government. The House of Representatives was controlled by the Australian Labor Party. The Senate was, as usual in Australia since 1949, not under the control of the governing party. This is an invariable consequence of the electoral systems for the two chambers. The House of Representatives has since 1919 used what in Australia is called 'preferential voting', and in the United Kingdom is called 'the alternative vote' in single-member districts. The Senate has since 1948 used 'single transferable vote' (STV), voting by state. Both of these were adopted for partisan reasons (McLean 1996); both have predictable consequences. Preferential voting concentrates power on the two leading parties, especially the top vote-getter; STV disperses it among minor parties. The resulting balance of power particularly favours minor parties in the lower-population states, since each state has equal representation in the Senate. Therefore, there was nothing intrinsically unusual in the situation that in 1975 the Australian Senate was under opposition control. But neither the Constitution nor the politicians had readied themselves for the situation this created. Representation by state rather than by population in the Senate is a fundamental condition of federalism in both Australia and the United States, which could not have become federal states without this concession to their thinly populated component units. In Australia, the Liberal–National alliance is relatively stronger in rural than in urban areas, and therefore in the thinly populated states more than the densely populated states. Although there was a convention that when a Senator resigned or died, the Premier of the state in question would appoint a member of the same party to fill the vacancy, that convention was not written down. It has been written now, via a constitutional amendment which was part of the fallout from 1975.

The United States has lived with divided government for 220 years with just one existential crisis—the American Civil War. Australia has lived with it for a century with just one existential crisis, the dismissal of Prime Minister Gough Whitlam by Governor General Sir John Kerr on Armistice Day in 1975. Was the existential crisis avoidable? And does it have any lessons for the United Kingdom?

In October 1975, Malcolm Fraser, the Liberal leader, announced that he would use his control of the Senate—which arose from two anti-Labor State Premiers having appointed anti-Labor Senators to fill gaps left by the death or resignation of two Labor Senators—to block supply by voting against the Whitlam government's appropriation (budget) bills. This is what the House of Lords did in 1909. But unlike them Fraser controlled an elected chamber, so he could claim more legitimacy, even though Australia has inherited the Westminster rule that the lower house is responsible for public expenditure. Whitlam took on the Lloyd George role. He was clearly gaming the situation in the hope that either Fraser would blink first and would vote supply, or that the electorate would blame Fraser for the ensuing chaos when government services started to fail and civil servants were not paid. Equally, Fraser was clearly gaming the situation in the hope that Whitlam would blink first, or if not that the electorate would blame Whitlam for the crisis.

Governor General Kerr sought an opinion from the Chief Justice of the High (supreme) Court, who advised him that he did have the power to dismiss Whitlam. On 11 November he duly did so without warning—his reasoning being that any warning might have caused Whitlam to request the Queen to dismiss the Governor General first. In the event, as it was the middle of the night in the United Kingdom when the crisis broke, nobody, including Kerr's Official Secretary, succeeded in getting through to the Queen or her secretaries:

> I identified myself to the operator and asked to be connected to the Queen's private secretary...I was asked whether I realised what time it was in London. I replied that I did, and that the matter was urgent (Smith 2005: 254).

The switchboard, on Smith's account, did not seem to try very hard to wake the Queen's private secretary or his deputy, but got the number 3 in the office, who happened to be Australian.

There was some prior collusion between Kerr and Fraser, although how much remains in dispute. On his nomination by the Governor General as caretaker Prime Minister, Fraser got the Senate to unblock supply, and won the ensuing general election. Kerr was widely blamed for the crisis and more or less disappeared from public life for the remainder of his term before retiring to England.

The National Archives of Australia contain fascinating files on 'The Dismissal', which were opened to public inspection in 2006. One 340-page file mostly comprises extracts from (mainly British) constitutional histories, which revisit the constitutional crises of 1910–14, and the roughly analogous Canadian dismissal crisis of 1926.[3] Most authors in the folder support the view that George V had the power to dismiss Asquith. An exception is Ivor Jennings, who, as noted above, was a bitter opponent of Dicey. Jennings believed that the monarch could only act on advice. Asquith in 1914, like Whitlam in 1975, was not going to advise the head of state to dismiss him. If the King dismissed his ministers, he could not avoid being seen as partisan, Jennings pointed out in a section sidelined by the Attorney General's office (Jennings 1959: 416, as annotated in National Archives of Australia, Attorney General's Department A/75/7778, '*Governor-General* v. *Prime Minister*: whether the Governor-General has power to dismiss a Prime Minister', December 1975, at f. 109).

Kerr found out the hard way what George V would certainly have found if he had done what Dicey and the Unionists wanted him to do. Dismissing a government of one party makes you inevitably seen as a partisan of the other—with good grounds in both the George V and John Kerr cases, although probably not in the Canadian case of 1926. (The defence of Sir John Kerr by his Official Secretary, Sir David Smith, and the constitutional issues raised by Sir David, are considered later in this chapter.) The best way for a head of state to avoid such a dilemma is by not letting it arise in the first place. If the head of state has no power to dismiss a government, the parties lose the ability to play the backward induction game played by Bonar Law and Asquith in 1912–14, and by Whitlam and Fraser in 1975. If it is common knowledge that there is no third party available to resolve disputes arising from divided government, then the parties know that they will have to sort it out for themselves. If the electorate perceives the parties to be playing silly games, the parties will suffer, and they should bargain in that knowledge. This will be the case between the House of Commons and any reformed House of Lords.

In a related area, the risks to the UK head of state at the *start* of a government have diminished substantially since the days of Victoria and George V. When a monarch had discretion regarding who to approach to form an administration, the monarch had some liberty to express his or her personal tastes. Victoria tried to block Gladstone this way, but luckily for the survival of the monarchy the politicians to whom she turned in a vain effort to avoid Gladstone would not let her. Since 1965, all the United Kingdom's major political parties have elected their own leaders, and there is no discretion left for the monarch of the sort that Victoria tried to exploit in 1880.

Another possible danger for the head of state is the case where a prime minister offers to resign and the head of state tries to dissuade the prime minister from doing so. This situation arose in the United Kingdom in August 1931, when Prime Minister Ramsay MacDonald could not persuade his minority Labour government colleagues to accept public expenditure cuts. When he offered to resign, George V urged him to stay on for the duration of economic crisis, to be joined by the leaders of the other parties in a 'National Government' strictly for the duration of the crisis. When it came to the General Election in October of the same year, the other parties forgot about the 'temporary' nature of the promises and the king failed to enforce them. Bogdanor (1995: 104–12) argues persuasively that this was not George V's finest moment. His well-meaning actions destroyed MacDonald's career and, for a long time, his posthumous reputation.

What about the 'hung parliament' scenario that all the texts discuss? Some precedents are clear, some less so. Bogdanor (1995, p. 158) is in the unfortunate position of having to treat the letter to the *Times* in 1950 from George VI's secretary writing as 'Senex' ('Old Man') as part of the British Constitution, although an ambiguous one.

It seems clear, from the most recent precedent in February 1974, that if an incumbent prime minister has lost his majority at a general election, but that no other party has gained a clear majority, the incumbent has the right to make the first attempt at building a coalition. Edward Heath did so, and resigned only when it became clear that he could not do a deal which would stick with either the Liberals or the Ulster Unionists.

The rest is less clear. The texts say that the sovereign should invite the leader of the largest party, or the leader of the party most likely to be able to build a majority in the Commons, to form an administration. Unfortunately, as Bogdanor points out, there is no guarantee that these two are the same person. To go for the first interpretation favours (in the United Kingdom context) the Conservative and Labour parties, who may choose to form a minority government; to go for the second favours the Liberal Democrats as the centre party.

HOW WELL HAVE THEY DONE?

It seems, therefore, that the role of head of state ineradicably involves exercising political judgement. What is the track record of the British monarchy in this regard?

It is customary for books on the British monarchy, especially at the coffee-table end of the market, to assert that the Queen is wonderful, the monarchy is wonderful, the British Constitution is wonderful, and everything is for the best in the best of all possible worlds. The data in Table 12.2 cast some doubt on this. Table 5.5, on monarchical veto plays, is also relevant.

Since Parliament chose the present reigning dynasty of the United Kingdom, there have been the eleven monarchs listed in Table 12.2. Of these

Table 12.2 The current UK dynasty as heads of state.

Monarch	Reigned	Performance as head of state
George I	1714–27	Did not speak English. Quarrelled with heir. Spent considerable time governing Hanover. Efficient, Patron of Handel
George II	1727–60	Quarrelled with heir. Efficient
George III	1760–1820	Quarrelled with heir. Too ill to reign 1788–9, 1801, 1804, 1810–20. Vetoed Catholic emancipation, 1801
George IV	1820–30	'Torrents of debts' (*DNB*). Hated his wife. Alcoholic. Tried to block Catholic relief. 'There never was an individual less regretted by his fellow-creatures than this deceased King'—*The Times*, 29.06.1830. Art patron
William IV	1830–7	'One of the least wise of British monarchs'—Asquith to George V, 1913
Victoria	1837–1901	Tried to destabilize Gladstone and Rosebery 1885–94. Wrote plain-text letter denouncing death of Gordon 1885, delivered to Gladstone at Carnforth station
Edward VII	1901–10	Most successful royal racehorse owner; independently initiated talks leading to alliance with France 1903.
George V	1910–36	Encouraged Unionist revolt; signalled support for Curragh 'mutineers'. Collected stamps
Edward VIII	1936	Nazi sympathizer as king. Composed bagpipe tunes
George VI	1936–52	Model constitutional monarch
Elizabeth II	1952–	Model constitutional monarch

Sources: *Oxford Dictionary of National Biography*, online; Matthew (1999); Jenkins (1964); Nicolson (1952); McKinstry (2005).

eleven, three, including Queen Elizabeth II, have performed as exemplary heads of state (the others being George II and George VI). The performance of the remaining eight raises questions. Victoria and George V have been discussed. The most ardent royalist would have difficulty in defending three of the rest (George IV, William IV, and Edward VIII, who abdicated when it became clear that he could not get his way over the Prime Minister). Of those not mentioned hitherto, George I spent substantial time governing Hanover; George III vetoed Catholic emancipation and for four periods was too ill to reign; and Edward VII not only resisted the creation of peers, but also pursued an independent foreign policy that may have led to closer entanglements with France and Russia than his governments would have chosen. However, it is fair to add that the unelected Edward VII bears less responsibility than the unelected Henry Wilson for committing the United Kingdom to what became the First World War.

Given that the idea that monarchs are touched by the divine went out of fashion in the seventeenth century, what arguments are put up to justify the hereditary principle? The best argument is a negative one. Any elected head of state, it is argued, is partisan, or was once a partisan. That is why they are in the frame to be considered for the role of head of state. Only a random selection, as modified by the rules of succession and occasional parliamentary intervention (as in 1701 and 1936), can guarantee a non-partisan who will take a long-term view. The most sophisticated version of the argument I know is due to the economist Mancur Olson:

> The historical prevalence of dynastic succession, in spite of the near-zero probability that the oldest son of a king is the most talented person for the job, probably owes something to an intuitive sense that everyone in a domain, including the present ruler, gains when rulers have a reason to take a long-term view. In an absolutist regime, it may be advantageous to all concerned if a consensus emerges about who the next ruler will probably be. This not only reduces the likelihood of a battle over succession but also increases confidence and thus investment, income, and tax receipts even in the present. (Olson 2000: 28)

In this perspective, the argument for the hereditary principle is an argument for stability and against short termism. As everybody knows who the next monarch is likely to be, everybody can plan on that assumption. Transaction costs are minimized. Also, the monarch has a vested interest in preserving the institution of monarchy so that her family may continue to enjoy the benefits. This vested interest can be seen in the actions of Lord Knollys in 1910, when he tried to save his kings from the risk to the monarchy that would have been involved in allowing Balfour to form a minority Conservative government.

Even then, the hereditary principle does not guarantee stability. The next monarch may be an infant (e.g. Henry VI), go mad (e.g. George III), or be utterly unfit for office (e.g. George IV). A record of three unambiguously good, three unambiguously bad, and five so-so does not speak terribly well for the hereditary principle as regards the present British dynasty. But there is no reason to suppose that another dynasty of monarchs would be better. Furthermore, it is worth asking some vulgarly Marxist questions about the British monarchy. Are the monarch's family disproportionately likely to enter certain occupations, and/or have certain material interests?

Yes and yes. For wholly understandable reasons, relations of the British monarch are more likely than the population at large to become military officers. They are probably more likely than members of the aristocracy from which they are drawn to be military officers, although I have no data on that point. If, therefore, there is, as in 1914, a dispute over whether and on what conditions the military may be sent to aid the civil power, the monarch may have distinctive opinions. George V did. But such disputes are in their nature likely to arise only when the state is in need of protection.

Consider again the advice reaching George V between 1912 and 1914. The Royal Archives contain six bulky files on Home Rule and one on the Curragh. George V and his secretary Stamfordham[4] received a great deal of advice, some of it solicited, some not. Advice from government ministers came sparely and formally. Asquith advised the King that it was his constitutional duty to act on the advice of ministers and not to seek alternative sources of advice. In one of his most forthright papers, he wrote:

> [I]t is not the function of a Constitutional Sovereign to act as arbiter or mediator between rival parties and politics; still less to take advice from the leaders on both sides, with the view to forming a conclusion of his own (*Memo*, December 1910, quoted in Spender and Asquith 1932, I: 306).

However, George V did precisely what his Prime Minister had formally asked him not to do. Worse, rather than 'take advice from the leaders on both sides', he sought advice from one side only, namely the Unionist Opposition. Most of the unsought advice in the file also comes from Unionists. The seven files contain not a single message either to or from the Irish Party, which held 74 seats, and the balance of power, in the elected house of the Parliament of 1910.[5] (There are no messages to or from Labour politicians either; but they held no power in the Commons—McLean 2001a, Tables 4.1–4.3). The King took his advice on Ireland almost entirely from Unionists. Southern Irish landlords advised him that the people, and the Catholic Church, no longer wanted Home Rule. He and his secretary did not check these claims with representatives of either. However, the archbishop of Canterbury, the leader of a church that was disestablished in Ireland in 1869 and was only the third-largest denomination there, was one of those efforts to mediate and arbitrate were encouraged. On the other hand, there are copious messages in the Royal Archives to the King from, or on behalf, of the Irish Unionists, who held 17 seats in the elected house of the Parliament of 1910, and did not hold the balance of power. However, their leaders were threatening armed insurrection against His Majesty's Government. This seems, prima facie, an odd reason for His Majesty to accord them special attention.

Of course, it was appropriate for the king to talk to Opposition politicians, as he did intensively, for instance at Balmoral in autumn 1913. But it is surprising to find, according to Bonar Law's note of his discussion with the king on that occasion, that the king seems to have told Law—who, at the time, 'could imagine no lengths of resistance' to which the Ulster Protestants might go 'in which I would not be prepared to support them'—that he planned to ask his ministers to dissolve Parliament before the Government of Ireland Bill became law. 'I expressed to His Majesty my belief that such a letter. . . might save the situation . . . His Majesty stated it was his intention to send it in the latter half of October'.[6] A mediator must be in the middle, not to one side. In 1913, George V was not capable of mediation, much though he wished to be.

The problem remains if we look at the advice offered to the King by courtiers with no formal partisan identification. Besides the archbishop, these included Sir Francis Hopwood, Lord Esher, and the King's equerry and assistant private secretary, Clive Wigram. All were instinctive Unionists; all of them hostile to the advice His Majesty's ministers were sending. For example: 'I have strong doubts whether Seely's so-called "order" to officers is not ultra vires'; 'The defeat of the Government candidate at Lanark will do much good'; 'The Ulstermen are grim, dogged, determined "ghazis" with good leaders and a certain amount of discipline, but the Southerners will have no leaders and can only be "Franc Tireurs"'.[7]

For centuries, power and land have been intertwined in the United Kingdom. Until recently the House of Lords was almost exclusively a landed chamber, and the landed interest is still disproportionately represented there (Chapter 11). The monarch is one of the United Kingdom's largest land-owners. Publicity issued on behalf of the Royal Household is careful to stress that much of the royal real estate, including the Crown Estate, the Duchy of Lancaster, and the Duchy of Cornwall (the latter two primarily agricultural holdings) are not owned by the Sovereign or her heir personally, and that their income is used to defray royal and other public expenditure. Elizabeth II does own personally the two holiday estates of Balmoral in Scotland and Sandringham in Norfolk. Besides those, it would be very surprising if the monarch and the Prince of Wales did not take a trustee's interest in the issues of land policy (such as the terms and conditions of European Union farm payments) that affect such large landholdings as the Duchies of Lancaster (18,700 ha; capital value £400 million) and Cornwall (54,700 ha; capital value £600 million).[8]

HOW ELSE MIGHT IT BE DONE?

Defenders of monarchy are usually driven back on an adaptation of Winston Churchill's famous comment on democracy: 'the worst form of Government except all those other forms that have been tried from time to time' (in House of Commons, 11.11.1947). It is said that an elected head of state would either be a political partisan or a superannuated footballer. Perhaps; but it could depend on the method of election.

A head of state may be elected directly or indirectly. An example of a directly elected, but non-executive presidency is that of Ireland. Here are the relevant clauses of the Irish Constitution (English-language version):

[Article 12]

1. The President shall be elected by direct vote of the people.
2. Every citizen who has the right to vote at an election for members of Dáil Éireann [the Parliament of Ireland—IM] shall have the right to vote at an election for President.
3. The voting shall be by secret ballot and on the system of proportional representation by means of the single transferable vote.

   3.1 The President shall hold office for seven years from the date upon which he enters upon his office, unless before the expiration of that period he dies, or resigns, or is removed from office, or becomes permanently incapacitated, such incapacity being established to the satisfaction of the Supreme Court consisting of not less than five judges.

   3.2 A person who holds, or who has held, office as President, shall be eligible for re-election to that office once, but only once.

[Article 13]

1.1° The President shall, on the nomination of Dáil Éireann, appoint the Taoiseach, that is, the head of the Government or Prime Minister.

2° The President shall, on the nomination of the Taoiseach with the previous approval of Dáil Éireann, appoint the other members of the Government.

    3° The President shall, on the advice of the Taoiseach, accept the resignation or terminate the appointment of any member of the Government.

2.1° Dáil Éireann shall be summoned and dissolved by the President on the advice of the Taoiseach.

    2° The President may in his absolute discretion refuse to dissolve Dáil Éireann on the advice of a Taoiseach who has ceased to retain the support of a majority in Dáil Éireann.

    3° The President may at any time, after consultation with the Council of State, convene a meeting of either or both of the Houses of the Oireachtas.

    4. The supreme command of the Defence Forces is hereby vested in the President.[9]

An example of an indirectly elected non-executive presidency is that of Germany:

[Article 54]
[Election]

1. The Federal President shall be elected by the Federal Convention without debate. Any German who is entitled to vote in Bundestag elections and has attained the age of forty may be elected.

2. The term of office of the Federal President shall be five years. Re-election for a consecutive term shall be permitted only once.

3. The Federal Convention shall consist of the Members of the Bundestag and an equal number of members elected by the parliaments of the Länder on the basis of proportional representation.

4. The Federal Convention shall meet not later than thirty days before the term of office of the Federal President expires or, in the case of premature termination, not later than thirty days after that date. It shall be convened by the President of the Bundestag.

5. After the expiration of a legislative term, the period specified in the first sentence of paragraph (4) of this Article shall begin when the Bundestag first convenes.

6. The person receiving the votes of a majority of the members of the Federal Convention shall be elected. If after two ballots no candidate has obtained such a majority, the person who receives the largest number of votes on the next ballot shall be elected.

[Article 60]

[Appointment and dismissal of federal judges, federal civil servants, and military officers; pardon]

1. The Federal President shall appoint and dismiss federal judges, federal civil servants, and commissioned and non-commissioned officers of the Armed Forces, except as may otherwise be provided by a law.[10]

Both the Irish and the German Constitutions contain provisions for the impeachment and dismissal of the president, and for his or her incapacity.

Do these constitutions protect their countries from electing political hacks, retired sportsmen, or people with skeletons in their cupboards? There are too few cases for systematic comparison with the record of monarchs but it is possible to make some tentative points. There have been eight presidents of Ireland since the Constitution came into force in 1937. All were nominees of political parties. Judging by standard biographical sources, two of the eight (Seán T. Ó Ceallaigh, 1945–59, nominated by a dominant prime minister; and Cearbhall Ó Dálaigh, 1974–6) were disastrous in office. There have been nine presidents of the Federal Republic of Germany since the Basic Law was enacted in 1949. All were nominees of political parties. Judging by standard biographical sources, only one of the nine (Heinrich Lübke, 1959–69) was a disaster in office. He had been nominated by a dominant Chancellor of his own party, Konrad Adenauer.

These anecdotes suggest, although of course they do not prove, that the probability of a bad elected president is lower than the probability of a bad monarch; and a president can always be denied re-election. Normally, democratic constitutions, including those of Ireland and Germany, set a maximum term for their presidency. A monarch is for life, unless deposed, which also means that the probability of a monarch being too ill to reign is higher than for a president.

However, given that in practice only political parties normally have the resources to nominate and pursue a presidential candidacy, how big is the risk of a president's being simply a weak and compliant puppet of the party that nominated him? The risk is certainly there, with one clear case in Germany and one at least arguable case in Ireland. The remedy is in the hands of the people, directly or indirectly.

The Irish Constitution prescribes the electoral rule for the election of the president as (what in the United Kingdom is called) 'alternative vote' (AV). It is the same rule as that used to elect members of the Australian House of Representatives. Although the text of the Constitution prescribes STV for Irish presidential elections, that system is properly applicable only to the case of a multi-member district. When applied to an election to a single position, STV collapses into AV. Each voter casts a ranked ballot paper. Any candidate who achieves more than 50 per cent of the vote is immediately elected. If none is, the candidate with the fewest first preferences drops out and his or her votes are transferred to the next stated preference (if any). This process is iterated until one candidate has more than half of the valid votes cast.

It has one notable merit and one notable drawback. Its notable merit is that it cannot select a *Condorcet loser*—that is, a candidate who would lose to each of the others in exhaustive pairwise comparisons. The successful candidate must have beaten at least one other in the (final) majoritarian vote. It gives some incentive to candidates to seek out the median-voter position, since a candidate may depend on the later preference votes of eliminated candidates. Some of these will be extreme, and some centrist. But (unless a Condorcet winner is eliminated, as will be described shortly) a candidate has more incentive to please the centrists than the extremists, because the final contest will choose whichever of the last two candidates is closer to the median voter.

On the basis of this reasoning (formally or informally), a number of political scientists have recommended AV as a suitable electoral system for (at least presidential elections in) divided societies—such as South Africa (Horowitz 1991) or Papua New Guinea (Reilly 2001). Both Horowitz and Reilly are serious institutional designers and their books are well argued.

However, a constitutional engineer could do still better. AV, like all electoral systems depending on elimination of unsuccessful candidates, has one serious defect. It may eliminate a *Condorcet winner* and/or a *Borda winner*. A Condorcet winner is a candidate who would beat each other in exhaustive pairwise comparisons. A Borda winner is the candidate who, on average, is ranked the highest. To see how this can arise, imagine a simple case (Table 12.3).

Table 12.3 The electoral system for the President of Ireland may eliminate a Condorcet winner.

Number of voters	41	10	10	39
First preference	Blue	Yellow	Yellow	Red
Middle preference	Yellow	Red	Blue	Yellow
Lowest preference	Red	Blue	Red	Blue

Under alternative vote, with sincere voting, Yellow (20 votes) is eliminated in the first round. In the second round, Blue beats Red by 51 votes to 49. However, Yellow is the Condorcet winner. In pairwise comparison, Yellow beats Blue by 59 votes to 41, and Red by 61 votes to 39. With partially informed sophisticated voting, where Yellow is known to be running third, the result is still a win for Blue over Red by 51/49, because Yellow voters all default to their second preference. With fully informed sophisticated voting, Yellow voters do not desert their top preference, as it is common knowledge that Red voters will support Yellow in order to prevent the election of Blue, and Blue voters have no counter-strategy.

Borda scores (last place = 0, middle = 1, top = 2):

   Blue: $(41 \times 2) + 10 = 92$
   Yellow: $(20 \times 2) + 80 = 120$ *Borda winner*
   Red: $(39 \times 2) + 10 = 88$

Table 12.3 illustrates a simple case with a technically 'well-behaved' electorate. There is some dimension such that everybody accepts that Red is at one end of it and Blue is at the other, with Yellow intermediate. Accordingly, all Blue supporters rank Red lowest, and all Red supporters rank Blue lowest. Yellow supporters divide into two groups, according to which of the others they rank second. This structure of opinion is called 'single-peaked'. From the median voter theorem, when preferences are single-peaked, the median voter's optimum will win in any well-behaved choice procedure. However, if all voters express their sincere preferences on the ballot paper, Yellow is eliminated in the first round and in the second Blue narrowly beats Red. Yet, Yellow was the Condorcet winner. To calculate the Borda winner, award 0 points for a last place, 1 for a second place, and 2 for a top place. Here again Yellow is the winner, being therefore the candidate who on average the voters rank the highest.

There is a huge technical literature on the properties of the Condorcet and Borda criteria, and social choice theorists are not wholly agreed which should have precedence in the cases where they point to different winners, or where there is no unique Condorcet winner. Fortunately, a non-technical book like this can avoid this literature entirely, because nobody has ever proposed a rule different from both the Condorcet rule and the Borda rule to determine the 'true' democratic winner of a contest.

The Condorcet and Borda rules must not be used to select a legislature, where multiple seats are at stake. Whether the country uses single-member or multi-member districts, it should use a different rule, or combination of rules. But to elect a single president, the technical literature is unanimous: only two rules are in contention. In a technical paper written jointly with an economist (McLean and Shephard 2004), I gave details of an algorithm that could be used, and a little piece of software that works in the case with a small number of voters. The software selects the Condorcet winner if one exists. If none exists, because the candidates are in a cycle (where A beats B, who beats C, who (beats D, who . . .) beats A), it selects the Borda winner. This combined selection criterion was first suggested by Black (1958). Various academics and NGOs have software available for larger elections. The procedure for voters is identical with that used at an Irish presidential (or Australian House of Representatives) election: each voter has only to rank the candidates in order of preference. Behind the scenes, however, the ballots are handled in a different, and mathematically more defensible, way.

Should a head of state for the United Kingdom be elected directly (as in Ireland) or indirectly (as in Germany)? I surmise that the drafters of the German Basic Law were mesmerized by Hitler. He never actually won a democratic election, but he was undoubtedly popular in the early years of his *Führership*. Therefore, like the framers of the US Constitution 150 years earlier, the German framers proposed indirect election by an ad hoc body of electors, bringing together the *Bundestag* and the newly formed *Länder*. No doubt they felt that a demagogue was less likely to be elected by an indirect process than by a direct popular election. For no doubt similar reasons, when the proposal to make Australia a republic was put to a referendum in 1999, the proposition was:

> To alter the Constitution to establish the Commonwealth of Australia as a republic with the Queen and Governor-General being replaced by a President appointed by a two-thirds majority of the members of the Commonwealth Parliament.

This proposition was widely supported by political elites, including (rather remarkably) both Gough Whitlam and Malcolm Fraser. However, although most of the Australian public were thought to favour a republic, the proposal was defeated by a margin of 55 to 45. Detailed evidence shows that this arose because two groups of people were dissatisfied, those who wanted to retain the monarchy, and those who favoured a directly elected president. Among the latter, the ballot proposition was derided as a stitch-up by politicians.

A deliberative poll took place in October 1999, where a nationally representative random sample of Australian voters was invited to Canberra to hear detailed argument for and against the ballot proposition, and for and against indirect election. The voters were polled before and after deliberation (Tables 12.4 and 12.5).

Table 12.4 shows that a weekend of deliberation left the sample both more favourable towards the proposal, and less uncertain about it. Table 12.5 shows, first, that the status quo of retaining the monarchy, which actually won in the referendum, was unpopular going into, and still less popular coming out of, the deliberation. It also shows a sharp swing of opinion

Table 12.4 Australian Deliberative Poll: before-and-after opinion on the ballot proposition.

	Before deliberation (%)	After deliberation (%)	Difference (%)
Approve the proposed alteration to the constitution?			
Yes	53	73	+20
No	40	27	13
Uncommitted	7		7

Source: Center for Deliberative Democracy, Stanford University

Table 12.5 Australian Deliberative Poll: first preferences.

	Before deliberation (%)	After deliberation (%)	Difference (%)
Change to a republic with a President directly elected by the people	50	19	−31
Change to a republic with a President appointed by Parliament	20	61	+41
Not change anything, keeping the Queen and the Governor General in their current roles	26	15	−11
None, don't know	4	5	+1

Source: Center for Deliberative Democracy, Stanford University

from directly elected to indirectly elected—that is, to the proposal on the ballot. It implies that, if all Australians had been exposed to the same level of argument about the three possible options, the ballot proposition would have been carried.

Why, though, are people such as the American and German framers, and Australian constitutional experts, so worried about a directly elected head of state? The root feeling was made explicit by Alexander Hamilton in *The Federalist Papers,* which were written in 1787–8 in an attempt to persuade New Yorkers to elect people in favour of ratification to their state constitutional convention. Defending the Electoral College, which was planned to be an ad hoc body of electors in each state who would meet for the sole purpose of voting on presidential nominees and transmitting their findings to the national capital, Hamilton writes:

> The choice of *several* to be an intermediate body of electors will be much less apt to convulse the community with any extraordinary or violent movements than the choice of *one* who was himself to be the final object of the public wishes. . . . This process of election affords a moral certainty that the office of President will seldom fall to the lot of any man who is not in an eminent degree endowed with the requisite qualifications. Talents for low intrigue, and the little arts of popularity, may alone suffice to elevate a man to the first honors in a single state; but it will require other talents, and a different kind of merit, to establish him in the esteem and confidence of the whole union. (*Federalist* # 68; Madison, Hamilton, and Jay 1788/1987: 393–5)

But is it really true, in modern conditions, that an ad hoc assembly (as in Germany and, theoretically, the United States) or the legislature (as proposed for Australia) is better than the people at electing someone endowed with the requisite qualifications—or less likely than the people to elect someone with talents for low intrigue, and the little arts of popularity? There are certainly instances when the people have been fooled. There are also instances when the people have rejected the candidates of the leading parties. The election of Mary Robinson as President of Ireland in 1990 was one of the latter.

The most eloquent defender of Sir John Kerr has been not Kerr himself (Kerr 1979), but his Official Secretary in 1975, Sir David Smith (Smith 2005). Smith was a career civil servant who moved from the Department of the Prime Minister to the Governor General's Office in 1973 and stayed there until his retirement in 1990, when he was awarded a knighthood in the personal gift of the Queen—the last Australian to receive this honour for services in Australia, as Australia withdrew from granting knighthoods in 1986. In the 1998 constitutional convention, he was an appointed delegate and one of the intellectual leaders of the monarchist side, and he remains an active supporter of Australians for a Constitutional Monarchy. His arguments against an elected head of state therefore have considerable weight.

> Unlike an elected president, a Governor-General comes to that high office without having to seek it, and without having to defeat others to attain it or to retain it. As a result, an appointed Governor-General is able to represent national unity in a way that no elected president would be able to do, for an appointed Governor-General has no political constituency to represent and no supporters to reward. (Smith 2005: 124–5)

In a footnote, Sir David draws attention to a campaign speech by Mary Robinson in which she reportedly said: 'As President directly elected by the people of Ireland, I will have the most democratic job in the country.' It is odd that Sir David defends a non-elected head of state through a favourable contrast between the most unpopular (non-elected) Governor General in Australian history and the most popular (elected) President in Irish history. President Robinson has the better of that argument—*providing* that the terms of election, eligibility, and re-eligibility are right. If a directly elected president is re-eligible for election, she will indeed want to maximize her chances of re-election. These are unlikely to be best served either by rubber-stamping the actions of the current government, or by dismissing it.

However, in a sense, the dispute between direct election and indirect election advocates is a second-order matter. Return to Olson's point that it is vanishingly improbable that the eldest son of the current monarch is the best-fitted person in the country for the role of head of state (and remember George IV if you need reminding). The chances of an election selecting that person are no doubt low; but they are higher than those of the hereditary principle and the rules of succession which privilege males.

As to unelected Governors General, Sir David's argument fails. If Sir John Kerr had been elected, he would have had more authority, not less. He could have defended his actions without reference to the Queen, which raised, and has continued to raise, an irrelevancy that has prevented Australians from seeing that they already live in a federal republic to all intents and purposes, but one with a defective procedure for nominating the head of state.

However, the arguments of this chapter do not depend on personalities. They emphatically do not depend on the personality of the current or future monarchs. The transition from a monarchy to a republic need not, and probably ought not, to occur at the death of a particular monarch, but on an appointed day specified in the legislation after the election of the first republican head of state. As monarchs, and people in the line of succession to the monarchy, have been brought up in reasonable (perhaps stochastic) expectation of getting the job, it would be appropriate to compensate them for the loss of that expectation. It would also be appropriate to allow them to retain courtesy titles. They might even wish to run for election to the post of head of state.

THE ROYAL PREROGATIVE

One benefit of abolishing monarchy in the United Kingdom is that the royal prerogative would go too, clearing the way for serious thought about the freedom of the executive to act without explicit parliamentary authority. This would continue a movement started in the UK government's 2007 Green Paper on the constitution. The *Oxford English Dictionary* defines 'prerogative' in the relevant sense as *The special right or privilege exercised by a monarch over all other persons*, and adds an explanatory note:

> In Great Britain, the royal prerogative includes the right of sending and receiving ambassadors, making treaties, making war and concluding peace, conferring honours, nominating to bishoprics, choosing ministers of state, summoning Parliament, refusing assent to a bill, and of pardoning those under legal sentence; with many other political, ecclesiastical, and judicial privileges. Though notionally unrestricted, the exercise of the royal prerogative is practically limited by the rights of parliament or of other bodies or persons and the constitutional obligation to take the advice of ministers. (*Oxford English Dictionary* (OED) online, s.v. *prerogative*, noun, sense 2a).

In its etymology, the word is from post-classical Latin via Norman French; so it was introduced to English law by post-Norman Conquest monarchs and their lawyers. This leaves open the fascinating antiquarian issue of how far, if at all, the royal prerogative applied in Scotland before 1707. I do not attempt to answer that question. Remarkably, as the Green Paper states (para. 21), 'The precise scope of the prerogative executive powers is uncertain: there is no authoritative list.' However, its list is similar to the *OED*'s:

The Government exercises prerogative powers to:

- Deploy and use the Armed Forces overseas
- Make and ratify treaties
- Issue, refuse, impound and revoke passports
- Acquire and cede territory
- Conduct diplomacy
- Send and receive ambassadors
- Organize the Civil Service.

The Government makes recommendations to the Monarch to exercise her powers to:

- Grant honours or decorations
- Grant mercy
- Grant peerages
- Appoint Ministers.

(HM Government 2007, Box 2).

From these combined lists, the Government in 2007 withdrew there and then from nominating to bishoprics (para. 57–66; see Chapter 13) and announced its intention to put other prerogative powers on a statutory footing. It proposes to make dissolving Parliament the subject of a Commons vote (though this makes little practical difference); to give a statutory basis to the civil service; and to give the Commons the right to vote on the deployment of armed forces abroad and the ratification of treaties. It announced that it would consult on other options. As any option which requires a vote of both houses of parliament must proceed by political consensus, it is clear that the government in office in 2007 does not plan to move on them immediately.

Would the abolition of the monarchy leave any of the powers on either the *OED* or the HM Government list orphaned? No. Any which, according to the consultations envisaged in the Green Paper, should not be brought under parliamentary control would therefore remain as prerogatives of the head of state. The grant of honours or decorations seems an obvious example. It is easy to see why giving that unfettered power to Parliament or the executive would be a bad idea, and that giving it explicitly to the head of state would be a good one. It would help the head of state to consolidate her role as a non-partisan unifier of the nation.

Appendix to Chapter 12

'The Constitutional Position of the Sovereign': Letters between King George V and Prime Minister H. H. Asquith, Autumn 1913[11].

Letter I. KGV to HHA, 11 August 1913

HM Yacht *Victoria and Albert*

Although I have not spoken to you before on the subject, I have been for some time very anxious about the Irish Home Rule Bill, and especially with regard to Ulster.

The speeches not only of people like Sir E. Carson,[12] but of the Unionist leaders, and of ex Cabinet Ministers; the stated intention of setting up a provisional Govt in Ulster directly the Home Rule Bill is passed; the reports of Military preparations, Army drilling etc.; of assistance from England, Scotland and the Colonies; of the intended resignation of their Commissions by Officers in the Army, all point towards rebellion if not Civil War; and, if so, to certain bloodshed.

Meanwhile, there are rumours of probable agitation in the country; of monster petitions, addresses from the House of Lords, from Privy Councillors, urging me to use my influence to avert the catastrophe which threatens Ireland.

Such vigorous action taken, or likely to be taken, will place me in a very embarrassing position in the centre of the conflicting parties backed by their respective Press.

Whatever I do I shall offend half the population.

One alternative would certainly result in alienating the Ulster Protestants from me probably for ever, and whatever happens the result must be detrimental to me personally and to the Crown in general.

No Sovereign has ever been in such a position, and this pressure is sure to increase during the next few months.

In this period I shall have a right to expect the greatest confidence and support from my Ministers, and, above all from my Prime Minister.

I cannot help feeling that the Government is drifting and taking me with it.

Before the gravity of the situation increases, I should like to know how you view the present state of affairs, and what you imagine will be the outcome of it.

On the 24th July I saw Mr Birrell,[13] who admitted the seriousness of the outlook.

He seemed to think that perhaps an arrangement could be made for Ulster to 'contract out' of the Home Rule Bill, say for 10 years, with the right to come under the Irish Parliament, if so desired, after a referendum by her people, at the end of that period. But it was for the Opposition to come forward with some practical proposal to this effect.

Is there any chance of a settlement by consent as suggested by Lord Loreburn, Lord Macdonnell, Lord Dunraven, Mr W. O'Brien, Mr Birrell, Lord Lansdowne, Mr. Bonar Law and others?[14]

Would it be possible to have a Conference in which all parties should take part, to consider the whole policy of devolution, of which you, in introducing the Home Rule Bill in April 1912, said 'Irish Home Rule is only the first step?'

Would it not be better to try to settle measures involving great changes in the Constitution, such as Home Rule all round, Reform of the House of Lords etc., not on Party lines, but by agreement?

Letter II HHA to KGV, [11] September 1913

[HHA's handwritten covering letter, from Hopeman, Morayshire, states: 'Mr Asquith has not, so far, shown this paper to any of his colleagues; it is (what he understood your Majesty to desire) a personal communication from the PM to the King.' He describes the following letter as a corrected proof. It is printed in the style of a Cabinet paper of the time.]

The constitutional position of the sovereign

I propose to deal in this memorandum with the position of a Constitutional Sovereign in relation to the controversies which are likely to arise with regard to the Government of Ireland Bill. In a subsequent paper I will deal (1) with the actual and prospective situation in Ireland in the event of (a) the passing, (b) the rejection of that Bill; and (2) with the possibility and expediency of some middle course.

In the old days, before our present Constitution was completely evolved, the Crown was a real and effective, and often a dominating factor in legislation. Its powers were developed to considerable lengths by such kings as Henry VIII, and enforced with much suppleness and reserve by Queen Elizabeth; but the Tudor Sovereigns had a keen eye and a responsive pulse to the general opinion of the nation. The Stuarts, who followed, pushed matters to extremes, with the result that Charles I lost his head, and James II his throne. The Revolution put the title to the Throne and its prerogatives on a Parliamentary basis, and since a comparatively early date in the reign of Queen Anne, the Sovereign has never attempted to withhold his assent *from a Bill which had received Parliamentary sanction.*[15]

We have had, since that date, Sovereigns of marked individuality, of great authority, and of strong ideas (often from time to time, opposed to the policy of the Ministry of the day) but none of them—not even George III, Queen Victoria or King Edward VII—have ever dreamt of reviving the ancient veto of the Crown. We have now a well-established tradition of 200 years, that, *in the last resort*, the occupant of the Throne accepts and acts upon the advice of his Ministers. The Sovereign may have lost something of his personal power and authority, but the Crown has been thereby removed from the storms and vicissitudes of party politics, and the monarchy rests upon a solid foundation which is buttressed both by long tradition and by the general conviction that its personal[16] status is an invaluable safeguard for the continuity of our national life.

It follows that the rights and duties of a constitutional monarch in this country in regard to legislation are confined within determined and strictly circumscribed limits.

He is entitled and bound to give his Ministers all relevant information which comes to him; to point out objections which seem to him valid against the course which they advise; *to suggest (if he thinks fit) an alternative policy.* Such intimations are always received by Ministers with the utmost respect, and considered with more care and deference than if they proceeded from any other quarter. But in the end, the Sovereign always acts upon the advice which Ministers, after full deliberation and (if need be) reconsideration, feel it their duty to offer. They give that advice well knowing that they can, and probably will, be called to account for it by Parliament.

The Sovereign undoubtedly has the power of changing his advisers, but it is relevant to point out that there has been, during the last 130 years, one occasion only on which the King has dismissed the Ministry which still *possessed the confidence of the House of Commons.* This was in 1834, when William IV (one of the least wise of British monarchs) called upon Lord Melbourne to resign. He took advantage (as we now know) of a hint improvidently given by Lord Melbourne himself, but the proceeding was neither well advised nor fortunate. The dissolution which followed left Sir R. Peel in a minority, and Lord Melbourne and his friends in a few months returned to power, which they held for the next six years. The authority of the Crown was disparaged, and Queen Victoria, during her long reign, was careful never to repeat the mistake of her predecessor.

The Parliament Act was not intended in any way to affect, and it is submitted has not affected, the Constitutional position of the Sovereign. It deals only with differences between the two Houses. When the two Houses are in agreement (as is always the case when there is a Conservative majority in the House of Commons), the Act is a dead letter. When they differ, it provides that, after a considerable interval, the thrice repeated decision of the Commons shall prevail, without the necessity for a dissolution of Parliament. The possibility of abuse is guarded against by the curtailment of the maximum life of any given House of Commons to five years.

Nothing can be more important, in the best interests of the Crown and of the country, than that a practice, so long established and so well justified by experience, should remain unimpaired. It frees the occupant of the Throne from all personal responsibility for the Acts of the Executive and the legislature. It gives force and meaning to the old maxim that 'the King can do no wrong.' So long as it prevails, however objectionable particular Acts may be to a large section of his subjects, they cannot hold him in any way accountable, and their loyalty is (or ought to be) wholly unaffected. If, on the other hand, the King were to intervene on one side, or in one case—which he could only do by dismissing Ministers in *de facto* possession of a Parliamentary majority—he would be expected to do the same on another occasion, and perhaps for the other side. Every Act of Parliament of the first order of importance, and only passed after acute controversy, would be regarded as bearing the personal *imprimatur* of the Sovereign. He would; whether he wished it or not, be dragged into the arena of party politics; and at a dissolution following such a dismissal of Ministers as has just been referred to, it is no exaggeration to say that the Crown would *become the football of contending factions.*

This is a Constitutional catastrophe which it is the duty of every wise statesman to do the utmost in his power to avert.

Letter III. HHA to KGV, [19] September 1913

[HHA's handwritten covering letter, again from Hopeman, states: 'In accordance with what he knows to be Your Majesty's wish, Mr Asquith has expressed himself... with complete freedom & unreserve'. The following letter is again printed in the style of a Cabinet paper of the time.]

Most secret. II. The Government of Ireland Bill

I proceed to consider the prospective situation in Ireland in the event of the passing or of the rejection of the Bill.

If the Bill becomes law (whether or not its passing is preceded by another general election) there will undoubtedly be a serious danger of organised disorder in the four north-eastern counties of Ulster. It is, in my opinion, a misuse of terms to speak of what is likely to happen as Civil War. The total population of the area concerned is little over 1,000,000. It. is divided between Protestants and Roman Catholics—and in that part of the world political and religious differences roughly coincide—in the proportion of 7 to 3 (Protestants 729,624, Roman Catholics 316,406). In 2 of the 4 counties (Armagh and Londonderry) the Protestant preponderance is not greater than 6:5.[17] It is not, therefore, the case of a homogeneous people resisting a change to which they are unitedly opposed. On the contrary, there will be a considerable and a militant minority strongly in favour of the new state of things, and ready to render active assistance to the forces of the executive. In the remainder of Ulster, and in the three other provinces of Ireland, there will be an overwhelming majority of the population on the side of the law.

But, while anxious that things should be seen in their true perspective, I have not the least disposition to minimise the gravity of the situation which will probably arise. The importation of rifles has, so far, been on a small scale, and the drilling and training of volunteers, though it is no doubt accustoming numbers of men to act together, to obey orders, and to develop *esprit de corps*, is not likely to produce a body which can stand up against regular troops. But the genuine apprehensions of a large majority of the Protestants, the incitements of responsible leaders, and the hopes of British sympathy and support, are likely to encourage forcible resistance (wherever it can be tried); there is the certainty of tumult and riot, and more than the possibility of serious bloodshed.

On the other hand, if the Bill is rejected or indefinitely postponed, or some inadequate and disappointing substitute put forward in its place, the prospect is, in my opinion, much more grave. The attainment of Home Rule has for more than 30 years been the political (as distinguished from the agrarian) ideal of four-fifths of the Irish people. Whatever happens in other parts of the United Kingdom, at successive general elections, the Irish representation in Parliament never varies. For the last 8 years they have had with them a substantial majority of the elected representatives of Great Britain. The Parliament of 1906 was debarred by election pledges from dealing with the matter legislatively, but during its lifetime, in 1908, the House of Commons affirmed by an overwhelming majority a resolution in favour of the principle. In the present Parliament, the Government of Ireland Bill has passed that House in two successive sessions, with British majorities which showed no sign of diminution from first to last. If it had been taken up by a Conservative Government, it would more than a year ago have been the law of the land. It is the confident expectation of the vast bulk of the Irish people that it will become law next year.

If the ship, after so many stormy voyages, were now to be wrecked in sight of port, it is difficult to overrate the shock, or its consequences. They would extend into every department of political, social, agrarian and domestic life. It is not too much to say that Ireland would become ungovernable—unless by the application of forces and methods which would offend the conscience of Great Britain, and arouse the deepest resentment in all the self-governing Dominions of the Crown.

III.

It follows, from what has been said above, that while in my opinion—from the point of view of social order—the consequences of the passing of the Bill would be unquestionably less serious than those of its rejection, yet no forecast, in either event, can be free from anxiety. Any practicable means of mitigation—still more, of escape—deserves, therefore (whencesoever it is suggested), impartial and mature consideration.

The demand, put forward recently by Mr. Balfour, for a General Election, between now and the beginning of next session, is open to objections of the most formidable character. (1) If such an election resulted in a majority for the Government, and the consequent passing of the Irish Bill next session, the recalcitrance of North-East Ulster would not in any way be affected. Sir E. Carson, and his friends have told the world, with obvious sincerity, that their objections to Home Rule have nothing to do with the question whether it is approved or disapproved by the British electorate. It is true that the Unionist Leaders in Great Britain have intimated that, in such an event, they would not give 'active countenance' (whatever that may mean) to the defiance of the law. But what effect can that have on men who have been encouraged to believe, and many of whom do believe, that under Home Rule their liberties and their religion would be in jeopardy? (2) If the election resulted in a Government defeat, the circumstances are such that neither in Ireland nor in Great Britain would it be accepted as a verdict adverse to Home Rule. There may not be much active enthusiasm for Home Rule in the British constituencies, but the evidence afforded, not only by the steady and persistent majorities in the House of Commons, but by the bye-elections, tends to show that (at the lowest) it meets with acquiescence as an inevitable necessity in itself, and as a first step towards further devolution. All the most trustworthy observers agree that, even where the bye-elections have gone against the Government, the attempt (wherever made) to arouse interest and resentment by pushing to the forefront the case against Home Rule and the supposed wrongs of Ulster, has met with no success. The General Election would be fought, as the bye-elections have been, not predominantly on Home Rule, but on the Insurance Act, the Marconi contract, and a score of other 'issues' which happened for the moment to preoccupy public attention. (3) The concession of the demand for a General Election, at this stage, would be in the teeth of the intentions of the Parliament Act. One of the primary and most clearly avowed purposes of that Act was to abrogate the power of the House of Lords to force a dissolution. The assumption which underlies the whole measure is, that a Bill which can survive the ordeal of three sessions, prolonged over two years, in the House of Commons, ought without the need of another election, to pass into law.

It is quite another matter to suggest that, after the Bill has passed, a General Election should take place before it has come into active operation. Parliament will then have completed, or nearly completed, four out of its possible five years; and if the country were either on general or particular grounds averse to the Government, the new Parliament could consider, before anything irreparable has been done, whether to repeal or to amend the Irish Government Act. If, moreover, it were known beforehand that this would happen, any outburst of disorder in Ulster would everywhere be regarded as premature and inexcusable.[18]

There remains the proposal, to which Lord Loreburn has during the last week given his authority, for settlement by Conference. I wrote to Lord Loreburn, as soon as I read his letter in *The Times* to ask him to tell me precisely what he meant. I expressed sympathy with the spirit of all that he had written, and acquiescence in the reasoning of much, though not the whole, of his argument. But I pointed out that the parties concerned in this controversy, including Sir E. Carson and Mr. Redmond, are not likely, at the moment, to accept an invitation (from any quarter) to come into a room and sit round a table, for the purpose of talking in the air about the Government of Ireland, or about Federalism and Devolution. It is no good blinding one's eye to obvious and undeniable facts, and one of those facts, relevant to the present case, undoubtedly is, that there is a deep and hitherto unbridgeable chasm of *principle*[19] between the supporters and the opponents of Home Rule. It is a question not of phraseology but of substance. Four-fifths of Ireland, with the support of a substantial British majority in the present and late Houses of Commons, will be content with nothing less than a subordinate legislature with a local executive responsible to it. They insist, moreover, that (whatever may be done with Devolution elsewhere) the claim of Ireland is peculiar, and paramount in point of time and urgency. A settlement which ignored these conditions would be no settlement. But within these conditions—so I said to Lord Loreburn—there is (so far as I am concerned) no point—finance, Ulster, Second Chamber, representation of minorities, etc., upon which I am not ready and anxious to enter into conference, and to yield to any reasonable suggestion.

For a Conference to be fruitful, there must be some definite basis upon and from which its deliberations can proceed. I fear that at present (it may be different nearer the time) no such basis can be found. I shall be only too glad if that fear can now or hereafter be satisfactorily dispelled.

I feel bound to add, that after the experience of 1910, when there was on both sides perfect goodwill and a sincere desire for agreement, that an abortive Conference would be likely to widen differences and embitter feeling.

H.H.A

Letter IV. KGV to HHA, 22 September 1913

Balmoral Castle, 22nd September 1913.

My dear Prime Minister,

I am most grateful to you for your very clear and well reasoned Memorandum which you have been good enough to draw up for me on the Government of Ireland Bill.

Acting upon your own suggestions that I should freely and unreservedly offer my criticisms, I do so upon quotations taken from it.

Referring to the Constitutional position of the Sovereign, you say 'in the end the Sovereign always acts upon the advice which Ministers feel it their duty to offer... and his subjects cannot hold him in any way accountable'.

Fully accepting this proposition, I nevertheless cannot shut my eyes to the fact that in this particular instance the people will, rightly or wrongly, associate me with whatever policy is adopted by my advisers, dispensing praise or blame according as that policy is in agreement or antagonistic to their own opinions.

While you admit the Sovereign's undoubted power to change his advisers, I infer that you regard the exercise of that power as inexpedient and indeed dangerous.

Should the Sovereign *never* exercise that right, not even, to quote Sir Erskine May, 'in the interests of the State and on grounds which could be justified to Parliament'? Bagehot wrote, 'The Sovereign too possesses a power according to theory for extreme use on a critical occasion, but which in law he can use on any occasion. He can *dissolve*.'.

The Parliament Act 'was not intended in any way to affect, and it is submitted has not affected the Constitutional position of the Sovereign'.

But the Preamble of the Bill stated an intention to create a new Second Chamber; that this could not be done immediately; meanwhile provision by the Bill would be made for restricting the powers of the House of Lords.

Does not such an organic change in the Constitutional position of one of the Estates of the Realm also affect the relations of all three to one another; and the failure to replace it on an effective footing deprive the Sovereign of the assistance of the Second Chamber?

Should the Home Rule Bill become law I gather you consider that there is a 'certainty of tumult and riot and more than a possibility of serious bloodshed', but you do not anticipate 'anything which could rightly be described as Civil War'.

If, however, the union which you contemplate of the 'considerable and militant minority' of Roman Catholics in North-East Ulster with the forces of the executive is carried into effect, will not the armed struggle between these sections of the people constitute Civil War, more especially if the forces of Ulster are reinforced from England, Scotland and even the Colonies, which contingency I am assured is highly probable[?] Do you propose to employ the Army to suppress such disorders?

This is, to my mind, one of the most serious questions which the Government will have to decide.

In doing so you will, I am sure, bear in mind that ours is a voluntary Army; our Soldiers are none the less Citizens; by birth, religion and environment they may have strong feelings on the Irish question; outside influence may be brought to bear upon them; they see distinguished retired Officers already organising local forces in Ulster; they hear rumours of Officers on the Active List throwing up their Commissions to join this force. Will it be wise, will it be fair to the Sovereign as head of the Army, to subject the discipline, and indeed the loyalty of his troops, to such a strain[?]

Have you considered the effect upon the Protestant sentiments in these Islands and the Colonies of the coercion of Ulster?

I quite admit the grave prospects resulting from a rejection of the Bill.

But is the demand for Home Rule in Ireland as earnest and as National to-day as it was, for instance, in the days of Parnell?

Has not the Land Purchase Policy settled the agrarian trouble, which was the chief motive of the Home Rule agitation?

I am assured by resident Landowners in the South and West of Ireland that their tenants, while ostensibly favourable to Home Rule, are no longer enthusiastic about it, and are, comparatively speaking,[20] content and well-to-do.

The hierarchy of the Church of Rome is indifferent and probably at heart would be glad not to come under the power of an Irish Parliament.

The application of forces and methods to govern Ireland, were the Bill rejected, would in your opinion 'offend the conscience of Great Britain'.

But surely not more so than their application against Ulster?

With regard to your objections to a General Election between now and the beginning of next Session.

It is the case, unfortunately, that Sir Edward Carson and his friends declare that they would not be influenced by a verdict at the Polls in favour of Home Rule. And here let me assure you that I view with the gravest concern the advocacy of what Sir Edward Carson openly admits to be illegal measures in the resistance of North-East Ulster to the constituted law and authority of the land. Still we have the assurance of the Unionist leaders that in the event of the Country declaring in favour of Home Rule, they will support the Government instead of supporting Ulster, as they intend to do if an appeal to the Country is refused.

Is due consideration given to the fact that although Home Rule has been before the Country for 30 years, the present Bill differs materially from any previous Home Rule Bill; that it has never been before the Country; that it is opposed by practically the whole of the House of Lords; by one third of the House of Commons; by half the population of England, and that it was forced through the House of Commons, pages of it never having been discussed[?]

I recognise your argument that the proposed General Election would not be fought on Home Rule, but on a 'score of other issues', so that you would not obtain a mandate *pur et simple* upon Home Rule.

But I suppose this argument might be equally urged to show that the General Election of December 1910 gave no verdict in favour of Home Rule.

Would it not be right in order to ensure a lasting settlement, to make certain that it is the wish of my people that the Union of Ireland shall be repealed by a measure which was not put before them at the last Election?

Is there any other Country in the world which could carry out such a fundamental change in its Constitution upon the authority of a single chamber?

Is there any precedent in our own Country for such a change to be made without submitting it to the Electorate?

To the suggestion that a General Election should take place after Assent has been given to the Bill, I see the most serious objections.

Granted that this policy is adopted, I assume that once the Bill is passed, outbreaks will occur in Ulster if they have not done so at an earlier date.

Meanwhile Great Britain and Ireland will be plunged into the throes of a General Election.

If the Government are returned to power, Ulster will probably resist more vigorously than ever.

On the other hand, if the Government are defeated, a new Ministry will be formed, Parliament reassembled, the Home Rule Bill perhaps repealed, followed by revolt in the South and West of Ireland, and finally the Sovereign's Assent asked for to repeal the Act to which only a few months before he had affixed his signature.

I can hardly think that Ministers contemplate placing the Country and the Sovereign in such a position.

I heartily welcomed Lord Loreburn's weighty letter suggesting a Conference, and I hope to hear that you have received a satisfactory reply to the letter you have addressed to him on the subject.

Recollecting my conversations with you on August 11th, and with Mr Birrell a fortnight earlier, I trust that some agreement may be found on the lines then suggested, such as leaving out North-East Ulster from the Scheme for a certain period, say five or ten years, with the power to come under the Irish Parliament, if so desired, after the question is put to the test of a Referendum in the reserved Counties.

The objection urged that this arrangement would involve the desertion of the Protestants in other parts of Ireland, is met by the fact that the Nationalist minority in Ulster would be placed at a similar disadvantage.

It seems inconceivable to me that British commonsense will not ultimately find a solution to this terrible prospect of rebellion and bloodshed in so rich and flourishing a part of my Dominions.

Assuming that the aim of both political Parties is to secure good Government, prosperity and loyal contentment for the Irish people, it must be admitted that these objects cannot be attained by the policy so far advocated by either Liberal or Conservative Governments.

Therefore, we can only hope for the attainment of these objects by common agreement upon some alternative course.

Nevertheless, I entirely recognise all the grave difficulties which must confront anyone who endeavours to secure by consent the settlement of a question which has divided Ireland for many generations.

I rejoice to know that you are ready and anxious to enter into a Conference if a definite basis can be found upon which to confer.

For my part, I will gladly do everything in my power to induce the Opposition to meet you in a reasonable and conciliatory spirit.

For it behoves us all to withhold no efforts to avert those threatening events which would inevitably outrage humanity and lower the British name in the mind of the whole civilised world.

I have endeavoured to comment frankly upon your Memorandum, and I trust that in your next letter you will give your views upon the various points referred to before I have the pleasure of seeing you here on the 6th October.

The Memorandum has been seen by no one except my Private Secretary, nor have I mentioned the fact that I have received it to anyone.

Believe me, My dear Prime Minister, Very sincerely yours, GEORGE R.I.

Letter V. HHA to KGV, 01 October 1913

Most secret

1. In regard to the Constitutional position of the Sovereign, I cannot usefully add much to my previous memorandum. When Bagehot says that The King 'can dissolve', he, of course, means upon the advice of Ministers, who will make themselves responsible for what is done. As has been already pointed out, the Crown can always change its advisers, provided that others are ready and willing to take their place; but the dismissal of Ministers, still in possession of the confidence of the House of Commons, with the view of forcing a dissolution, is a step which has only been taken once in more than 100 years, and then with consequences which were very injurious to the authority of the Crown. In my opinion, a statesman sincerely anxious to maintain the Constitutional rights of the Sovereign in their true and full sense, would be very slow to advise its repetition.
   Bagehot was neither a professor nor a lawyer, but a shrewd and accomplished man of business; and his description of the actual—as distinguished from the legal and technical—functions and powers of the Throne remains, after 50 years, more accurate, as well as more vivid, than that of any other writer.

2. The use of coercion, in Ulster, or in the rest of Ireland. Either alternative is in the highest degree repellent; but unless we are to abandon once and for all the reign of law, every Act of Parliament must be carried into execution; and if its execution is resisted, it is the duty of the State to see that that resistance is overborne by whatever modes of enforcement are appropriate and adequate in the particular case. This might necessitate in the last resort, either in the one case or the other, the use of the Army, though not until other and more indirect means had been tried and proved to be ineffectual. There is, in my opinion, no sufficient ground for the

fears—or hopes—expressed in some quarters, that the troops would fail to do their duty.

The recent performances of Sir E. Carson—e.g., the semi-regal allocution which the 'Chief of Staff' of his 'General' has just issued, expressing his approval of the bearing &c of the volunteers at the Belfast review—have done much to shock the commonsense, and to alienate the sympathy and goodwill, of moderate men in Great Britain.

3. The proposal of a General Election. I dealt very fully with this matter in my previous memorandum.

Nothing is historically more certain than that at the General Election of December 1910 it was common ground between all parties that the passing of the Parliament Act would be immediately followed by the introduction of a Home Rule Bill. *Every elector on both sides gave his vote in that knowledge and with that belief.* The evidence is overwhelming; but it is sufficient to cite Lord Lansdowne's declaration at Portsmouth, at the height of the contest, that 'Mr Asquith had made it perfectly clear' that this would be the sequence of events. That Home Rule would forthwith become a reality was, indeed, one of the principal arguments used to dissuade the electors from voting for candidates who favoured the Parliament Bill.

It is true that the precise terms of the Bill were not before the electorate. But they knew that it must proceed upon the basis of a subordinate legislature for Ireland with an executive responsible to it. The actual Bill differs from its predecessors in finance and other matters; particularly, in the additional safeguards which it provides for the rights and liberties of minorities. But it embodies the same principle. I must add that during a Parliamentary experience of nearly 30 years, I have never known a measure the detailed provisions of which were more thoroughly discussed and overhauled in Committee and upon Report. No point which was even of secondary importance escaped attention. No doubt it is susceptible of further improvement; and it is much to be regretted that the House of Lords, instead of opposing in two successive sessions an absolute *non-possumus* to the second reading, did not introduce, by way of amendment, proposals for dealing with Ulster and other controverted matters, which might now be forming the basis for conference and adjustment.

A General Election subsequent to the passing of the Act, and before the new system of Irish Government comes into full operation is, as a matter of dates, almost, if not quite, inevitable.

I am still as anxious as anyone can be that the dangers to social order, undoubtedly incident either to the passing or the rejection of the Bill (and the latter is in my opinion by far the more formidable contingency), should be averted, by some special arrangement in regard to the North East, which is not inconsistent with the fundamental principle and purpose of the Bill.

HHA 1st October 1913

13

Established Churches

The Religious Establishment and Free Speech Act 2015 need have only three sections. As noted in the Introduction, the wording of the substantive section is lifted unaltered from the First Amendment to the US Constitution.

1. Parliament shall make no law respecting an establishment of religion, or prohibiting the free exercise thereof; or abridging the freedom of speech, or of the press; or the right of the people peaceably to assemble, and to petition the government for a redress of grievances.
2. Consequential repeals are listed in the Schedule hereto.
3. This Act shall not be brought into force until the repeal of such parts of the *Act for securing the Protestant Religion, and Presbyterian Church Government in Scotland* and the *Act for securing the Church of England as by Law established* as are recited and incorporated into the Act of Union 1706 shall have been ratified in a referendum, such repeal being supported by a majority of those voting in Scotland and a majority of those voting in England.

In this chapter I discuss how it arises that two incompatible forms of Protestant truth, in Scotland and England, are constitutionally protected in the United Kingdom, whereas no religious truth, Protestant or other, is constitutionally protected in Wales or Northern Ireland. I aim to show how there would be no losers from religious disestablishment except those with vested interests. Finally, to avoid being caught in contradiction, I show why, although the Religious Establishment etc. Act repeals a number of obnoxious statutes which require the monarch to be a Protestant and not to marry a Roman Catholic, the only repeal which must be ratified by referendum is that of the establishment clauses of the Act of Union 1706. If the Monarchy (Abolition) Act discussed in Chapter 12 comes into force before the Religious Establishment etc. Act, then the restrictions on the monarch's rights to marry and profess religion will in any case have become redundant.

I shall assume that by 2015, unelected religious representatives have already disappeared from the second chamber as a result of the reforms discussed in Chapter 11. But I shall explain why the arguments put forward in a Royal Commission report as recently as 2000 for retaining religious representation in the UK Parliament are spectacularly threadbare.

TWO PROTESTANT TRUTHS

In Chapter 3, we studied the background to the Act of Union. Because it was a genuine treaty and both the English and the Scots had some veto power, each side was able to insert protection of things that mattered to them, which for both of the dissolving Parliaments included their respective national churches. The words of the preamble of the (English) Act of Union 1706 are completely clear:

> W H E R E A S Articles of Union were agreed on . . . by the Commissioners nominated on Behalf of the Kingdom of *England* . . . and the Commissioners nominated on the Behalf of the Kingdom of *Scotland*, under your Majesty's Great Seal of *Scotland* . . . : And whereas an Act hath passed in the Parliament of *Scotland*, at *Edinburgh*, the sixteenth Day of *January* in the fifth Year of your Majesty's Reign, wherein 'tis mentioned, That the estates of Parliament considering the said Articles of Union of the two Kingdoms, had agreed to and approved of the said Articles of Union, with some Additions and Explanations, and that your Majesty, with the Advice and Consent of the Estates of Parliament, for establishing the Protestant Religion and Presbyterian Church Government within the Kingdom of *Scotland*, had passed in the same Session of Parliament an Act, intituled, *An Act for the securing of the Protestant Religion and Presbyterian Church Government*, which by the Tenor thereof was appointed to be inserted in any Act ratifying the Treaty, and expressly declared to be a Fundamental and Essential Condition of the said Treaty of Union in all Times coming: The Tenor of which Articles, as ratified and approved of, with Additions and Explanations by the said Act of Parliament of *Scotland*, follows:

The Act for the Security of the Church of Scotland, as incorporated in the Act of Union, stipulates:

> it being reasonable and necessary that the true Protestant Religion, as presently professed within this Kingdom, with the Worship, Discipline, and Government of this Church, should be effectually and unalterably secured: Therefore her Majesty, with Advice and Consent of the said Estates of Parliament, doth hereby establish and confirm the said true Protestant Religion, and the Worship, Discipline and Government of this Church, to

continue without any Alteration to the People of this Land in all succeeding Generations... And it is hereby statuted and ordained, That this Act of Parliament, with the Establishment therein contained, shall be held and observed in all Time coming, as a fundamental and essential Condition of any Treaty or Union to be concluded betwixt the two Kingdoms, without any Alteration thereof, or Derogation thereto in any Sort for ever:

And the incorporated English Act states:

And whereas it is reasonable and necessary, that the true Protestant Religion professed and established by Law in the Church of *England*, and the Doctrine, Worship, Discipline, and Government thereof, should be effectually and unalterably secured; Be it enacted by the Queen's most Excellent Majesty, by and with the Advice and Consent of the Lords Spiritual and Temporal, and the Commons, in this present Parliament assembled, and by Authority of the same, That an Act made in the thirteenth Year of the Reign of Queen Elizabeth, of famous Memory, intituled, An Act for the Ministers of the Church to be of sound Religion; and also another Act made in the thirteenth Year of the Reign of the late King Charles the Second, intituled, An Act for the Uniformity of the Publick Prayers and Administration of Sacraments, and other Rights and Ceremonies, and for establishing the Form of making, ordaining, and consecrating Bishops, Priests, and Deacons in the Church of England (other than such Clauses in the said Act, or either of them, as have been repealed or altered by any subsequent Act or Acts of Parliament) and all and singular other Acts of Parliament now in Force, for the Establishment and Preservation of the Church of *England*, and the Doctrine, Worship, Discipline, and Government thereof, shall remain and be in full Force for ever.

Note that the words 'true Protestant religion' thus appear twice in the Act of Union: the first time to refer to the Presbyterian church 'established' (which word also appears twice) in Scotland; the second time to refer to the Church of England. At most one of them can be the true Protestant religion. The problem is with the word 'true', not the words 'Protestant religion'. The true Protestant religion must either permit bishops or must not permit them, to take only the most obvious difference between the established Church of Scotland and the established Church of England.[1]

WHY DISESTABLISHMENT IS GOOD FOR (ALMOST) EVERYBODY

In 1707 'England' included Wales. The first, and for 150 years the only, official statistics on church attendance in Great Britain came in the Census of 1851. Table 13.1 shows the main results.

Table 13.1 Number of persons present at the most numerously attended services on Sunday 30 March 1851.

	Church of England	Protestant dissent	RC	Other	All	Total population	Attendances as % of population	C of E as % of attendances
England	2,838,318	2,629,590	243,701	21,110	5,732,719	16,738,986	34.25	49.51
Wales	132,940	481,192	5,688	3,683	623,503	1,188,914	52.44	21.32
Scotland					740,794	2,888,742	25.64	

Source: cols 1–6 *Census Reports 1851: England and Wales, and Scotland. Religious Worship/ E & W Table N. Sc Table B.* Cols 7–8: author's calculations. The census takers for England and Wales warned that there could be over- and under-counting of individuals who attended more than one service; who attended services of more than one denomination; or who attended a service that was not the most numerously attended on Census Sunday. The Scottish enumerators merely reported attendances in 'morning', 'afternoon', and 'evening', and did not discriminate by denomination. The figures for 'morning' (the highest) are shown. A Scottish report by denomination is, however, available at PP 1854: lxi, *Census of Great Britain 1851: Religious Worship and Education, Scotland, Report and Tables*, Table 1. It shows Established church attendances as just ahead of Free Church, but behind Free Church and United Presbyterian (voluntarist) combined.

The result of the 1851 religious census was such a shock to the Church of England that it was never repeated. It shows that even in England it accounted for fewer than half of all attendances, while in Wales it was a small minority. Up to 1851, an argument for establishment of the Church of England could be made along the lines: *Christianity is true and it is not unjust for a state to select the church of a majority of the population for some special mark of an underlying ideological preference for Christianity, so long as this is combined with practical liberty and equality for others. In short, a Christian state can be as just as a secular one.* After 1851 it was no longer possible to make this argument.

Wales was the most church-going of the three territories, while Scotland was apparently the least (but the numbers were calculated on a different basis there, so this conclusion may be wrong). Anglican clergy, led by Samuel Wilberforce, the Bishop of Oxford, led a campaign of spin against the results. Dissenting ministers, they said, were ignorant folk who could not count; and anyhow, they exaggerated the size of their flocks. Modern research (Crockett and Crockett 2006) discounts the spin. If you assume that a rounded return (say 50 or 100) implies that the reporting minister is exaggerating and an exact return (43, 79) implies that he has counted accurately, then the incidence of exaggerated (at least of rounded) returns is highest in the denominations that were declining in 1851 and lowest among those that were growing. The former comprises the Church of England and 'Old Dissent'—that is, the seventeenth-century sects. The latter comprises 'new Dissent'—the varieties of Methodism—and the Catholic Church. Thus the overall numbers reported in 1851 are exaggerated, but the relativities between denominations are approximately correct. If they are biased, they are biased in favour of the Church of England and Old Dissent.

The 1851 census may have called establishment into question even in England. It destroyed its moral basis in Wales. From then on, disestablishment became the rallying cry of popular Welsh politics. It was one of Lloyd George's first campaigns. However, until 1911 the House of Lords, which always had a Conservative majority and twenty-six Anglican bishops, could block any non-financial legislation. It was not worth even trying to enact Welsh disestablishment till then. Under the Parliament Act 1911, it could go forward on the votes of the Commons only but had to be re-presented three times if rejected by the Lords. It was indeed rejected three times by the Lords, with sixteen of the eighteen Church of England bishops who voted opposing it on the first two iterations. It was enacted in September 1914, but as the First World War had broken out it, together with Irish Home Rule, was suspended, and not brought into operation until 1920.

The Church in Wales has not relatively declined since 1920. Not until after Disestablishment did it begin seriously to engage with the Welsh language.

Prior to 1920 there was no official Welsh-language liturgy. The opinion of many Welsh clergy, apparently including Archbishop of Canterbury Rowan Williams, is that disestablishment has done the Welsh Church no harm and may have done it some good. 'It's possible to have very fruitful, very constructive relations with government and public life without all the apparatus of legal establishment as it's evolved in England,' said the Archbishop in a BBC profile recorded while he was still Archbishop of Wales but broadcast after his elevation to Canterbury (quoted in McLean and Linsley 2004: 12). As with Northern Ireland, nobody now proposes that any church should be established in Wales. We saw in Chapter 8 that not only is no church established in Northern Ireland, but the Government of Ireland Act 1920 expressly forbade the establishment of any church there, using the exact language of the US First Amendment that this chapter proposes to extend to the rest of the United Kingdom.

Much discussion of church establishment confuses the United Kingdom, or Great Britain, with England. Compare and contrast an archbishop:

> From the perspective of the Church of England, establishment helps to underwrite the commitment of a national church to serve the entire community and to give form and substance to some of its deepest collective needs and aspirations . . . At times of national celebration and mourning, for example, we expect great cathedrals to be a focal point of attention. That was true in the aftermath of the tragedies of September 11th [2001]. It was true . . . with the passing away of the Queen Mother. It will be the case again . . . when we celebrate and give thanks at the Queen's Golden Jubilee. (George Carey, Archbishop of Canterbury preceding Williams, 23 April 2002)

with a Prime Minister's Private Office:

> The Welsh Church [is] disestablished and ha[s] no claim on Westminster Abbey. ('Note for the Record', from Prime Minister's Private Office, 27 October 1966. Prime Minister Harold Wilson rejected calls for a Westminster Abbey service in memory of the 144 victims (109 of them schoolchildren) of the Aberfan coal tip disaster in South Wales, which had taken place on 21 October. (McLean and Johnes 2000: 224.)

Lord Carey, like many others, upholds the establishment of the Church of England on the grounds that it is a national church. But it is a national church only in England. Its status might be thought to give it certain privileges *in England*—say to run some state schools in England. It cannot be an argument for giving it special status *in the United Kingdom*.[2] It is multiply entangled with the UK Parliament. Twenty-six of its bishops sit in the UK House of Lords. The UK Prime Minister retained residual rights over appointing its bishops until the Government unilaterally withdrew in July 2007 (HM

Government 2007). Its finances and even its doctrine are nominally under the control of the UK Parliament. Its status as the national church of only one of the four parts of the United Kingdom, even though it is by far the largest part, cannot justify these entanglements. The onus is on the proponents of establishment to say why they should continue, not on its opponents to say why they should be dissolved. Though the entanglements between the Church of England and the UK state have endured for hundreds of years, they are at best anomalous, and at worst (as at Aberfan) insulting to the people of the other three nations of the United Kingdom.

I believe that disestablishment of the Church of England would be good for

1. Everybody in Wales, Scotland, and Northern Ireland;
2. All non-Anglican Christians in England who care about church unity;
3. All adherents of non-Christian faiths in England;
4. All people of no religion in England; and
5. All members and supporters of the Church of England who wish to control the government, theology, and finance of their church.

Establishing the relative numbers in those groups is difficult because religious statistics are notoriously slippery (and some of the groups listed are neither counted nor, probably, countable). However, a (voluntary) question about religious adherence was asked in the 2001 Census, and social surveys ask about religious affiliations from time to time. The 2001 Census results and the latest available survey results are in Tables 13.2 and 13.3.

The Census (Table 13.2) asked different questions in different parts of the United Kingdom, reflecting various religious sensitivities. The headline results are that 71 per cent of the population described themselves as 'Christian', with 23 per cent either stating that they had no religion or declining to answer the question. The largest non-Christian faith community, in 2001, were Muslims, followed by Hindus, Sikhs, and Jews. However, when the tables summarized as Table 13.2 were first published, I noticed an oddity.

Table 13.2 reports about 180,000 people as having identified themselves as of a religion other than those specifically tabulated. However, an urban myth circulating before the Census had said that if enough people described themselves as 'Jedi', the government would be required to recognize Jedi as a religion. About 390,000 people did so, and the Census authorities obligingly issued a press notice giving their spatial distribution. Jedi were thickest on the ground in Brighton (where they formed 2.6 per cent of the population), next thickest in Oxford, and thinnest in Easington, County Durham (only 152, or 0.2 per cent of the Easingtonians were Jedi in 2001).[3] As the 390,000 Jedi exceeded the 180,000 total for all 'other religions' put together in Table 13.2, I asked the Census authorities what was going on, to be told that citizens

Table 13.2 The UK population: by religion, April 2001.

United Kingdom	England & Wales[a]	Scotland[b]	Northern Ireland[c]	UK	UK %
Christian	37,338,486	3,294,545	1,446,386	42,079,417	72
Roman Catholic	*	803732	678462	n/a	n/a
Other Christian	*	344562	102221	n/a	n/a
Church of Scotland	*	2146251	*	n/a	n/a
Presbyterian Church in Ireland	*	*	348742	n/a	n/a
Church of Ireland	*	*	257788	n/a	n/a
Methodist Church in Ireland	*	*	59173	n/a	n/a
Buddhist	144,453	6,830	533	151816	0.3
Hindu	552,421	5,564	825	558810	1.0
Jewish	259,927	6,448	365	266740	0.5
Muslim	1,546,626	42,557	1,943	1591126	2.7
Sikh	329,358	6,572	219	336149	0.6
Other religion	150720	26974	1143	178837	0.3
All religions	40321991	3389490	1451414	45162895	76.8
No religion	7709267	1394460	45909	n/a	15.5
Not stated	4010658	278061	187944	n/a	7.3
All no religion/not stated[d]	11719925	1672521	233853	13626299	23.2
Base	52041916	5062011	1685267	58789194	100

[a]'What is your religion?'
[b]'What religion, religious denomination, or body do you belong to?'
[c]'Do you regard yourself as belonging to any particular religion?'
 If yes, 'What religion, religious denomination, or body do you belong to?'
[d]Includes 233,853 cases in Northern Ireland, where data is only available as a combined category.
*Answer category not provided as a tick-box option in this country.
Source: Census, April 2001, Office for National Statistics.

identifying themselves as Jedi were classed as 'no religion'. This seems a piece of unwarranted presumption by the Office for National Statistics, who may be punished for it in another world. Self-identified Jedi outnumbered each of Jews, Sikhs, and Buddhists.

Table 13.3 shows that a remarkable social change has taken place in the United Kingdom since 1964. The first known reliable survey to ask people's religious affiliation was the British Election Survey (BES) in that year. The question has been repeated in either BES or British Social Attitudes (BSA) periodically since then, and in most years since 1983. There are a few restrictions in the data, noted in the footnotes to Table 13.3. Northern

Table 13.3 GB religious belonging and attendance, 1964–2005.

	1964 %	1970 %	1983 %	1992 %	2005 %
Belongs to a religion, ever attends services, etc.	74	71	55	37	31
Belongs to a religion, never attends services, etc.	23	24	30	31	31
Does not belong to religion	3	5	26	31	38

Source: BSA: *the 23rd Report* Table 1.3. Original data from British Election Study (<1983); BSA (>1970). Coverage: Great Britain south of the Caledonian Canal. 'Belonging' question: *What is your religion?* (1964); *Do you regard yourself as belonging to any particular religion? IF YES: Which? IF 'Christian' PROBE FOR DENOMINATION* (>1964). 'Attendance' question: *Apart from such special occasions as weddings, funerals and baptisms, how often nowadays do you attend services or meetings connected with your religion?*

Fuller information including denominational breakdowns is available at the British Social Attitudes Information System [http://www.britsocat.com/].

Ireland is excluded, which probably depresses the proportion giving a religious affiliation. So is the far north of Scotland, which probably makes no difference (despite *The Wicker Man*). The question asked in 1964 probably suppressed some 'no religion' answers. However, with all these qualifications, two facts jump out. Firstly, since 1964, the proportion of the British people who state that they belong to a religion and ever go to its services has dropped from three-quarters to a third. In the 2005 data, for the first time, 'no religion' is the most popular choice, offered by 38 per cent of respondents. Secondly, the number who claim to belong to a religion but never attend its services apart perhaps from weddings, funerals, and other special events now equals the number who ever attend an ordinary service, at 31 per cent.

Notoriously, the answers people get on religious affiliation and belief depend on the questions asked. The data in Tables 13.2 and 13.3 were collected by different methods, a few years apart, and they do not tell an identical story. Nevertheless, it can be reliably assumed that a large proportion of those who stated a religious affiliation in the 2001 Census were among those who never attend events connected with their religion except perhaps weddings and funerals.

Those who defend religious establishment (other than for reasons of pure self-interest) nevertheless have serious concerns, which any constitutional reform must address. They may be summarized as the 'national church', the 'national heritage', and the 'respect for faith' problems. In the following text I argue that although all of these are real problems, none of them is solved, and the third at least is worsened, by the special establishment of the Church of England.

WHY THERE IS NO CASE FOR RELIGIOUS REPRESENTATION IN PARLIAMENT

Bishops have sat in (what was then) the English Parliament since the Middle Ages. As Lord Wakeham and his colleagues point out in the Report of the Royal Commission on the House of Lords, they sat there because of their land and power as much as their religion (Wakeham 2000, paragraph 15.1). Bishops were among the largest landowners, and axiomatically therefore among the most powerful people in the land. If and when kings needed Parliaments, they needed bishops in them.

The first English monarch to call himself Supreme Head of the Church in England was Henry VIII, and the title changed to Supreme Governor under Elizabeth I. The Act of Supremacy 1534 states

> Be it enacted by Authority of this present Parliament, That the King our Sovereign Lord, his Heirs and Successors, Kings of this Realm, shall be taken, accepted and reputed the only supreme Head in Earth of the Church of England, called Anglicana Ecclesia; (2) and shall have and enjoy, annexed and united to the Imperial Crown of this Realm, as well the Title and Stile thereof, as all Honours, Dignities, Preheminences, Jurisdictions, Privileges, Authorities, Immunities, Profits and Commodities to the said Dignity of supreme Head of the same Church belonging and appertaining; (3) and that our said Sovereign Lord, his Heirs and Successors, Kings of this Realm, shall have full Power and Authority from Time to Time to visit, repress, redress, reform, order, correct, restrain and amend all such Errors, Heresies, Abuses, Offences, Contempts and Enormities, whatsoever they be, which by any manner spiritual Authority or Jurisdiction ought or may lawfully be re- formed, repressed, ordered, redressed, corrected, restrained or amended, most to the Pleasure of Almighty God, the Increase of Virtue in Christ's Religion, and for the Conservation of the Peace, Unity and Tranquillity of this Realm; any Usage, Custom, foreign Laws, foreign Authority, Prescrip- tion, or any other Thing or Things to the contrary hereof notwithstanding.

If the monarch was to be the supreme governor of the Church of England, it followed that he must have the right to appoint its bishops. The vestiges of this power remain with 'the Crown', although 'the Crown' has meant since George I 'the monarch acting on the advice of his or her ministers'. Mr Gladstone spent months trying to find a Welsh speaker for a Welsh diocese. Henry VIII's power to appoint bishops attenuated into Margaret Thatcher's, John Major's, and Tony Blair's. Prime Ministers exercising this power included three from a Church of Scotland Presbyterian background: Sir Henry Campbell-Bannerman (1906–8); Andrew Bonar Law (1922–3), and

Ramsay MacDonald (1924, 1929–35); and one Welsh nonconformist, David Lloyd George (1916–22). Gordon Brown, the fourth Scottish Presbyterian Prime Minister, surrendered this power in July 2007.

If Church and State were one from Henry VIII's time onwards, the State was content to let the Church exercise social control. They had a common interest in an educated and reasonably docile population. Therefore, the State was content for the church to control much of education (including Oxford and Cambridge Universities); to be responsible for policing marriage and for the control of antisocial behaviour. When the church defined marriage it was simultaneously defining what was not a marriage.

These elements of establishment were overthrown in the English Civil War between 1640 and 1660. When restored in 1660 they were less complete than before. Restoration governments tried to suppress the most dangerous Dissenting sect—the Quakers—but gave up doing so for them, the Baptists, Presbyterians, and the Congregationalists by the Toleration Act 1689. The Quakers were even eventually allowed (and still are) to register their own marriages, under the Marriage Act 1753. The exemption from the requirement to marry in the parish church applied to Jews as well. However, the covert attempts of King Charles II and the overt attempts of his brother and successor James II to institute Roman Catholicism led to the 'Glorious Revolution' of 1688–9. Catholicism was a political more than it was a religious threat to the revolutionaries of 1688. A pro-Catholic king might lead England into alliance with her oldest enemies, France or Spain. After the deposition of James II and the Parliamentary invitations to William of Orange and his wife Mary to become monarchs of England and Scotland, a series of Acts, still in force, were enacted in England to ensure that the monarch remained a Protestant. They include the 1688 Bill of Rights; the Coronation Oath Act, 1688, and the Act of Settlement 1701. These Acts (which antedate the 1706 Act of Union) affirm that the Crown is held on condition that the holder should be in communion with the Church of England. The monarch may not become a Roman Catholic nor marry a Roman Catholic. The Act of Settlement lays down the rules for a Protestant succession to Queen Anne, who was (correctly) expected to die without living heirs.

In 1927, the Church of England offered its proposed new Prayer Book for Parliamentary approval. It was rejected twice—on the votes of Scots, Welsh, and Northern Irish MPs, who should probably not have voted at all as it was a purely English question. However, its alleged popery warmed Protestant hearts that beat fastest outside England; and their rejection of an English prayer book was perhaps revenge for the English bishops' earlier rejections of Irish and Welsh disestablishment.

Since the 1927 fiasco, both sides have agreed to keep Parliament out of the thicket of Church of England doctrine and theological discipline. It suits neither side that Parliament should be tangled in it, although 21 conservative MPs (including Ian Paisley and Ann Widdecombe) voted against the Church of England's proposals for the ordination of women in 1993, which were carried by a large majority (HC Deb 29 October 1993 vol 230 cc1082–151). In this respect, establishment is a dead letter.

The finances of the Church of England are in the hands of the Church Commissioners. The Second Church Commissioner (a back-bench member of the governing party: since 1997 Sir Stuart Bell MP) is answerable in the Commons for them. This is a thoroughly unsatisfactory arrangement for both church and state. For the church, because it denies Church of England members responsibility for their own finances—so that when the Church Commissioners blunder they have no redress. For the state, because most of the time MPs have no interest in Church of England finances. When they do enquire, the Second Commissioner may be unable to answer, for instance because the Commissioners have no jurisdiction over cathedrals, which appear to be entirely unregulated. The state nominates six Church Commissioners, but to judge by the following plaintive comment from the Commission to the then Department of Constitutional Affairs (DCA), they take no part:

> (T)he Commissioners wish to add that the attendance as a matter of course of at least one of the six ex officio 'State' Commissioners at the Commissioners' AGM in June of each year would be greatly valued. (A. Whittam Smith to DCA, 12.11.2003, at http://www.dca.gov.uk/consult/lcoffice/responses/lc037.pdf)

The Royal Commission on the House of Lords recognized that 26 bishops, all male and all from the same denomination, sitting in the United Kingdom's legislature were an anachronism that could no longer be supported. They proposed a reduction of Church of England bishops to 16, with ten other Christian representatives, (five of them from Wales, Scotland, and Northern Ireland) and five representatives of non-Christian faiths.

This recommendation fell flat. The relativities were wrong. Based on official numbers available in 2000 (now superseded by Tables 13.2 and 13.3), I calculated that, to achieve religious parity, the 16 all-male bishops of the Church of England would have to be joined by 61 other religious representatives, to a total of 77. Most of these would have to be female, to help meet the Royal Commission's commitment to gender diversity in the reformed House (McLean and Linsley 2004, Table 2). The Royal Commission's recommendation was not derived from the evidence before it. It received 31 representations on the future of bishops in the Lords. Of these

31, 16 opposed their continuation; three supported it; and 12 expressed no opinion. The Church of Scotland, the Baptist Union, and two conferences of Roman Catholic bishops all submitted cogent evidence as to why their denomination did not wish to be represented in the legislature (Cm 4534, Vol. II: written evidence on CD-ROM). For Catholics, it contradicts canon law; for the Church of Scotland, it contradicts its Reformation theology, described below; for the Baptists, it contradicts the separation of church and state. Needless to say, no humanist or secularist submission supported the continuation of bishops in the Lords.

In the face of such a dramatic evidential deficit, it is not surprising that no serious constitutionalist seems to believe that the bishops can survive in a reformed upper house. Their position is pointedly not mentioned in the July 2007 Green Paper (HM Government 2007)—but then neither is the Lords reform of which religious representation forms part. However, the UK government line until recently linked the government role in appointing bishops with the bishops' seats in the Lords. As the first has now gone, the second seem unlikely to survive.

WHAT ESTABLISHMENT MEANS—OUTSIDE ENGLAND

The same word 'established' appears in the Scottish Act that is rehearsed and incorporated in the 1707 Act of Union. But the Scots had a very different understanding of it. They still do.

The 'two swords' dispute lay at the heart of medieval theology and political thought. What was the relationship between the secular state and the Church? Was one subordinate to the other, or were they in some sense coequal? What did it mean to render unto Caesar the things that are Caesar's and render unto God the things that are God's? This controversy did not go away with the Protestant Reformation. If anything, it intensified. In England, the Church was at one with the state from 1534. In Scotland, the main Reformers believed in the doctrine of 'two swords' or, more strictly, 'two realms'. In church matters, the Church was to be sovereign. King James VI (to become King James I of England) was therefore not the governor of the Church of Scotland, but 'Gods sillie vassal' as Andrew Melvill, the successor of John Knox, plucked his sleeve to tell him in 1596. In Melvill's theology, the Church ran its own God-given internal jurisdiction, and the civil magistrate's religious responsibility was confined to the external protection of the Church. Hence, to fast-forward, the monarch is not the governor of the Church of Scotland. The Queen is bound, by the Act of Security 1707, to uphold the true Presbyterian doctrine of the Church of Scotland, but this gives her no special status there. Her representative at the General Assembly of the Church of Scotland, the Lord High Commissioner, is not a member of the Assembly nor does he give it instructions. In 1707 the Scots did not object to the English legislation stipulating that the monarch must be in communion with the Church of England's being carried over into the United Kingdom. The Scottish Calvinist understanding is that the role of the civil magistrate is to protect Christ's Kirk, not to interfere in its governance.

In the seventeenth century the Stuart kings tried and failed to retain episcopacy in Scotland. During the English Civil War, the Scots Presbyterians tried and failed to impose their Westminster Confession on England. The stand-off was ratified in the Treaty and Acts of Union in 1707. Almost immediately, Parliament enacted what some Scottish church people regarded as a breach of the Act of Union, by restoring lay patronage—that is, the right to nominate ministers. This entangled the civil magistrate in the internal jurisdiction of the Church. When the latter broke into factions, the former was drawn in. In the end, the courts and the General Assembly appointed rival ministers to the parish of Marnoch, Aberdeenshire, in 1841. This provoked the Disruption of 1843, where a third of the General Assembly seceded and marched off to form the Free Church of Scotland in a hall they had already prudently hired (Rodger 2008).

The lesson of the Disruption for politicians was that they meddled in the affairs of the Church of Scotland at their peril, and to no gain. Many secessions and reunions later, in 1921, the Church of Scotland, and the remaining large free church were ready to (re-)unite. The Church of Scotland Act of that year is a declaratory act in which Parliament declares, in effect, that it accepts the theology of Andrew Melvill in regard to Scotland. It declares that its schedule, drawn up by the church and entitled 'Articles declaratory of the constitution of the church of Scotland in matters spiritual' is the constitution of the Church of Scotland, and that those articles 'shall prevail' against any parliamentary enactment that seems to contradict them.

The establishment of the Anglican Church in Ireland began with the Tudors, although the Protestant Reformation did not touch most of Ireland. Where it did—especially in Ulster—Protestants were as likely to be Presbyterian as Anglican. The Presbyterian churches had spread from Scotland but were never established—in the legal sense—in Northern Ireland. In the rest of Ireland, only a small group of landowners and professional people were, or became, Anglican. The large majority—about 7/8 in 1845—of the population remained Roman Catholic, despite Oliver Cromwell's attempts to extirpate them. By the Act of Union 1801, the two established Churches, England and

Ireland, became the United Church of England and Ireland. The Monarch, from being two Supreme Governors in one person, became one Governor.

By 1845 the state, in the shape of Sir Robert Peel's Tory government, had ceased pretending that the established Church of Ireland was ever likely to become a national church for the people of Ireland. In the lapidary words of the Duke of Wellington, 'we cannot avoid their being Roman Catholics' (*Hansard*, Lords, 2 June 1845, see Chapter 11). By re-endowing the Catholic seminary at Maynooth, Peel and Wellington ensured that Irish priests were at least educated in Ireland, where the state could overhear what they were taught, rather than in Rome or some equally dangerous overseas Catholic city. The Maynooth Grant was bitterly unpopular among the Protestant Ultras who formed a sizeable faction in both houses of Parliament, but it was a recognition of reality. The logical next step was to disestablish the Church of Ireland, a step taken by Gladstone's first Liberal government in 1869 and in force since 1870. No church is now established in Northern Ireland. With the division of society there into two large confessional groups of roughly equal size, it is inconceivable that any could be. As noted, the Government of Ireland Act 1920 forbade it.

In Wales, Table 13.1 shows that the established Anglican Church had lost ground rapidly by 1851—less through its own decline than through the rapid rise of the distinctly Welsh 'Calvinistic Methodists' (in truth Calvinist, but not Methodist). Disestablishment was therefore on the agenda as soon as something resembling manhood suffrage was achieved in Wales, namely from the general election of 1868 (Morgan 1963/1991). However, Welsh MPs knew that any attempt to disestablish or disendow the Welsh Church would be blocked in the unelected House of Lords. Therefore, disestablishment required both a Liberal government and the removal of the Lords' veto. The fact that it was a manifesto commitment of the 1892 Liberal government cut no ice with Queen Victoria, nor would it with the Lords if it had reached there (McKinstry 2005; see Chapter 14). As noted earlier, disestablishment was enacted in 1914, but its operation was immediately suspended because the First World War had broken out. Elsewhere (Peterson and Mclean 2007) we have shown that, although Parliament had decided that the pre-1662 endowment of the Welsh Church should go to the local authorities and the University in Wales, the beneficiaries only received a small fraction of what Parliament had intended them to get—and that not until the late 1940s. Welsh disestablishment was an instance of what has more recently been labelled the 'West Lothian Question'. An action that affected only Wales, supported by the majority of MPs from Wales, was blocked for over fifty years by the vetoes of legislators who were not from Wales.

There are thus (different) established churches in two of the four parts of the United Kingdom, and none in the other two. All other faith communities are regulated by charity law, and by general law as it affects their contracts, employment practices, health and safety standards, and so on. I now consider how this disparate and inconsistent set of regulations might be made fair and uniform for those of any faith community and of none.

HOW RELIGION SHOULD BE REGULATED

On 5 March 2008, the House of Lords voted to abolish the common-law offences of blasphemy and blasphemous libel. Two bishops voted with the majority; three with the minority. The Archbishops of Canterbury and York had earlier signalled that they did not object to the move, but they queried its timing. A government minister pointed out that it had been discussed in Parliament four times since 1995. The Lords' vote was triggered by an earlier government concession in the Commons. The Liberal Democrat MP Evan Harris had introduced a Commons amendment to the same effect. Although Labour MPs were whipped to oppose the amendment, government whips had warned ministers that the amendment would be carried, so the government agreed to sponsor a government amendment in its place. The clause was later carried in the Commons and was enacted in England and Wales on the 8 July 2008 by s79 of the Criminal Justice and Immigration Act 2008.

This little story has a number of morals. The blasphemy laws protected only Christians, and perhaps not all of those. Muslim lobbyists had earlier pressed for the protection to be extended to them. But that was impracticable, not least because the British government protests against sentences of blasphemy handed down in various other countries, such as Pakistan, Afghanistan, and Sudan. Faced with the choice between extending blasphemy protection to all faiths and to none, the UK government opted for the latter.

Another moral is that the dog did not bark. According to the Lexis-Nexis database, not a single newspaper worldwide reported the Lords' vote the following day: The only report in the database is from the Press Association's Lords correspondents. This may suggest that religious regulation is strictly a matter for religious enthusiasts. In this section I argue that, on the contrary, it is an important constitutional matter for religious and non-religious people alike. I return to the three reasons, suggested above, that have been put forward for retaining the special establishment of the Church of England.

The Church of England is required by law to offer its services to any parishioner in every parish in the land, and it maintains a presence in every parish. It is precisely at the times of greatest joy and greatest sorrow—typified by weddings and funerals—that people who never normally go near a church or cleric may feel the need to do so. Therefore the fact that half of the religious people in the United Kingdom are wedding-and-funeral people only (Table 13.3) does not mean that the regulation of religion is unimportant.

One argument of those who wish to retain establishment is that disestablishment would weaken this commitment (see e.g. Avis 2000). Another is that establishment recognizes the unique role of the Church of England in protecting the nation's heritage. A third, more fundamental than either, is that faiths need protection, and establishment offers that protection.

As to a 'national church', we have seen that even an Archbishop of Canterbury can become confused. The Church of England is the national church of England. It is not the national church of the United Kingdom. Its special role in various 'national' events in the UK state or civil society is therefore based on a mistake.

But a national network of pastoral support is something most governments would like to encourage. The Church of Scotland also aspires to be a national church with a presence in every parish and the duty to offer marriages and funerals to all parishioners. Giving all faiths the protection that the Church of Scotland has would put the Church of England in no worse position than it is now to offer its national services. The disestablished church in Wales still offers national coverage as it did before 1914.

Establishment offers the Church of England no material help in protecting its heritage, and in one respect may be a hindrance. There is no state support for maintaining the buildings, music, or libraries of the Church of England. The main scheme for helping to repair historic churches, run by the Heritage Lottery Fund, is (as it should be) open to all churches, although the source of money causes trouble to those that have a testimony against gambling, including Methodists and Quakers.

In recent UK discussion, however, these issues have both been overshadowed by something which now looms much larger. This is the degree of protection that faiths may reasonably expect—respect for their beliefs, practices, and rights to discipline their own members.

This has been a battleground between liberals and communitarians for two centuries. On the liberal side, the most ringing statements were made by Thomas Jefferson and John Stuart Mill. In 1802, President Jefferson found it expedient to answer a petition he had received from a Baptist delegation in Connecticut. Several of the New England states still had state establishment, against which the Danbury (CT) Baptists had protested. Jefferson wrote:

> Believing with you that religion is a matter which lies solely between Man & his God, that he owes account to none other for his faith or his worship, that the legitimate powers of government reach actions only, & not opinions,

I contemplate with sovereign reverence that act of the whole American people which declared that their legislature should 'make no law respecting an establishment of religion, or prohibiting the free exercise thereof,' thus building a wall of separation between Church & State. Adhering to this expression of the supreme will of the nation in behalf of the rights of conscience, I shall see with sincere satisfaction the progress of those sentiments which tend to restore to man all his natural rights, convinced he has no natural right in opposition to his social duties.[4]

And in *On Liberty* (1859), J. S. Mill launched a tirade which is addressed nominally to Muslims (rare in England in 1859), but actually to evangelical Christians, who were numerous:

Suppose now that in a people, of whom the majority were Mussulmans, that majority should insist upon not permitting pork to be eaten within the limits of the country. This would be nothing new in Mahomedan countries. Would it be a legitimate exercise of the moral authority of public opinion? and if not, why not? The practice is really revolting to such a public. They also sincerely think that it is forbidden and abhorred by the Deity. Neither could the prohibition be censured as religious persecution. It might be religious in origin, but it would not be a persecution for religion, since nobody's religion makes it a duty to eat pork. The only tenable ground of condemnation would be that with the personal tastes and self-regarding concerns of individuals the public has no business to interfere (Mill 1859/1910: 142).

The communitarian response takes many forms. Note that neither Jefferson nor Mill denies that a faith community may discipline its own members. But there is a painful issue: how much freedom should they have, in a plural state, to discipline their members without state interference? The second issue is whether, and if so how, a faith community may regulate the behaviour of those who are not its own members, or who have lapsed from membership. The third is how far if at all the state may protect believers from religious hatred.

A communitarian response of particular interest is that of Archbishop Rowan Williams in February 2008, when he stirred up a storm of criticism for saying in a radio interview that Sharia law was 'unavoidable' in the United Kingdom. In the lecture that occasioned the interview he was more subtle:

it might be possible to think in terms of what . . . Ayelet Shachar, in a highly original and significant monograph on *Multicultural Jurisdictions: Cultural Differences and Women's Rights* (2001), . . . calls 'transformative accommodation': a scheme in which individuals retain the liberty to choose the jurisdiction under which they will seek to resolve certain carefully specified matters, so that 'power-holders are forced to compete for the loyalty of their shared constituents' . . . This may include aspects of marital law, the regulation of financial transactions and authorised structures of mediation and conflict resolution—the main areas that have been in question where supplementary jurisdictions have been tried, with native American communities in Canada as well as with religious groups like Islamic minority communities in certain contexts . . . [A] communal/religious nomos, to borrow Shachar's vocabulary, has to think through the risks of alienating its people by inflexible or over-restrictive applications of traditional law, and a universalist Enlightenment system has to weigh the possible consequences of ghettoising and effectively disenfranchising a minority, at real cost to overall social cohesion and creativity. Hence 'transformative accommodation': both jurisdictional parties may be changed by their encounter over time, and we avoid the sterility of mutually exclusive monopolies.[5]

Were Jefferson and Mill guilty of promoting 'a universalist Enlightenment system', in its turn guilty of 'ghettoizing and effectively disenfranchising a minority, at real cost to overall social cohesion and creativity'? If so, what should constitution-writers do about it?

Note that Archbishop Williams, like every communitarian who is trying to make a cross-community argument, is arguing not merely that his own faith community should have a protected sphere, but that all should. He could have argued, as his predecessor vigorously did, for the continued special establishment of the Church of England. But he does not.

There are some obvious difficulties with the Archbishop's position (see also Witte 2008). It is perfectly correct to say that there are some religious jurisdictions with the power to settle disputes among their own members. The Jewish Beth Din is an example. The Church of Scotland courts are in a special position, examined later. There is nothing unreasonable in the suggestion that Sharia tribunals should be added to the list, to rule, as the Archbishop suggests, on 'aspects of marital law' or 'the regulation of financial transactions'. This is fine if both parties accept the jurisdiction. But what if one does not? Both the jurisprudence of the Beth Din and that of Sharia courts have been criticized for treating women less favourably than men. What if a woman aggrieved by their ruling, say on a divorce, appeals to the secular courts?

The Archbishop suggests, following Shachar, that in those circumstances there might be a 'transformative accommodation', in which both jurisdictions compromise their claims. They might. But in the last resort, there must be a supreme tribunal. It is hard to see how, in the United Kingdom, this can be anything other than the standard court system.

The most interesting case in this area concerns the Church of Scotland courts. Helen Percy was a minister of the Kirk, admitted to the ministry in rural Angus. She was disciplined by the Church courts for an alleged improper liaison with a parishioner. She resigned her post and demitted status as a minister, but then had second thoughts and raised an employment tribunal action alleging sexual discrimination, on the grounds that the Kirk had treated her less favourably than in other cases where a male minister had been disciplined for sex with a female parishioner. All the courts up to the Court of Session (the highest civil court in Scotland) accepted the Kirk's defence that the discipline complained of was in the sphere of 'doctrine, worship, government, and discipline in the Church' that is reserved exclusively to the Kirk under the terms of the Church of Scotland Act 1921, and that therefore the secular courts, including employment tribunals, had no standing in the case.

The relevant Article from the 1921 Articles Declaratory helps to illuminate both the strengths and the difficulties of the position advocated by the Archbishop.

> This Church, as part of the Universal Church wherein the Lord Jesus Christ has appointed a government in the hands of Church office-bearers, receives from Him, its Divine King and Head, and from Him alone, the right and power subject to no civil authority to legislate, and to adjudicate finally, in all matters of doctrine, worship, government, and discipline in the Church, including the right to determine all questions concerning membership and office in the Church, the constitution and membership of its Courts, and the mode of election of its office-bearers, and to define the boundaries of the spheres of labour of its ministers and other office-bearers. Recognition by civil authority of the separate and independent government and jurisdiction of this Church in matters spiritual, in whatever manner such recognition be expressed, does not in any way affect the character of this government and jurisdiction as derived from the Divine Head of the Church alone, or give to the civil authority any right of interference with the proceedings or judgments of the Church within the sphere of its spiritual government and jurisdiction. (Church of Scotland Act 1921. Schedule, Article IV)

However, in *Percy*, the House of Lords, with one dissenting voice, reversed the Court of Session and sent the case back to an employment tribunal for adjudication (it was actually then settled out of court).[6] The Lords held:

> That the provision of a remedy for unlawful discrimination in the employment field was a civil matter, not a spiritual one; that, therefore, notwithstanding that the applicant's complaint of sex discrimination arose out of the disciplinary proceedings instituted against her, it did not come within

the ambit of 'matters spiritual' so as to be excluded from the jurisdiction of the civil courts by section 3 of the Church of Scotland Act 1921; and that, accordingly, the employment tribunal had jurisdiction to determine the complaint.

Thus, though the Church of Scotland has a legally protected sphere within which it may determine doctrine, worship, and discipline without interference from the civil magistrate, it must abide by the law against sex discrimination. (Speech of Lord Hope of Craighead in *Percy*. See further Cranmer and Peterson 2006; Rodger 2008.) Rivers (2000: 138), writing before *Percy*, states that 'The Church of Scotland enjoys an autonomy greater than any other religious body in the UK'. *Percy* has thrown this into doubt. Similarly, the Bishop of Hereford was held to have unjustly discriminated against a gay church worker by refusing to appoint him to a post, contrary to the Employment Equality (Sexual Orientation) Regulations 2003.[7] In 2007 also, Catholic adoption agencies were denied an exemption from regulations stipulating that all adoption agencies must be willing to handle applications from same-sex couples to adopt a child. The Catholic Church announced that it would sooner close its agencies than abide by this ruling. Archbishop Williams mentioned this case in his sharia speech, stating that the regulations should not have been imposed on the Church. (Although nothing in the regulations precludes the Roman Catholic Church from running its private affairs according to the light of Catholic social teaching—the ruling stemmed from the agencies' interactions with local authorities.)

There are in fact some religious exemptions from general employment and discrimination law. Religions are allowed to restrict some appointments to members of one gender, and to refuse to appoint to the ministry people who do not share their faith. They may give their co-religionists preference for employment in faith schools. The sphere of exemption offered by the 1921 Act to the Church of Scotland is thus recognized for other faiths also, but its boundaries are fiercely contested. This contest is inevitable in any plural society as militants on both sides pick test cases to fight. Have the governors of a faith school the right to deny promotion to teachers who do not share their faith? Has a schoolchild the right to wear a certain form of religious dress not permitted by her school's dress code? Has a registrar the right to refuse to officiate at civil partnerships?[8] As noted in Tables 13.4 and 13.5, religious people in the United Kingdom have systematically different social attitudes to non-religious people. The contest cannot be finally settled in the constitution. In the end, the courts and employment tribunals will be the place where religious claims and equal-opportunity claims must be balanced against one

Table 13.4 Attitudes to homosexuality by religion, 2005.

		Is sex between same-sex adults wrong?					
		Always wrong	Mostly wrong	Sometimes wrong	Rarely wrong	Not wrong at all	Total
Religion	C of E/Anglican						
	Count	199	89	57	52	190	587
	% within religion	33.9	15.2	9.7	8.9	32.4	100.0%
	Other Christian						
	Count	205	76	44	50	174	549
	% within religion	37.3	13.8	8.0	9.1	31.7	100.0%
	Non-Christian						
	Count	30	10	6	6	17	69
	% within religion	43.5	14.5	8.7	8.7	24.6	100.0
	No religion						
	Count	161	60	59	65	378	723
	% within religion	22.3	8.3	8.2	9.0	52.3	100.0
Total	Count	595	235	166	173	759	1928
	% within religion	30.9	12.2%	8.6	9.0	39.4	100.0

p of χ^2 < 0.001.
Source: BSA online.

Table 13.5 Attitudes to the monarchy by religion, 2005.

		Respondent's view importance monarchy continue?						
		Very important	Quite important	Not very important	Not at all important	Should be abolished	Don't know	Total
Religion	C of E/ Anglican							
	Count	168	104	28	9	14	1	324
	% within religion	51.9	32.1	8.6	2.8	4.3	3	100
	Other Christian							
	Count	102	116	39	21	22	3	303
	% within religion	33.7	38.3	12.9	6.9	7.3	1.0	100
	Non-Christian							
	Count	9	12	6	6	4	2	39
	% within religion	23.1	30.8	15.4	15.4	10.3	5.1	100
	No religion							
	Count	77	145	95	33	49	3	402
	% within religion	19.2	36.1	23.6	8.2	12.2	0.7	100
Total	Count	356	377	168	69	89	9	1068
	% within religion	33.3	35.3	15.7	6.5	8.3	8	100

p of $\chi^2 < 0.001$.
Source: BSA online. Question asked of half sample only.

another. This may lead to the 'transformative accommodation' the Archbishop seeks.

Regulation also involves finance. Here the regime for religious regulation is improving and could be improved further. Until 2006, religious charities in the United Kingdom were exempt or excepted from regulation, leading to anomalies such as the Bradford Cathedral case mentioned above. Under the Charities Act 2006, most formerly unregulated charities, including religious denominations, come under regulation for the first time. This means that their accounts must be in order, must be professionally examined or audited, and comply with the 'Statement of Recommended Practice' for charity accounting. These are weasel words—it is actually a statement of mandatory practice for all but the smallest organizations.

Since 1601, 'the advancement of religion' has been accepted as a charitable purpose. To the dismay of some secularists, the 2006 Act does not change this. But it adds a separate requirement that all charities must not only have a charitable purpose but also must demonstrate public benefit from that purpose. Holding religious services open to the public will probably satisfy the public benefit test (Charity Commission 2008a, 2008b). Religious charities which do not do that may have some work to do in showing that they meet the public benefit test.

Thus through the rather unlikely channel of the Charities Act 2006, the United Kingdom may be slowly working towards (as Christians might say) 'rendering unto Caesar the things which are Caesar's, and unto God the things that are God's' (Matthew 22:21). The Religious Freedom etc. Act would help still more.

The troubled legislative history of what became the Racial and Religious Hatred Act 2006 helps to show why my proposed Act would clear the waters. The terrorist attacks of 2001 and 2005 have focused policy makers' minds on the threat to public order from alienated Muslims (and terrorists who claim to act in the name of Islam). Accordingly, the UK government was sympathetic to demands from moderate Muslims that their religion should get similar protection to Christianity, which in 2001 was still protected by the blasphemy laws. The government introduced legislation to this effect, but was repeatedly defeated in the House of Lords. The original version would have criminalized the *expression* of religious hatred. Some critics pointed out that this version might catch the Hebrew Bible, Christian Bible, and the Quran themselves. For instance, there is a great deal of smiting in the Hebrew Bible (the Christian Old Testament). And the crucifixion narratives in the Gospels according to Matthew and John pin the blame for the death of Jesus on the Jews. In October 2005, the House of Lords amended the government bill to restrict its scope to 'acts *intended* to stir up religious hatred' (Lords Hansard

25.10.2005, available at: http://www.publications.parliament.uk/pa/ld200506/
ldhansrd/vo051025/text/51025–12.htm; Racial and Religious Hatred Act 2006
(c.1), Schedule; my emphasis). The Commons voted to accept the Lords'
amendments: the first instance in the 2005 Parliament of the loss of a
manifesto bill. As it is hard to prove intention except in the most extreme
cases, the Act is probably a dead letter.

It may be helpful to draw a distinction between religious autonomy and
religion-blindness. Religious autonomy means allowing each religion to have
a sphere of spiritual self-government like the Church of Scotland's. Several
denominations in England and Northern Ireland are regulated under public
or private Acts of Parliament of the Victorian era that were presumably
designed to allow them, like railway companies and canals, to make their
own by-laws and run their internal affairs. Religion-blindness would entail
hostility to *any* religious exemptions from (especially) employment and
gender-equality legislation. I think that complete religion-blindness is a bad
idea. For both principled and pragmatic reasons I think that the state should
not be insisting that all posts of minister of religion must be open to people of
either sex. That exemption protects the spiritual autonomy of religions. But
the exemption should not be drawn so that it covers cleaners, youth workers,
or teachers. If all religions explicitly had the same degree of protection as the
Church of Scotland (perhaps the Church of Scotland before *Percy*), religious
people would be better off and non-religious people would be no worse off
than now.

AMENDING THE ACT OF UNION 1706

It is one of the principal themes of this book that the Act of Union 1706 is a
constitutional treaty between two sovereign states which voted to dissolve
themselves into a new state. There is no continuing international body to
enforce the Treaty of Union. Therefore, the clauses of the 1706 Act which
declare that such-and-such must be protected 'forever' must be entrenched.
(How entrenchment might be done, in general, is discussed below.) As we
have seen, the failure of Parliament to respect the intentions of the 1706/7
signatories of the Treaty as early as 1712[9] led to a great deal of trouble in
Scotland which was not resolved until 1843 (perhaps 1921).

The 'forever' clauses of the Act of Union 1706 include Section XI, which
entrenches the English and Scottish church establishments. There was
neither constitutional court nor international tribunal to which those who
were aggrieved by the Patronage Act 1711 could complain that it was

unconstitutional because it breached one of the 'forever' clauses of the Act of Union. If anything is a constitutional statute which deserves some entrenchment, it is the Act of Union. Therefore, the Religious Freedom etc. Act of 2015 needs to do better than the Patronage Act 1711. It must make the repeal of Section XI of the 1706 Act legitimate by either a Parliamentary supermajority, or a referendum, or both. Furthermore, the referendums must be symmetrical. The section protects two establishments 'forever'. It should not be repealed unless the referendum both in Scotland and in England goes in favour. It would be polite to ask people in Wales and Northern Ireland as well, but it would be inconsistent to let their votes bind either the Scots or the English.

Part V:

Things to Put In

14

We the People

It is now time to take stock. In this book so far, I hope I have shown that:

1. The United Kingdom exists by virtue of a constitutional contract between two previously independent states.
2. The Diceyan tradition is vacuous, not least because Professor Dicey vigorously emptied it.
3. A superior way to study the constitution is to consider the veto plays and credible threats available to politicians since 1707.
4. The idea that the people are sovereign dates back to the seventeenth century (maybe the fourteenth in Scotland), but has gone underground in English constitutional writing.
5. The constitution of the United Kingdom was too weak to withstand the Unionist coup d'état of the years 1909–1914;
6. Devolution and Europe (the former in three guises, the latter in two) have taken the United Kingdom along a constitutionalist road since 1972, and perhaps since 1920.
7. No intellectually defensible case can be made for retaining an unelected house of Parliament, an unelected head of state, or an established church.

The structure of this final chapter is as follows. First, I revisit the anti-constitutionalist case to see whether it can be made to stand up without a Diceyan strut. Then, I consider what sort of constitutional laws there should be, if there is to be a distinct class of constitutional statutes. Related to this is a discussion of how, or whether, such laws should be entrenched. The implications of entrenchment for majority rule are discussed. Finally, I discuss how UK policy makers might make the United Kingdom a regime whose constitution frankly admits that it depends on the people of the United Kingdom.

DICEYANISM WITHOUT DICEY

At various points, I have acknowledged that a powerful strand of political and legal writing on the United Kingdom is deeply suspicious of a written constitution, judicial review, and entrenchment of legislation. These are not all the same thing, of course; one could have one or two without the other(s). But they are all, potentially, counter-majoritarian in the sense noted by the American jurist Alexander Bickel (1962: 16–17):

> [J]udicial review is a counter-majoritarian force in our [the US] system . . . [W]hen the Supreme Court declares unconstitutional a legislative act . . . it thwarts the will of representatives of the actual people of the here and now.[1]

In this section, I therefore review whether Diceyanism can stand up without Dicey. By Diceyanism I mean a faith in the sovereignty of Parliament, justified not on the grounds Dicey gives, but essentially on the grounds that legislators are elected and judges are not. Thus defined, I think it is fair to say that there are two centuries of writers in this tradition, going back to Jeremy Bentham and John Austin, and in more recent times represented most notably by Ivor Jennings, Harold Laski, J. A. G. Griffith, Richard Bellamy, and Jeremy Waldron. Those who reach Dicey's conclusion without necessarily accepting Dicey's arguments may usefully be labelled 'parliamentary sovereigntists'.

Bentham was a utilitarian before he was a democrat. He attacked the American and French declarations of rights of his day not because they were counter-majoritarian but because they were either meaningless or pointless. Of the French Declaration of the Rights of Man and the Citizen of 1789, Bentham wrote:

> Suppose a declaration to this effect: No man's liberty shall be abridged in any point. – This, it is evident, would be a useless extravagance which must be contradicted by every law that came to be made. Suppose it to say, No man's liberty shall be abridged but in such points as it shall be abridged in by the law. This, we see, is saying nothing: it leaves the law just as free and unfettered as it found it. (quoted by Schofield 2006: 60)

However, this anti-rights argument was later linked to one in favour of parliamentary sovereignty. For Bentham's follower John Austin (1832/1999) it was a necessary truth that there could only be one sovereign—an argument derived from Hobbes in the seventeenth century. Law was the command of that sovereign.

In Bentham's and Austin's time, the distinction between Bagehot's dignified and efficient constitutions was already evident to anybody who thought about the matter, even though they wrote decades before Bagehot. Legally, the sovereign of the United Kingdom was the monarch. The Church of England still prays daily to 'Our Sovereign Lady Queen Elizabeth'. The central department of state is HM Treasury, where HM stands for Her Majesty's. The Department that collects tax is Her Majesty's Revenue and Customs. The courts are all hers as well.

But the efficient sovereign was (except from 1909 to 1914) the party which controlled Parliament. Parliamentary sovereigntists, as I suggested earlier, followed the 'court' as opposed to the 'country' interpretation of the revolutions of 1688–9. Parliament elected the sovereign monarch in 1688–9, and later altered the line of succession. (Actually, as I have shown, *two* Parliaments elected the same monarchs and later altered the line of succession in different ways, but this important detail is lost in many accounts.) Gradually, through the nineteenth century, the doctrine solidified that the party entitled to form the government was the party that had the confidence of the House of Commons. Many people who have featured in this book contributed to this doctrine. They include writers such as Bagehot, but more importantly politicians such as Wellington, Gladstone, and Asquith. As the latter waspishly advised George V, the last monarch to dismiss a government that retained the confidence of the Commons was William IV, 'one of the least wise of British monarchs' (Appendix to Chapter 12). However grumpily, George V took Asquith's advice and did not dismiss him, as A.V. Dicey and Sir William Anson apparently hoped he would. By contrast, there was no Asquith (or Knollys) around to save the monarchy in Australia on Armistice Day 1975. It was the middle of the English night.

For twentieth-century sovereigntists, therefore, the elected government has the right to use its parliamentary sovereignty in any way it chooses, just because it is the *elected* government. In mid-century this idea was developed most firmly by writers on the political left (such as Jennings, Laski, and Griffith). For all these writers, parliamentary sovereignty enabled a radical reforming government, such as those of 1906 and 1945, to make dramatic changes in policy, but to command the loyalty of the civil service and the courts, and the legitimacy of the population. As Griffith put it, decrying those judges who at the time were developing doctrines of judicial review and judicial law-making (overt or covert) in what they called the public interest:

> The judicial conception of the public interest, seen in the cases discussed in this book, is threefold. It concerns, first, the interests of the State (including its moral welfare) and the preservation of law and order, broadly interpreted; secondly, the protection of property rights; and thirdly the promotion of certain political views normally associated with the Conservative party. (Griffith 1977: 195)

Accordingly, it was writers on the political right who deplored the 'elective dictatorship' of Labour governments. The phrase was due to the Conservative politician and lawyer Lord Hailsham (1976) who, like Dicey and Anson before him, seemed bothered by the elective dictatorship of left-wing governments but not by the elective dictatorship of a Conservative government such as the one he joined in 1979. As Lord Chancellor under Mrs Thatcher until 1987, he sponsored no legislation to make her governments less dictatorial.

Sovereigntists now may be still on the political left; but they are probably a minority there. Most constitutional writers now seem to endorse the entrenchment (in some form) of human rights; many support limitations on parliamentary sovereignty. Against them, writers such as Bellamy (2007) and Waldron (1999, 2006) 'defend . . . democracy against judicial review' in Bellamy's words (2007: 260). I will consider the most outspoken of these defenders, Jeremy Waldron. Like other writers in this tradition, including Bellamy and Griffith, Waldron insists that there is no *a priori* reason why judges should be more protective of human rights than legislatures. Judges, too, can rule against human rights, as the US Supreme Court did in the notorious *Dred Scott* and *Korematsu* cases.[2] When judges do consider human rights, they often do so in a rule-bound way that does not go to the heart of the issues; but if they do go to the heart of the issues, they are merely expressing the ethical opinions of nine individuals who happen to comprise the current bench of the Court. Contrast the happy procedures of an elected legislature:

> In countries that do not allow legislation to be invalidated in this way, the people themselves can decide finally, by ordinary legislative procedures, whether they want to permit abortion, affirmative action, school vouchers, or gay marriage. They can decide among themselves whether to have laws punishing the public expression of racial hatred or restricting candidates' spending in elections. If they disagree about any of these matters, they can elect representatives to deliberate and settle the issue by voting in the legislature. That is what happened, for example, in Britain in the 1960s, when Parliament debated the liberalization of abortion law, the legalization of homosexual conduct among consenting adults, and the abolition of capital punishment. On each issue, wide-ranging public deliberation was mirrored in serious debate in the House of Commons. (Waldron 2006: 1349)

By contrast, according to Waldron and those who agree with him, the rights and wrongs of abortion (and school prayer, gay marriage, the death penalty, and limits to the right to bear arms) in the United States are stuck in the courts, addressed by a nine-strong 'legislature' who are not specially equipped for moral reasoning; and electoral politics is distorted into the channel of electing candidate X so as to get Justice Y on to the Supreme Court.

The toughest case, however, is that of 'discrete and insular minorities'. The phrase was coined by US Justice Harlan Stone in one of the 1938 New Deal regulatory cases. Before the 'switch in time' that 'saved nine', the Court had struck down several New Deal statutes as inconsistent with the Bill of Rights or other counter-majoritarian clauses of the Constitution. The 'old Court' had struck down business regulation and labour protection on the grounds that they interfered with the rights of business to run its affairs as it pleased. After the switch, one of the regulatory cases that reached the Supreme Court challenged the validity of the Federal Filled Milk Act, under which filled milk, such as that produced by a firm called Carolene Products, had been banned from interstate commerce.[3] The firm offered to prove that its milk was safe, and that the statute violated its rights of economic freedom and due process. Justice Stone, speaking for the post-switch Court, reversed the decision of lower courts, which had found for the firm, and declared that normally the court would not interfere with regulatory statutes unless it could be shown that they had no rational basis. The court therefore deferred to the legislature and pulled out of an area of judicial law-making. However, a footnote warned that if a statute appeared to violate the rights of 'discrete and insular minorities', the court should remain ready to protect the human rights of members of such minorities.

Do discrete and insular minorities exist in the United Kingdom; and does the need to protect them give rise to a case for judicial review? The first of these is (for any country) an empirical question, hotly contested since the days of James Madison.

> Among the numerous advantages promised by a well constructed union, none deserves to be more accurately developed than its tendency to break and control the violence of faction. . . . A religious sect, may degenerate into a political faction in a part of the confederacy; but the variety of sects dispersed over the entire face of it, must secure the national councils against any danger from that source: A rage for paper money, for an abolition of debts, for an equal division of property, or for any other improper or wicked project, will be less apt to pervade the whole body of the union, than a particular member of it[.] (Madison, *The Federalist* number 10, paragraphs 1, 22. Madison, Hamilton, and Jay 1788/1987: 122, 128).

In *The Federalist* number 10, Madison argues that an 'extended republic' is itself the cure for faction. To switch from Madison's language to that of Justice Stone, a large state is less likely to discriminate against discrete and insular minorities than is a small one.[4] In 1943, Joseph Schumpeter (1943/ 1954: 240–2) wrote:

> Suppose that a community, in a way which satisfies the reader's criteria of democracy, reached the decision to persecute religious dissent. The instance

is not fanciful ... [He goes on to give examples of the persecution of (the wrong kind of) Christians and Jews in supposed democracies.] Let us transport ourselves into a hypothetical country that, in a democratic way, practices the persecution of Christians, the burning of witches, and the slaughtering of Jews. We should certainly not approve of these practices on the ground that they have been decided on according to the rules of democratic procedure. But the crucial question is: would we approve of the democratic constitution itself that produced such results in preference to a non-democratic one that would avoid them?

To Schumpeter's crucial question, proponents of strong judicial review answer *No*; Waldron and those who argue like him answer *Yes*. I am not ready to take sides without a little empirical investigation. Does the UK

Table 14.1 Does the UK Parliament protect discrete and insular minorities from the tyranny of the majority?

Discrete and insular minority	Failure to protect	Protection
Church of Scotland supporters	Patronage Act 1711 (repealed 1874)	Church of Scotland Act 1921
Welsh people	Blocking of Welsh Church Bills 1868–1920	Welsh Language Acts 1967, 1993
Irish people	Government of Ireland Bills 1893, 1912 blocked until 1920	
Roman Catholics	Ecclesiastical Titles Act 1851	Government of Ireland Act 1920
Gay people	'Section 28' of the Local Government Act 1988, repealed in 2000 (Scotland) and in 2003 (England and Wales)	Sexual Offences Act 1967 c.60
		Civil Partnerships Act 2004
Murderers		Murder (Abolition of Death Penalty) Act, 1965, c.71.
People seeking an abortion		Abortion Act, 1967, c.87
Fetuses	Abortion Act, 1967, c.87	
Asylum seekers	Aliens Act 1905	Human Rights Act 1998
People charged with terrorism-related offences	Terrorism Acts 2000, 2001, 2005, 2006	Human Rights Act 1998

Sources: Justis and Westlaw legal databases; standard histories; Waldron (2006)

Parliament protect or persecute discrete and insular minorities? If and when Parliament persecutes them, do the courts step in to protect them?

Table 14.1 lists the main discrete and insular minorities in the United Kingdom that have been subject to relevant legislation (or failure to legislate). They include the cases listed by Waldron earlier, but I have tried to go wider.

Table 14.1 shows that there is evidence on both sides. Without commenting on all the cases listed, I may make a few points.

1. The most enduring cases relate to Scotland, Ireland, and Wales. Irish Home Rule was blocked and Welsh disestablishment delayed by the unelected parts of Parliament. Home Rule was also blocked by the Unionist coup d'état and paramilitary revolt. An elected Parliament, *ceteris paribus*, would have enacted Irish Home Rule in 1893 and Welsh disestablishment during the Parliament of 1868–74 (or at latest that of 1880–5). By contrast, the Rosebery government of 1894–5 faced veto threats from both unelected chambers. The queen said she was 'horrified' by Government proposals for Welsh and Scottish disestablishment, and refused to have them in her speech. The Queen's Speech lays out the government legislative programme. Rosebery counter-threatened 'The Government came in . . . on Welsh and Scottish disestablishment . . . We could not exist for a moment without dealing with these questions.' The queen grumpily gave way. But disestablishment had no chance of enactment without Lords reform. She violently objected to that as well, telling Rosebery that the Lords are 'part and parcel of the much vaunted and admired British constitution'. He retorted, as his Home Secretary Asquith was later to do, 'the moment a Liberal government is formed, this harmless body assumes an active life and its activity is entirely exercised in opposition to the Government'. This so horrified the queen that she started plotting with the opposition, asking Lord Salisbury 'Is the Unionist Party fit for a dissolution?' It seems that she was on the point of 'doing a William IV' on Rosebery. However, his administration imploded, and the Unionists won the next election without the queen's help. (All letters in this paragraph are from McKinstry 2005, quoted: 305, 306, 327–30).

2. In most cases the prejudice precedes the protection, but gay rights offer a partial counter-example which shades Waldron's encomium.

3. In relation to anti-Catholic legislation, Mr Gladstone called the 1851 Act (which forbade the Catholic Church to establish territorial dioceses in the United Kingdom) one of the three 'actual misdeeds of the Legislature during the last half-century' (Gladstone's diary quoted in Matthew 1998: 238). As noted in Chapter 8, the Government of Ireland Act 1920 contains at s.5 a re-enactment of the Establishment and Free Exercise

clauses of the US First Amendment: the Parliament of Northern Ireland may not 'make a law so as either directly or indirectly to establish or endow any religion, or prohibit or restrict the free exercise thereof'. This was introduced, probably, to protect *Protestants* in the South, but had the effect also of protecting Catholics in the North.

4. In some cases, abortion being an obvious example, protection of one insular and discrete minority entails harm to another.

Have the UK courts protected the subject when Parliament has failed to? Although not sufficiently expert to generalize, I would hazard, 'Not until recently'. Bad and embarrassing Acts (such as the Ecclesiastical Titles Act and Section 28) have been allowed to wither away for lack of prosecutions rather than face a head-on legal challenge which would certainly have failed. When the courts have applied (or discovered, or invented) common law principles bearing on minority rights, they might go either way. Griffith (1977) lists cases in which the courts, for instance, invented the crime of conspiracy to corrupt public morals, and supported the expulsion of a trainee teacher from college because she had a man in her room.[5]

However, since the enactment of the Human Rights Act 1998, the UK legal climate seems to have changed dramatically (Bogdanor 2006; Hazell 2008). As noted earlier, the 1998 Act gives direct effect to the European Convention on Human Rights in UK law. That convention in turn derived from the Holocaust and World War II, when everybody knew that Schumpeter's cases were not fanciful. Under the Human Rights Act, courts may not directly strike down a UK statute (whereas under the European Communities Acts they may), but they may make a declaration of incompatibility. Those made in the first few years of the act were listed in Table 10.1. Reference to that table will remind the reader that we are very much in the territory of discrete and insular minorities.

Some commentators believe that 'there will inevitably be a conflict and a struggle' between UK courts and governments on this (Bogdanor 2006). Others see it as an opportunity for comity.

> Such modifications may prompt a constitutional crisis that may result either in Parliament or the courts gaining legal ascendancy over the other institution through a modification of our current constitutional arrangements. As such, comity between the two institutions may help to enhance healthy checks and balances between Parliament and the courts. Neither can gain ascendancy without running the risk that this will also result in a loss of their current powers. (Young 2009: 169–70)

By comity Young has in mind, I think, something like the 'switch in time' of the New Deal Supreme Court, as interpreted by Ackerman (1998). Rather than all-out war, the two institutions each see that the other has its own legitimacy, and each defers to the other. Justice Stone's withdrawal of the Court from aggressive enforcement of the claimed rights of corporations which were not insular and discrete minorities is a case in point. As noted in Chapter 10, a precondition for comity between the UK executive and judiciary is full separation of powers between them. This came for the first time with the Constitutional Reform Act 2005.

Without exhaustive research involving a careful definition of the population of cases, it is thus impossible to say which out of Parliament and the Courts is the better guarantor of minority rights. It is interesting, however, that the cases in which Parliament has most firmly written minority rights into statute refer to Northern Ireland. Examples have included the guarantee of religious freedom in the 1920 Act and the (attempted) entrenchment of proportional representation for Stormont. The Parliaments that enacted these sections knew that the conditions Madison outlined in *The Federalist* number 10 did not apply to Northern Ireland. There, both main 'religious sects' had 'degenerated into a political faction'. And one was bigger than the other.

Two more general lessons appear to emerge from this discussion. First, Waldron assumes, as part of the set-up of his 'core ... case against judicial review', that the territory has a statute—not necessarily entrenched—protecting human rights. The United Kingdom has such a statute. This is to acknowledge that counter-majoritarian rights protection has a place even in a Waldronesque democracy without judicial review. A democracy with no statutory rights protection is, he makes plain, not within the scope of his argument against judicial review. No contemporary lawyer known to me is making the confident claim to parliamentary sovereignty against the courts that was made by the mid-twentieth-century Diceyans discussed earlier. Politicians—especially Home Secretaries—may make the claim, but it is not backed up by analysis. It seems that Waldron has no problem with the United Kingdom's (non-entrenched) Human Rights Act.

Second, those who still stake a claim to parliamentary sovereignty may only do so if parliament is elected. Dicey's doctrine has collapsed into the vacuous claim that 'Parliament is supreme because it is.' There is a respectable, non-Diceyan, argument for Parliamentary supremacy. It runs *Parliament is elected; civil servants and judges are not. Therefore it is for Parliament, not for civil servants or judges, to decide questions of morality and rights.* This argument may be made, with some caution, for the UK Parliament since 1999. For all Parliaments before then it fails for a very basic reason.

Until 1999, it was nonsense to claim that Parliament was elected. In reading the canon of commentators, I am surprised how often those on the political left (including Laski, Jennings, and Griffith) seem to fall for the nonsense.

Parliament (in the mouths of lawyers) was not elected. One house out of three was elected. True, the powers of one of the unelected houses were curbed in 1911. True, the second non-elected house had not seriously threatened a veto since 1914. But lawyers need to pay some attention to basic political science here. The House of Lords largely set the terms for its own withdrawal, by means of the Salisbury(–Addison) convention(s) discussed earlier. But that convention covers only bills in the winning party's manifesto; the Liberal Democrats have abandoned it; and the Lords' powers of delay remain potent in the last two years of each Parliament. What political scientists call the 'rule of anticipated reactions' means that there are some reforms that a non-Conservative administration would not even try to introduce before 1999. It was common knowledge that it would be a waste of time. And time—especially parliamentary time—is scarce. The reforms of the 1960s, listed in Table 14.1, that so impress Waldron were possible only because a liberal Home Secretary, Roy Jenkins, allowed their proponents parliamentary time (Jenkins 1992: 175–213). Although not government bills, they required government action. Lloyd George was a better political scientist than Sir Ivor Jennings when he asked why 500 men chosen accidentally from the ranks of the unemployed should have a parliamentary veto.

Even in the post-1999 Parliament, two of its three houses remain unelected. The monarchy is unelected in the same way as it has been since 1714. It was elected then (and in 1689 and in 1660), but all these dates are a long time ago. The Lords are differently unelected than before 1999. Instead of being un-electedly and automatically Conservative, they are unelectedly and contin-gently balanced across parties. Only contingently, because there is nothing in statute to prevent a future Prime Minister from stuffing the house with partisan nominees.

Therefore, anyone serious about the idea that 'we, the people' either do or should ultimately decide policy must support an elected head of state and an (at least predominantly) elected upper house. Equally, anyone serious about retaining the normative doctrine of Parliamentary supremacy has to explain why anyone should defer to a body, two of whose three chambers are unelected.

The three elected houses should each be elected by a different electoral system. The head of state should probably be chosen by a Condorcet meth-od—that is, any method which guarantees that the chosen head of state defeats each of the other candidates in exhaustive pairwise comparison. The upper house—let's call it the Senate—should be elected by proportional representation with long, non-renewable fixed terms, and with members ineligible to move immediately either to or from the Commons. If (and only if) these arrangements are in place, a democrat could be content with the Commons remaining elected by the highly non-proportional system of simple plurality rule—that is, the present system, with single-member districts. Or the Commons could be elected using the Alternative Vote system, as in Australia. This could deliver even less proportional results than the existing first-past-the-post system, but that could be tolerable if the Senate were elected under PR. Any arrangement short of that could risk degenerating into the elective dictatorship that Lord Hailsham deplored, but did nothing to rectify when in power.

A particularly dangerous option that appeals to some conservatives on the left should be mentioned. This is elective dictatorship by unicameral first-past-the-post. Abolition of the House of Lords was a 1983 Labour manifesto commitment.[6] It was dropped in 1987 but it continues to appeal to some, especially on the Labour left. In the 2003 Commons votes on Lords reform, the motion to abolish the second chamber attracted 174 votes (McLean, Spirling, and Russell 2003, Table 1). In the 2007 votes, it was widely reported that the unexpectedly large majority for an all-elected chamber was swollen by strategic votes of unicameralists who realized that an all-elected upper house had no realistic chance of enactment. Of the available options, it was argued that such unicameralists favoured the status quo because an all-unelected Lords is the likeliest kind to be cowed by an elected Commons playing the legitimacy card. By voting for an impossible option (a well-known Trotskyist tactic) they therefore maximized the chances for the status quo.

Before 1999, unicameralists on the left saw (more clearly than the constitutional authorities of their day) that policies of an anti-Conservative government could still often be vetoed by the Conservative median peer. They could appeal to an idea that has since been formalized by Persson and Tabellini (2005) and by Iversen and Soskice (2006). Both of those pairs of political economists argue that, compared to regimes with proportional representation, regimes with single-member districts and a first-past-the-post electoral system have fewer veto players, less stability, and more decisiveness. In its February 1974 manifesto, Labour called for a 'fundamental and irreversible shift of wealth and power towards working people and their families' (*Times Guide* 1974: 311). A fundamental shift probably required the decisiveness of a first-past-the-post unicameral majority. An irreversible shift would have required something different again.

First-past-the-post unicameralism faces three big problems. One is that median peer is, since 1999, no longer a Conservative. The left-wing unicameralists have lost their strongest democratic argument, which is exactly Lloyd George's: Why should 500 men and women chosen accidentally from the ranks of the unemployed have veto power in a purported democracy? True, the Lords remain unelected, so the unicameralists are not bereft of an argument. But the Lords now roughly reflect party balance in the country. The British House of Lords is now a slightly superior version of the Canadian Senate. The loss of the best unicameralist argument exposes the grave weaknesses of other parts of their claim.

To see those, take that phrase 'fundamental *and irreversible*'. Radical governments could indeed make fundamental changes more easily in the United Kingdom than in other regimes. Examples from the governments of 1906 and 1945 pepper this book and standard histories. That is why the Marxist political scientist Harold Laski was a constitutional conservative. In particular, in 1906–10, the Lords did not veto protection of trade unions, old age pensions, or social insurance. But *irreversible*? First-past-the-post can elect radical governments of the right as well as the left. That happened in 1979. The Conservative administration elected then and in office until 1997 reversed many policies which had been thought irreversible by most commentators. Likewise, the Tory House of Commons elected in 1710 reversed what the Scots Union negotiators had thought an irreversible guarantee when it enacted the restoration of patronage in the Church of Scotland. The decisiveness of a unicameral first-past-the-post parliament cuts both ways.

To counter that, an irreversible-shiftist can only make two moves. One is to demand entrenchment and guarantees against future change. But this is to contradict the shiftist's starting position, which demands the opposite. The other, more worryingly, devalues democracy. This is the third and deepest objection to United Kingdom first-past-the-post unicameralism. First-past-the-post has two technical properties: bias and responsiveness. A system is responsive if a given change in the gaining party's vote share yields a greater change in its seat share. That is not necessarily a bad thing. It is what makes radical change possible. But a system may also be biased. That is, at equal vote

Table 14.2 Bias in the UK electoral system: the Parliaments of 1951 and February 1974.

Party	1951			February 1974		
	Vote share	Seat share	Ratio	Vote share	Seat share	Ratio
Conservative	48.0	51.4	1.07	38.2	46.8	1.22
Labour	48.8	47.2	0.97	37.2	47.4	1.27
Liberal	2.6	1.0	0.38	19.3	2.2	0.11
Sc. and W. nationalist	0.1	0.0	0.00	2.6	1.4	0.55
NI Unionist	included with Cons			1.5	1.7	1.18
NI nationalist	0.4	0.5	1.09	0.7	0.2	0.23
Other	0.2	0.0	0.00	0.5	0.3	0.58

Sources: Times Guide 1951, 1974; Butler and Kavanagh 1974; author's calculations

shares it awards one party more seats than the other. The danger then is of an elective dictatorship which not only does not have *majority* support but does not even have *plurality* support. The two contentious cases in modern UK history are the Parliaments of 1951 and February 1974 (Table 14.2).

For each election, Table 14.2 gives three columns of data. The first shows the vote share for each party or coalition; the second its seat share; and the third, the ratio of the second to the first. The ratio column illustrates both the responsiveness and the bias in the system. In both elections, minor parties did very badly (ratios far below 1), unless geographically concentrated like the Ulster parties. The lead party has a ratio above 1. That measures responsiveness. But in both of these elections, the winner in votes was not the winner in seats. In 1951, Labour was the victim of this bias; in February 1974 the Conservatives were. In 1951 Labour got 13.95 million votes—more than it ever has before or since. But the Conservatives won an absolute majority of seats and governed on their own for a Parliament of standard length.[7] In February 1974 almost the reverse happened. Labour got fewer votes but more seats than the Conservatives. True, they did not win an overall majority, although they just did on similar vote shares in the following general election in October of the same year. Would either of those victories have entitled the winner to make a fundamental and *irreversible* shift in power?

Unicameralism combined with PR *is* a defensible constitutional option, which has existed in New Zealand since 1996. It would have rather similar effects to the Australian-style system discussed earlier. But, as no UK lobby or think tank is currently proposing it, I do not discuss it further here.

WHAT SORT OF WRITTEN CONSTITUTION?

Two restrictions on parliamentary sovereignty in the United Kingdom are already in place. As explained in Chapter 9, the UK courts now treat EU law as trumping domestic law. And, as explained in Chapter 10, the Human Rights Act 1998 empowers a court to issue a declaration of incompatibility. Such a declaration states that a UK statute cannot be read consistently with the European Convention on Human Rights (ECHR), but does not repeal it. Parliament is invited to decide how (or whether) to remedy the situation. These could be seen as examples of 'strong' and 'weak' judicial review respectively. The first question for constitutional reformers is then: *How strong should judicial review be in a future UK Constitution?*

Here it seems to me that the arguments of Griffith, Bellamy, and Waldron have considerable force. Judges are not elected. At the moment, neither is

Parliament, but once it is, it will be able to claim the democratic legitimacy that judges never can. The strong judicial review of UK legislation for compatibility with EU directives that has existed since *Factortame* is therefore rather uncomfortable. Whence do the judges of the European Court of Justice derive their authority? Not, on any defensible reading, from the people of the European Union (EU). Some good questions asked by Enoch Powell and Sir Derek Walker-Smith in 1972 have never been adequately answered. On the other hand the weak judicial review enshrined in the ECHR and the Human Rights Act seems a good way to protect discrete and insular minorities. As Young (earlier) says, it may lead to 'comity' such that judges do not challenge the right of Parliament to legislate, and parliaments do not (seriously) challenge the right of judges to determine rights claims under the ECHR and the HRA. Determining these claims *is* one of those things for which judges are better equipped than politicians or administrators. For rights claims may conflict. We saw in previous chapters that claims for freedom of religion under Article 9 of the ECHR have come into conflict with other rights claims, such as anti-discrimination claims by gay and lesbian people.

Sir John Laws has suggested an alternative approach: speaking as a judge, in the *Thoburn* case, and extra-judicially in articles and speeches. In *Thoburn*, he said

> We should recognise a hierarchy of Acts of Parliament: as it were 'ordinary' statutes and 'constitutional' statutes. The two categories must be distinguished on a principled basis. In my opinion a constitutional statute is one which (a) conditions the legal relationship between citizen and state in some general, overarching manner, or (b) enlarges or diminishes the scope of what we would now regard as fundamental constitutional rights. (a) and (b) are of necessity closely related: it is difficult to think of an instance of (a) that is not also an instance of (b). The special status of constitutional statutes follows the special status of constitutional rights. Examples are Magna Carta 1297 (25 Edw 1), the Bill of Rights 1689 (1 Will & Mary sess 2 c 2), the Union with Scotland Act 1706 (6 Anne c 11), the Reform Acts which distributed and enlarged the franchise (Representation of the People Acts 1832 (2 & 3 Will 4 c 45), 1867 (30 & 31 Vict c 102) and 1884 (48 & 49 Vict c 3), the Human Rights Act 1998, the Scotland Act 1998 and the Government of Wales Act 1998. The 1972 [European Communities] Act clearly belongs in this family. It incorporated the whole corpus of substantive Community rights and obligations, and gave overriding domestic effect to the judicial and administrative machinery of Community law. It may be there has never been a statute having such profound effects on so many dimensions of our daily lives. The 1972 Act is, *by force of the common law,* a constitutional statute. (Laws LJ in *Thoburn*: 280–1, My emphasis)

I agree with Lord Justice Laws's list of constitutional statutes, although I would also wish to add, at least, the Parliament Acts 1911 and 1949, the Northern Ireland Act 1998, the Government of Wales Act 2006, the Church of England Assembly (Powers) Act 1919, the Church of Scotland Act 1921, and the current Representation of the People and Parliamentary Constituencies Acts. Laws's list with these additions would cover what Herbert Hart famously called the 'rules of recognition' and 'rules of change' in the United Kingdom (see Introduction). The Parliament Acts undoubtedly meet criteria (*a*) and (*b*); the devolution statutes should be treated as a group; the protection of the spiritual independence of the Churches of Scotland and (to a much lesser degree) of England is a baseline constitutional matter that Parliament should not again be allowed to violate by simple majority vote; and the current statutes governing the election and constituencies of MPs, in my view, also meet Laws's criteria (*a*) and (*b*), although the matters they deal with are unexciting except for MPs and those who would supplant them.

What is more difficult is his assertion that the laws on his list are constitutional statutes because the common law says they are. How am I to know whether 'the common law' is or is not 'what one particular judge, sitting in one particular court, at one particular time, says it is'?

HOW WOULD WE THE PEOPLE ORDAIN TO OURSELVES A CONSTITUTION?

One way to proceed would be to hold a directly-elected UK Constitutional Convention. Among its tasks would be to decide which statutes are 'constitutional', and to make a rule for deciding whether a future statute will come into that class. It would then prescribe the super-majority procedure for amending constitutional statutes. That might, for instance, entail a greater than simple majority in both the Commons and the Senate in favour of amendment; and/ or a referendum, which could be binding or non-binding. At the same time it could decide on the substantive constitutional changes discussed in this book, including the creation of an elected Senate and head of state and the disestablishment of the Church of England. We might call this the Big Bang approach. At the end of it, the members of the Constitutional Convention would declare, as their US forebears did in 1787, that the text should open *We the People of Urania*[8] do ordain and establish this Constitution for the United Republic of Great Britain and Northern Ireland. The draft from the Constitutional Convention would then be sent for ratification in each of the four nations of the United Kingdom (which at the same time would, of course, become the UR).

At this point even a friendly critic would probably urge me to get real. What chance is there of a constitutional convention being convened? If convened, of producing a unanimous constitution draft? And if produced of the draft being ratified? Each of these is unlikely; their combination is multiplicatively unlikely. The history of some successful and some near-miss constitutional conventions is relevant here.

The US Constitutional Convention of 1787 was called when it became obvious to some politicians including Alexander Hamilton, John Jay, and James Madison that the existing constitution, the Articles of Confederation, was falling apart. The Articles required the unanimous agreement of all states for any action; therefore nothing was being done. The immediate urgency of war with Britain had disappeared in 1783; but the United States would be desperately unprepared for any new war with Britain, France, or Spain, none of which was unlikely. Nevertheless, Rhode Island refused to send a delegation at all; and several other state delegations contained grumpy Anti-Federalists, as the opponents of the Constitution became called. The draft Constitution contained provisions for its own ratification (nine states minimum) and amendment.

Americans revere their Constitution; they do not often observe that it was both *unconstitutional* and highly *improbable*. It was unconstitutional because the Articles of Confederation required unanimity for anything, including therefore their own amendment. The Constitution amends the Articles of Confederation: how then could the Framers say that the assent of nine states would suffice to bring the new constitution into force? Because they had to. Unanimity would have given a veto to the absent Rhode Island, which would certainly have used it. Several (more than three) of the other states were believed to have Anti-Federalist majorities, however public opinion was to be tapped. The ratification by nine states is therefore so improbable that it deserves the detailed study it has too rarely had (but, see Riker [1996]). Part of the Federalists' strategy was to create a cascade. The most Federalist states ratified first, beginning with Delaware, where the state convention ratified unanimously. It was followed by New Jersey and Georgia; then things started to get harder for the Federalists. They predicted that the swing states would be New York and Virginia. The Constitution might—just—get nine states without them, but they would leave two big holes in the United States. Hamilton, Jay, and later Madison therefore got together to write the 85 *Federalist* papers for the New York newspapers in the hope of getting that state to ratify. Part-way through, Madison had to rush home to argue for ratification in his home state of Virginia, where some of the social and political leaders were Anti-Federalist. There is not room here to explain how the Federalists pulled it off (Riker 1996), but they did, on one condition: that the country-Whig Bill of Rights must be added by the first Congress, as it duly was. Once the twelve[9] remaining states had ratified, tiny Rhode Island could not hold out, and it ratified grumpily in 1790.

The cascading strategy was so successful that it was tried elsewhere. It succeeded in Australia in 1900 and (just) in Wales in 1997; it failed in Canada in 1982–92 and to date has failed in the EU. In all these cases, the constitution-writers required unanimous consent of the previously-existing units for a new constitution. In all cases some units were keen and some were hostile. In Australia, the most hostile state was Western Australia, whose economic interests differed from the others'. The other states nevertheless went ahead with the second constitutional convention that produced a constitution. By Rhode Island logic, Western Australia joined after the draft has already been presented to Queen Victoria (which is why the preamble does not mention Western Australia). The state government website records that

> Western Australian political representatives who either opposed Federation outright or who wanted to hold out for more concessions from the other colonies, failed completely in their attempts to secure the support of the British Government. It was clear that Federation would go ahead with or without Australia's western third. (http://www.liswa.wa.gov.au/federation/fed/index.htm, consulted 15.01.09).

Western Australia voted to secede in 1933, but its petition to the UK Parliament to amend the Australia Act got nowhere.

By the same cascading logic, the UK government arranged in 1997 for the devolution referendum in lukewarm Wales to take place a week after that in enthusiastic Scotland. The Welsh *Yes* was achieved by the narrowest possible margin; so the cascade probably worked. However, in Canada the cascading strategy has failed. Three successive attempts to get unanimous approval for the Constitution have foundered on the opposition of Quebec, or the prairie provinces, or First Nations. The EU has similarly failed to get its Lisbon draft constitution ratified by the most Eurosceptic member states.

The requirements for a successful constitutional convention seem therefore to include a national emergency; substantial national unity; and politicians' willingness to coerce holdouts. The conditions applied in the United States in 1787 and in Australia in 1900, but not elsewhere. They do not apply in the United Kingdom today.

Are we then at an impasse? Sir John Laws's declaration that constitutional statutes are entrenched at common law will not do; nor will Lord Bridge's fictional history of Parliament's discussion of sovereignty in 1972; and a constitutional convention would probably not succeed. I suggest that the way out is to accept that the United Kingdom is indeed at a constitutional moment, but that the measure of that is electoral acceptance. In saying so I am heavily influenced by Ackerman's characterization of the US Constitution (1991, 1998) in *We the People*. This was introduced in Chapter 2. To recapitulate, Ackerman shows that each of the United States's great constitutional moments was unconstitutional. The Constitution was not duly ratified by the procedures laid down in the previous constitution. If the Thirteenth Amendment was validly ratified, then the Fourteenth cannot have been. And the switch in time that saved nine, of which Stone's footnote in *Carolene Products* was part, was not done by constitutional amendment at all. President Roosevelt, in issuing his threat to the Old Court, was influenced by Asquith's move against the House of Lords (although he wrongly attributed it to Lloyd George—Chapter 2). The Court followed the election returns.

In this characterization, the US constitutional moments are 1787–91; 1864–8; and 1932–6. (I think Ackerman should have added the period from 1954 to 1965.) The UK constitutional moments are 1647–60; 1688–1707; 1832; and 1909–14. What about the period since 1997? Since then, a UK government has been repeatedly re-elected (as in 1906–14 and the US cases). This is a necessary but insufficient criterion. The previous administration was repeatedly re-elected (in 1979, 1983, 1987, and 1992). But Mrs Thatcher, for all her transformative energies, was not a *constitutional* reformer any more than Mr Churchill or Mr. Attlee. However, a case can be made that the Labour governments of 1997–2009 have instituted a 'fundamental and irreversible' change while not saying they would, whereas Labour vainly aspired to do so from 1974 to 1983. Devolution is probably irreversible unless the people of a devolved territory ask for it to be reversed. The separation of powers embodied in the Constitutional Reform Act 2005 is probably irreversible. Membership of the Council of Europe and of the EU is irreversible unless, again, the people reverse it. Equally, all main parties in the United Kingdom are now formally committed to a predominantly elected upper house. The same cannot be said of the Human Rights Act 1998. However, the change in *legal* culture of which it forms part seems hard to reverse.

How then might a future UK Parliament implement the distinction between constitutional and other statutes which everybody seems to agree now exists? I suggest the following (I hope painless) procedure: A statute is constitutional if a qualified majority of each house decides so. A 'qualified majority' might be defined as 'two-thirds of those present and voting' or 'more than half of the total membership of the House', or more stringently via a higher threshold. Once a statute had been declared constitutional, it would require the same qualified majority vote in each house to change its constitutional status or to repeal.

What statutes should be put up for this treatment? If I were advising a reform administration I would start with Laws's list, and add the statutes that (as an American might say) will 'guarantee a republican form of government' once the monarchy has been abolished. These are, principally, the consolidated Representation of the People and Parliamentary Constituencies Acts.

This may seem a weak and naïve form of entrenchment. Weak, because it does not go even as far as existing EU law and judicial practice, which treats the 1972 and 1986 European Communities Acts as trumps in a stronger sense than I am proposing. Naïve, because (a critic will say) a determined government could easily railroad repeal of rights protection, or accretion of power to itself, through a complaisant Parliament, perhaps during a war or national emergency.

The weakness is deliberate. It is hard to think of a *democratic* justification for the strong entrenchment that elevates EU law above Member State law. Did we the people so ordain? It is true that we, or our parents and grandparents, voted to confirm UK membership of the EU in 1975. But as shown above, on none of the three key occasions, in 1972, 1975, and 1986, did we the people discuss the constitutional implications of what we, or our representatives, were proposing to do. A lot of us the people did not understand what those implications were. I certainly did not, when as a young political scientist I voted *Yes* in 1975. I never then thought that thirty years on I would be writing, in effect, *Enoch was right!*

Any justification of this strong entrenchment has to be pragmatic. I think it runs as follows. The EU is one of the supranational bodies of which the United Kingdom is a member. Others include the United Nations, the World Trade Organization, and the International Monetary Fund. Supranational bodies, to which states freely sign up, issue binding instructions to states. Sometimes, somebody has to. Some public goods and public bads are supranational. The goods include free trade and world peace; the bads include species extinction and global warming. Because of multiple free-riding dilemmas, the goods cannot be achieved and the bads averted, by states acting alone, *even when their governments know that they are freeriding*. Overfishing is a case in point. That was the fundamental issue in *Factortame*. Left to themselves, sovereign states permit overfishing, leading to the exhaustion of fish stocks, even though they knew all along that this was self-destructive in the long run. It is the classic tragedy of the commons (Hardin 1968). The EU decided on a common fisheries policy to mitigate the tragedy. The UK Merchant Shipping Act undermined the common fisheries policy. Therefore there were defensible grounds for invalidating it. Protection of supranational public goods is therefore warranted, even though there is no world, nor European, elected government. In McLean (2008) I explore this idea further in the context of global warming, imagining a fantasy President Gandalf Skywalker elected when the UN votes to turn itself into a world government in 2012.

Is my proposed entrenchment not only weak but naïve? In times of war and crisis, parliaments have enacted laws that have severely restricted liberties. The US Congress enacted the Alien and Sedition Acts 1798 during a panic about war with France. The UK Parliament enacted the Official Secrets Act 1911 during a war scare and Defence of the Realm (and similar) Acts during the real First and Second World Wars. If Parliament can do that, it could also remove entrenchment from, and indeed repeal, the Human Rights Act or whatever other protection of human rights were currently entrenched. Surely strong entrenchment and strong judicial review would do better?

Not necessarily. As noted previously, in *Korematsu* v. *United States*, (1944), the US Supreme Court upheld the Roosevelt Administration's forced removal of Japanese-Americans. Roosevelt's behaviour was no different to Churchill's, when he interned 'enemy aliens' (including many refugees from Nazism) on the Isle of Man during the First World War. But the supposed entrenchment of human rights in the US Constitution made no difference to the outcome in the United States.

My proposed entrenchment (and therefore disentrenchment) also demands the assent of supermajorities in two houses elected with different terms, different mandates, and on different electoral systems. In the political science language of Chapter 2, the effect of this is to contract the win set of the status quo, or (equivalently) to make the outcome set more stable. A single-chamber elective dictatorship can do anything it likes, as not only Lord Hailsham but Thomas Jefferson observed.[10] In substantive policy areas this may be good; in constitutional policy it is surely bad.

WE THE PEOPLE HAVE THE LAST WORD

I therefore propose that there be two classes of entrenchment. The EU constitution would remain strongly entrenched, for pragmatic not democratic reasons. This should remain so unless or until the UK Parliament and a popular referendum both support the United Kingdom's withdrawal from the EU. Other constitutional statutes would be weakly entrenched in the way just described. They would include the Human Rights Act (perhaps in re-enacted form as a British Bill of Rights). They would also include the Free Speech and Religious Freedom Act 2015 envisaged earlier.

The role of the courts in relation to all entrenched legislation except the 1972 and 1986 European Communities Acts would then be the role assigned to them under the Human Rights Act 1998. They could invalidate any executive act that they found inconsistent with a constitutional statute. They could insist on reading statutes in a way compatible with the Human Rights Act. In relation to conflicting statutes, the courts would have the power to issue directions of incompatibility, but not to repeal or invalidate any statutory provision that they found to be incompatible with any constitutional statute. It would then be up to the Parliament to consider the incompatibility, and to resolve it if it so chose. This would be, let us remember, a democratic Parliament. A governing party that decided to ignore a declaration of incompatibility would not only have to carry the Senate[11] but also the people in the next general election.

One form of constitutional adjudication that already exists, but has never been used, is adjudication of the *vires* of Acts of the Scottish Parliament, National Assembly of Wales, and Northern Ireland Assembly. The devolution acts assigned this role to the Judicial Committee of the Privy Council (the same body that Joseph Chamberlain vainly tried to make the ultimate arbiter of the Australian Constitution). With the creation of the new Supreme Court of the United Kingdom in 2009, this role transfers to that court.

I have noted that the UK Parliament has not hesitated to limit the powers of its subordinate assemblies on 'Bill of Rights' matters. The Stormont Parliament created by the 1920 Act was neither allowed to establish religion nor to restrict the free exercise thereof. All the devolved assemblies are expressly required to act in a way that complies with the Human Rights Act 1998. To that extent, the Supreme Court will already have a human rights constitutional jurisdiction from the moment it opens for business.

Such a constitution would, I believe, embody Ackerman's happy 'dualistic' medium. I share his objection to 'monists' who say (in the UK context) that Parliament is supreme; that the constitution is what happens; and that restrictions on Parliamentary supremacy are unwarranted. The monist position is much weaker in the United Kingdom than in the United States because the UK Parliament is not fully elected. I also share his objection to 'rights foundationalists'. Less prominent in United Kingdom than in US debate, there are nevertheless those who believe that Parliament can never be trusted, but that courts can, to protect fundamental rights. There is no conclusive evidence for either part of this claim. A third class of opponent discussed by Ackerman is the 'Burkean' whom he characterizes as one who believes that the accumulated wisdom of the common law reconciles democracy with rights. (Ackerman 1991: 17–19). In this characterization, Laws LJ is a classic Burkean.

Like Ackerman I disagree with the Burkean position, for two reasons. First, if a judge says that, for instance, the common law dictates that such-and-such are constitutional statutes, then how can this statement be checked, verified, or (above all) falsified? Second, whose common law? If the United Kingdom is a treaty state, uniting two regimes one of which elevated the common law in (what might anachronistically be called) a Burkean way and the other did not, who has the right to say that common law is trumps in the new state? Nothing in the Act of Union says so.

Therefore, the constitutional proposals in this book spring from a 'dualist' perspective similar to Ackerman's. Yes, the people should be recognized as sovereign. Therefore, the two unelected chambers of Parliament must become elected chambers. And the People should have a voice in referendum on certain fundamental changes, such as any proposal for Scotland or Northern Ireland to leave the United Kingdom, or for the United Kingdom to leave the EU. But at the same time there should be a weak embedding of two sorts of counter-majoritarian rules. The first sort embeds the format of Parliament and (perhaps) other core democratic bodies, so as to make it difficult for current parliamentary majorities to change them, perhaps for immediate partisan advantage. One such embedding has been in place since 1911, in the Parliament Act, s.2 (1). By that subsection, 'a Bill containing any provision to extend the maximum duration of Parliament beyond five years' may not be enacted without Lords' consent. When the 'Second Chamber constituted on a popular instead of hereditary basis' envisaged in the preamble to the 1911 Act comes into existence, that embedding will become consistent with democracy.

The second weak embedding is of human rights. The creative device of a 'declaration of incompatibility', dreamt up by Lord Lester and others, seems as good a way as any of preserving comity between the legislature and the courts.

I let Thomas Rainborough have the last word. Sir Stephen Sedley (an Appeal Court judge) and others have recently pointed out that the Levellers wanted both popular sovereignty and some entrenched constitutional law. Their *Remonstrance* of 1646 claims that MPs are elected 'to deliver us from all kinds of bondage ... for effecting whereof, we possessed you with the same power that was in ourselves, to have done the same: for we might justly have done it ourselves without you ... But ye are to remember, this was only of us but a power of trust ... We are your principals, and you our agents'. Their *Case of the Army, Truly Stated,* called for 'a law paramount be made ... to be unalterable by parliaments' to fix the term and frequency of parliaments. The second edition of the *Agreement of the People,* published a year after Putney, demanded that:

No representative shall in any wise render up, or give, or take away any of the foundations of common right, liberty or safety contained in this Agreement, nor shall level men's estates, destroy [property], or make all things common. (All quoted from Sedley 2008. See also M. Loughlin 2007)

The American Framers knew of the Levellers only indirectly. They might be astonished to realize how many of their ideas are in the Levellers' manifestoes. If the proposals in this book are taken up, then perhaps it will become clear that the poorest he (and she) that is in England (and Scotland, Wales, and Northern Ireland) has a life to live as the greatest he (etc.); and therefore that every person who is to live under a Government ought first to consent to put him or herself under that Government.

Notes

INTRODUCTION

1. A Convention Parliament is one that has assembled without a sovereign to call it together.
2. Jefferson was not, strictly, a Framer, as he was in Paris as American Minister in 1787. However, he made his views known through frequent letters to his friend and Framer James Madison.
3. Successively the European Economic Community/ies, the European Community, and the European Union (EU). I use the latest acronym, anachronistically, for convenience.
4. Why 1706? Because England was still using the old calendar, in which the new year began on 25 March. In this respect, if no other, Scotland was ahead of England in 1707.
5. A powerful leader in the *Manchester Guardian*, 24.03.1914, denounces the 'contingent mutiny of the cavalry officers in Ireland'.
6. *R. (Jackson and others)* v. *Attorney general.* [2006] 1 A.C. 262. Speech by Lord Steyn, para. 95. Between them their Lordships cited Dicey twenty times in total in their speeches in this case. Note the word 'our', both in the speeches in *Jackson* and in the Jowell and Oliver law text just quoted. Who 'we' are is not explained.
7. In a letter to Lord Stamfordham, George V's secretary, when (as Roberts knew but Stamfordham and the king did not) the Curragh 'mutiny' had just broken out, Roberts wrote, 'I consider it my duty as the Senior Officer in the Army to bring this serious state of affairs to His Majesty's notice' (20.03.1914. Royal Archives, Windsor, PS/PSO/GV/C/F/674/2).
8. Especially *R.* v. *Secretary of State for Transport ex parte Factortame Ltd (No. 2)* [1991] 1. A.C. 603.
9. In the 1930s, the Scottish committee for the History of Parliament pointed out to the London committee that 1707 inaugurated a new Parliament and a new state, and that therefore the historical volumes must break at that point. Professors Lewis Namier and Jack Plumb were appalled at this impudence. Plumb described the Scots' request as 'fatuous'; Namier refused to go to Edinburgh to discuss it, saying, 'My answer is "no Berchtesgarden"' (i.e. Neville Chamberlain's visit to appease Hitler at the latter's country retreat). Plumb and Namier got their way (Hayton 2008: quoted at p. 413).
10. This is not to say that such a vote would be self-enforcing. Hazell (2008*a*) has argued persuasively that there would have to be two referendums in Scotland: first, to open negotiations for independence and second, to ratify the deal that would subsequently be struck between the Scottish and UK governments defining the terms of separation.

CHAPTER 1

1. Senex (1950), from Times Online archive. My emphasis. For the Byng and Duncan cases see Bogdanor (1995, 156–61).
2. Dicey cites this as page 153. He does not say what edition he is using, but his page references are about four pages away from those in the scanned copy of the first edition cited here.
3. Blackstone here cites John Locke's *Second Treatise of Government* (Locke 1690/ 1988, §149 and 227). His quotation of Locke is not exact.
4. Dicey gives the page range of the immediately preceding passage as i: 160–1.
5. Respectively, *Attorney-General for the Commonwealth of Australia* v. *Colonial Sugar Refining Company, Limited* (1914) A.C. 237, and *Webb* v. *Outrim* [1907] A.C. 81. The sources disagree about the spelling of Out[t]rim's surname.
6. King Edward VIII gave his own Royal Assent to his own abdication: His Majesty's Declaration of Abdication Act, 1936 c.3.

CHAPTER 2

1. They may be treated differently as they pass through Parliament, for example, by being discussed by a committee of the whole house. But the courts insist that they examine only the 'roll of Parliament', not how a particular statute became law.
2. The pre-1982 Constitution of Canada was the British North America Act 1867. Although known in Canada as the Constitution Act, it was an Act of the United Kingdom Parliament, which the Canadian constitutional negotiators of 1982 had to ask the UK Parliament to repeal. However, the delay in patriation until 1982 was due to Canadian failure to agree on a constitution, not due to British obstruction.
3. Including Rhode Island, which boycotted the entire Constitutional Convention.
4. While conceding that Ackerman overstates his case for rhetorical effect. For a corrective see Rakove (1999).
5. For other, less buccaneering, readings of the Fourteenth Amendment see, for example, Nelson (1988) and Kyvig (1996).
6. For the *Dred Scott* case see Chapter 14.
7. Father Charles E. Coughlin (1891–1979), popular and populist anti-Semitic broadcaster.

CHAPTER 3

1. For the principal characters discussed in the history chapters of this book see the appendix, *Dramatis personae*.
2. Jacobite poem written or revised by Robert Burns, 1791, set to a traditional tune.
3. In February 1692, on orders sanctioned by William III and his Scottish ministers, a regiment whose colonel was the Duke of Argyll massacred MacIain, the leader of the Macdonalds of Glencoe, and about thirty-eight of the clan, for MacIain's alleged refusal to take a loyalty oath to King William, which he had in fact taken,

albeit late. The Macdonalds were Catholics, and the regime suspected all the highland Catholic clans of Jacobitism. The regiment had been the guests of the Macdonalds before the massacre.

4. *Jacobite*: supporter of (the Catholic) King James (Latin *Jacobus*) II, deposed in 1689, and of his son James Stuart ('The Old Pretender') and grandson Charles James Stuart ('Bonnie Prince Charlie', 'The Young Pretender'). The Jacobite Risings of 1715 and 1745 were failed attempts to restore James, the 'Old Pretender', to the throne; Charles came to Scotland to lead the 1745 rebellion.

5. Full documentation of sources and methods, and some flow-of-the-vote tables, are in McLean and McMillan (2005).

6. See his speeches delivered in parliament in September 1703, reprinted in Robertson (1997: 168–71). He denounced the Act as 'a design of the blackest nature, hurtful and ignominious to the nation' (quoted in Robertson 1997: 171).

7. Clerk of Penicuik records that Hamilton 'was so unlucky in his privat circumstances that he wou'd have complied with anything on a suitable encouragement' (Clerk 1892: 57).

8. He challenged Roxburgh to a duel in 1705, over Roxburgh's defection from the anti-Union cause. The dispute was settled without violence on the sands of Leith, after Roxburgh complained of a leg injury (Scott 1992: 129).

9. The significance test used is the non-parametric chi-square (χ^2) statistic. This gives the probability that the association shown has arisen by chance.

10. A more detailed breakdown is in McLean and McMillan (2005), and their Table 2.3.

11. Those who know the tune 'Old 124th' could try singing these lines to themselves, to that tune. Could the poet's choice of the metre and phrases of the 124th (unusual among the Scottish Metrical Psalms, most of which are in 'Common Metre') be designed to evoke the spirit of the 124th, which was seen by the Covenanters as 'Scotland's psalm of deliverance'.

12. Both dates are resonant in Ulster Protestant history. Twelfth of July is the date on which the Orange Order and other Protestant marching bodies celebrate the victory of 'King Billy'. But 1 July 1916 was the first day of the Battle of the Somme, in which the all-Protestant Thirty-Sixth Ulster Division (the former Ulster Volunteer Force) marched across no-man's land to destruction, in the sure and certain faith that God was on their side.

13. In imitation of the citizen militias that had helped the Americans win their war, and of the Scottish militia that Scots country whigs since Fletcher had seen as bastions of independence from government, Volunteer movements sprang up around Ireland in the 1770s. They were especially strong in Protestant areas. In 1798, the paramilitaries (to use an anachronistic term) were to split four ways: some loyal to the Crown, some in the non-sectarian United Irish rebellion; and some as sectarian protectors of their communities (Protestant Orangemen, Catholic Defenders, and Whiteboys).

CHAPTER 4

1. Cabinet memorandum by the Chancellor of the Exchequer, 'The Taxation of Land Values', 13.03.09. UK National Archives, CAB 37/98 # 44.
2. Sir George Murray to Lord Rosebery, 31.12.08. Rosebery MSS, National Library of Scotland, NLS MS 10049. One of Sir George's successors in post, Sir Gus O'Donnell, who went on to be Cabinet Secretary, comments, 'Events of this sort are worth remembering when reference is made to a bygone age of unimpeachable propriety and professionalism in the civil service' (O'Donnell 2005 p. 78).
3. These are three of the names on Asquith's (or his chief whip's) draft list: Jenkins (1964): 539–42.
4. The terms of the settlement are given in Halévy (1961: 394). Balfour: as quoted by Offer (1981: 357). 'Shillings of British artisans': Offer (1983: 134).
5. T. E. Scrutton (1920), quoted by Offer, *Property and Politics*, p. 369. *Inland Revenue Commissioners* v. *Smyth (King's Bench Division)* (1914) 3 KB 406.

CHAPTER 5

1. As often in Irish history, a lot hangs on terminology. Were the events of this chapter correctly describable as a mutiny or not? No officer disobeyed an actual order. However, the *Manchester Guardian* (24.03.1914) condemned their actions, in a leader probably by C. E. Montague, as 'the contingent mutiny of the cavalry officers in Ireland'. A recent paper arguing that it is correctly describable as a mutiny is O'Domhnaill (2004). Strachan (1997), the fullest modern scholarly discussion, comes closer than most authorities to accepting that it was a true mutiny. However, we retain the distancing quotation marks in this chapter.
2. See Dicey (1885/1915: liii): 'The Parliament Act enables a majority of the House of Commons to resist or override the will of the electors or, in other words, of the nation'.
3. The Wilson diaries, which are in negative microfilm, are very hard to read; the transcriptions in Beckett (1986) are sometimes incorrect. Where possible therefore I take citations to the diaries from my reading of the original rather than from Beckett.
4. In terms of his position as DMO, not of his formal rank. As a major general, he ranked equally with Sir Charles Fergusson and below Sir Arthur Paget, Sir Spencer Ewart, and Sir John French, all of whom he despised and outmanoeuvred. He drew much of his political capital in the Army from his association with the revered Field Marshal Lord Roberts.
5. A label applied by the former Unionist leader A. J. Balfour, which stuck.
6. Gough gave his copy to his solicitor and refused all requests to return it. Quotations in this paragraph are from the version in Beckett (1986: 218–9).
7. IWM HHW 1/23, Wilson diary, various dates between 21 and 29.03.1914. Lord Morley (Lord President of the Council) had been with Seely while he drafted the

'peccant paragraphs'. Lord Chancellor Haldane had preceded Seely as Secretary for War.

8. Fergusson to his brother, 25.03.1914, in Beckett (1986: 339–42). The letters from or on behalf of the king are Beckett's Documents 170–87, 193, 214, 227. That the king was beside himself with fury is clear from a letter in his own hand to Asquith on 21 March: 'As you will readily understand, I am grieved beyond words at this disastrous and irreparable catastrophe which has befallen my Army ... It is deplorable to think that gallant Officers have been drawn to take such fatal steps ... Now I must complain that I have been kept in complete ignorance ... I must request that no further steps are taken without my being consulted'. Bodleian Library, Oxford: MS Asquith 40 f.27.

9. Thus, as should be evident, we side with Smith (1993) against those who put Law's behaviour down to inexperience, irresolution, or capture by extremists. Law *was* a calculating extremist. As he said to the Scottish Unionist MP Sir Henry Craik in March 1914, 'The government are trying to carry through the measure in an entirely unconstitutional way and they cannot be prevented from succeeding unless action is taken by us which goes much beyond ordinary Parliamentary opposition'. BLP 34/2/39 Law to Sir H. Craik, 16.03.1914, quoted by Smith (1993: 162).

10. Versified by the English hymn-writer Isaac Watts. But the (Ulster-) Scots have always thought it one of their special Psalms, along with Psalm 124.

11. Police report, Larne, 25.04.14, in MS Asquith 41, ff. 36–7. Sir William Adair was a retired General in the Royal Marines. An intercepted Co. Fermanagh UVF mobilisation order in the Mottistone Papers, Box 16, gave two grades: against the police, 'Mobilization No. I—Without arms, but bring a truncheon or blackthorn'. Against the military presumably a Mobilization No. II 'With arms' would have been ordered.

12. In one of his anti-Home Rule polemics, Dicey (1890) claims that the verdict of the Parnell Commission on alleged intimidation by the Irish Land League proves, to a criminal standard of proof, that Parnell and his colleagues were guilty of a criminal conspiracy 'by a system of coercion and intimidation' (Dicey 1890: 189) and of treason and sedition. However, the great ideologue of the rule of law never applied a comparable analysis to the Larne conspirators.

13. Appendix to Chapter 12. Compare Law's memo to the king, 1912, in Nicolson (1952, p. 201) for the similarity of language.

14. The main exceptions are Dangerfield (1970; originally published in 1935), Jenkins (1964), Stewart (1967), and Jackson (2003). Of these, Dangerfield has been perhaps written off as shrill (which he was, about industrial unrest and suffragism, which were smaller threats than he made them out to be). Jenkins is so urbane that readers seem to have missed his passionate unspoken contempt for the king and Law. Stewart is an uninhibited, but scholarly, celebration of the Goughites and the UVF. Professor Jackson reports that his revelation from the Crawford papers was ignored by British conservative reviews of his book, and celebrated by Irish republican reviewers (personal communication, 30.03.07).

15. Bogdanor (1995: 116, 118, and 128) (source of quotation).
16. For example: Persson and Tabellini (2005), Iversen and Soskice (2006).
17. Steve Bruce, *God Save Ulster! The Religion and Politics of Paisleyism* (Oxford: Oxford University Press, 1986); *The Edge of the Union* (Oxford: Oxford University Press, 1994).

CHAPTER 6

1. However, in his review of Dicey in a centenary symposium, Bogdanor (1985) took a similar position to that argued in this chapter:
2. Or if, as Professor Alvin Jackson has suggested (personal communication) he means the two elections of 1910, he ignores the fact, pointed out by Asquith in his final letter to the king (Appendix to Chapter 12), that all politicians on both sides said the elections were about home rule.
3. Union with Scotland Act 1706, c.11, s.2.

CHAPTER 7

1. A word of obscure etymology denoting the Khoekoe and San people of southern Africa; but by Salisbury's time usually used to mean 'A person of inferior intellect or culture; an uncivilized or ignorant person' *OED* s. v. *Hottentot*, sense 2, marked 'derogatory (offensive)'.
2. Why would Salisbury accept the overrepresentation of Ireland when he had a chance to insist otherwise? At the 1881 Census Ireland contained 14.73 per cent of the UK population but the 1885 redistribution left it with 15.67 per cent of the seats. Its overrepresentation would increase to 1918. As to Catholic Ireland, Salisbury might already have been thinking of an Irish–Tory pact, which his Irish minister Carnarvon did offer in 1885, only to be repudiated by Salisbury. As to Protestant Ireland, Jackson (1989: 25–27) suggests that Salisbury disliked the Irish Tories because of their support for Gladstone's 1881 Land Act. The 1885 redistribution *weakened* the Irish Protestant position in the Commons. It abolished small boroughs and, as in the rest of the United Kingdom, expanded the rural franchise. The first harmed Protestants; the second, especially when coupled with the non-reduction of Ireland's seats to its population share, benefited Catholics. Because there was no redistribution between 1885 and 1918, the rapid growth of Belfast and industrial Ulster failed to counter this. Hence, the anomaly that, both in 1886 and 1912, the Catholic-Nationalist Irish Party held more seats in Ulster than did the Unionists.
3. Collins's note of his conversation with Lloyd George on 05.12.21 is reproduced in Dail Eireann (1972: 304–306). For a discussion of Lloyd George's game see McLean (2001: 176, 184) where I maintain, perhaps controversially, that Lloyd George told no lies. He did not hoodwink Collins; Collins hoodwinked himself.

CHAPTER 8

1. Students from ordinary Scottish schools were not eligible for maintenance grants at English universities until the early 1960s. I was one of only the third or fourth cohort of ordinary Scots who could afford to attend Oxford or Cambridge.

2. The Northern Ireland Civil Service is administratively distinct and handles pay and recruitment separately. No deep constitutional issue arises from this.

3. Source for this paragraph: personal knowledge. I was an elected member of Tyne & Wear Metropolitan County Council 1973–9, being successively vice-chair and chair of its Economic Development Committee. With the Leader of the Council, I was responsible for the council's policy towards the Scotland and Wales Bill.

4. Jack Rakove has shown that American constitutionalists between 1776 and 1787 focused intensely on the status of the English Convention Parliament, though so far as is known, not on the Scots one (1999: 1046–53). His anti-Ackerman reading of 1787 depends on the following argument. The Framers of 1787 knew that the state constitutions were mostly defective. Like the Convention Parliaments of 1689, they were unconstitutional since the colonial governors had not agreed to constitutions that deposed them. But, with a war on, none of the states except Massachusetts had time or energy to have their constitution ratified by the people. In that reading, therefore, the 1787 Constitution has more legitimacy than either the preceding Articles of Confederation or the state constitutions.

5. 'The Sewel Convention applies when the UK Parliament legislates on a matter which is devolved to the Scottish Parliament. It holds that this will happen only if the Scottish Parliament has given its consent' (Bowers 2005).

6. But it could be argued that the king was indeed rewarding Crawford and the similarly-honoured Wilfrid Spender, the paramilitaries' quartermaster-general, for their services to the British Empire, in which of course he had a vested interest which happened to differ from that of the elected government. McNeill (1922: 284) notes that Crawford and Spender were honoured for war service; 'but Ulstermen did not forget service of another sort to the Ulster cause before the Germans came on the scene'. He seems to overlook the Germans who sold Crawford his guns.

7. See <http://www.statistics.gov.uk/SIC/nugget.asp?ID=447>

8. The Barnett Formula was originally so named neither by Lord Barnett nor by HM Treasury, but by a public finance academic, David Heald (Heald 1980).

9. Scottish Office, 'Needs Assessment Studies'. National Archives of Scotland SOE6/1/1708-9, released June 2008.

10. See <http://wales.gov.uk/icffw/home/news/chairannounced/?version=2&lang=en>

11. See the National Conversation website front page <http://www.scotland.gov.uk/Topics/a-national-conversation? accessed 24 December 2008.

CHAPTER 9

1. See <http://europa.eu/index_en.htm> and <http://www.coe.int/DefaultEN.asp>
2. See <http://europa.eu/scadplus/glossary/Luxembourg_compromise_en.htm>
3. The margin of victory was 67.2 per cent to 32.8 per cent. *Yes* won in every sub-region of the country except Shetland and the Western Isles. The region with the lowest *Yes* margin was Northern Ireland, where Ian Paisley had warned that 'the Virgin Mary is the Madonna of the Common Market' and that the EEC was 'a Roman Catholic super-state' (Butler and Kitzinger 1976: 156; chapter 11, Table 1).
4. The live list at <http://ec.europa.eu/unitedkingdom/press/euromyths/index_en.htm> contained 47 headings (including 'Bombay mix' and 'Vultures') as of October 2008, with a link to other, archived myths.
5. In *Marbury v. Madison*, 5 U.S. (1 Cranch) 137 (1803), the US Supreme Court under Chief Justice John Marshall, held that the Court had the power to review the constitutionality of legislation, and proceeded to rule the Judiciary Act 1789 unconstitutional. This got Marshall out of a hole, and defined the jurisprudence and power position of the Court. See, generally, Ackerman (1991).
6. And to a line of other judgments in the same sense, some before and some after UK accession. They are discussed in every public law text, for example, Craig (2007).
7. String 'Van Gend' searched on <http://hansard.millbanksystems.com> on 22.10.2008.
8. There is a good mathematical reason for doing this (Penrose 1946), but the adoption of the square-root rule for the Council of Ministers seems to be a happy accident. The huge literature on this up to 1998 is summarized in Felsenthal and Machover (1998), especially in chapter 5. Since then the literature has continued to grow as abortive treaty revisions have tried to rebalance the ratios of member states' bloc votes.
9. Pronounced Co-field. This section draws on *The Times* 10.01.07; *Guardian* 11.01.07; *Independent* 20.01.07; and on Cockfield (1994).
10. 'The bounty to the white-herring fishery is a tonnage bounty, and is proportioned to the burden of the ship, not to her diligence or success in the fishery; and it has, I am afraid, been too common for the vessels to fit out for the sole purpose of catching, not the fish but the bounty' (Smith 1776/1981, IV.v.a.32).

CHAPTER 10

1. Although Lester and Beattie do not say so, Lester was a special adviser to Jenkins at the time. See Jenkins (1992: 375–6).
2. Secretary of State for the Home Department, *Rights Brought Home: the Human Rights Bill* Cm 3782: 1997.
3. See <http://nhrc.nic.in/> accessed 29 October 29, 2008.

4. Respectively, *Shabina Begum* v. *Denbigh High School* [2006] UKHL 15; *X* v. *Y School* [2007] EWHC (Admin); *Playfoot* v. *Millais School* [2007] EWHC 1698 (Admin). See further www.ReligionLaw.co.uk, consulted 31.10.08.

5. As usual, W. S. Gilbert was the most acute Victorian critic: 'And if he commit himself for contempt of his own Court, can he appear by counsel before himself, to move for arrest of his own judgement? Ah, my Lords, it is indeed painful to have to sit upon a woolsack which is stuffed with such thorns as these!' *Iolanthe*, Act I, Lord Chancellor's opening speech.

6. 'A Conservative Government will . . . [r]eplace the Human Rights Act, which has undermined the Government's ability to deal with crime and terrorism, with a British Bill of Rights'. See <http://www.conservatives.com/Policy/Where_we_stand/Democracy.aspx> accessed 31 October 31, 2008.

7. *Justice* 2007 paragraph 23. The deeply conservative, but covertly gay, poet A. E. Housman got there first:

> Oh who is that young sinner with the handcuffs on his wrists?
> And what has he been after that they groan and shake their fists?
> And wherefore is he wearing such a conscience-stricken air?
> Oh they're taking him to prison for the colour of his hair.

(Housman, Additional Poems 18. Written 1895 after the conviction of Oscar Wilde; published posthumously in 1939.)

CHAPTER 12

1. France: Constitution of the Fifth Republic, Article 5, my translation. There is no official translation, nor exact English equivalent of *veiller à* or *arbitrage*. These (deliberately?) ambiguous words were no doubt intended to give Charles de Gaulle, first President of the Fifth Republic, the maximum freedom of manoeuvre. Germany: Basic Law, Article 56, authorized English translation at http://www.bundestag.de/htdocs_e/parliament/function/legal/germanbasiclaw.pdf, consulted 12.03.08. USA: Constitution, Article II Section 1.

2. > 'Just the place for a Snark! I have said it twice:
   > That alone should encourage the crew.
   > Just the place for a Snark! I have said it thrice:
   > What I tell you three times is true.'
   > *The Hunting of the Snark*, Fit the First, stanza 2.

3. However, the Canadian High Commission in Canberra warned the Australian Attorney General's department that the cases were not comparable. NAA, A/75/7778, f. 46.

4. Whose grandson became a long-serving Private Secretary to Queen Elizabeth II.

5. However, Sir Francis Hopwood met Sir Kenelm Digby, who had called on Lady Matthew, the (Protestant) widow of Lord Justice Matthew, an Irishman and a Catholic, and also John Dillon's mother-in-law. Lady Matthew had reported to

Sir Kenelm what she believed to be Dillon's (and Redmond's) views. RA, PS/PSO/
GV/C/K/2553/3/91, 23.02.14. Some scholars, for example Fair (1971) and
J. Loughlin (2007), paint a more sympathetic picture of George V in this period.
They state that he was personally in favour of Home Rule; that he insisted on the
removal of the most anti-Catholic parts of his Coronation oath (Nicolson 1952:
62–3); and that at the abortive Buckingham Palace conference in July 1914 he
struck up a rapport with Redmond sufficient to encourage Redmond to commit
the Irish Volunteers to the army at the outbreak of war. I concede all of these
points; but I do not think they mitigate the king's failure to consult in 1913, nor
his one-sided rage at ministers (and Sir Charles Fergusson) over the Curragh.

6. Memo by Bonar Law, Balmoral, 16.09.13. RA, PS/PSO/GV/C/K/2553/2/16.

7. Letters to Lord Stamfordham, all in RA PS/PSO/GV/C/K/2553: from Hopwood
   21.03.14 (/4/38); Esher 14.12.13 (/3/30); Wigram 04.12.13 (/3/15). *Ghazi*:
   'A champion, esp. against infidels; also used as a title of honour.'—*OED* online,
   consulted 01.05.2008. Wigram's letter reports a long conversation he had had
   with Nevile Chamberlain about Ireland and so the views quoted may be Chamberlain's rather than Wigram's.

8. These are rounded-off figures taken from their respective websites and published
   accounts.

9. Text from web site of the Taoiseach [Prime Minister] of Ireland at http://www.
   taoiseach.gov.ie/attached_files/html%20files/Constitution%20of%20Ireland%20
   (Eng)Nov2004.htm, consulted 18.03.2008.

10. Basic Law of Federal Republic of Germany, official translation at http://www.
    bundestag.de/htdocs_e/parliament/function/legal/germanbasiclaw.pdf, consulted
    18.03.2008.

11. The five letters, and Asquith's covering notes, are mainly quoted from the versions
    in the Royal Archives. RA

    PS/PSO/GV/C/K/2553/1/70
    PS/PSO/GV/C/K/2553/2/9–10
    PS/PSO/GV/C/K/2553/2/21–22
    PS/PSO/GV/C/K/2553/2/26
    PS/PSO/GV/C/K/2553/2/45.

    They have been collated with the versions in the Asquith Papers (Oxford,
    Bodleian Library, MS Asquith 38) and with the printed versions listed
    below. There is one material difference, noted ad loc., among the three
    states of Asquith's Letters II and III. State 1 is HHA's holograph; State II is
    the first proof received by the king; State III is the later proof in the Asquith
    Papers. The king's versions can be dated by Asquith's covering letters to
    11 and 19 September. The proofs in the Asquith MSS are dated by the
    printers to 13 and 22 September. Other changes between States II and III
    (e.g. substitution of 'seven' for '7' etc) are not material.

    Letters I and IV are quoted in Nicolson (1952: 223–4, 225–9). However,
    the version of Letter I received by Asquith differs somewhat from that

quoted by Nicolson. The version in the Royal Archives has some sheets missing, so we take the recipient's copy in MS Asquith 38 as the most authentic. Letters II and III are quoted in Spender and Asquith (1932: II, 29–34), and in Jenkins (1964: 543–9). The heading to letter III is, however, given incorrectly by Jenkins. Neither source indicates the underlinings and sidelinings made by the recipient. Both have minor errors of transcription. Letter V has not been previously published to the best of our knowledge. I am most grateful to Mrs Jill Kelsey, Deputy Registrar, The Royal Archives, for casting a second pair of eyes over the Royal Archives' copies of the letters, and correcting several transcription errors.

12. The principal people named in these letters are in the *Dramatis Personae* in the endmatter of this book.

13. Augustine Birrell, Chief Secretary for Ireland. The king's description of Birrell's views does not tally with the note made by Stamfordham after the meeting of 24 July, which states that Birrell 'discounted the seriousness of the state of things in Ulster'. [Royal] [A]rchives PS/PSO/GV/C/K/2553 (1)/45. Nor does it tally with Birrell's own version, as reported to HHA on 24 July: MS Asquith 38/109, which begins 'Had an interview with HM. alone . . . I found it very difficult . . . to stem his torrent of *Hearsay*'.

14. Respectively: retired Liberal Lord Chancellor, who in office had vigorously opposed what he proposed in his letter to *The Times*; permanent under-secretary for Ireland, 1901–8; Irish Protestant landowner and peer; MP (Independent Nationalist) for Cork City; Chief Secretary for Ireland; Unionist leader in the Lords and southern Irish landowner; Leader of the Opposition.

15. This and later underlined passages are underlined in the king's copy, presumably either by the king or by Lord Stamfordham, whose working files these are.

16. HHA actually wrote 'impersonal', although this is hard to read because of a deletion. Version III restores 'impersonal'. The king received, apparently by accident, a version which probably appealed more to him than what the prime minister had written. Bodleian Library, MS Asquith 38/160 (holograph); 38/158 (final version).

17. This sentence is added in MS, not (I think) in HHA's hand, in the king's copy. It is not in HHA's holograph but is printed in the final version (Bodleian MS Asquith 38/ 167; 38/162).

18. This paragraph is sidelined in the King's copy.

19. Stress in original.

20. 'comparatively speaking' added in MS, not in the king's hand, in recipient's copy: MS Asquith 38/202.

CHAPTER 13

1. It may be objected that whether or not to have bishops is a matter of *order*, not of doctrine. The Kirk did not finally establish the Presbyterian form of government until 1688/9. But behind that was the issue of the role of *Crown* v. *the Kirk*. When Andrew Melvill told James VI that he was 'not a Lord, nor a Heid, bot a

member . . .' of Christ's Kirk in Scotland (this chapter) he was, I believe, making a claim to possess (the unique) Protestant truth.

2. For a more sophisticated and better-informed defence of establishment, see, however, Leigh (2004) and Adhar and Leigh (2005).

3. Data from http://www.statistics.gov.uk/census2001/profiles/rank/jedi.asp consulted 31.01.2008.

4. Cited from http://www.loc.gov/loc/lcib/9806/danpre.html, consulted 10.03.08. This Library of Congress site gives fascinating links to the political context of the letter, and makes available Jefferson's original text, with his deletions restored with the assistance of the FBI.

5. Cited from http://www.archbishopofcanterbury.org/1575, consulted 10.03.08. The quotation from Shachar (2001: 122).

6. *Percy* v. *Board of National Mission of the Church of Scotland* [2005] UKHL 73. [2006] 2 AC 28; Rodger (2008).

7. 'Bishop loses gay employment case', BBC News online at http://news.bbc.co.uk/1/hi/wales/6904057.stm, consulted 11.03.08. The diocese was later required to pay £47,000 in compensation (and an estimated £50,000 in costs) and the bishop required to take equal-opportunities training. Hannah Fletcher, 'Bishop ordered to have equality training over gay discrimination', *The Times*, 09.02.2008.

8. The main test cases brought by religious advocates, with a summary of the outcomes, are *Shabina Begum* v. *Denbigh High School* [2006] UKHL 15 (Article 9 of the European Convention on Human Rights does not prevent a school from banning wearing of the jilbab); *Azmi* v. *Kirklees Council* [2007] UKEAT 0009/07 (a teaching assistant may be forbidden from wearing a face veil in class); *Playfoot* v. *Millais School Governing Body* [2007] EWHC (Admin) (a school was allowed to ban a Christian student from wearing a 'purity ring'); *Ewada* v. *British Airways* (employment tribunal 2008) (an employee could be banned from wearing a cross at work); *Sarika Singh* v. *Aberdare Girls School* [2008] EWHC 1865 (a school could not ban a Sikh pupil from wearing a Kara bracelet); *Ladele* v. *London Borough of Islington* (employment tribunal 2008): a registrar who had been disciplined for refusing to conduct civil partnership ceremonies had suffered religious discrimination. Transcripts are conveniently available at www.religionlaw.co.uk/casescivil.htm. I acknowledge the work of Neil Addison in compiling the list. Rivers (2000) examines the likely impact of the Human Rights Act s.13, which requires a court to 'have particular regard to the importance . . . of the Convention right to freedom of thought, conscience, and religion'.

9. In the Patronage Act 1711—but Parliament was still using old-style dates, where the new year started on 25 March. The year was actually 1712.

CHAPTER 14

1. A good entry point to the huge US debate on this is Ely (1980) and the review of it by Cox (1981).

2. *Dred Scott* v. *Sanford*, 60 U.S. (19 How.) 393, 425–27 (1857); *Korematsu* v. *United States*, 323 U.S. 214 (1944). The 1857 Court held that Dred Scott, a slave who had

been moved to a free state, was not and never could be a citizen of the United States. The 1944 Court refused to strike down the compulsory removal of Japanese-American citizens after Pearl Harbor.

3. *United States* v. *Carolene Products Company*, 304 U.S. 144 (1938). Wikipedia (entry for *Carolene Products*, consulted 12.01.09) tells me that filled milk is 'skimmed milk compounded with any fat or oil other than milk fat, so as to resemble milk or cream'. All other facts in this paragraph are from Ackerman (1998): 368-82, 489-90. Ely (1980) is a *Carolene*-footnote-based monograph on the proper scope of judicial review.

4. A reader may object that in other numbers of *The Federalist*, especially number 51, Madison comes up with a different solution to the same problem. In number 51 the solution to faction, including the tyranny of the majority, is a set of checks and balances, both vertical (federal–state) and horizontal (separation of legislative, executive, and judicial powers). However, I believe, as do other scholars, that number 10 represents what Madison really thought, whereas numbers 45–51 represent what it was prudent to say in the New York papers in the hope of getting New York to ratify the Constitution. Furthermore, if we trace #10 back to two earlier documents, we may see that the argument began as one about 'religious sects', not one about 'a rage for paper money'. Madison is siding with Adam Smith in an argument Smith had with David Hume about established churches. Smith (and Madison) opposed them; Hume supported them (McLean 2003*b*, 2004; Kernell 2003).

5. *Shaw* v. *Director of Public Prosecutions* [1961] 2 W.L.R. 897; *Ward* v. *Bradford Corporation* (1972) 70 L.G.R. 27.

6. Although the wording of the commitment was slightly odd:

> We shall . . . Take action to abolish the undemocratic House of Lords as quickly as possible and, as an interim measure, introduce a Bill in the first session of parliament to remove its legislative powers – with the exception of those which relate to the life of a parliament.
>
> Source: *Times Guide to the House of Commons 1983*: 325.

7. The reasons for, and components of, bias in the UK electoral system are discussed in for example McLean (2001*a*: Chapter 4) and Rossiter et al. (1999).

8. For the sake of fluency I am assuming that during its lifetime the Constitutional Convention has established a Committee on Style which proposes that the full title of the state is 'the United Republic of Great Britain and Northern Ireland' which may be rendered in short form as 'Urania', with the adjective 'Uranian'. The Committee will have been influenced by Tom Nairn's coinage (2000) 'Ukania'.

9. Eleven the first time around. The first North Carolina state convention rejected the Constitution. It revisited it only after eleven other states had ratified.

10. 'All the powers of government, legislative, executive, and judiciary, result to the legislative body [in the Virginia Constitution of 1776]. The concentrating these in the same hands is precisely the definition of despotic government. It will be no alleviation that these powers will be exercised by a plurality of hands, and not by a

single one. 173 despots would surely be as oppressive as one'. (Jefferson 1784, Query 13)

11. A possible objection is that the Senate could not *force* a government which had decided to ignore a declaration of incompatibility to pay attention, since ignoring it would take the form of doing nothing about the offending statute. But the Senate (assuming it was more constitutionalist than the Commons, as it would likely be given the methods of election I propose) would possess the counter-threat that it could block other legislation until the Commons was prepared to bargain about the declaration of incompatibility. The same threat would be open to the Commons if the boot was on the other foot.

Dramatis Personae

Some of the historical actors discussed in this book are extremely well known. This cast list is restricted to those whom the reader may not instantly recognize, or whose appearance in this book is for an activity for which they are not particularly recognized. (*ODNB: Oxford Dictionary of National Biography,* online edition consulted in January 2009.)

Argyll, John Campbell, second Duke of (1678–1743) Soldier. Lord High Commissioner to the Scottish Parliament, 1705.

Asquith, Herbert Henry (1852–1928) Liberal politician; Prime Minister 1908–15. Master of the formal memorandum and the witty character-sketch, which in 1912–15 was often sent to Venetia Stanley with whom (by letter) he was passionately in love.

Balfour, A. J. (1848–1930) Succeeded his uncle Lord Salisbury as Conservative leader and Prime Minister, 1902; resigned as Conservative leader, 1911, but remained Unionist elder statesman. Golfer and philosopher.

Belhaven, John Hamilton, second Baron (1656–1708). Anti-Union member of the last Scottish Parliament. Famous for anti-Union speech, 1706.

Beresford, John (1738–1805) Irish politician. Privy Councillor, Member of Parliament for County Waterford and revenue commissioner.

Campbell-Bannerman, Sir Henry (1836–1908) Radical ('pro-Boer') Scottish Liberal politician; Prime Minister 1906–8.

Carson, Sir Edward (1854–1935) Irish Protestant lawyer and politician. MP (Unionist) for Dublin University. Acted for Marquess of Queensberry in Oscar Wilde libel case. Leader of Irish Unionists in Commons 1910. Though a southern Irish Anglican, he became the inspirational leader of the Ulster Protestant paramilitary revolt, 1912–14.

Carstares, William (1649–1715) Scottish church leader; chaplain of William of Orange and Principal of University of Edinburgh.

Castlereagh, Robert Stewart, Viscount (1739–1821) Irish Privy Councillor. Enthusiastic and influential supporter of the Irish Union with Great Britain. Later (as Lord Londonderry) Foreign Secretary and Leader of the House of Commons in the Westminster Parliament.

Chalmers, Sir Robert (1858–1938) Chairman, Board of Inland Revenue 1907–11; permanent secretary to the Treasury 1911–13; became governor of Ceylon after falling out with Lloyd George.

Clare, John Fitzgibbon, first Earl of (1748–1802) Lord Chancellor of Ireland. A supporter of Union with Great Britain, his speech of 1800 in the Irish House of Lords marked him as the chief propagandist of the measure.

Clerk of Penicuik, Sir John (1684–1755) Diarist and Scottish Union negotiator who wrote a memoir of the Union.

Cockfield, Arthur, Lord (1916–2007) Conservative politician; Secretary of State for Trade 1982–3. Sent by Margaret Thatcher to be UK Commissioner in the European Commission, 1984–9. Turned single-mindedly to completing the single market, personally drafting the Single European Act implemented in the United Kingdom by the European Communities (Amendment) Act 1986, which led directly to *Factortame*. Not reappointed Commissioner in 1989.

Cornwallis, Charles, first Marquess (1738–1805) Lord-Lieutenant of Ireland, 1797–1801. Previously, unsuccessful British general in American War of Independence: surrendered to George Washington at Yorktown, 1781. Governor General of India 1786–93.

Craig, James (later Lord Craigavon) (1871–1940) Leader of Ulster revolt, later first Prime Minister of Northern Ireland. Belfast-born son of a whiskey distiller. Service in Boer War. MP (Unionist) for East Down 1906–18. '[N]ot an original thinker, nor even a very clever man; but he had the ability to win and keep the confidence of his constituents and his fellow Unionist MPs'—*ODNB*.

Cromwell, Oliver (1599–1658) Leader of parliamentary army in English Civil War. Signed death warrant of Charles I, 1649, then appointed general in charge of English army. Conquered Scotland at battle of Dunbar (1650) and subjugated Ireland. Appointed Lord Protector of England, Scotland, and Ireland 1653.

Defoe, Daniel (1661–1731) Novelist; English spy.

Dicey, A. V. (1835–1922) Vinerian Professor of English Law and fellow of All Souls College, Oxford, 1882–1909. Main exponent of the doctrine of parliamentary sovereignty. Increasingly shrill Unionist ideologue, 1885–1914; coauthored book on 1707 Union with Historiographer-Royal for Scotland, 1920.

Dundas, Henry, first Viscount Melville (1742–1811) Scottish politician. Close ally of Pitt the Younger during the passage of Irish Union.

Edgeworth, Richard Lovell (1744–1817) Engineer and educational writer. British born, but settled in Ireland.

Edward VII (1841–1910) King of Great Britain and Ireland and Emperor of India 1901–10. Son of Victoria, father of George V. Bon vivant, pro-French, Unionist (although not as ideologically so as his mother and son).

Fergusson, Sir Charles, of Kilkerran, seventh Bart. (1865–1951) Army officer. After service in Sudan and Egypt (but not South Africa), in 1914 he held the position of divisional commander of the 5th Division of the British Army, headquartered in the Curragh. The most important and most effective influence in limiting the damage caused by the 'mutiny', an action for which he got no thanks from those whose army he helped to save. Later Governor-General of New Zealand.

Fletcher of Saltoun, Andrew (1655–1716) Member of the last Scottish Parliament. Leading ideologue of the anti-Union side; a country Whig.

Foster, John, first Baron Oriel (1740–1828) Irish politician. As speaker of the Irish House of Commons, he was opposed to the Union, and Catholic emancipation.

Fox, Charles James (1749–1806) English politician. As an opposition leader during the passage of the Act of Union he had an ambivalent position on the statute itself, but was generally sympathetic to Irish patriotism.

George V (1865–1936) King of Great Britain, (Northern) Ireland, and the British dominions overseas 1910–36. Son of Edward VII. An instinctive Unionist before 1914; his advisers were even more so.

George, David Lloyd (1863–1945) Chancellor of the Exchequer 1908–15; Prime Minister 1916–22. Born in Manchester but brought up in Welsh-speaking Wales (and turned his language skills to political advantage). The supreme heresthetician of British politics.

Godolphin, Sidney, first Earl of (1645–1712) English politician; Lord Treasurer between 1703 and 1710.

Gough, Brigadier-General (Sir) Hubert (1870–1963) Cavalry officer. Brought up in Ireland, where 'all our relations were anti-Home-Rulers' (ODNB), in 1914 he was brigadier-general commanding the 3rd cavalry brigade at the Curragh. On-the-spot leader of the 'mutiny' with excellent connections to Unionist politicians and royal circles.

Grattan, Henry (*bap.* 1746–1820) Gifted patriotic orator, and Irish politician under the patronage of the first Earl of Charlemont. Opponent of the Union, although suffered from an illness during its passage which prevented him from campaigning against the measure.

Grenville, William Wyndham, Baron Grenville (1759–1834) As British foreign secretary and a close ally of Pitt, he was a key figure in the creation of the Irish Union.

Hamilton, James Douglas, fourth Duke of (1658–1712) Leader of anti-Union faction in last Scottish Parliament. His domineering mother was more single-minded than him. Missed crucial vote because of "toothache". May have been scheming to restore his claim to the line of royal succession.

Harper, (Sir) Edgar (1860–1934) Land valuation expert, London County Council and London School of Economics. Chief valuer, Inland Revenue, 1915–25.

Ilbert, Sir Courtenay (1841–1924) Constitutional draftsman in India; clerk of the House of Commons 1902–21.

Knollys, (pronounced "Knowles") Francis, first Viscount (1837–1924), private secretary to Prince of Wales, later Edward VII, 1870–1910; joint private secretary to George V 1910–13. Played crucial role, unappreciated by his employer, in saving the British monarchy in November 1910.

Lansdowne, fifth marquess (Henry Charles Keith Petty-Fitzmaurice) (1845–1927) of Irish landowner; Unionist leader in House of Lords 1903–16. At Eton, was fag master to his Commons counterpart A. J. Balfour.

Law, Andrew Bonar (1858–1923) Leader of the Unionist (Conservative) Party 1911–21; Prime Minister 1922–3. Of Scots-Canadian presbyterian origins: the first non-Anglican to lead the Conservatives.

Loughborough, Alexander Wedderburn, baron, later first Earl of Rosslyn (1733–1805) —British Lord Chancellor at the time of the Irish Union, he was a close advisor to King George III.

Mar, John Erskine, sixth Earl of (c.1675–1732) Court politician whose income did not match his ideas of family greatness. Scottish Union Commissioner 1706. Changed sides to lead Jacobite rising, 1715. Died in exile and poverty.

Marlborough, John Churchill, first Duke of (1650–1722) British military leader; victor of Blenheim and Ramillies.

Midleton, St John Brodrick, first Earl of (1856–1942) Irish landowner; leader of the southern Irish landed interest in the House of Lords.

Mottistone: *see* Seely

Murray, Sir George (1849–1936) Joint permanent secretary to HM Treasury 1903–7; sole permanent secretary 1907–11. Denounced his Chancellor behind his back to a political opponent (Lord Rosebery), whose private secretary Murray had been.

Oxford, Robert Harley, first Earl of (1661–1724) English politician; English Commissioner for Union.

Pakington, Sir John (1671–1727) Tory high church leader in English Parliament; opposed Union on grounds that it was inconsistent to support two established churches.

Parnell, Charles Stewart (1846–91) Leader of the Irish Party in the 1880s. MP (Irish Party) 1875–91. Organized Land League to boycott and intimidate landowners 1879–82. Lost leadership 1890 on grounds of his affair with Katharine O'Shea, wife of another Irish Party MP.

Parnell, Sir John (1745–1801) Irish Chancellor of the Exchequer from 1785 until dismissed in 1799 for his opposition to Union. Great-grandfather of Charles Stewart Parnell.

Paterson, William (1658–1719) Scottish banker; founder of Bank of England; promoter of Darien company.

Pitt, William ('the Younger') (1759–1806) British politician; Chancellor of the Exchequer 1783; Prime Minister 1784–1801and 1804–6.

Powell, J. Enoch (1912–1998) Politician. MP (Cons.) for Wolverhampton SW 1950–74; (Ulster Unionist) for Down South 1974–87. Passionate advocate of numerous causes, including parliamentary supremacy, the Union, and opposition to non-white migration to the United Kingdom.

Queensberry, James Douglas, second Duke of (1662–1711) Commissioner to the Scottish Parliament and Secretary of State 1703–5; commissioner 1706. Ancestor of Lord Alfred Douglas (see Carson; Rosebery).

Rainborough [Rainborowe, Rainborow], Thomas, d. 1648. Colonel in Oliver Cromwell's Parliamentary army, later transferred to navy. Spokesman for Levellers in Putney Debates, 1647. Killed by royalists in a skirmish.

Redmond, John (1856–1918) Leader of the Irish Party 1900–18. Militant nationalist on the stump; more accommodating in private. Refused offer of a place in the coalition Cabinet 1915. Destroyed personally and politically by the British suppression of the Easter Rising 1916, after which his party was electorally swamped by Sinn Fein.

Roberts, Field-Marshal Lord (1832–1914) Boer War hero. Of Anglo-Irish extraction but served mostly in the British Empire. Commander-in-chief of British Army 1900–04. In spring 1914 approved letter to be issued in his name advising soldiers unwilling to serve in Ulster to disobey any order to do so.

Rosebery, Archibald Philip Primrose, fifth Earl of (1847–1929) Racehorse owner; Prime Minister 1894–5; while Prime Minister was debilitated by his fringe involvement in the Oscar Wilde—Alfred Douglas affair (Rosebery's private secretary and perhaps lover, who committed suicide in 1894; was Douglas's brother); severed relations with Liberals 1905 but by 1909 still seen by some as a cross-party figure who might broker Lords reform.

Roxburgh[e], John Ker, fifth Earl and first Duke of (d. 1741) Member of the last Scottish Parliament. A member of the *Squadrone Volante*, who switched position from an anti-English to a pro-Union stance over the life of the Scottish parliament of 1703 to 1707. Scottish representative peer, 1707.

Salisbury, Robert Gascoyne-Cecil, third Marquis of (1830–1903) Unionist Prime Minister 1885–6, 1886–92, and 1895–1902. Wily, depressive, extreme conservative; bolstered Unionist veto over all Liberal policies in the House of Lords.

Seafield, James Ogilvy, first Earl of (1664–1730) Commissioner for Union with England; Scottish representative peer, 1707.

Seely, J. E. B. (later Lord Mottistone) (1868–1947) Liberal politician. Served in Boer War. Elected as a Conservative in 1900, crossed floor over protection and 'Chinese labour'. Minister from 1908; Secretary for War 1912–14. Issued orders for protection of munitions in Ulster, March 1914, that led to Curragh 'mutiny'; then gave guarantees to Gough (q.v.) that army would not be used to coerce Ulster. Resigned as minister after Curragh; served as staff officer in the First World War. Nicknamed, sarcastically, 'Modest One' in later life.

Stamfordham, Lord (Arthur Bigge) (1849–1931) Assistant private secretary to Queen Victoria 1879–95; private secretary 1895–1901. Private secretary, Duke of York (later George V), 1901–31.

Tone, Theodore Wolfe (1763–98) Irish Protestant agitator for Catholic emancipation; led the 1798 rebellion.

Tweeddale, John Hay, second Marquis of (1645–1713) Lord High Chancellor of Scotland 1704–5. Became head of *Squadrone Volante*; made representative peer, 1707.

Wellington, Arthur Wellesley, first Duke of (1769–1852) Irish Protestant soldier and politician. Victor of Peninsular War and Waterloo. Prime Minister (Ultra) 1828–30. Leader of the Lords in the Peel Administration 1841–6, where he accepted concessions to Irish Catholics that he had earlier resisted, and used his unique authority to get Peel's controversial legislation through the Lords.

Whiteboys, late eighteenth-century Irish Catholic rural protest movement, who took direct action against Church of Ireland tithes and landlords' rents.

Wilson, (Field-Marshal Sir) Henry (1864–1922) Army officer and plotter. Commandant, Staff College, Camberley, 1907–10; Director of Military Operations, War Office, 1910–14; enthusiastic encourager of Curragh 'mutineers', 1914. Assassinated by Irish nationalists.

References

Unpublished sources

Public Record Office of Northern Ireland, Belfast
  Carson Papers, PRONI D1507.
  Fred Crawford, 'Diary of the gunrunning' PRONI D1700/5/17/2/4.
Churchill College, Cambridge
  Sir William Bull Papers. MSS Bull.
National Archives of Australia, Canberra
  Papers on dismissal of Prime Minister by Governor-General 1975. Attorney-General's Department, *Governor General–Prime Minister: Whether the Governor General has the power to dismiss a Prime Minister.* A432, A1975/7778.
  http://www.naa.gov.au/about-us/publications/fact-sheets/fs240.aspx
  The Dismissal–Advice–Opinion of Solicitor General and Attorney General regarding exercise of the Governor General's powers in constitutional crisis. (The 'Byers–Enderby memorandum' and associated papers). M4081/1. http://naa12.naa.gov.au/scripts/ItemDetail.asp?M=0&B=5450308
National Archives of Scotland, Edinburgh
  Scottish Office, Needs Assessments Studies. 1984–5. SOE6/1/1708–9.
National Library of Scotland, Edinburgh
  Rosebery MSS, NLS MS 10049.
National Archives, Kew
  Cabinet papers CAB 37 (1909–14).
British Library, London
  Walter Long MSS, British Library Add mss 62406.
HM Treasury, London
  1976–9 Needs Assessment: background and service-by-service papers released to me under a Freedom of Information request 2005.
Imperial War Museum, London
  Diaries of (Sir) Henry Wilson. HHW 1.
Parliamentary Archives, London
  Bonar Law Papers. MSS BL.
Bodleian Library, Oxford
  H. H. Asquith Papers, MSS. Asquith.
  Letters of H. H. Asquith to Venetia Stanley. MSS. Eng. c. 7091–8.
  A perfect list of the several persons residenters in Scotland, who have subscribed as adventurers in the joynt-stock of the Company of Scotland trading to Africa and the Indies. Edinburgh, 1696. (5 Delta 277 (4)).

Scottish Parliament 1703–7. Voting list of 6 May 1703.
Nuffield College, Oxford.
Mottistone (J.E.B. Seely) Papers. MSS Mottistone
Royal Archives, Windsor
Correspondence of George V and of Lord Stamfordham with various politicians, 1913–14. PS/PSO/GV/C/K/2553.
Correspondence about the Army in Ireland, 1914. PS/PSO/GV/C/F/674.

Published sources

Ackerman B (1991) *We the People I: Foundations.* (Cambridge, MA: Belknap Press).
—— (1998) *We the People II: Transformations.* (Cambridge, MA: Belknap Press).
Adair D (1974) *Fame and the Founding Fathers,* edited by T. Colburn. (New York: Norton).
Adhar R and Leigh I D (2005) *Religious Freedom in the Liberal State.* (Oxford: Oxford University Press).
Adonis A (1993) *Making Aristocracy Work: The Peerage and the Political System in Britain, 1884–1914.* (Oxford: Clarendon Press).
Anson W (1914) 'Resistance of Ulster: A Comparison and an Analysis', letter to *The Times,* 31 March. From the *Times Online* database.
Austin J (1832/1999) *The Province of Jurisprudence Determined.* (London: John Murray; facsimile reprint by Lawbook Exchange Ltd, Union, NJ).
Avis P (2000) *Church, State and Establishment.* (London: Society for Promoting Christian Knowledge).
Balinski M L and Young H P (2001) *Fair Representation: Meeting the Ideal of One Man, One Vote,* 2nd edn. (Washington, DC: Brookings Institution Press).
Barbour J S (1907) *A History of William Paterson and the Darien Company.* (London: William Blackwood and Sons).
Bayly C A (2000) 'Ireland, India and the Empire: 1780–1914', *Transactions of the Royal Historical Society,* 6th series, 10: 377–97.
Beckett I W F (1986) *The Army and the Curragh Incident, 1914.* (London: Bodley Head for the Army Records Society).
Beckett J C (1966) *The Making of Modern Ireland 1603–1923.* (London: Faber & Faber).
Bellamy R (2007) *Political Constitutionalism: A Republican Defence of the Constitutionality of Democracy.* (Cambridge: Cambridge University Press).
Bentley M (2001) *Lord Salisbury's World: Conservative Environments in Late-Victorian Britain.* (Cambridge: Cambridge University Press).
Bickel A (1962) *The Least Dangerous Branch: The Supreme Court at the Bar of Politics,* 2nd edn. (New Haven, CT: Yale University Press).
Black D (1958) *The Theory of Committees and Elections.* (Cambridge: Cambridge University Press).
Blackstone W (1765–9) *Commentaries on the Laws of England.* (Oxford: Printed at the Clarendon Press). Quoted from the scanned version at http://www.yale.edu/

lawweb/avalon/blackstone/blacksto.htm#intro. The scanning introduces errors, particularly reading long 's' as 'f', which I have silently corrected.

Blake G (1995) 'Some Lessons from the 1924–25 Irish Boundary Commission', *IBRU Boundary and Security Bulletin*, Winter 1995–1996. At http://www.dur.ac. uk/resources/ibru/publications/full/bsb3–4_blake.pdf.

Blake R (1955) *The Unknown Prime Minister: The Life and Times of Andrew Bonar Law 1858–1923*. (London: Eyre and Spottiswoode).

Bogdanor V (1985) 'Dicey and the Reform of the Constitution', *Public Law*, 1985: 652–72.

—— (1995) *The Monarchy and the Constitution*. (Oxford: Oxford University Press).

—— (1996) *Politics and the Constitution: Essays on British Government*. (Aldershot: Dartmouth).

—— (2003). *The British Constitution in the 20th Century*. (Oxford: Oxford University Press for the British Academy).

—— (2006) *The Conflict Between Government and the Judges*. Oxford: Foundation for Law, Justice and Society, Available at http://www.fljs.org/uploads/documents/ Bogdanor_Policy_Brief%231%23.pdf, consulted 12.01.09.

—— (2007) Review of Robert Hazell 'The English Question', *Public Law*, 2007: 169.

—— (2008) 'The Consistency of Dicey: A Reply to McLean and McMillan', *Public Law*, 2008: 19–20.

Bolton G C (1966) *The Passing of the Irish Act of Union: A Study of Parliamentary Politics*. (Oxford: Oxford University Press).

Bowers P (2005) *The Sewel Convention*. House of Commons Library Standard Note: SN/PC/2084. At http://www.parliament.uk/commons/lib/research/notes/ snpc-02084.pdf, accessed 15.12.2008.

Bowring J (ed.) (1843) *The Works of Jeremy Bentham, vol. 2*. (Edinburgh: William Tait).

Braithwaite W J (1957) *Lloyd George's Ambulance Wagon*. (London: Methuen).

Brown K M (1992) *Kingdom or Province? Scotland and the Regal Union 1603–1715*. (Basingstoke: Macmillan).

—— Geoghegan P, and Kelly J (2003) *The Irish Act of Union, 1800: Bicentennial Essays*. (Dublin: Irish Academic Press).

Budge I, Klingemann H D, Volkens A, Bara J, and Tanenbaum E (2001) *Mapping Policy Preferences: Estimates for Parties, Electors, and Governments 1945–1998*. (Oxford: Oxford University Press).

Butler D E and Kavanagh D (1974) *The British General Election of February 1974*. (London: Macmillan).

—— and Kavanagh D (1980) *The British General Election of 1979*. (London: Macmillan).

—— and Kitzinger U (1976) *The 1975 Referendum*. (London: Macmillan).

—— Adonis A, and Travers T (1994) *Failure in British Government: The Politics of the Poll Tax*. (Oxford: Oxford University Press).

Butt Philip A (1975) *The Welsh Question*. (Cardiff: University of Wales Press).

Calman Sir Kenneth (chairman) (2008) *The Future of Scottish Devolution within the Union: A First Report.* Edinburgh: Commission on Scottish Devolution. At http://www.commissiononscottishdevolution.org.uk/uploads/2008–12–01-vol-1-final--bm. pdf, consulted 15.12.2008.

Calvert H (1968) *Constitutional Law in Northern Ireland: A Study in Regional Government.* (London: Stevens).

Campbell J (1993) *Edward Heath: A Biography.* (London: Jonathan Cape).

Ceadel M (2004) 'Cecil (Edgar Algernon) Robert Gascoyne [Lord Robert Cecil], Viscount Cecil of Chelwood (1864–1958)', *Oxford Dictionary of National Biography,* Oxford University Press, Sept 2004; online edn, Jan 2008 [http://www.oxforddnb. com/view/article/32335, accessed 10 Oct 2008].

Cecil Lady Gwendolen (1921–32). *Life of Robert, Marquis of Salisbury,* 4 vols (London: Hodder & Stoughton).

Charity Commission (2008*a*). *Charities and Public Benefit: The Charity Commission's General Guidance on Public Benefit.* (Liverpool: Charity Commission).

—— (2008*b*). *Public Benefit and the Advancement of Religion: Draft Supplementary Guidance for Consultation.* At http://www.charitycommission.gov.uk/Library/public-benefit/pdfs/pbarsum.pdf

Chhibber P and Kollman K (2004) *The Formation of National Party Systems: Federalism and Party Competition in Canada, Great Britain, India, and the United States.* (Princeton, NJ: Princeton University Press).

Claim of Right (1989) 'The Claim of Right of 1988'. Edinburgh: Scottish Constitutional Convention. At http://www.alba.org.uk/devolution/claimofright.html. Publication date given as 1989 because it was then that the Claim was formally signed.

Clerk J (1892) *Memoirs of the Life of Sir John Clerk of Penicuik, Baronet, Baron of the Exchequer, Extracted by Himself from His Own Journals 1676–1755,* edited by John M Gray. (Edinburgh: Edinburgh University Press).

Cockfield Francis Arthur, Baron *The European Union: creating the single market* (London: Wiley Chancery Law).

Colomer J M (1995) *Game Theory and the Transition to Democracy: The Spanish Model.* (Aldershot: Edward Elgar).

Constitution Unit (2007) *Monitor* 36, May. At http://www.ucl.ac.uk/constitution-unit/files/publications/monitor/Monitor_36.pdf.

Cox A (1981) Review of *Democracy and Distrust: A Theory of Judicial Review* by John Hart Ely. *Harvard Law Review* 94:3, pp. 700–16.

Cox G W (1997) *Making Votes Count: Strategic Coordination in the World's Electoral Systems.* (Cambridge: Cambridge University Press).

Command Papers (all published by HMSO, London):

   Cmnd 3301 (1967) *Legal and Constitutional Implications of United Kingdom Membership of the European Communities.*

   Cmnd 4715 (1971) *The United Kingdom and the European Communities.*

   Cmnd 5999 (1975) *Membership of the European Community.*

*Complaynt of Scotland (c.*1549) Probably by Robert Wedderburn. Available at http://www.scotsindependent.org/features/scots/complaynt/index.htm.

Conservative Party (2001) *Time for Common Sense: 2001 Conservative Party General Election Manifesto* at http://www.conservative-party.net/manifestos/2001/2001-conservative-manifesto.shtml#democracy.

Craig F W S (1974) '*British Parliamentary Election Results 1885–1918.* (London: Macmillan).

Craig P (2007) 'Britain in the European Union', in J Jowell and D Oliver (2007 eds), *The Changing Constitution.* (Oxford: Oxford University Press), pp. 84–107.

Cranmer F and Peterson S (2006) 'Employment, Sex Discrimination and the Churches: The Percy Case', *Ecclesiastical Law Journal* 8, 392–405.

Crockett A and Crockett R (2006) 'Consequences of Data Heaping in the British Religious Census of 1851', *Historical Methods: A Journal of Quantitative and Inter-disciplinary History,* 39:(1): 24–46.

Crowson N J (2007) *The Conservative Party and European Integration Since 1945: At the Heart of Europe?* (Abingdon: Routledge).

Cullen L M (1968) *Anglo-Irish Trade 1660–1800.* (Manchester: Manchester University Press).

—— (2000) 'Alliances and Misalliances in the Politics of the Union', *Transactions of the Royal Historical Society,* 6th series, 10: 221–41.

Dáil Eireann (1972) *Private Sessions of the Second Dail. Minutes of Proceedings 18.8.1921 to 14.9.1921 and Report of Debates 14.12.1921 to 6.1.1922.* Dublin: Stationery Office.

Dalrymple, J 1st Viscount Stair (1681) *The Institutions of the Law of Scotland,* 2 vols. (Edinburgh).

Dangerfield G (1970) *The Strange Death of Liberal England.* (London: Paladin). Originally published 1936.

Devine T M (2003) *Scotland's Empire, 1600–1815.* (London: Allen Lane).

Dicey A V (1885/1915) *Introduction to the Study of the Law of the Constitution.* London: Macmillan. Citations in text are to the 8th (1915) ed., the last edited by Dicey, republished in facsimile Indianapolis: Liberty Classics (1982).

—— (1886) *England's Case Against Home Rule.* (London: John Murray).

—— (1887) *Letters on Unionist Delusions.* (London: Spectator).

—— (1890) *The Verdict: A Tract on the Political Significance of the Report of the Parnell Commission,* 2nd edn. (London: Cassell).

—— (1893/1911) *A Leap in the Dark: A Criticism of the Principles of Home Rule as Illustrated by the Bill of 1893,* 2nd edn. (London: John Murray).

—— (1905) *Lectures on the Relation Between Law and Public Opinion in England During the Nineteenth Century.* (London: Macmillan).

—— (1913) *A Fool's Paradise: Being a Constitutionalist's Criticism on [sic] the Home Rule Bill of 1912.* (London: John Murray).

—— and Rait R S (1920) *Thoughts on the Union Between England and Scotland.* (London: Macmillan).

Dickson P G M (1967) *The Financial Revolution in England: A Study in the Development of Public Credit 1688–1756.* (London: Macmillan).

Ditchfield G M, Hayton D, and Jones C (eds) (1995) *British Parliamentary Lists, 1660–1800: A Register*. (London: Hambledon Press).

Dorey P (2008) 'Stumbling Through "Stage Two": New Labour and House of Lords Reform', *British Politics* 3: 22–44.

Doyle W (2000) 'The British-Irish Union of 1801: The Union in a European Context', *Transactions of the Royal Historical Society*, 6th series, 10: 165–80.

Dunlop A I (1967) *William Carstares and the Kirk by Law Established*. (Edinburgh: Saint Andrew Press).

Duverger M (1954) *Political Parties*. (New York: Wiley).

Dymond G and Deadman H (2006) *The Salisbury Doctrine*. House of Lords Library Note LLN 2006/006, 30 June. At http://www.parliament.uk/documents/upload/HLLSalisburyDoctrine.pdf.

Ehrman J (1969) *The Younger Pitt: The Years of Acclaim*. (London: Constable).

Electoral Commission (2003) *Distribution Between Electoral Regions of UK MEPs*. London: Electoral Commission.

—— (2007) *Distribution Between Electoral Regions of UK MEPs: Recommendation July 2007*. London: Electoral Commission. At http://www.electoralcommission.org.uk/__data/assets/electoral_commission_pdf_file/0017/16073/MEPs-Report-Web-Final_27140–20067__E__N__S__W__.pdf.

Ely J H (1980) *Democracy and Distrust: A Theory of Judicial Review*. (Cambridge, MA: Harvard University Press).

Ensor R C K (1936) *England 1870–1914*. (Oxford: Clarendon Press).

Fair J D (1971) 'The King, the Constitution, and Ulster: Interparty Negotiations of 1913 and 1914', *Eire-Ireland* 6(1): 35–52.

Felsenthal D S and Machover M (1998) *The Measurement of Voting Power*. (Cheltenham: Edward Elgar).

Ferguson W (1968) *Scotland, 1689 to the Present*. (Edinburgh: Oliver & Boyd).

—— (1977) *Scotland's Relations with England: A Survey to 1707*. (Edinburgh: John Donald).

Fletcher of Saltoun, Andrew (1698). 'Two Discourses Concerning the Affairs of Scotland' in J Robertson (ed., 1997), *Andrew Fletcher: Political Works*. (Cambridge: Cambridge University Press), pp. 33–81.

—— (1703) 'Speeches by a Member of the Parliament which Began at Edinburgh the 6th of May, 1703', in J Robertson (ed., 1997), *Andrew Fletcher: Political Works*. (Cambridge: Cambridge University Press), pp. 129–73.

Fortescue J W (1914) *Military History*. (Cambridge: Cambridge University Press).

Foster R F (1989) *Modern Ireland 1600–1972*. (Harmondsworth: Penguin). Originally published by Allen Lane in 1988.

—— (1995) *Paddy & Mr Punch: Connections in Irish and English History*. (London: Penguin).

Freedom House (annual since 1972) *Freedom in the World*. Washington DC: Freedom House. At http://www.freedomhouse.org/uploads/FIWAllScores.xls.

Fry M (2001) *The Scottish Empire*. (Edinburgh: Tuckwell Press and Birlinn).

Galligan B (1995) *A Federal Republic: Australia's constitutional system of government.* (Cambridge: Cambridge University Press).

Geoghegan P M (1999) *The Irish Act of Union: A Study in High Politics 1798–1801.* (Dublin: Gill and Macmillan).

George H (1882/1911) *Progress and Poverty.* (London: Dent/Everyman).

Gilbert B B (1978) 'David Lloyd George: The Reform of British Landholding and the Budget of 1914', *Historical Journal* 22: 117–41.

Gilbert W S (1882) *Iolanthe: Or the Peer and the Peri.* (London: Chappell). Available at: http://math.boisestate.edu/gas/iolanthe/iollib.pdf.

Gillingham J (2003) *European Integration, 1950–2003: Superstate or New Market Economy?* (Cambridge: Cambridge University Press).

Goldie M (1996) 'Divergence and Union: Scotland and England, 1660–1707', in B Bradshaw and J Morill (eds), *The British Problem, c.1534–1707: State Formation in the Atlantic Archipelago.* (London: Macmillan), pp. 220–45.

Griffith J A G (1977) *The Politics of the Judiciary.* (Glasgow: Fontana/Collins).

Gwynn D (1950) *The History of Partition (1912–1925).* (Dublin: Browne & Nolan).

Hadfield B (1989) *The Constitution of Northern Ireland.* (Belfast: SLS Legal).

Hague W (2004) *William Pitt the Younger.* (London: HarperCollins).

Hailsham Lord (Quintin Hogg) (1976). 'Elective Dictatorship'. The Richard Dimbleby Lecture. At http://law.uts.edu.au/~chriscl/hailsham.html.

Halévy E (1961) *A History of the English People in the Nineteenth Century, vol. 5: Imperialism and the Rise of Labour,* paperback edn. (London: Ernest Benn).

Hall F G (1949) *The Bank of Ireland 1783–1946.* (Dublin: Hodges Figgis).

Hallerberg M (2004) *Domestic Budgets in a United Europe: Fiscal Governance from the End of Bretton Woods to EMU.* (Ithaca, NY: Cornell University Press).

—— and Maier P (2004) 'Executive Authority, the Personal Vote, and Budget Discipline in Latin American and Caribbean Countries', *American Journal of Political Science* 48(3): 57–187.

Hand G (ed.) (1969) *Report of the Irish Boundary Commission 1925.* (Dublin: Irish University Press).

Hardin G (1968) 'The tragedy of the commons', *Science,* vol. 162. no. 3859, pp. 1243–8, 13 December.

Hart H L A (1961) *The Concept of Law.* (Oxford: Clarendon Press).

Hayton D (1996) 'Traces of Party Politics in early Eighteenth-Century Scottish Elections' in C Jones (ed.), *The Scots and Parliament.* (Edinburgh: Edinburgh University Press), pp. 74–99.

—— (2008) 'Adjustment and Integration: The Scottish Representation in the British House of Commons, 1707–14', *Parliamentary History* 27: 410–35.

Hazell R (ed.) (1999) *Constitutional Futures: A History of the Next Ten Years.* (Oxford: Oxford University Press).

—— (2008a) 'The Acts of Union – the Next Thirty Years'. Sunningdale Accountability Lecture 29 January. At https://www.ucl.ac.uk/constitution-unit/files/staff/Accountability_Lecture.pdf, consulted 21.05.08.

—— (ed.) (2008*b*) *Constitutional Futures Revisited: Britain's Constitution to 2020*. (Basingstoke: Palgrave Macmillan).

Heald D (1980) 'Territorial Equity and Public Finances: Concepts and Confusion'. University of Strathclyde, Centre for the Study of Public Policy, Studies in Public Policy no. 75.

HM Government (1975) *Britain's New Deal in Europe*. (London: HMSO).

—— (2007) *The Governance of Britain*, Cm 7170. Norwich: HMSO. Available online at http://www.official-documents.gov.uk/document/cm71/7170/7170.pdf.

—— (2008) *The Governance of Britain – Constitutional Renewal*, Cm 7342. Norwich: HMSO. Available online at http://www.justice.gov.uk/docs/constitutional-renewal-white-paper.pdf.

HM Government Scotland Office (2008). *Government Evidence to the Commission on Scottish Devolution*. Available at http://www.commissiononscottishdevolution.org.uk/uploads/2008–11–10-hmg.pdf.

HM Treasury (1979) *Needs Assessment Study – Report*. (London: HM Treasury).

Hiebert J (1996) *Limiting Rights: The Dilemma of Judicial Review*. (Montreal: McGill-Queens University Press).

—— (2002) *Charter Conflicts: What Is Parliament's Role?* (Montreal: McGill University Press).

Hopkinson M (2002) *The Irish War of Independence*. (Dubliln: Gill and Macmillan).

Horowitz D L (1991) *A Democratic South Africa? Constitutional Engineering in a Divided Society*. (Berkeley, CA: University of California Press).

Howe G (1973) 'The European Communities Act 1972', *International Affairs* 49(1): 1–13.

Ickes H L (1953) *The Secret Diary of Harold L. Ickes: The First Thousand Days 1933–1936*, edited by J. D. Ickes. (New York: Simon & Schuster).

Insh G P (1932) *The Company of Scotland Trading to Africa and the Indies*. (London: Charles Scribner's Sons).

Iversen T and Soskice D (2006) 'Electoral Institutions and the Politics of Coalitions: Why Some Democracies Distribute More Than Others', *American Political Science Review*, 100: 165–81.

Jackson A (1989) *The Ulster Party: Irish Unionists in the House of Commons, 1884–1911*. (Oxford: Clarendon Press).

—— (1999) *Ireland 1798–1998: Politics and War*. (Oxford: Blackwell).

—— (2003) *Home Rule: An Irish History 1800–2000*. (London: Weidenfeld & Nicolson).

Jalland P (1980) *The Liberals and Ireland: The Ulster Question in British Politics to 1914*. (Brighton: Harvester).

Jay D (1937) *The Socialist Case*. (London: Faber & Faber).

Jenkins R (1964). *Asquith*. (London: Collins).

—— (1968) *Mr Balfour's Poodle*, 2nd edn. (London: Collins).

—— (1992) *A Life at the Centre*. (London: Pan Books).

Jennings W I (1933/1965) *The Law and the Constitution*, 5th edn. (London: University of London Press).

—— (1941) *The British Constitution*. (Cambridge: Cambridge University Press).

—— (1959) *Cabinet Government*, 3rd edn. (Cambridge: Cambridge University Press). Originally published in 1936.

Johnston E M (1963) *Great Britain and Ireland 1760–1800: A Study in Public Administration*. (Edinburgh: Oliver and Boyd).

Johnston-liik E M (2002) *History of the Irish Parliament 1692–1800*. (Belfast: Ulster Historical Foundation).

Joint Committee On Human Rights (2008) *Thirty-First Report*, Session 2007–08. At http://www.publications.parliament.uk/pa/jt200708/jtselect/jtrights/173/17302.htm.

Jones W D (2001) '"Bold Adventurers": A Quantitative Analysis of the Darien Subscription List (1696)', *Scottish Economic and Social History*, 21(1): 22–42.

Jowell J (2007) 'The Rule of Law and Its Underlying Values', in J Jowell and D Oliver (eds), *The Changing Constitution*. (Oxford: Oxford University Press), pp. 5–24.

—— And Oliver D (eds) (1985, 1989, 2000, 2007) *The Changing Constitution*. (Oxford: Oxford University Press). 2nd edn. 1989. 4th edn. 2000, 6th edn. 2007.

Jupp P (2000) 'Britain and the Union, 1797–1801', *Transactions of the Royal Historical Society*, 6th series, 10: 197–219.

Justice (2007) *A British Bill of Rights: Informing the Debate*. (London: Justice). Available at http://www.justice.org.uk/publication/listofpublications/index.html

Kernell S (2003) 'Introduction and The True Principles of Republican Government: Reassessing James Madison's Political Science', in S Kernell (ed.), *James Madison: The Theory and Practice of Republican Government* (Stanford, CA: Stanford University Press): 1–13 and 92–125.

King A (2007) *The British Constitution*. (Oxford: Oxford University Press).

Kyvig D E (1996) *Explicit and Authentic Acts: Amending the U.S. Constitution, 1776–1995*. (Lawrence, KS: University Press of Kansas).

Labour Party (1997) *New Labour Because Britain Deserves Better: Britain Will Be Better with New Labour*. London: Labour Party. At http://www.bbc.co.uk/election97/background/parties/manlab/labman.html.

—— (1999) *Reforming the House of Lords for the New Millennium: Submission by the Labour Party to the Royal Commission on the reform of the House of Lords*. (London: Labour Party).

Latham J (1952) 'Interpretation of the Constitution' in R Else-Mitchell (ed.), *Essays on the Australian Constitution*. (Sydney: Law Book Co. of Australia), pp. 1–50).

Lawson P (1993) *The East India Company: A History*. (London: Longman).

Lecky W E H (1902) *A History of Ireland in the Eighteenth Century*, vol. 2. (London: Longmans).

Leigh I D (2004) 'By Law Established? The Church of England and Constitutional Reform', *Public Law*, 266–73.

Lester A and Beattie K (2007) 'Human Rights and the British Constitution' in J Jowell and D Oliver (eds), *The Changing Constitution*. (Oxford: Oxford University Press), pp. 59–83.

Locke J (1690/1988) *Two Treatises of Government* edited by Peter Laslett. (Student edn, Cambridge: Cambridge University Press).

Loughlin J (2007) *The British Monarchy and Ireland: 1800 to the Present.* (Cambridge: Cambridge University Press).

Loughlin M (2007) 'The Constitutional Thought of the Levellers', *Current Legal Problems*, 60: 1–39.

Low S (1904) *The Governance of England.* (London: T. Fisher Unwin).

Maccormick N (1998) 'The English Constitution, the British State, and the Scottish Anomaly', *Proceedings of the British Academy*, 101: 289–306.

Madison J (1787/1987) *Notes of Debates in the Federal Convention*, edited by A Koch. (New York: W. W. Norton).

—— Hamilton A, and Jay J (1788/1987) *The Federalist*, edited by Isaac Kramnick. (New York: Viking Penguin).

Mallet B (1913) *British Budgets 1887–8 to 1912–13.* (London: Macmillan).

Marquand D (2008*a*) *Britain since 1918: The Strange Career of British Democracy.* (London: Weidenfeld & Nicolson).

—— (2008*b*). 'The Democratic Republican Tradition in Britain' in S White and D Leighton (eds) *Building a Citizen Society: The Emerging Politics of Republican Democracy.* (London: Lawrence & Wishart), pp. 23–32.

Mathieson W L (1905) *Scotland and the Union: A History of Scotland from 1695 to 1747.* (Glasgow: James Maclehose and Sons).

Matthew H C G (1995) *The Gladstone Diaries xi. 1883–1886.* (Oxford: Clarendon Press).

—— (1999) *Gladstone 1809–1898.* (Oxford: Oxford University Press).

Marx K (1852) 'The elections in England – Tories and Whigs', *New York Daily Tribune* August 21. In *Karl Marx and Frederick Engels on Britain* (Moscow: Foreign Languages Publishing House, 1962), pp. 351–7.

McCavery T (2000) 'Politics, Public Finance and the British–Irish Act of Union of 1801', *Transactions of the Royal Historical Society*, 6th series, 10: 353–75.

McCrudden C (2007) 'Northern Ireland and the British Constitution under the Belfast Agreement', in J Jowell and D Oliver (eds), *The Changing Constitution.* (Oxford: Oxford University Press), pp. 227–70.

McDowell R B (1943) *Irish Public Opinion 1750–1800.* (London: Faber and Faber).

—— (1979) *Ireland in the Age of Imperialism and Revolution 1760–1801.* (Oxford: Clarendon Press).

Macinnes A I (1990) 'Influencing the Vote: The Scottish Estates and the Treaty of Union, 1706–1707', *History Microcomputer Review*, 11–25.

Mackay of Clashfern, Lord (chairman) (1999) *Report of the Constitutional Commission.* (London: Mackay Commission).

McKenzie R T and Silver A (1968) *Angels in Marble: Working-Class Conservatives in Urban England.* (London: Heinemann).

McKinstry L (2005) *Rosebery: Statesman in Turmoil.* (London: John Murray).

McLean I (1969) *Scottish Nationalism: Its Growth and Development, with Particular Reference to the Period since 1961.* Oxford University B. Phil Thesis in Politics.

—— (1995) 'Are Scotland and Wales Over-represented in the House of Commons?', *Political Quarterly* 66: 250–68.

—— (1996) 'E.J. Nanson, Social Choice and Electoral Reform', *Australian Journal of Political Science* 31(3): 369–85.

—— (2001a) *Rational Choice and British Politics: An Analysis of Rhetoric and Manipulation from Peel to Blair.* (Oxford: Oxford University Press).

—— (2001b) 'The national question', in A. Seldon (ed.), *The Blair Effect: The Blair Government 1997–2001.* (London: Little, Brown), pp. 429–47.

—— (2003a) 'Two Analytical Narratives about the History of the EU', *European Union Politics* 4(4): 499–506.

—— (2003b) 'Before and After Publius: The Sources and Influence of Madison's Political Thought' in S Kernell (ed.), *James Madison: The Theory and Practice of Republican Government* (Stanford, CA: Stanford University Press), pp. 14–40.

—— (2004) 'Thomas Jefferson, John Adams, and the *Déclaration des droits de l'homme et du citoyen*' in R Fatton Jr and R K Ramazani (eds), *The Future of Liberal Democracy: Thomas Jefferson and the Contemporary World* (New York: Palgrave Macmillan), pp. 13–30.

—— (2005) *The Fiscal Crisis of the United Kingdom.* (Basingstoke: Palgrave).

—— (2006) *Adam Smith, Radical and Egalitarian: An Interpretation for the 21st Century.* (Edinburgh: Edinburgh University Press).

—— (2008) 'Climate Change and UK Politics: From Brynle Williams to Sir Nicholas Stern', *Political Quarterly*, 79: 184–93.

—— (2009) 'Lessons from the Aberfan Disaster and Its Aftermath', *British Academy Review*, 12: 49–52.

—— and Foster C D (1992) 'The Political Economy of Regulation: Interests, Ideology, Voters and the UK Regulation of Railways Act 1844', *Public Administration* 70: 313–31.

—— and Johnes M (2000) *Aberfan: Government and Disasters.* (Cardiff: Welsh Academic Press).

—— and Linsley B (2004) *The Church of England and the State: Reforming Establishment for a Multi-faith Britain.* (London: New Politics Network).

—— and McMillan A (2005) *State of the Union: Unionism and the Alternatives in the United Kingdom since 1707.* (Oxford: Oxford University Press).

—— and Shephard N (2004) *A Program to Implement the Condorcet and Borda Rules in a Small-n Election.* Nuffield College Working Papers in Politics, 2004-W11. At: http://www.nuffield.ox.ac.uk/Politics/papers/2004/McLean%20and%20Shephard.pdf.

—— Spirling A, and Russell M (2003) 'None of the Above: The UK House of Commons Votes on Reforming the House of Lords, February 2003', *Political Quarterly*, 74(3): 298–310.

—— Lodge G, and Schmuecker K (2008) *Fair Shares? Barnett and the Politics of Public Expenditure.* (London and Newcastle-upon-Tyne: IPPR and IPPR North).

McNeill P G B and MacQueen H L (eds) (1996). *Atlas of Scottish History to 1707.* (Edinburgh: University of Edinburgh Press).

McNeill R (1922) *Ulster's Stand for Union.* (London: John Murray).

Mill J S (1859/1910) *On Liberty.* (London: Dent/Everyman).

Ministry of Justice (2008) *An Elected Second Chamber: Further reform of the House of Lords.* Cm 7438. (London: TSO). Available online at http://www.justice.gov.uk/docs/elected-second-chamber.pdf.

—— (2009) *Responding to Human Rights Judgments: Government Response to the Joint Committee on Human Rights' Thirty-first Report of Session 2007–08*. Cm 7524. (London: TSO). At http://www.justice.gov.uk/docs/responding-human-rights-judgments.pdf.

Mitchell J (2006) 'Undignified and Inefficient: Financial Relations Between London and Stormont', *Contemporary British History*, 20/1: 57–73.

Mitchison R (1983) *Lordship to Patronage: Scotland 1603–1745*. (London: Edward Arnold).

Moravcsik A (1998) *The Choice for Europe: Social Purpose and State Power from Messina to Maastricht*. (Ithaca, NY: Cornell University Press).

Morgan K O (1963/1991) *Wales in British Politics*, 4th edn. (Cardiff: University of Wales Press).

—— and Morgan J (1980) *Portrait of a Progressive: The Political Career of Christopher, Viscount Addison*. (Oxford: Clarendon Press).

Morris-Jones W H (1948) 'Parliament Bill, 1947: Agreed Statement on Conclusion of Conference of Party Leaders, February–April, 1948. (Cmd. 7380)', *The Modern Law Review*, 11(3): 332–5.

Murray B K (1980) *The People's Budget 1909/10*. (Oxford: Clarendon Press).

Muscatelli A (Chairman) (2008) *First Evidence from the Independent Expert Group to the Commission on Scottish Devolution*. Edinburgh: Heriot-Watt University. At http://www.hw.ac.uk/reference/ieg-first-evidence.pdf, consulted 15.12.2008.

Nairn T (2000) 'Ukania under Blair', *New Left Review*, January–February. Available online at http://www.newleftreview.org/?view=2095, consulted 14.01.09.

Namier Sir L and Brooke J (eds) (1964) *The House of Commons, 1754–1790*, 3 vols. (London: Published for the History of Parliament Trust by HMSO).

Nelson W E (1988) *The Fourteenth Amendment: From Political Principle to Judicial Doctrine*. (Cambridge, MA: Harvard University Press).

Nicolson H (1952) *King George V: His Life and Reign*. (London: Constable).

Oates W (1972) *Fiscal Federalism*. (New York: Harcourt Brace Jovanovich).

O'Brien P K (1988) 'The Political Economy of British Taxation, 1660–1815', *Economic History Review*, 2nd series, 41(1): 1–32.

O'Domhnaill R (2004) 'Curragh Mutiny in Historical, Legal and Constitutional Perspective', *Royal United Services Institute Journal* 149(1): 80–4.

O'Donnell G (2005) 'The Economy and the State' in Office of the Civil Service Commissioners, *Changing Times: Leading Perspectives on the Civil Service in the 21st Century and Its Enduring Values* (London: OCSC, n.d., *c*.2005), pp. 76–87.

Offer A (1981) *Property and Politics 1870–1914: Landownership, Law, Ideology and Urban Development in England*. (Cambridge: Cambridge University Press).

—— (1983) 'Empire and Social Reform: British Overseas Investment and Domestic Politics', *Historical Journal*, 26: 119–38.

Olson M (2000) *Power and Prosperity: Outgrowing Communist and Capitalist Dictatorships*. (New York: Basic Books).

ONS (Office for National Statistics) (2007) *UK Electoral Statistics—Local Government and Parliamentary Electors 2007*. At http://www.statistics.gov.uk/ STATBASE/Product.asp?vlnk=319.

Parliament Bill: Agreed Statement on Conclusion of Conference of Party Leaders, February–April 1948 Cmd 7380. (London: HMSO).

Penrose L S (1946) 'The Elementary Statistics of Majority Voting', *Journal of the Royal Statistical Society*, 109: 53–7.

Persson T and Tabellini G (2002) 'Do Constitutions Cause Large Governments? Quasi-experimental Evidence', *European Economic Review*, 46: 908–18.

—— (2005) *The Economic Effects of Constitutions*, MIT Paperback edn. (Cambridge, MA: MIT University Press).

Peterson, M (ed.) (1984) *Thomas Jefferson: Writings*. (New York: Library of America).

Peterson S and Mclean I (2007) 'Of Wheat, the Church in Wales and the West Lothian Question', *Welsh History Review* 23(3): 151–74.

Powell E (1977) *Joseph Chamberlain*. (London: Thames & Hudson).

Prochaska F (2004) 'Lascelles, Sir Alan Frederick (1887–1981)', in H C G Matthew and B Harrison (eds), *Oxford Dictionary of National Biography* (Oxford: Oxford University Press). Online edn, edited by Lawrence Goldman, January 2008. http://www. oxforddnb.com/view/article/31334 (accessed September 11, 2008).

Pryde G S (1950) *The Treaty of Union of Scotland and England*. (London: Nelson).

Pugh M (1985) *The Tories and the People 1880–1935*. (Oxford: Basil Blackwell).

Rait R S (1901) *The Scottish Parliament before the Union of the Crowns*. (London: Blackie and Son).

Rakove J N (1999) 'The Super-Legality of the Constitution, or, a Federalist Critique of Bruce Ackerman's Neo-Federalism', *Yale Law Journal* 108: 1931–58.

Reilly B (2001) *Democracy in Divided Societies: Electoral Engineering for Conflict Management*. (Cambridge: Cambridge University Press).

Reilly R (1979) *William Pitt the Younger*. (New York: G. P. Putnam's Sons).

Riker W H (1986) *The Art of Political Manipulation*. (New Haven, CT: Yale University Press).

Riker W H (1996) *The Strategy of Rhetoric: Campaigning for the American Constitution*. (New Haven, CT: Yale University Press).

Riley P W J (1964) *The English Ministers and Scotland 1707–1727*. (London: Athlone Press).

—— (1968) 'The Scottish Parliament of 1703', *Scottish Historical Review* 47(143): 129–50.

—— (1978) *The Union of England and Scotland: A Study in Anglo-Scottish Politics of the 18th Century*. (Manchester: Manchester University Press).

Rivers J (2000) 'From Toleration to Pluralism: Religious Liberty and Religious Establishment under the United Kingdom's Human Rights Act' in R J Adhar (ed.) *Law and Religion* (Aldershot: Ashgate), pp. 133–61.

Robertson J (1995) 'An Elusive Sovereignty: The Course of the Union Debate in Scotland 1698–1707' in J Robertson (ed.), *A Union for Empire: Political*

Thought and the British Union of 1707 (Cambridge: Cambridge University Press), pp. 198–227.

—— (ed.) (1997) *Andrew Fletcher: Political Works*. (Cambridge: Cambridge University Press).

Robson W A (1928) *Justice and Administrative Law: A Study of the British Constitution*. (London: Macmillan).

Rodger of Earlsferry, Lord (2008) *The Courts, the Church and the Constitution: Aspects of the Disruption of 1843*. (Edinburgh: Edinburgh University Press).

Rose K (1983) *King George V*. (London: Weidenfeld & Nicolson).

Rossiter D J, Johnston R J, Pattie C J, Dorling D F L, Macallister I and Tunstall H (1999) 'Changing Biases in the Operation of the UK's Electoral System, 1950–97', *British Journal of Politics and International Relations*, 1: 133–164.

Russell M (2007) 'Peers' and Public Attitudes to the Contemporary House of Lords: Briefing for a seminar in the *House of Lords*, 12 December 2007', London: Constitution Unit. At http://www.ucl.ac.uk/constitution-unit/files/research/parliament/lords/survey-results2007.pdf.

—— (2009) 'House of Lords Reform: Are We Nearly There Yet?', *Political Quarterly*, 80 (1): 119–25.

—— and Sciara M (2007) 'The Policy Impact of Defeats in the House of Lords'. Paper presented to the *Political Studies Association Conference, University of Bath*, 11–13 April 2007.

Saville R (1996) *Bank of Scotland: A History 1695–1995*. (Edinburgh: Edinburgh University Press).

Schofield P (2006) *Utility and Democracy: The Political Thought of Jeremy Bentham*. (Oxford: Oxford University Press).

Schumpeter J A (1943/1954) *Capitalism, Socialism, and Democracy*, 4th edn. (London: Unwin University Books).

Scott P H (1992) *Andrew Fletcher and the Treaty of Union*. (Edinburgh: John Donald).

Scott W R (1911) *The Constitution and Finance of English, Scottish and Irish Joint-Stock Companies to 1720: Vol. III, Water Supply, Postal, Street-Lighting, Manufacturing, Banking, Finance and Insurance Companies. Also Statements Relating to the Crown Finances*. (Cambridge: Cambridge University Press).

Shachar A (2001) *Multicultural Jurisdictions: Cultural Differences and Women's Rights*. (Cambridge: Cambridge University Press).

Sedley S (2008) 'The Spark in the Ashes: The Constitutional Ideas of the Levellers in the English Civil War' in C Geiringer and D Knight (eds), *Seeing the World Whole: Essays in Honour of Sir Kenneth Keith* (Wellington: Victoria University Press).

Senex [said to be Sir A. F. Lascelles] (1950) 'Dissolution of Parliament: Factors in Crown's Choice', letter to *The Times*, 2 May. From the *Times Online* database.

Sharp A (1998) *The English Levellers*. (Cambridge: Cambridge University Press).

Smith A (1776/1981) *An Inquiry into the Nature and Causes of the Wealth of Nations*, 2 vols. (Indianapolis: Liberty Fund).

Smith J (1993) 'Bluff, Bluster and Brinkmanship: Andrew Bonar Law and the Third Home Rule Bill', *Historical Journal*, 36: 161–78.

Smith Sir David (2005) *Head of State: The Governor-General, the Monarchy, the Republic and the Dismissal.* (Sydney: Macleay Press).

Smout T C (1963) *Scottish Trade on the Eve of Union 1603–1707.* (Edinburgh: Oliver & Boyd).

—— (1964) 'The Anglo-Scottish Union of 1707: I. The Economic Background', *Economic History Review* 41(3): 439–67.

—— (1969) *A History of the Scottish People 1560–1830.* (London: Collins).

Sorabjee S J (2004) 'Rights and Human Rights in the Modern World: the experience of working the Bill of Rights in the Indian Constitution' in R Fatton Jr and R K Ramazani (eds), *The Future of Liberal Democracy: Thomas Jefferson and the Contemporary World* (Basingstoke: Palgrave Macmillan 2004), pp. 115–21.

Speck W A (1994) *The Birth of Britain: A New Nation 1700–1710.* (Oxford: Blackwell).

Spender J A and Asquith C (1932) *Life of Herbert Henry Asquith, Lord Oxford and Asquith.* 2 vols. (London: Hutchinson).

Stair: *see* Dalrymple.

Stephen J (2007) *Scottish Presbyterians and the Act of Union 1707.* (Edinburgh: Edinburgh University Press).

Stewart A T Q (1967) *The Ulster Crisis.* (London: Faber & Faber).

—— (1993) *A Deeper Silence: The Hidden Roots of the United Irish Movement.* (London: Faber & Faber).

Stone Sweet A (2000) *Governing with Judges: Constitutional Politics in Europe.* (Oxford: Oxford University Press).

Strachan H (1997) *The Politics of the British Army.* (Oxford: Clarendon Press).

Strauss E (1951) *Irish Nationalism and British Democracy.* (London: Methuen).

Surridge K (1997) All You Soldiers Are What We Call Pro-Boer: The Military Critique of the South African War, 1899–1902', *History*, 82: 582–600.

The Acts of the Parliaments of Scotland: 1424–1707 (2nd edn, 1966). (London: HMSO).

Times (1951) *The Times House of Commons 1951.* (London: Times Books).

—— (1974) *The Times Guide to the House of Commons February 1974.* (London: Times Books).

—— (1983) *The Times Guide to the House of Commons June 1983.* (London: Times Books).

Tomkins A (2005) *Our Republican Constitution.* (Oxford: Hart Publishing).

—— (2008) 'Republican Constitutionalism and Constitutional Reform' in S White and D Leighton (2008) *Building a Citizen Society: The Emerging Politics of Republican Democracy.* (London: Lawrence & Wishart), pp. 33–43.

Tsebelis G (1995) 'Decision-making in Political Systems—Veto Players in Presidentialism, Parliamentarism, Multicameralism and Multipartyism', *British Journal of Political Science* 25(3): 289–325.

Tsebelis G (2002) *Veto Players: How Political Institutions Work.* (Princeton, NJ: Princeton University Press).

Wakeham Lord (Chairman) (2000*a*) *A House for the Future: Report of the Royal Commission on the Reform of the House of Lords*, Cm 4534. (London: The Stationery

Office). Part I Report. Part II Evidence. Available at: http://www.archive.official-documents.co.uk/document/cm45/4534/4534.htm

—— (2000*b*) *A House for the Future: A Summary.* (London: The Stationery Office).

Waldron J (1999) *Law and Disagreement.* (Oxford: Clarendon Press).

—— (2006) 'The Core of the Case Against Judicial Review', *Yale Law Journal,* 115: 1346–406.

Weill R (2003) 'Dicey Was Not Diceyan', *Cambridge Law Journal,* 62(2): 474–94.

Whatley C A (1989) 'Economic Causes and Consequences of the Union of 1707: A Survey', *Scottish Historical Review,* 68(2): 150–81.

—— with Patrick D J (2006) *The Scots and the Union.* (Edinburgh: Edinburgh University Press).

White S and Leighton D (2008) *Building a Citizen Society: The Emerging Politics of Republican Democracy.* (London: Lawrence & Wishart).

Whitlam G (1979) *The Truth of the Matter.* (Ringwood, Victoria, Australia: Penguin).

Wicks E (2006) *The Evolution of a Constitution: Eight Key Moments in British Constitutional History.* (Oxford: Hart Publishing).

Witte J Jr (2008) 'The Archbishop and Marital Pluralism: An American Perspective'. *Ecclesiastical Law Journal,* 10: 344–7.

Young A (2006) 'Hunting Sovereignty: Jackson v. Her Majesty's Attorney-General', *Public Law,* 187–196.

—— (2009) *Parliamentary Sovereignty and the Human Rights Act.* (Oxford: Hart Publishing).

All UK statutes and court judgements are cited from the versions to be found in either the Justis or the Westlaw databases, except that pre-1707 Scottish Acts are cited from the *Acts of the Parliament of Scotland.*

Hansard (reports of debates in the House of Commons and the House of Lords) is quoted where possible from the wonderful online version being developed on behalf of the UK Parliament at http://hansard.millbanksystems.com/. This (currently a beta version) aims to put the entire content of *Hansard* since 1803 on the Web. Modern citations, from the online current versions produced by the House authorities at www.publications.parliament.uk, are given slightly differently.

Index